ARCHITECTURE AND CONSTRUCTION IN
CONCRETE

LINKS

ARCHITECTURE AND CONSTRUCTION IN CONCRETE

Author: Dimitris Kottas
Graphic design & production: Cuboctaedro, Neu Studio
Collaborators: Oriol Vallès, Roberto Bottura
Text: Contributed by the architects, edited by Naomi Ferguson

© Linksbooks
Jonqueres, 10, 1-5,
Barcelona 08003, Spain
Tel.: +34-93-301-21-99
Fax: +34-93-301-00-21
info@linksbooks.net
www.linksbooks.net

© This is a collective work. In accordance with Intellectual Property Law "collective works" are NOT necessarily those produced by more than one author. They have been created by the initiative and coordination of one person who edits and distributes them under his/her name. A collective work constitutes a collection of contributions from different authors whose personal contributions form part of a creation, without it being possible to separately attribute rights over the work as a whole.

© All rights reserved. No part of this book may be used or reproduced in any manner whatsoever without written permission except in the case of brief quotations embodied in critical articles and reviews.

ARCHITECTURE AND CONSTRUCTION IN
CONCRETE

LINKS

Contents

8 Building with concrete

20 Defects and deterioration of concrete

44 Concrete protection and repair

56 Concrete and agglomerate products

Zaha Hadid Architects
66 Phaeno Science Center Wolfsburg
78 Bergisel Ski Jump

Alberto Campo Baeza
88 Blas House

Besonias - Almeida -Kruk
98 Mar Azul House

Cloud 9
112 Villa Bio

Ken Architekten
126 Kindergartens Zentral I and II

Eisenman Architects
136 The Memorial to the Murdered Jews of Europe

Alan Dempsey & Alvin Huang
142 [C]space DRL10 Pavilion

Aranguren + Gallegos & Herrada + Maiz
150 Housing at Encinar de los Reyes

Bevk Perovic Architects
160 House H

Miralles Tagliabue - EMBT
168 Vigo University Campus

Carme Pinós
182 Cube Tower

Michael Shamiyeh / BAU|KULTUR
194 Seifert House

Shuhei Endo
204 Transtreet G

UN Studio van Berkel & Bos
212 NMR Facilities

Justo García Rubio
222 Casar de Cáceres Sub-Regional Bus Station

Pezo von Ellrichshausen Architects
234 Poli House

Designliga
246 Bench

Kei'ichi Irie + Power Unit Studio
254 Y House

Mathias Klotz (KLOTZ & ASSOC.)
264 Eleven Women House

Introduction

In recent years, concrete has to a large extent recovered its reputation as an innovative and versatile material after its long association with the repetitive gray blocks of the postwar. Concrete need not be gray and orthogonal blocks are not the only forms it can be used to create.

Concrete is a highly industrial material that has evolved considerably over the last thirty years. Innovations such as glass-reinforced concrete have created more durable concretes, as well as concretes with greater ductility and elasticity. Even what were seen as its defining characteristics, such as its strength and opacity, are no longer inherent properties of the material. There are now various types of translucent concrete on the market that incorporate fiber optics or other transparent materials as aggregates. There have also been innovations in finishes for concrete, including techniques for printing images, even to near photographic quality, on its surfaces. Important advances have also been made in the environmental sustainability of concrete. The use of recycled materials as aggregates is now a fairly common practice, while at the other end of the scale, the addition of titanium dioxide to the concrete mix creates a concrete which absorbs atmospheric pollution.

This book, organized in two sections, comprises a presentation of the properties of this fascinating group of materials followed by a selection of contemporary projects that demonstrate the possibilities of their utilization. The first section presents all that the informed reader could want to know about cement and concrete, from technical properties to the characteristics of the most recent cement-based materials. The second section illustrates the importance of these materials in contemporary architecture with a range of projects from leading architectural practices, which have pushed the boundaries of the constructional possibilities of concrete with designs of exceptional quality and daring. This volume constitutes an invaluable reference resource for anyone designing with concrete.

Building with concrete

Building with concrete

Composition

Concrete (from the Latin 'concretus', meaning compact or condensed, a participle of the verb 'concrescere'- to grow together) is the result of mixing cement, or a similar binder material, with aggregates (gravel and sand) and water, to form a mass that can be molded and compacted with relative ease. The chemical process of hydration then reduces the plasticity of the mass and, after a few hours, it begins to take on the appearance and characteristics of a compact solid, similar to stone. The final product, hardened concrete, is a highly mechanically resistant material. The most common way of indicating the proportions of the constituent materials is with a numeric proportion. For example, 1.3.4 indicates: one part cement, 3 parts fine aggregate (sand) and 4 parts coarse aggregate (gravel). Combining steel and concrete produces reinforced concrete.

Cement

Cement could be considered as the soul of concrete. The history of cement reflects the history of mankind who, in the search for increased comfort and security, has built with the materials available in the environment. Many historians cite Ernest L. Ransome, builder and inventor, as the catalyst in helping to make reinforced concrete the widely used construction material that it is today. Throughout the 19th and early 20th centuries many binder materials were patented, which we know today as cement. The most widely known type of cement is Portland cement, a fine powder composed of compounds containing calcium, silica, alumina, iron and magnesium, and which hardens when mixed with water.

Cement is the fundamental material of concrete, as the type of cement used greatly influences the characteristics of the resulting concrete. The strength of the concrete depends largely on the proportions of the water: cement mix. Certain alkaline compounds in the cement also protect the steel reinforcement from corrosion.

Thus the proportion of water to cement, as well as the type of cement, determine to a large extent the strength and durability of reinforced concrete elements.

The cements used in reinforced concrete structures are hydraulic cements, which have the ability to harden in water due to the process of hydration. These cements can be classified as:

- Portland cements
- Portland-composite cements
- Blast-furnace cements
- Pozzolanic cements
- Composite cements
- Natural cements
- Calcium aluminate cements
- Cements with additional, specific properties

Portland cement

Of all the types of cement this is the one most commonly used in reinforced concrete structures.

The production of Portland cement involves the mixing of crushed limestone with clays or other excavated raw materials. This mix is then heated in a kiln where, once the right temperature is reached, a chemical reaction occurs that forms calcium silicates. This heated substance, called 'clinker' is usually in the form of small gray-black pellets. The clinker is then cooled and pulverized into a very fine powder and fortified with a small amount of gypsum.

The constituents of the resulting cement can be classified into principal, or active, and secondary constituents. The former help to create the positive properties that are characteristic of the particular cement, while the latter are those that tend to weaken the concrete or mortar in which the cement will be used

Types of cement and their constituents in proportion to total mass

Type	Designation according to EN-197	Clinker	Blastfurnace Slag (S)	Natural Pozzolana (P)	Fly Ash (V)	Calcium Carbonate (T)	Other constituents
Portland cements	CEM I	100	0	0	0	0	0
	CEM I	95-99	—	—	—	—	1-5
White Portland cements	I-CEM I	95-100	—	—	—	—	0-5
Portland-composite cement	CEM II	65-88	6-27	6-23		0-5	—
Portland slag cement	CEM II	65-94	6-35	—	—	—	0-5
Portland pozzolana cement	CEM II	72-94	—	6-28	—	—	0-5
Portland fly ash cement	CEM II	72-94	—	—	6-28	—	0-5
Portland calcareous cement	CEM II	80-94	—	—	—	6-15	0-5
White Portland cement with additives	CEM II	75-94	—	—	—	—	6-25
Blast-furnace cements	CEM III	40-64	36-60	—	—	—	0-5
	CEM III	20-39	61-80	—	—	—	0-5
Pozzolanic cement	CEM IV	-60	—	< 40		—	0-5
Composite cement	CEM V	20-64	36-80			—	0-5
Composite white cement	CEM V	40-70	—	—	—	—	30-60
Calcium aluminate cements	CEM VI	100	—	—	—	—	—

and whose quantities should therefore be reduced as much as possible.

The principal constituents are:

- Tricalcium silicate
- Dicalcium silicate
- Tricalcium aluminate
- Tetracalcium aluminoferrite

The secondary constituents are:

- Burnt lime (calcium oxide)
- Free magnesium (magnesium oxide)
- Sulfates
- Alkalis

Amongst the principal constituents the silicates are those that give mechanical strength to the cement.

Tricalcium silicate is responsible for initial hardening (or 'setting') and early strength. Even though both tricalcium and dicalcium silicates eventually reach the same strength, the hardening curves differ between the two. The dicalcium silicate does not contribute to the strength of the concrete at first, but after 28 days its contribution is equal to that of the tricalcium silicate.

The other two principal constituents (tricalcium aluminate and tetra calcium aluminoferrite) do not contribute greatly to the strength of the cement. The aluminate has the effect of accelerating the hardening process in the first few hours but its presence reduces the durability of the concrete in the long term since it leaves it susceptible to attack from sulfates. The tetracalcium aluminoferrite barely contributes to increasing strength during setting.

Portland cement is specified according to its minimum compressive strength (in kg/cm^2, or psi) after 28 days, determined by laboratory testing of a sample taken from the mix on site.

Portland-composite cement

This is made of Portland cement clinker, a setting regulator that makes up a minimum of 80% of the total mass, and a maximum of 20% of slag or pozzolana. It is also specified according to its compressive strength after 28 days.

Additives are products that give the cement added, beneficial properties. Certain blast-furnace slags have hydraulic properties, while pozzolana is a natural product that forms a hydraulic compound when it comes into contact with calcium in water.

Blast-furnace cement

Similar to the type mentioned above, this cement is made of Portland cement clinker, a setting regulator that makes up between 20 and 80% of the total mass, and blast-furnace slag, that must constitute at least 20% of the mass.

Pozzolanic cement

This is made of Portland cement clinker and a setting regulator (less than 80% of total mass), with pozzolana constituting a minimum of 20% of the total mass. In the European regulations EN-197, it is classified as type CEM/IV.

Composite cement

This contains Portland cement clinker, a minimum of 65% of a setting regulator, and inert additives (that do not react with cement and water) that make up the remaining mass. These types of cement are not suitable for use in structural concrete.

Natural cement

This is obtained by grinding the clinker of naturally occurring cement. The various types, also specified according to compressive strength after 28 days, can be sorted into 'slow' and 'fast' natural cements.

Calcium aluminate cement

This is obtained by the grinding of clinker consisting of hydraulic calcium aluminates. As such it is totally different in terms of raw materials, constituents, production and characteristics, to those cements made of Portland cement clinker.

Cements with additional properties

These are cements that not only comply with the basic requirements of their relevant categories but also possess additional, specialized, properties:

High early strength Portland cement: achieves a minimum compressive strength of 250kg/cm^2 (3555 psi) within 48 hours.

Sulfate resistant Portland cement: has a reduced susceptibility to attack by dissolved sulfates in water or soils, due to a lower proportion of tricalcium aluminate.

Low heat Portland cement: Sdefined as producing a heat on the seventh day of hydration of 65 cal/g (65 BTU/ lb), and on the 28th day of 75 cal/g (75 BTU/ lb).

White cement: possesses a minimum of 70% whiteness, measured by the level of light it reflects compared to a reference value, based on the reflectance of magnesium oxide powder.

Aggregates

Aggregates are normally divided into two types: fine and coarse aggregates. Fine aggregate is natural or artificial sand with a grain size of no more than 10 mm (less than ½ in). An aggregate with a grain size

Aggregates used in concrete		
	Density (kg/m^3, slugs/ft^3)	Examples
Lightweight aggregates	<2200	Pumice, slag wool, expanded clay, expanded shale
Normal aggregates	2300-3000	Dense natural stone (crushed or not), high density industrial products (e.g. blast-furnace slag)
Heavy aggregates	>3100	Iron ore pellets, steel pellets

Two unconventional aggregates (pellets of air-dried mud and burnt mud powder).

of less than 0.08 mm (1/320 in) can be detrimental to the concrete, especially if this size is similar to that of the dry cement particles. Coarse aggregates are those that do not pass through a No. 16 mesh and can be up to 152 mm (6 in) in diameter. The conventional maximum aggregate size is between 19 mm and 25 mm (around 1 in).

It is important to choose hard, strong, clean aggregates that are free of clay or contaminants that could affect the hydration of the cement.

In general the density of the aggregate is a good indicator of its quality, as low-density aggregate is porous and lacks strength.

The aggregates' properties greatly influence the properties of the concrete as the aggregate makes up 70 to 80% of the volume of the finished concrete.

Additives

Additives are considered to be the fourth ingredient in concrete and are products that are added during mixing. Their purpose is to modify, beneficially, certain characteristics of the concrete, both when it is plastic and once it has hardened.

Choosing the right type of additive is the first important step as there is a wide range of suppliers and it is important to know beforehand exactly what effect is desired from the additive. It is also vital to know what secondary effects the additive produces as in certain cases these could negate any initial benefits, resulting in it being wiser not to use the additive.

As opposed to the other constituents in concrete, there are no rules or guidelines that prescribe the qualities that an additive should possess, so it is necessary to take great care in choosing a trustworthy supplier who can guarantee a good quality product. This is especially important because additives do not generally improve the concrete in proportion to how much is used and so they must be used in the precise quantities indicated by the supplier.

Additives should therefore only be used on sites where a high level of quality control can be guaranteed for checking the material when it arrives on-site, and during dosage and construction.

Mix proportions

As well as the constituents that together make concrete, a formwork (or 'shuttering') is necessary in order to produce concrete elements, and steel reinforcement needs to be added in structural elements. The formwork is normally made of wood and can form anything from simple, cubic shapes to more sophisticated volumes depending on the nature of the project. The steel used for reinforcement can be high or low strength, depending on the size and strength of the required element. The plastic concrete mix is poured into the formwork and, once it has hardened, the formwork is removed. At this point the face of the concrete can be polished or given any number of finishes.

In any project that uses reinforced concrete two relationships between constituents of the concrete are of vital importance: the interaction between aggregate and cement, and the interaction between water and cement. When other factors (problems due to the quality of the constituents used, for example) are not relevant these two relationships determine the compactness, stability, durability, strength and 'health' of the concrete over time.

Types of additives

Plasticizers

Superplasticizers

Air entraining agents

Water repelling agents

Retarders

Accelerators

Hydration stabilizers

The potential quality of a concrete structure depends a great deal on the quantity of cement used. Reference doses should be considered as a rule of thumb and, often, are not met on normal building sites. They are also sometimes exceeded in chemically harsh environments or if a particularly high strength is required. Note, however, that the cement should never exceed 30% of the total volume.

The extra strength that adding more cement provides does not increase in direct proportion to the quantity used but rather decreases in effectiveness above a certain amount. However, the increase in binding strength, protection of the reinforcement from corrosion, and thermal insulation do increase proportionally with the amount of cement.

An excess of water will produce a reduction in strength and adherence to the reinforcement and will increase the probability of cracks due to shrinkage, as well as increasing the likelihood of corrosion of the reinforcement due to the higher level of porosity. Ready mixed concrete frequently tends to suffer from this problem because water is added in order to allow more time for the transportation to the site and to facilitate the pumping of the concrete.

Shrinkage (a reduction in volume due to a loss of water) is a phenomenon inherent in concrete while it is setting and before it is completely hard, i.e. when the mass is still plastic. Cracks due to drying shrinkage can appear in floor slabs while it is setting, especially if the fresh concrete slab is restrained from shrinking freely by other structural elements such as columns. It is common to find such cracks in tall buildings, as they tend to have very rigid floor beams and columns. The likelihood of these cracks appearing is increased when: the concrete is poured in hot weather or in a place that receives a lot of sunshine, the top layer of water on the concrete is struck off too soon, or if there are excessive vibrations from machinery on site.

Chemical attack from chlorides, from the reaction between the alkalis in the cement and the aggregate, from carbonation and from pyrite (iron disulfide) can all damage the concrete and corrode the steel reinforcement. If there are chlorides present in the concrete then this corrosion can occur even if the concrete has a high overall pH value (more than 9) because the chloride ions convert the constituent water into an electrical conductor. Sodium chloride can be inherently present in the concrete from the aggregate or constituent water and it can also penetrate into the set concrete through the pores. Sodium chloride is dangerous when it forms more than 0.1% of the volume of the concrete because it threatens the passivating capability that the concrete provides for the steel and can cause the concrete to break off in small areas. These weak points are then further eroded and can eventually expose the reinforcement, which can then be corroded and pitted, even to breaking point.

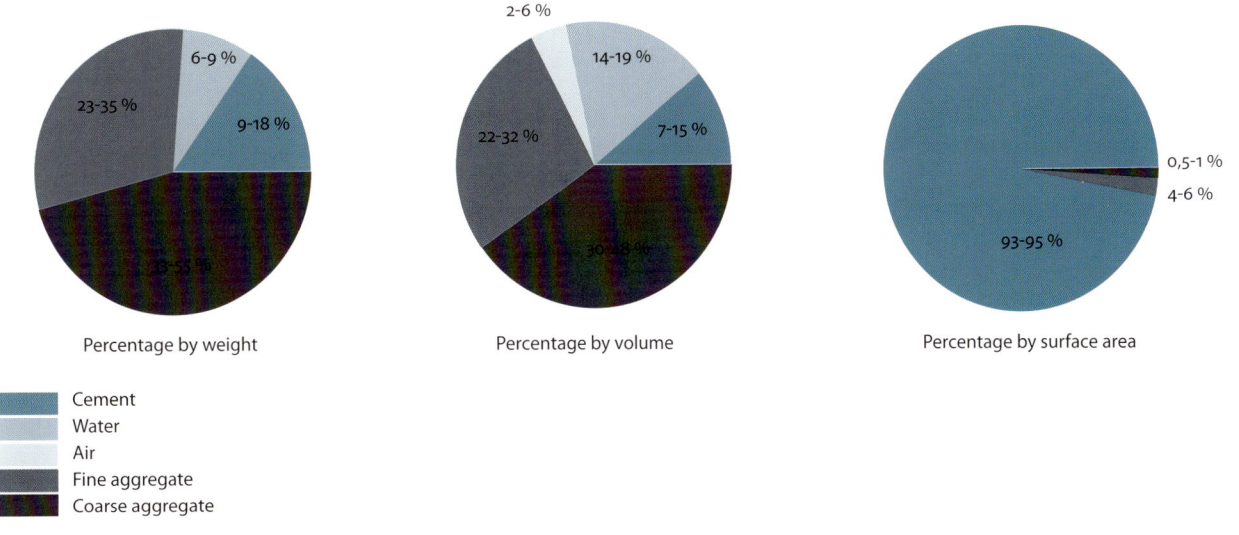

The composition of concrete

Types of concrete

High strength concrete
This is used in particularly corrosive environments, or in structures that have to support exceptionally high loads.

Uses:
- Reinforced concrete structural elements under compression, such as columns and walls
- Reinforced concrete structural elements subjected to bending stress, such as beams, slabs and retaining walls
- Reinforced concrete foundations and tie beams
- Bridge decks

Advantages:
- A better cost effectiveness in columns
- Savings in the structure, especially in columns, due to smaller sizing and less steel
- Space saving due to smaller sections
- Better durability due to low porosity, particularly suitable in chemically corrosive environments
- Allows bigger spans between supports

Lightweight ('cellular') concrete
A low-density concrete that has improved thermal and acoustic insulating properties.

Uses:
- Flat roofs
- Groundwater drainage
- In refurbishment of existing structures

Advantages:
- Good fire resistance
- Good thermal and acoustic insulation
- A lower coefficient of thermal expansion
- Savings in building structure are possible because of the decreased weight

Radiation shielding concrete
This type of concrete is ideal for use in barriers against nuclear radiation due to its higher density (>2800 kg/m^3/ 5.33 slugs/ ft^3).

Uses:
- Protective barriers against the passage of nuclear radiation
- Foundations in tall, slender structures as the extra weight helps prevent buckling

Advantages:
- Better protection against X-rays and Gamma rays
- High level of absorption of radiation and fast neutrons
- Forms durable barriers that require little maintenance

Antibacterial concrete
Resists the growth and spread of bacteria (both gram-positive and gram-negative) and mold, both internally and on its surface.

Uses:
- Grain silos
- Food manipulation premises
- Buildings for livestock
- Recycling plants
- Hospitals and health centers
- Swimming pools
- Infrastructure for the supply of drinking water

Advantages:
- In the quantities applied the biocide used is non-toxic to people, animals and plants
- The concrete is not otherwise altered by the introduction of the antibacterial agent/ fungicide
- The concrete does not require an additional finish of paint, or resin etc

Self-compacting concrete
Concrete that is able to flow and consolidate/compact under its own weight, without the need for any additional compacting. This type of concrete is particularly suitable for deep foundations where low or no-nexistent segregation of the constituents is required.

Uses:
- Pad foundations, beam foundations, strip foundations
- Piles, retaining walls and floor slabs

Advantages:
- Faster construction
- Retains its shape and does not disintegrate when submerged under water
- Reduces the likelihood of defects in piles
- Low permeability
- Reduces the risk of seepage at the top of the pile

Shotcrete
Shotcrete is concrete pumped through a hose and pneumatically projected at high velocity onto a surface. 'Shotcrete' is a general term that applies to both

wet-mix (in which ready mixed concrete is pumped through the hose) and dry-mix processes (in which the dry cement mixture is pumped through a hose to the nozzle, at which point water is injected immediately before application). The latter is also known as 'Gunite'. It allows the application of concrete over irregular surfaces that lack formwork or supports that could otherwise retain fresh concrete.

Uses:
- Tunnel construction
- Stabilization of slopes
- Formation of water reservoirs, swimming pools and canals
- Repairing existing structures
- Applying fire protection around steel

Advantages:
- Allows the patching up of damaged reinforced concrete structures without the need for partial or total demolition
- In the case of dry-mix, its application can be very precise with little risk of rebound

Pouring concrete

Before pouring the concrete a mold releasing agent should be applied to the inner face of the formwork (or 'shuttering') to prevent the concrete from sticking to the formwork, which would complicate its removal and ruin the concrete's finish. The type of releasing agent used depends on the material of the formwork panels (whether phenolic or metallic plywood).

Types of formwork and their application

Type of formwork	Material	Application	Number of times that it can be reused (after appropriate treatment)
Rough timber boards	Fir or spruce	General purpose	4-5
Smooth timber boards	Planed fir or spruce	Exposed surfaces	~10
Tongue and groove timber boards	Sandblasted fir or spruce	Exposed surfaces with a wooden texture	~10
Panels made of timber boards	Impregnated fir or spruce boards 500 x 1500 mm (1ft 6 in x 5 ft)	General purpose	~50
Resin-coated plywood panels	Resin-coated plywood	General purpose	~30
Film faced plywood	Plywood with a sodium or paper coating	General purpose	~30
Polyester plywood panels	Plywood with a polyester coating	Smooth surfaces	~100
Plastic coated plywood panels	Phenolic or melamine plywood	Smooth surfaces	80-100
Polysulfide rubber molds	Polysulfide rubber	Smooth surfaces with a fine texture	30-50
Rubber molds	Silicone rubber	Smooth surfaces with a fine texture	~50
Polystyrene	Polystyrene blocks	Smooth surfaces with a fine texture	1-5
Steel panels	Rolled steel	General purpose	~500
Steel tubes	Rolled steel	Smooth surfaces	1

The use of specialist formwork and surface treatments can create a huge variety of finishes.

The concrete should be poured in successive layers not exceeding 500 mm, and in accordance with the speed suggested by the manufacturer. This is to avoid the risk of damage to the previous layer that the pressure from pouring could produce. The formwork should be removed only after a minimum time has elapsed, which will depend on the characteristics of the site but, normally, is between 24 and 48 hours after pouring.

In order to achieve the required quality of concrete, it is necessary to leave enough time for proper hardening to occur, which will depend on the type of concrete used and the relation between self weight and design loads. This can take between 14 and 28 days, until which time the centering (supports) should not be removed.

Formwork

Formwork is the name given to the temporary structures, made of panels of timber or metal, used to mold fresh concrete into shape. Once the concrete has hardened to a sufficient degree, the formwork can be removed. The panels nearly always require a structure ('falsework', or 'centering') to support them that is also normally made of metal or wood. Different types of formwork systems allow the building of walls, floors, columns, paving and stairs. Reinforcement has to be put into place before the concrete is poured. The primary functions of the formwork are: to achieve the desired shape and protect the setting concrete from knocks, extreme temperatures, and the loss of water.

Today the most widely used panels are industrially produced, prefabricated panels that, unlike traditional ones, can be reused and adapted to each specific project. These panels can be light, or they can be very heavy and need cranes for their installation on site. There are horizontal systems for slabs and vertical ones for walls, though of course almost anything can be made to measure if a project requires it. There is a wide array of systems available on the market. Choosing the right one for a project will depend on the budget, the equipment, space and time available, and the surface finish required.

When creating large, continuous areas with reusable panels, it is useful to have scaffolding that permits easy removal and repositioning of the panels. For large scale projects, systems are available that use self-supporting panels or incorporate mechanisms that allow horizontal sliding, or vertical slipping, of the formwork without the need for cranes. The latter are most commonly available in sizes between 1 and 3 m (3 and 10 ft).

The most commonly used material for formwork is timber (normally pine, beech or birch), either cut into planks or used as a veneer in panels, in thicknesses of between 12 and 35 mm (1/2 in and 1 ½ in), and normally impregnated with acetic anhydride or coated with phenol for longer durability.

Other materials that lend themselves to being quickly installed on site are steel, plastic and plastic-laminated cardboard. The latter is around 9 mm (1/4 in) thick and is particularly suitable for round, square or rectangular columns. It is available for column diameters of between 150 and 1500 mm (6 in and 5 ft) and heights of between 3 and 12 meters (10 and 40 ft). It is an excellent material that retains a high level of moisture and is therefore well suited to molding.

Formwork for creating walls and columns consists of panels (250, 500, 750 and 900 mm/ 10, 20, 30 and 35 in wide, and between 0,6 and 3 m / 23 in and 10 ft high), corner pieces for the inside and outside faces at corners, and adjustable metal connectors covered in PVC. The latter pass through the width of the wall or column, serving to tighten and then release the mold, and can be taken out of the concrete when the formwork is removed.

Creating cylindrical walls in concrete, whether the radius is small (3 to 5 m / 10 to 16 ft) or big (more than 5 m / 16 ft), is a difficult task. One challenge is to achieve a flat, level finish along the top of the wall, and another is to construct formwork capable of withstanding the pressure that the wet concrete exerts on the formwork walls. Many supports, both under compression and tension, are needed to keep the formwork from buckling.

For the construction of round columns, both single use and reusable formworks are available. The former are usually made of cardboard with an impermeable liner of plastic or aluminum. The plastic-lined formwork is more rigid, allowing taller structures (up to 12 m / 40 ft with a diameter of 200 mm / 8 in) to be built. Reusable formwork can be made from steel components (separate panels requiring ties and supports) or from simple, steel box-frames.

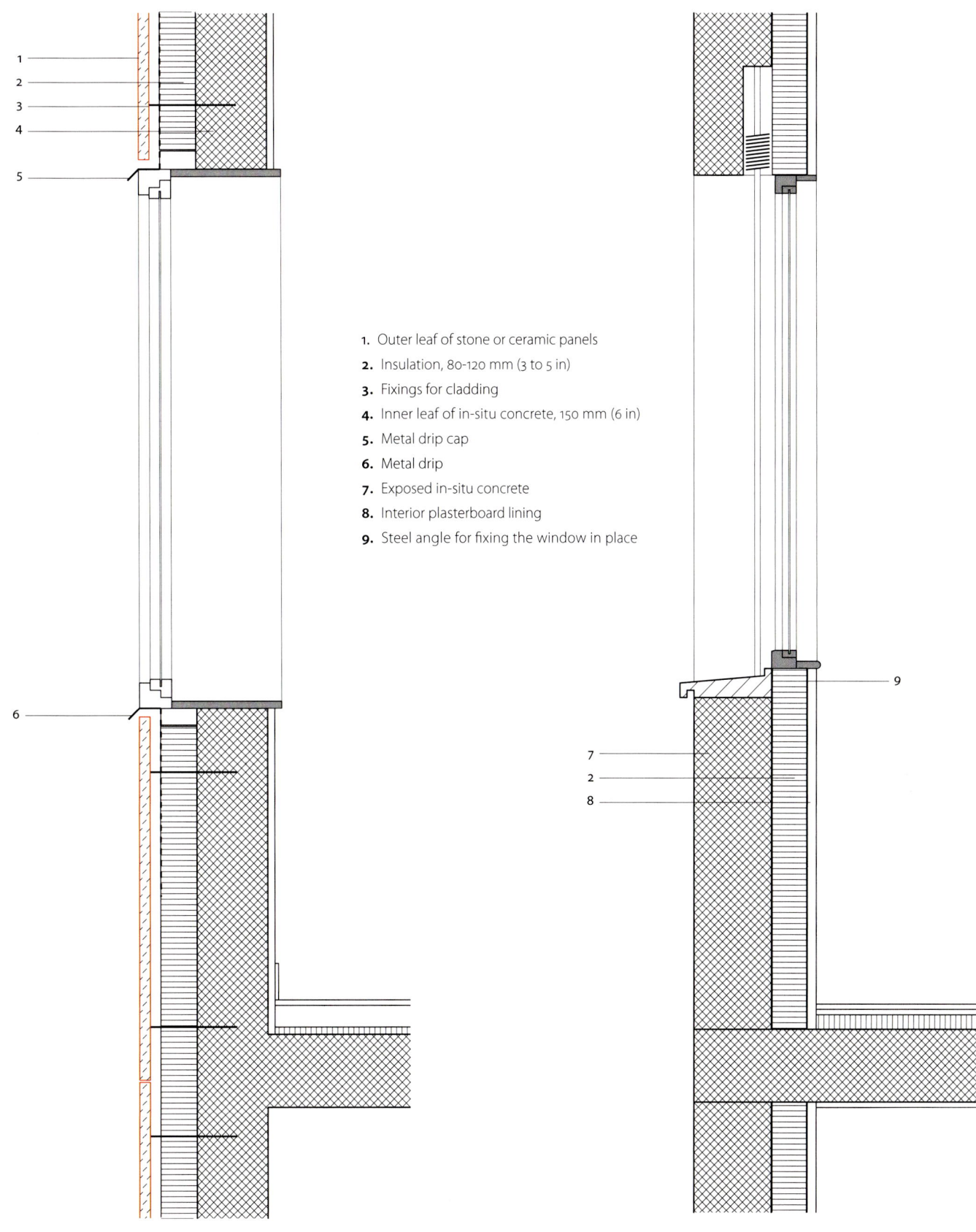

1. Outer leaf of stone or ceramic panels
2. Insulation, 80-120 mm (3 to 5 in)
3. Fixings for cladding
4. Inner leaf of in-situ concrete, 150 mm (6 in)
5. Metal drip cap
6. Metal drip
7. Exposed in-situ concrete
8. Interior plasterboard lining
9. Steel angle for fixing the window in place

A concrete structure with a heavy panel ventilated façade, and an exposed concrete façade

Building with concrete

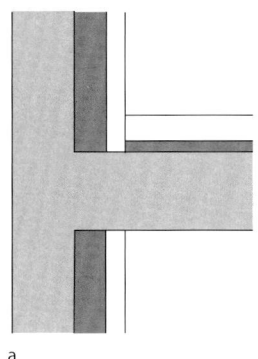

Floor slabs can be cast with reusable phenolic plywood panels supported by aluminum centering or with metal or plastic coffers supported by steel centering. Both of these systems allow for easy disassembly, with the metal studs being removed last.

Removal of formwork

Formwork is in most cases provisional, being removed once the concrete has hardened enough for it to resemble an 'artificial stone'. The time required for this to occur depends on the type of concrete and the type of formwork used.

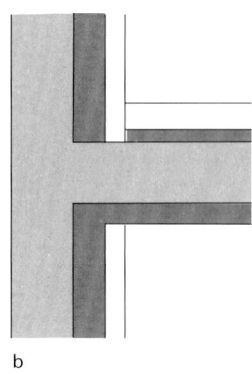

Exposed concrete

Modern architects have made much use of exposed concrete surfaces in their designs. To achieve a good quality of finish, especially in complex projects, requires good communication between all of the involved parties: architect, project manager, contractor, engineer, formwork manufacturer and concrete manufacturer. There are many possible finishes that can be applied to exposed concrete. It can be vibrated, sprayed to expose the aggregate, textured, polished, dyed, etc.

'Exposed concrete' means that the concrete is not hidden behind any other material, so that the appearance of the concrete determines the appearance of the building. It is thus sometimes helpful to classify concrete according to its final appearance, e.g. white concrete, exposed aggregate concrete, fiber reinforced concrete, etc.

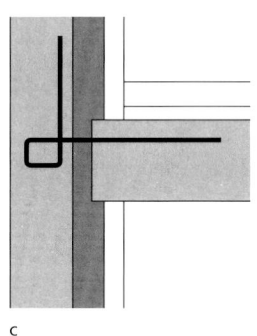

The best formwork panels to use when the concrete will be left exposed are smooth and impermeable, and are normally made of metal because they can be reused more times than wood based panels. Depending on the situation, a releasing agent may also be applied to the panels.

Insulation of exposed concrete:
a. normal insulation, concrete causes thermal bridging.
b. continuous insulation over the ceiling, the compactness of the structure is preserved, though the heat lost is inevitable.
c. gap between the slab and the wall, special insulation conditions are needed, but this is the method that guarantees a better insulation.

Defects and deterioration of concrete

The presence of defects and the deterioration of concrete can be due to many different causes. It is vital to understand these causes before undertaking any construction project that uses concrete. During the design stage factors that influence the sizing and appearance of concrete elements, as well as specific challenges relating to the site, should be considered. During the construction phase, a good knowledge of the potential weaknesses of concrete will help in deciding the correct specification of materials and doses and in checking quality on site.

In the case of existing buildings that show signs of deterioration, access to expert knowledge about the diverse signs and causes of damage is of the utmost importance for correct diagnosis and subsequent repair. The possible causes of damage can be classified as follows:

- damage caused by the **ingredients of the concrete**
- damage due to **incorrect manufacture and construction**
- damage due to **weathering**
- attack by **external agents:**
    - chemical
    - physical
- damage due to **defects and deterioration of the steel reinforcement**

Concrete is generally considered to be a tough, homogenous, compact and inert material. However, upon closer inspection it reveals itself to be a heterogeneous, porous material that in certain situations can be highly susceptible to its environment.

In the case of reinforced concrete it is not only the thickness of the concrete covering surrounding the steel bars, but also its chemical composition, that determine the level of protection and passivation of the reinforcement.

Damage caused by the concrete constituents

The formation of concrete depends on the correct interaction between cement, aggregate, water and additives. The incorporation of steel adds the tensile strength that is needed for concrete to become adequate for structural use.

Quite often the cause of damage to concrete can be found in the use of bad quality constituents, or the unsuitability of the chosen constituents for the concrete's end use or location.

Defects in concrete are thus closely related to defects in the constituents and so it is important to know the standards with which they should comply in order to avoid short or long-term damage to the concrete.

Cement

Cement is the fundamental consituent of concrete, as the type of cement used greatly influences the characteristics of the resulting concrete. The strength of the concrete depends largely on the proportions of the water: cement mix. Certain alkaline compounds in the cement also protect the steel reinforcement from corrosion.

Thus the proportion of water to cement, as well as the type of cement, determine to a large extent the strength and durability of reinforced concrete elements.

There are many different kinds of cement and a deciding factor in choosing which type is most adequate is the corrosiveness of the environment in which the concrete will be placed. For example, a fairly common problem is sulfate attack caused by sulfates present in the cement dissolving in water. Although the probability of such attacks occurring could be reduced by using the most compact concrete possible, a more

Classification of cements

Type	Class	Category	Designation
Portland cement		350	P-350
		450	P-450
		550	P-550
Portland-composite cement		350	PA-350
		450	PA-450
		550	PA-550
Blast-furnace cement	I	350	S-I-350
	I	450	S-I-450
	II	350	S-II-350
	III	250	S-III-250
	III	350	S-III-350
Pozzolanic cement	I	250	PUZ-I-250
	I	350	PUZ-I-350
	I	450	PUZ-I-450
	II	250	PUZ-II-250
	II	350	PUZ-II-350
	II	450	PUZ-II-450
Composite cement		200	C-200
Calcium aluminate cement		550	A-550
Natural cement	Slow	30	NL-30
	Slow	80	NL-80
	Fast	20	NR-20

logical preventative measure would be to avoid the use of sulfate-rich cements altogether.

It is also worth noting the problems caused in the past through the extensive use of aluminate-rich cements in pre-stressed concrete floors. Many such structures date from the 1940s and 1950s, and in certain environmental conditions the damage can be widespread and serious from a structural point of view. As a result the use of such cements is now highly restricted.

Types of cement and their composition

The cements used in reinforced concrete structures are hydraulic cements, which have the ability to harden in water due to the process of hydration. These cements can be classified as:

1. Portland cements
2. Portland-composite cements
3. Blast-furnace cements
4. Pozzolanic cements
5. Composite cements
6. Natural cements
7. Calcium aluminate cements
8. Cements with additional, specific properties

1. Portland cement

Of all the types of cement this is the one most commonly used in reinforced concrete structures, although it should be noted that other cements might be preferable in certain situations, such as in foundations when the ground is rich in sulfates or if the structure will be in a particularly corrosive environment.

A study of the potential weaknesses of this kind of cement can help in understanding the negative effects they can have on the resulting concrete.

Errors in its preparation, heating, or grinding, and any error in its composition can all cause defects that will go on to have negative effects on the concrete.

Improper storage and handling when mixing the concrete are also possible sources of defects.

The production of Portland cement involves the mixing of crushed limestone with clays or other excavated raw materials. This mix is then heated in a kiln where, once the right temperature is reached, a chemical reaction occurs that forms calcium silicates. This heated substance, called 'clinker' is usually in the form of small gray-black pellets. The clinker is then cooled and pulverized into a very fine powder and fortified with a small amount of gypsum.

The constituents of the resulting cement can be classified into principal, or active, and secondary constituents. The former help give the cement the characteristics required for a specific purpose while the latter are those that tend to weaken the concrete or mortar and whose quantities should therefore be reduced as much as possible.

The **principal** constituents are:

- Tricalcium silicate
- Dicalcium silicate

- Tricalcium aluminate
- Tetracalcium aluminoferrite

The **secondary** constituents are:

- Burnt lime (calcium oxide)
- Free magnesium (magnesium oxide)
- Sulfates
- Alkalis

Among the principal constituents the silicates are those that give mechanical strength to the cement.

Tricalcium silicate is responsible for initial hardening (or 'setting') and early strength. Even though both tricalcium and dicalcium silicates eventually reach the same strength, the hardening curves differ between the two.

The other two principal constituents (tricalcium aluminate and tetracalcium aluminoferrite) do not contribute greatly to the strength of the cement.

The aluminate has the effect of accelerating the hardening process in the first few hours but its presence reduces the durability of the concrete in the long term since it leaves it susceptible to attack from sulfates.

Hydration and initial hardening of cement (and thus of the concrete) are greatly affected by the cement's composition. During hydration the aluminates are the first compounds to undergo chemical reactions, followed by the silicates.

'False set' is when the mix begins to set within the first few minutes of mixing beginning.

The most common cause of this effect is partial dehydration of the gypsum, which itself is due to excessive heat while grinding the clinker. A false set tends to result in an excessive amount of water being mixed into the concrete, which then reduces its strength and increases the likelihood of cracks occurring due to shrinkage.

Hardening is the phase after hydration and is when the mechanical strength of the cement increases progressively. Each constituent of the cement reacts at different times and to different degrees. The tricalcium aluminate reacts quickly but the process is over quite quickly (within the first 7 to 28 days). Tricalcium silicate greatly influences initial strength, while also continuing to increase strength over an extended period.

The dicalcium silicate does not contribute to the strength of the concrete at first, but after 28 days its contribution is equal to that of the tricalcium silicate.

The tetracalcium aluminoferrite barely contributes to increasing strength during setting.

Each constituent contributes in a different degree to the total **'heat of hydration'**.

Of the heat generated by the tricalcium aluminate, the tricalcium silicate generates half of that amount, the dicalcium silicate a quarter and the tetracalcium aluminoferrite between half and a quarter.

It is important to know what relative quantities of these constituents are present, so that the overall temperature can be estimated, thus avoiding unexpected excessive shrinkage that would cause cracks to appear.

The ability to resist freeze-thaw weathering depends largely on the proportion of tricalcium aluminate present, with durability improving when it represents a higher proportion of the cement.

Secondary constituents, unlike the primary constituents, have a destabilizing effect once hydration has finished. This is because during hydration they create fine powders that have high expansivity, a quality that is detrimental to the concrete.

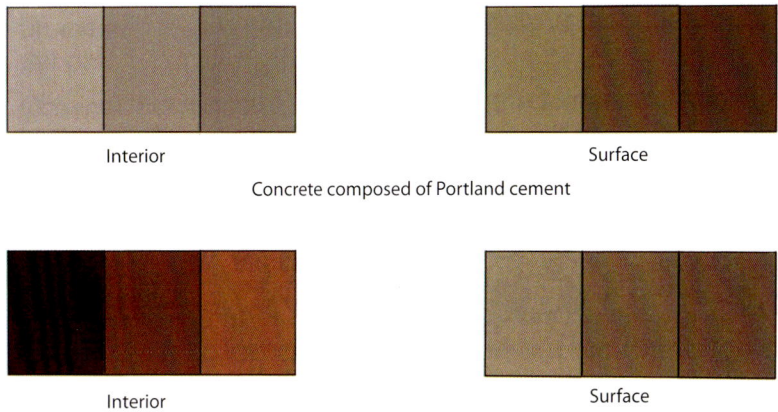

Colors of different types of concrete

As burnt lime (also known as quicklime) hydrates, it undergoes an exothermic reaction that causes it to expand in volume and the increase in pressure within the concrete can cause cracks to appear on the surface and, in extreme cases, can even cause its disintegration. The product of hydration, calcium hydroxide ('slaked lime'), is also susceptible to the presence of water, both acidic and alkaline. Therefore cements rich in lime tend to be unpredictable and lacking durability.

The magnesium oxide also undergoes an increase in volume but over a longer period. In a Portland cement its dose must be no more than 5%.

The alkalis in cement can react with aggregates that are rich in silica, causing their expansion, and this has negative consequences for the concrete's durability as it reduces the adhesion between the binder and the aggregate which can cause the concrete to disintegrate. Cement that has low levels of alkalis should therefore be chosen if silica-rich aggregates are to be used.

As well as the negative effects due to their expansion, alkalis can also cause efflorescence, accelerate the setting process, increase drying shrinkage and they can corrode certain types of glass when the glass is placed in direct contact with the concrete.

Portland cement is specified according to its minimum compressive strength (in kg/cm^2 or psi) after 28 days, determined by laboratory testing.

2. Portland-composite cement

This is made of a minimum of 80% by mass of Portland cement clinker with a setting regulator, and a maximum of 20% of slag or pozzolana. It is also specified according to compressive strength after 28 days.

Certain blast-furnace slags have hydraulic properties, while pozzolana is a natural product that, when it comes into contact with calcium in water, forms a hydraulic compound.

3. Blast-furnace cement

Similar to the type mentioned above, this cement is made of a 20 to 80% by mass of Portland cement clinker with a setting regulator, and at least 20% blast-furnace slag.

4. Pozzolanic cement

This is made of Portland cement clinker and a setting regulator (less than 80% of total mass), with pozzolana constituting a minimum of 20% of the total mass. In the European regulations EN-197, it is classified as type CEM/IV.

5. Composite cement

This contains a minimum of 65% Portland cement clinker with a setting regulator, and inert additives (that do not react with cement and water), making up the remaining mass. These types of cement are not suitable for use in structural concrete.

6. Natural cement

This is obtained by grinding the clinker of naturally occurring cement. The various types, also specified according to compressive strength after 28 days, can be sorted into 'slow' and 'fast' natural cements.

7. Calcium aluminate cement

This is obtained by the grinding of clinker consisting of hydraulic calcium aluminates, which is made by fusing together a mixture of a calcium-bearing material (normally limestone) and an aluminum-bearing material (normally bauxite). As such it is totally different in terms of constituents, production and properties, to those cements made of Portland cement clinker.

8. Cements with additional properties

These are cements that not only comply with the basic requirements of their relevant categories but also possess additional, specialized, properties:

High early strength Portland cement: achieves a minimum compressive strength of $250 kg/cm^2$ (3555 psi) within 48 hours. It is classified into the following categories:

- P-350 ARI
- P-450 ARI
- P-550 ARI

Sulfate resistant Portland cement: has a reduced susceptibility to attack by dissolved sulfates in water or soils, due to a lower proportion of tricalcium aluminate.

It is classified into the following categories:

- P-350 Y
- P-450 Y
- P-550 Y

Low heat Portland cement: defined as producing a heat on the seventh day of hydration of 65 cal/g (65 BTU/lb), and on the 28th day of 75 cal/g (75 BTU/lb).

White cement: possesses a minimum of 70% whiteness, measured by the level of light it reflects compared to a reference value, corresponding to the reflectance of magnesium oxide powder.

Reference doses for the cement are necessary as a guide but can be adjusted to suit the situation. In general the quality of the concrete will depend a great deal on the dosage of cement.

Increasing the cement dose above the recommended amount given by the manufacturer will proportionally increase the level of protection surrounding the reinforcement as well as increasing adherence between the reinforcement and the concrete.

An increase in the strength of the concrete also occurs, but this is not in direct proportion to the quantity of cement used. Instead, the increase in strength follows a steadily decreasing curve until a dose of 420 kg/m^3 (0.8 slugs/ft^3) is reached, after which point adding more cement has absolutely no effect on strength.

One negative repercussion of adding more cement is that the probability of cracks appearing due to drying shrinkage is increased.

It is of vital importance that cement be stored correctly, in a dry, ventilated space (ensuring that the air used for ventilation is not humid) otherwise the cement, and the concrete in which it is used, will be defective.

Aggregates

The type of aggregate used in concrete has a strong influence on its strength and durability. Of particular importance are two qualities pertaining to fine aggregates: particle size and compactness.

An aggregate must be chosen that does not react with the cement and is resistant to the aggressive external agents that could attack the concrete.

For example, aggregates that contain mud, clay, or organic material can be harmful because these substances reduce the adhesion between the binder and the aggregate and they can be detrimental to the hydration, and hardening, of the concrete.

Sands and gravels from natural deposits, as well as crushed stone and blast furnace slag, can all be suitable aggregates as long as they have been tested accordingly in the laboratory.

Blast furnace slag is only suitable for use as a fine aggregate if it has been previously tested to check that it is stable, i.e. it does not contain unstable silicates or iron compounds. Stones that are soft, friable, porous, or contain pyrite, clay or iron compounds are not suitable for use as aggregate.

Certain kinds of aggregate can create expansive compounds when they react with the cement, which create internal stresses in the concrete and can reduce its strength and durability.

Among the materials that can cause this problem, are **quartz polymorphs** such as opal, cristobalite, andesite and tridymite. They react with the alkalis in the cement to form compounds of greater volume that can destroy the concrete.

Similarly, **sulfur** compounds can react with water to form expansive sulfoaluminates. This can happen even if there is no liquid water present as it can also be caused by high humidity.

The presence of clays in aggregates is a common cause of defects in concrete. Due to the fact that the cracks caused appear on the surface of the concrete soon after pouring, they are often swiftly repaired and thus the damage can go largely unnoticed.

Usually the presence of clays is a result of insufficient cleaning of the aggregate at the site of extraction, often a quarry or river. This can cause confusion when sorting the aggregate at the processing plant and, in general, has negative repercussions for the quality of the concrete.

Pyrites, and similar sulfur based minerals, can oxidize upon contact with the air, creating sulfates that then react with the tricalcium aluminate present in the cement to form expansive ettringite. In the normal manufacture of Portland cement, gypsum is added to the clinker during grinding and this gypsum reacts with the calcium aluminate within 24 hours, forming ettringite. However, the reaction leaves traces of aluminate that could later react with sulfates if they are present.

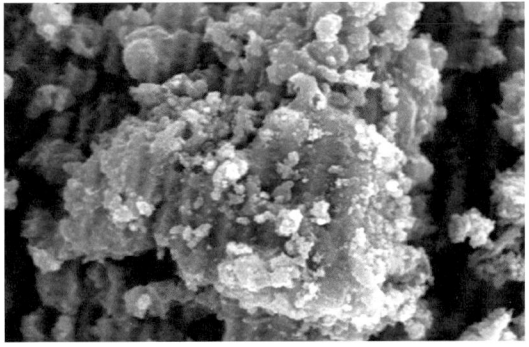

A common aggregate seen through a microscope (at 10 and 100 micrometres/ 400 and 4000 microinches)

Sulfates can be present in the aggregate or in water that is in contact with the concrete. The resulting reactions could produce expansive ettringite.

The effect of expansion could be cracks, or disintegration of the concrete, because such reactions occur before the concrete has fully hardened.

The three types of iron pyrite are:

- **Marcasite:** greenish yellow in color, it should not be used as an aggregate because it is susceptible to attack by atmospheric agents
- **Pyrrhotite:** differing from the other pyrites in possessing magnetic properties which, together with the fact that it is susceptible to attack from atmospheric agents, makes it unsuitable for use as aggregate
- **Yellow pyrite** often contains impurities and so, even if it otherwise would be a suitable aggregate, its use would be inadvisable

Pyrite has on occasion been used as an aggregate in concrete but the results in these cases have generally been unsatisfactory. All of the technical literature available on the subject reveals that it is best avoided as an aggregate material.

The strength of concrete is directly related to the compactness of the aggregates. This relationship can be measured by the difference between the real and apparent volume of the concrete.

A denser distribution of aggregate will leave less spaces for the binder to fill and will thus reduce the amount of cement required, which greatly reduces costs. A more dense concrete will also generally be more 'healthy' and durable than one that contains less aggregate. The density of a concrete element is thus a fundamental indicator of its quality.

The **particle size distribution of the aggregate** is another important factor. An incorrect distribution can cause a lack of compactness in the concrete.

This is usually dealt with in two ways. One way is to make up for the lack of fine aggregate by adding more cement, which implies that a significant part of the binder material is simply acting as a filler. As this is not what cement is supposed to be used for, doing this has two effects: increased costs and higher hydration temperatures, which has several repercussions.

The other method that is often used in order to compensate for an uneven particle size distribution is to use a more energetic compaction technique. This also achieves a smoother surface finish, which also makes the concrete appear more compact.

This smooth surface is the top layer of a thin coating of cement that forms the outer edge of the concrete element. It is the result of wet cement making its way out from the center of the element towards the inner face of the formwork by passing through the spaces left over between the particles of coarse aggregate. As such, it is a sign that there is a difference in composition across the section of the concrete element.

The shape of the coarse aggregate influences the quality of concrete. The ratio between the volume of the particle and the volume of a sphere is known as a particle's **sphericity** and if this value is below 0.15 the aggregate will require additional testing to check its suitability. As well as shape, another important characteristic of an aggregate is its density.

In general, the lower the density, the lower the quality of the aggregate. This is because low density is an indication of high porosity, which itself results in lower strength.

Given the fact that the aggregate makes up 70 to 80% of the volume of concrete, its quality greatly determines the quality of the concrete. A problem relating to fine aggregates is when they have a grain size of less than 0.08 mm (1/320 in). This is especially problematic when the fine aggregate size is similar to that of the dry cement.

When such cases occur, the grains of fine aggregate become mixed with the grains of cement during mixing. This then inhibits the hydration of the cement, creating irregularities that reduce the adhesion between the cement paste and the coarse aggregate.

The high specific surface area of these grains of aggregate also means that they absorb large amounts of water, which reduces the water available for the hydration of the cement. This has the effect of weakening the concrete.

In order to avoid this happening, the common solution is to increase the water dose (and, therefore, the ratio of water to cement) to achieve sufficient workability of the concrete.

However, this has the effect of reducing the concrete's mechanical strength, increasing the likelihood of shrinkage cracks and increasing the porosity (and hence, absorption of harmful agents) of the concrete. It also creates the problem of how to get rid of the surplus water that has not been used during hydration because it subsequently rises to the surface.

As it rises, it creates capillary pores that make the concrete more permeable. The scale of this problem depends on how much excess water was initially included.

Water

The defects in concrete that have their origins in the constituent water have two possible causes.

The first of these is the use of water containing impurities, which can create both short and long term problems. The second cause is related to dosage and occurs when the ratio of water to cement is too high.

As regards the first cause mentioned above, the outcome depends greatly on whether the concrete is reinforced or not. If the concrete does not have reinforcement then, to a certain degree, the use of impure water can have few harmful effects and produces no visible damage. However, in reinforced concrete the consequences can be more serious because the water can cause efflorescence and corrosion of the steel bars, due to the presence of chlorides. If impure water is used during curing it can cause even more harm than if it is introduced at the mixing stage.

If there are any doubts as to the quality of the water to be used in the construction of a concrete element (for example if no prior information is known about the water's characteristics) then it must be thoroughly tested before application. Regulations exist that establish advisable pH levels and the maximum permitted quantities of impurities, sulfates, chloride ions, carbohydrates and soluble substances.

Seawater: can be used for mixing concrete when reinforcement will not be used, although it must be noted that it can reduce the strength of the concrete by up to 15%. It is also likely to cause efflorescence, resulting in stains on the surface of the concrete. Seawater should never be used in pre-stressed concrete or concrete that contains calcium aluminate cement.

The maximum recommended amount of chloride ions in the water used in concrete is 6g/ litre (0.05 lb/ gallon). However, when there is no reinforcement up to 20g/ litre (0.17 lb/ gallon) can be present in the water without causing any harm, and when the concrete is pre-stressed an amount of more than 0.25g/ litre (0.002 lb/ gallon) will risk causing corrosion of the reinforcement.

If the limit of 6 g/litre is exceeded in regular reinforced concrete it can cause corrosion of the reinforcement. Once the reinforcement is corroded, it is less strong and the formation of oxidization layers on its surface exerts pressure on the surrounding concrete, causing it to disintegrate.

Sulfates: can be harmful to both the concrete and the reinforcement. The sulfates in water react with the tricalcium aluminate in the cement, forming expansive ettringite (tricalciumsulfo-aluminate hydrate, also known as 'Candlot's salt' or 'cement bacillus').

As the ettringite expands, it produces swelling and cracking in the concrete. If the cement used contains low levels of aluminate (e.g. sulfate-resistant Portland cement), the maximum permitted level of sulfate ions in the water can be increased to 5 g/litre (0.04 lb/ gallon). Attack by sulfates destroys the passivating layer around the reinforcement, leaving the bars vulnerable to corrosion, a process which is also expansive.

Carbohydrates: can impede the hydration of concrete, even when present only in small quantities. Water from sugar refineries, and water that has been in contact with sugars, glucose and other carboydrates, should never be used.

Water containing traces of **selenite** is rarely used in concrete but, if the concrete is in contact with groundwater that contains selenite, chemical attack can occur.

Additives

Additives are considered to be the fourth ingredient in concrete and are products that are added during mixing. Their purpose is to modify, beneficially, certain characteristics of the concrete, both when it is plastic and once it has hardened.

As opposed to the other constituents in concrete, there are no rules or guidelines that prescribe the required qualities that an additive should possess, so it is necessary to take great care in choosing a trustworthy supplier who can guarantee a good quality product.

Quality control during manufacture, in order to guarantee the uniform composition of the additive, is vital because the additive must produce the same effect across the entirety of the concrete element.

Additives do not generally improve the concrete in proportion to how much is used, so they must be used in the precise quantities indicated by the supplier.

Additives must be used in precise doses which have been tested on samples of the concrete before they can be used in construction.

The defects that are likely to arise from the use of additives could be due to:

- **Errors during manufacture**
- **Incorrect use**
- **Dosage errors**

In terms of the first point, suffice to say that the choice of a good quality manufacturer who can provide reliable test results should be enough to avoid the problem

Correct use will, first of all, depend on the correct choice of product. There is a wide range of suppliers and it is important to know beforehand exactly what effect is desired from the additive.

It is also vital to know what secondary effects the additive produces, as in certain cases these could negate any initial benefits, it being therefore wiser not to use the additive.

For example, if a hardening accelerator contains calcium chloride, it is likely to cause corrosion of the bars in reinforced and pre-stressed concrete.

Accelerators also increase drying shrinkage and are likely therefore to cause cracking to a degree that might not be permissible in exposed architectural concrete elements.

Plasticizers sometimes have the effect of delaying hydration, while in some cases they can provoke accelerated hydration, for example if used in large amounts in combination with cement that is low in gypsum.

Some accelerators have the effect of reducing mechanical strength and, as previously mentioned, can increase drying shrinkage and, subsequently increase the likelihood of corrosion of the reinforcement.

The most common problems associated with the use of color pigments in concrete

The pigment does not achieve the required tone and density of color
Coloration is not uniform: the fault of non-durable pigments or wet patches
Incompatible pigments are mixed together
Pigments are accidentally incorporated into the concrete
The pigment alters the characteristics of the concrete's constituents
The water: cement ratio is insufficient
Incorporating pigments forces changes to the construction schedule
It is difficult to control the color across construction joints
Uneven coloration due to the use of sub-standard formwork
The mold-releasing agent used is not appropriate for use with the chosen pigment
It is difficult to predict the effects that efflorescence will have on the color
The concrete lacks additional surface protection

Additives should only be used on sites where a high level of quality control can be guaranteed in the reception of material on-site, and during dosage and construction.

As such, the use of additives is less risky in those situations where quality control can be more systematic, for example when the concrete is mixed off-site, or when the concrete elements are entirely prefabricated off-site, under controlled conditions.

In general, the following rules apply to the use of additives:

- **The use of additives should be avoided whenever possible.** They can be avoided when other means can be used to achieve the desired properties in the concrete, e.g. by varying materials, dosage, manufacture, pouring or curing.
- **Tests must first be made** to check the full effects of the additive and dosages must be rigorously controlled when a particular effect is desired
- **Only good quality additives, that have undergone testing, should be used.** It is important to check the side effects that using the additive causes, so that an evaluation can be made as to whether it is ultimately worth using the additive or not.
- **The additives used must be stored correctly.** If the additive comes in the form of a liquid then it must be kept in a cool place and shaken before use, in case sedimentation has occurred. If the additive is a powder then it must be kept in a dry place to avoid lumps forming and any other changes that could alter its properties.
- Check the product's expiry date:
  The additive must be evenly distributed across the entirety of the concrete element in order to avoid any possible side effects resulting from its unevenness within the concrete
- **Additives can be incompatible with each other,** or with the binder material of the concrete. Some additives react well with certain types of cement but badly with others and tests should, therefore, be previously carried out with the specific cement that is to be used.
- **It is generally recommended to add the additive to the water used for mixing the concrete, before any other solid constituents are added** in order to achieve a more homogenous distribution of additive within the concrete. This does not apply to water-reducing additives or color pigments.
- **The uneven distribution of an additive can cause serious damage.** For example, if a hardening retarder is concentrated in certain areas it is possible that the concrete could collapse when the formwork is removed.
- **If the aggregate used is absorbent** (e.g. lightweight aggregate) it is necessary to wash it before adding it to the water that contains the additive because, otherwise, the aggregate will absorb part of the additive, reducing its effectiveness.
- **Water-reducing additives and color pigments must be dry-mixed with the cement.** A thorough mix is required to achieve an even distribution.
- **When air-entraining additives are used,** extra care must be taken during compaction of the concrete in order to ensure that not too much air is removed, especially if the purpose of using the additive is to improve resistance to freezing.

Defects in concrete arising from faulty manufacture and casting

The manner in which a concrete element is cast is a determining factor in its durability and robustness.

Errors made during casting will generally later cause the concrete to be weaker than predicted, and can also cause its appearance to be quite different to what was intended. The seriousness of these problems will depend on the gravity of the original mistake.

It is hoped that such mistakes can be avoided if the project leader is aware of the principles of proper dosage, mixing and casting and if the personnel on site are well qualified.

The most common causes of mistakes made during casting that can alter the properties of concrete are:

- **Incorrect dosage** due to human error or faulty equipment. In particular the most common pitfalls are the cement doses and the proportion of water to cement.
- **Transport and pouring** are two delicate stages because they inherently cause segregation of the constituents. This can create areas in the finished concrete that have holes, too much aggregate or insufficient density.
- **Insufficient vibrating** will result in a concrete that lacks density.
- **The shape of the formwork.** Of importance here is the width between the inner faces of the formwork and the size and distribution of the reinforcement. There has to be enough space between

bars, and in between bars and the inner face, for the wet concrete to pass through as otherwise hollows will form in the concrete in those areas that the mass could not reach. The formwork must also be watertight to avoid wet cement escaping. If cement were to escape it would produce areas of low compactness and reduce the protective coating around the reinforcement.

The properties that will be most affected by such errors are the concrete's **compactness** and **homogeneity**.

A concrete element can be considered to be homogenous when its composition is the same across the whole element. A homogenous concrete can therefore simultaneously be a concrete that lacks compactness.

A lack of homogeneity can be caused by the segregation of materials within the cast concrete. This can be due to the settlement of larger constituents as much as by lighter constituents floating towards the surface.

Holes, and a pitted surface, are the result of insufficient vibration of the concrete after pouring

Both phenomena can occur if the type and dosage of cement, quantity of water, and additives used are not correct. These errors occur during the mixing stage of construction.

Various other operations such as transport of mixed cement, pouring and compaction, and factors such as reinforcement layout and formwork design can also affect homogeneity.

Homogeneity will also depend to a large degree on careful compaction once the concrete has been poured. Compaction is a crucial stage in concrete construction.

The compactness of a concrete element largely depends on the correct dosage of constituents. Of fundamental importance are the proportions of water to cement and aggregate to cement. A proper cement dose is thus vital for each of these proportions to be correct. As well as aggregate, cement and water, a fourth 'constituent' plays a part in these relationships. This is air, which can cause gaps to form in the concrete.

The role that these constituents play in the compactness of concrete will now be analyzed in terms of their dosage and application.

Dosage

The dosage of cement can be a source of problems in concrete. When trying to achieve concrete of a specific strength, it is always advisable to try and do so using the least amount of cement possible. This is because a high cement dose will increase drying shrinkage, which can create internal cracks and visible fractures.

High doses also imply a high heat of hydration. This is something especially risky when casting during hot times of the year because the overall increase in temperature will exacerbate drying shrinkage and cracking.

Cement that includes inert additives of a similar grain size to that of the cement (also known as fillers) has a slower hardening time than that of pure cement. This should be borne in mind when dosing the concrete because it will affect how much cement and water are needed.

It is advisable to keep the cement dose to below 400 kg per cubic meter (0.77 slugs/ ft^3) in reinforced concrete and to below 550 kg per cubic meter (1 slug/ ft^3) in pre-stressed concrete.

The quantity of water used for mixing in relation to the quantity of cement is of fundamental importance. Theoretically, a proportion of water to cement of 0.18 is enough for proper hydration of the cement's active constituents to occur. However, higher proportions are invariably used in order to achieve sufficient **workability** in the mix.

Thus the quantity of water used in casting concrete is more than that simply needed for the hydration of the binder because, in order to be cast, the fresh concrete has to be fluid enough to enter and fully fill the formwork, and to be sufficiently compactable.

A proportion of water to cement of 0.6 to 0.8 is used in traditional concrete (i.e. concrete that has no water reducing additives and that is cast and compacted on site). The weight of water necessary for full hydration is equivalent to about 30% of the total weight of cement. The water left over after hydration leaves the concrete by evaporation, leaving small pores in the concrete. Hardened concrete with a porosity of less than 10% is considered to be of low porosity. If porosity exceeds 15% it is likely to affect the concrete's durability.

The network of pores is what later allows gases and liquids to penetrate into the concrete.

As such, the pores are the elements that facilitate the different types of corrosion that will be studied later in this chapter. An excess of water in the casting of concrete also produces an increase in contraction and a decrease in the concrete's strength.

In the field of restoration it is very common to find that the existing concrete was made with an excess of water. This is due in part to the fact that the technology of compaction was not as advanced as it is now, and extra water had to be added in order to make the fresh concrete workable using the methods of compaction that were available.

As an example, concrete with a cement dose of 350 kg per cubic meter (0.68 slugs/ft3) and a water : cement ratio of 0.5 requires 175 liters (0.34 slugs/ft3) of hydration water. Theoretically, only 63 liters (16.6 gallons) would have been necessary for the hydration, which leaves 112 liters (29.6 gallons) of water that must somehow make its way out of the fresh concrete.

A cubic meter of this concrete would therefore contain a network of 112,000 cubic centimeters (4 cubic feet) of capillary pores criss-crosssing the mass of cement, through which water and corroding agents could penetrate to the very core of the concrete.

This example illustrates how the quantity of water used for mixing the concrete later has a huge importance on its porosity and, therefore, its durability.

Air is not a constituent of concrete in the literal sense of the word but it does form a part of any element made from concrete. The proportion of air to concrete will depend on: the function that the concrete element must serve, the correct dosage of the concrete's constituents and the level of compaction that the concrete undergoes. In some cases, air plays an important role in helping the concrete achieve its purpose (e.g. in lightweight concrete), while in other cases its presence can be problematic, such as in high strength concrete. Air, which does not contribute to mechanical strength, is present in hardened concrete in the form of cavities. These can be both visible from the surface (open) and hidden inside the concrete (closed).

Both open and closed air holes reduce the mechanical strength of the concrete by replacing a certain volume of resistant material with air, which has no structural capability.

Open holes also have the effect of increasing the surface area of concrete in contact with the exterior. Compared to a more compact, less porous concrete, such an element will be more vulnerable to corrosion and hence less stable and durable because of the greater area of contact.

Therefore, more compact concrete is generally more resistant. Air, however, can sometimes be intentionally incorporated into the fresh concrete. For example, it can be added in order to improve resistance against freeze - thaw weathering.

Air-entraining additives work by creating small bubbles within the concrete that break the continuity of the capillary pores and thus reduce the risk of the concrete absorbing corrosive agents.

The quantity of water which enters the concrete is also reduced, and because the air pockets provide space for expansion, when the water freezes in cold weather it expands without generating internal pressures in the concrete which would cause its deterioration.

Air-entraining additives also play a secondary role as a lubricant in fresh concrete. Their ability to make the wet concrete more fluid allows for a lower dosage of water and a slightly lower dose of fine aggregate. The overall effect of these additives on the strength of the concrete is therefore beneficial, despite the fact that they add air to the concrete.

Cracking in concrete

The types of cracks studied in this section are those that arise from internal stresses in the concrete due to internal or external forces present during its preparation, pouring, hydration and subsequent hardening.

These stresses essentially derive from the presence of moisture in the concrete and so their causes can be classified as being hydro-thermo-mechanical in origin.

This category includes: drying shrinkage cracks, 'crazing' cracks, those cracks that are caused by thermal factors and all of those that occur while the concrete is still plastic, before it has fully hardened.

These cracks are analyzed here in the order in which they occur during the life of the concrete, with a distinction made between those that appear before and those that appear after hardening has begun.

Cracks that appear before the concrete starts to harden

The causes of these cracks develop when the concrete is still plastic, from a few minutes after the concrete is poured, to when hardening begins.

A distinction is made between two types of cracking of different characteristics: **plastic settlement** and **plastic shrinkage** cracking.

Plastic shrinkage cracking occurs most often in horizontal concrete elements, such as slabs, due to the high level of evaporation owing to the large area exposed to the air. Plastic settlement cracks, on the other hand, occur most frequently in thick concrete sections. The process of **bleeding** is what causes both types of cracking to occur. Bleeding is the name given to the phenomenon of water rising to the surface of the concrete in the hours immediately following pouring.

Gravity causes settlement of the solids in the wet concrete, leaving any water that has not been used in hydration exposed on the surface. Improving compaction reduces this effect.

Bleeding always occurs to some degree, regardless of the type of concrete, but the excess water on the surface is only visible when it cannot fully evaporate.

When the water cannot evaporate completely, a thin film of clear water can be seen on the surface of the concrete. This is not be confused with the watered mix that is applied between casting phases.

Some of the factors that influence the scale of bleeding are:

- **High ratios of water to cement** cause more bleeding than lower ratios
- **High rates of evaporation from the surface** in the period immediately following pouring and compaction cause increased bleeding
- **The thicker the concrete element, the longer the bleeding process will last**
- **The use of hardening retarders** generally increases bleeding

Plastic settlement cracks are almost always due to high levels of bleeding and, generally, appear within the first three hours after pouring. In some cases they can appear up to six or eight hours after pouring. They appear in those places where the natural settlement of the material is impeded in some way.

The most common types and locations of cracks are as follows:

- **Pronounced cracks situated immediately above horizontal reinforcing bars,** which could be the main reinforcement or stirrups.
- **Horizontal cracks in vertical elements** (columns, etc), where stirrups have impeded settlement.
- **Cracks that coincide with sudden changes in section** of the element. These are particularly common in waffle slabs and are due to the difference in settlement between thick and thin sections.
- **Cracks in thin concrete sections.** These occur when the network of reinforcement is so close to the surface that settlement essentially separates the concrete into two layers because the concrete above the reinforcement cannot settle as much as the concrete below the reinforcement.

Normally, these kinds of cracking are not of structural importance, but they can increase the likelihood of corrosion of the reinforcement because the bars can be left exposed.

Plastic shrinkage cracks appear within the first 8 hours after the concrete has been poured, although, in some cases, they can appear up to one day after pouring.

The cracks can be very wide at the surface (2-3mm (1/16-1/18 in) or even more), but the width reduces quickly with depth. It is also common for them to pass completely through a floor slab, something that marks them apart from plastic settlement cracks. They are especially common in floor slabs and ground floor slabs, and can follow several patterns.

They can form in diagonal lines, at an angle of approximately 45o from a corner, with a separation of between 200 mm and 2 m (8 in and 6 ½ ft) between them. They can also form concentrically, in a ripple pattern, or in a random, grid-like pattern.

Another common pattern is that they follow the lines of the reinforcing bars, or some similar geometrical characteristic of the element (changes in section, for example). They can also form around points at which pouring was interrupted.

The cause of these cracks, in general, is the rapid drying of the bleed water, for example when evaporation occurs at a faster rate than the bleeding. An evaporation rate of 1 kg/m² h (0.2 lb/ft² h) is considered to be a high rate of evaporation.

As an illustration, such a rate would be likely in the following conditions: a concrete with an internal temperature of 20oC in an atmosphere with a relative humidity of 80% with a 32 km/h (20 mph) wind at 5°C. The process of curing (adding additional water to the surface of the concrete) plays an important role in helping to avoid these cracks occurring because it compensates for high rates of evaporation, something that is especially likely in hot conditions.

Cracks that appear after hardening has begun
Initial **thermal cracks** and **crazing** can appear while the concrete is hardening, after hydration has occurred.

Drying shrinkage cracks can appear from when the concrete is nearly fully hardened up to a period of two to three years, and sometimes longer, after construction.

Initial thermal cracks normally appear between one and five days after pouring, when hydration has stopped.

They are a result of the heat generated within the mass of the concrete during hydration of the cement.

This heat generates an increase in volume that, in turn, generates stresses between the warmer and cooler parts of the concrete element. The warmer part would be at the core of the element, while cooler parts could be areas that are in contact with the air, or with concrete that was cast earlier. These areas of hardened concrete will impede the natural contraction of the fresh concrete.

The temperature difference between the inside of the concrete and the air outside is at its greatest between one and five days after pouring. In general, the internal temperature becomes equal to that of the environment between 7 and 14 days after pouring.

It is this fact that allows these cracks to be properly identified because drying shrinkage cracks tend to appear much later. The factors that influence the temperature difference between the concrete and the environment are:

Types of cracking in concrete

Before hardening

Freezing	
Plastic	Plastic shrinkage
	Plastic settlement
Movement during construction	Movement of the formwork
	Movement of adjacent structures

After hardening

Physical	Shrinkage of the aggregate
	Drying shrinkage
	Crazing
Chemical	Rusting of the reinforcement
	Alkali-aggregate reaction
	Carbonation
Thermal	Freeze - thaw
	Seasonal temperature changes
	Initial thermal cracks
Structural	Accidental additional live load
	Fatigue
	Errors in structural calculations

- **The initial temperature of the constituents and the materials used for casting the concrete, compared to the air temperature.** The difference between the two will be greater during cold weather
- **Thick sections of concrete produce more heat,** though this effect reduces in magnitude above a certain thickness
- **Concrete should not be hosed down with cold water immediately after the formwork is removed,** as doing so would create a thermal shock. Instead, an effort should be made to keep the concrete as warm as possible in the period immediately following the removal of the formwork.
- **The heat of hydration will be higher when there is more cement in the mix.** The heat of hydration also varies according to the type of cement used.
- **Limestone and granite aggregates have lower coefficients of thermal expansion than other materials.** Lightweight aggregates tend to work better under tension than regular aggregates.
- **Hydration enhancing additives cause heat to be generated more quickly.** Retarders can delay hydration, although this will not change the total amount of heat generated.
- **The width of the cracks can be reduced by increasing the amount of reinforcement,** possibly by using bars of smaller diameter in combination with the thinnest possible covering layer of concrete
- **Timber formwork retains more heat than metallic types,** but they also act as insulation, reducing the temperature gradient across the concrete element.
- **Premature removal of formwork** normally increases the difference in temperature
- **The cracks are more likely to occur where there are uneven internal stresses,** such as: sudden changes in section, the corners around openings or around the holes left by the formwork ties.

Thermal cracks are very common in retaining walls, slabs and, in general, thick elements. They are especially likely to occur when there is something that impedes the free expansion of the concrete. They are often confused with drying shrinkage cracks because they both tend to appear in the same places and they also share some of the same causes.

Crazing is the term given to thin, superficial cracks that appear between one and fifteen days after pouring, when the concrete is hardening. They are normally between 0.05 and 0.5 mm (1/520 and 1/52 in) wide and less than 10 mm (1/32 in) deep. They form a grid-like pattern of hairline cracks, spaced about 50 to 100 mm (2 to 4 in) apart.

They occur when the concrete is cast in extremely dry conditions, forcing it to shrink rapidly before it has developed sufficient tensile strength. Such conditions can occur in particularly windy, or dry weather conditions.

On occasion, these cracks can be so thin that their existence is only noticed after a significant amount of time has passed, when the collection of dirt and dust makes them more visible.

Other factors that influence the formation of these cracks are: the presence of physical restraints near the exposed surface, and a marked moisture gradient across the section of the element.

The best ways to avoid these cracks occurring are by: avoiding a concrete mix that has a high water or cement dose, achieving good compaction and avoiding the creation of very polished surfaces, that increase the proportion of cement paste in contact with the air.

Drying shrinkage cracks occur as a result of the contraction associated with a loss of moisture. The water is lost via physical and chemical processes during the final stages of hardening.

Similarly to the other types of cracks studied here, these cracks will only appear in concrete if its movement is in some way restricted, generating stresses that exceed the material's ability to resist tension.

These cracks can appear from two to three weeks after the concrete has been poured and, in normal conditions, can appear up to as much as one, two or three years later. The length of time will depend on the dryness of the environment surrounding the concrete.

Drying shrinkage cracks are often confused with initial thermal cracks because they often both appear in the same places, especially in retaining walls, and they look similar. Drying shrinkage cracks can be recognized because they have a more or less equal width along their length, are thin and vary in depth, sometimes crossing the whole thickness of the element.

Some of the factors that influence their formation are:

- **The loss of water through evaporation** is the main cause of drying shrinkage. As the amount of evaporation largely depends on the relative humidity of the air, a drier atmosphere will increase the scale of drying shrinkage and, therefore, the likelihood of

cracks appearing.
- **Curing,** even if it does not reduce the total amount of drying shrinkage, alleviates the problem by increasing the concrete's tensile strength during the early stages of hardening, thus minimizing the risk of cracking
- **The higher the water: cement ratio, the greater the drying shrinkage.** This is because the quantity of water evaporating will be higher.
- **If the element has a large surface area exposed to the air, in relation to its volume, then it is more likely to contract** because this will increase the amount of evaporation.
- **The use of aggregates with a low specific area** tends to reduce the likelihood of cracking.

Environmental factors that influence the durability of concrete

If we consider for a moment a hypothetical situation, in which the many other variables that can deteriorate concrete could be taken out of the equation, the single most important factor affecting durability would be the choice of a type of concrete that matches the aggressiveness of the environment in which it is placed.

However, in reality, a correct specification alone is not enough to guarantee good durability because errors can be made in the dosage and preparation of the concrete that will later produce weaknesses.

What happens frequently in construction is that the concrete specified does not suit the particular environment and protective treatments are applied after the concrete has hardened in order to compensate for any deficiencies.

It is worth noting that such a system can still produce an element that is adequate from a purely structural point of view, and if the treatment is adequate then the concrete can still ultimately have a long service life.

However, it must be pointed out that it is always much easier, cheaper and safer to take decisions to increase durability at the design stage rather than once construction has finished and that the cost of implementing remedial action steadily increases as time goes by.

In qualifying the 'aggressiveness of the environment', what is being referred to are those physical and chemical forces that act on concrete structures and which are distinct from mechanical actions and changes in volume due to hydro-thermal factors.

Environments can thus be analyzed and described according to the following categories: slightly aggressive (e.g. interior or semi-interior spaces in humid conditions), of medium aggressiveness (e.g. exteriors that are exposed to the weather and/ or non-aggressive soils), aggressive (e.g. industrial or marine environments, in contact with salt water and/ or acidic or aggressive soils) and chemically aggressive (e.g. chemical storage, in contact with bleach or fertilizer, etc).

The higher up the scale a certain environment is, the more resistant the concrete has to be in order to withstand corrosion. The property of the concrete that is most often adjusted in order to do this is its permeability. Generally, as concrete's impermeability is increased, so too is its compactness.

The most common recommendation as to how to achieve this is to reduce the proportion of water to cement but this is not always compatible with the need for the concrete to be workable during pouring.

As a result plasticizers tend to be used instead but these can have negative side effects, which can reduce the strength and durability of the concrete.

Other important factors are the grain size distribution of the aggregate and the technique used in testing the impermeability of the concrete.

As examples of the kind of damage that aggressive environments can cause, special mention is given here to marine environments, aggressive water and acid rain.

Marine environments create problems due to the concrete coming into contact with salt water and water vapor that contains salts, chlorides and sulfates. If seawater is used in mixing the concrete this will also produce chemical attack.

Water on the surface of the concrete, or in the internal pores, leaves crystallized salt on the concrete's surface once it has evaporated. This cryptoflorescence produces internal stresses that can cause weak, and even average strength, concrete to disintegrate.

This process also has the effect of creating areas of negative and positive polarity that, when water is present, create internal currents that can lead to electro-chemical corrosion of the reinforcement.

Aggressive water includes: blackwater, swamp water and groundwater that contains sulfates, which can react with concrete to form aluminates and gypsum.

The large size of the resulting crystals generates strong internal stresses that can crack and disintegrate concrete foundations, particularly at the edges and corners.

Acid rain generally affects the surface of the concrete. Rain is considered to be acid rain when it has a pH of 4 or less. Acid rain can contain sulfuric acid, nitric acid and heavy metals.

Damage arising from defects in the steel reinforcement

The great strength and flexibility that comes from combining steel with concrete is what lies behind reinforced concrete's widespread use as a structural material.

The reinforcement plays a very important role in structures due to its ability to resist tension.

There are basically three factors that explain why concrete and steel complement each other so effectively:

- **Coefficient of thermal expansion:** Both materials possess similar coefficients ($11 \times 10^{-6} \, k^{-1}$ for steel and $10 \times 10^{-6} \, k^{-1}$ for concrete)
- **Young's modulus:** Steel has a higher modulus ($2.1 \times 10^6 \, kp/cm^2 / 30 \times 10^6 \, psi$) than concrete ($2.5 \times 10^5 \, kp/cm^2 / 35 \times 10^5 \, psi$).
- **The alkaline nature of concrete:** Thus enabling it to act as a protective layer against corrosion of the reinforcement.

The defects in concrete derived from faults in the steel reinforcement are diverse, as are their precise origins. Here these defects are classified as follows:
- Damage arising from inherent defects in the steel
- Damage arising from corrosion of the reinforcement inside the concrete
- Damage arising from errors made in the placement of the reinforcement

Inherent defects in the steel
The steel manufacturer must guarantee the suitability of the metal for use in reinforced concrete structures by conducting laboratory tests. When such tests are properly carried out it is normally sufficient proof of the quality of the product. Normally, manufacturers provide the diameter, weight per meter length and the type of steel. They should also be able to provide detailed information about mechanical properties, properties related to achieving good adherence between the concrete and the steel and, in the case of corrugated bars, the bars' geometry.

The principal defects that reinforcement bars can suffer from are:

- **Impurities**
- **Surface defects**
- **Surface corrosion**

Impurities
Impurities can be substances left over from the alloy process, foreign substances and gases trapped in the steel. The former could be: phosphor, sulfur, manganese and silicon. The latter two are only considered to be impurities above certain levels.

Phosphor and sulfur are theoretically dangerous in quantities above 0.04%, but in reality they only pose a significant threat to the capability of the steel when they exceed this level constantly throughout the steel element.

Foreign substances are those that have a very high melting point (oxides, silicates, sulfates) and thus remain present in the formed steel.

Their very presence weakens the steel and they also have the effect of creating discontinuities in the steel, which then create points where internal stresses concentrate.

Gases can become incorporated into the steel when it is at a very high temperature and especially when it is molten. Molten steel dissolves a quite large amount of gases that then cannot be fully released while it is cooling. The most common gases that become trapped are atmospheric gases such as hydrogen, oxygen and nitrogen.

Surface defects
The most common defects are folds, which are a result of incorrect forging. The faces of the steel oxidize when hot and if not properly welded then this weak joint can produce a weak point in the reinforced con-

crete, which could crack

Another defect generated during the manufacture of the reinforcement is superficial scars in the steel that occur when it has cooled too quickly.

Surface corrosion

The previous two categories of defects originate in the manufacture of the steel. Surface corrosion, on the other hand, is generally a consequence of improper storage of the reinforcement or accidental exposure to a corrosive environment.

Frequently, reinforcing bars can be exposed to the atmosphere for a considerable amount of time while waiting to be used, and this allows for corrosion to begin. The frequent bending that reinforcing bars can be subjected to in order to facilitate transport and storage can also provoke corrosion.

Corrosion of steel reinforcement

Two of the processes through which steel can be weakened are corrosion and embrittlement. They both originate from contact with the air and the presence of moisture within the reinforced concrete.

Embrittlement of reinforcement is normally not too serious in regular reinforced concrete, but it can be particularly problematic in pre-stressed elements.

It is a result of hydrogen being present in the steel, either by coming into contact with a liquid that contains diffused hydrogen (such as an acid) or a gas that contains hydrogen (e.g. gases of hydrogen cyanide or hydrogen sulfide). Once hydrogen is absorbed into the steel it causes it to be more fragile and easily susceptible to breaking.

Corrosion occurs when layers of oxide form on the surface of the steel. As layers accumulate, the expansion creates stresses in the concrete, which can then disintegrate under the pressure.

The deterioration of steel reinforcement affects its appearance, thickness and, therefore, strength.

The presence of water or, at least, moisture is necessary for corrosion to occur. Variations in temperature also accentuate the effects of corrosion.

As such, understanding the characteristics of the environment surrounding the concrete is of vital importance when evaluating the possible extent of corrosion.

Broadly speaking, there are two ways in which corrosion can occur: chemically and electro-chemically. However it is also possible for the two processes to be at work simultaneously.

In general, when corrosion occurs chemically it affects the entire surface of the reinforcing and when it occurs electro-chemically it affects those points that have been converted into anodes.

Damage arising from incorrect placement of the reinforcement

As with concrete, care needs to be taken on site when preparing reinforcement. Proper handling will depend on decisions made during the **design stage, the cutting and bending** of the bars and the **placement** of the bars on site. The layout of the reinforcement is specified at the design stage of the project, with structural analysis needed in order to determine the size, quantity and layout of reinforcement.

This layout is then conveyed to the contractor through drawings. The bars will already have been cut and bent when they arrive on site and the contractor will refer to these drawings in order to place the reinforcement in the formwork.

Mistakes can be made at each of the stages highlighted above, usually as a result of insufficient technical understanding of how steel and concrete interact in reinforced concrete.

If the designer lacks this knowledge then the plans he/she produces will invariably contain errors. The most common error of this nature is a lack of information in the plans. For example, if the layout lacks detailed dimensions it leaves the contractor no choice but to measure off the drawings, which can lead to inaccuracies. Another common oversight is not giving clear indication of where the bars should overlap.

More often than not, the result of these oversights is that a person on site who lacks technical knowledge has to make decisions that could later have important consequences.

Incorrect cutting of reinforcing bars normally does not have structural implications and, in general, does not lead to serious problems.

The cases in which the incorrect cutting of reinforcing bars has caused serious problems, have generally been those where tolerances have been greatly exceeded.

The solution involves attaching extra reinforcement.

The most common error made in terms of bending the bars is the specification, or accidental execution of a bending radius that is smaller than what the steel used is capable of supporting.

This often happens when the tools needed for the correct bending and checking of diameters are not available on site and also frequently happens when thick bars, greater than 20 mm (3/4 in) in diameter, are used. The damage can be visible in the form of cracks at the inside of the bend that, if severe enough, can break the bar. This sort of damage is quite common nowadays because of the widespread use of more rigid steel bars.

The incorrect distribution of the reinforcement can be a source of problems in reinforced concrete if certain tolerances are not respected. An example would be if negative-moment reinforcement bars are not evenly distributed, resulting in too much overlap in some areas, and too little in others.

It is common to find reinforced concrete structures whose covering layer of concrete on top of the reinforcement lacks sufficient thickness. This makes the structure more susceptible to deterioration. One possible cause of this defect is the omission of formwork ties, whose purpose is to regulate the spacing between the sides of the mold.

Another mistake made during placement is the use of bars that are not completely straight, something that affects both tensile and compressive strength.

Any slight bend in a reinforcement bar will reduce its structural capacity.

This normally is of little consequence in elements that are in compression because the steel contributes relatively little compressive strength compared to that of the concrete.

However, if a bent bar has to work in tension then it will make cracking of the concrete more likely. This could be the case of a bar in an element which is normally under compression but has part of its load removed, causing the element to decompress and creating tension that the reinforcement would normally need to resist.

It is also common to find areas with excessive concentrations of reinforcement, which do not allow the wet concrete to pass and thus create holes in the finished concrete. This mistake is sometimes attributable to bad design, where not enough space was provided for the overlapping bars, and in other cases it is due to the incorrect execution of the bond between bars on-site.

Protection

The corrosion of reinforced concrete begins with the corrosion of the steel, so the provision of sufficient protection around the bars is vitally important. The layer of concrete around the bars provides protection and the inclusion of products that impede capillary absorption within the concrete also increases protection.

Another factor to bear in mind is that the nature of pre-stressed bars means that they are in a state that is not far from their elastic limit, and they are susceptible to electro-chemical corrosion. Several environmental conditions have to be present in order for this to occur.

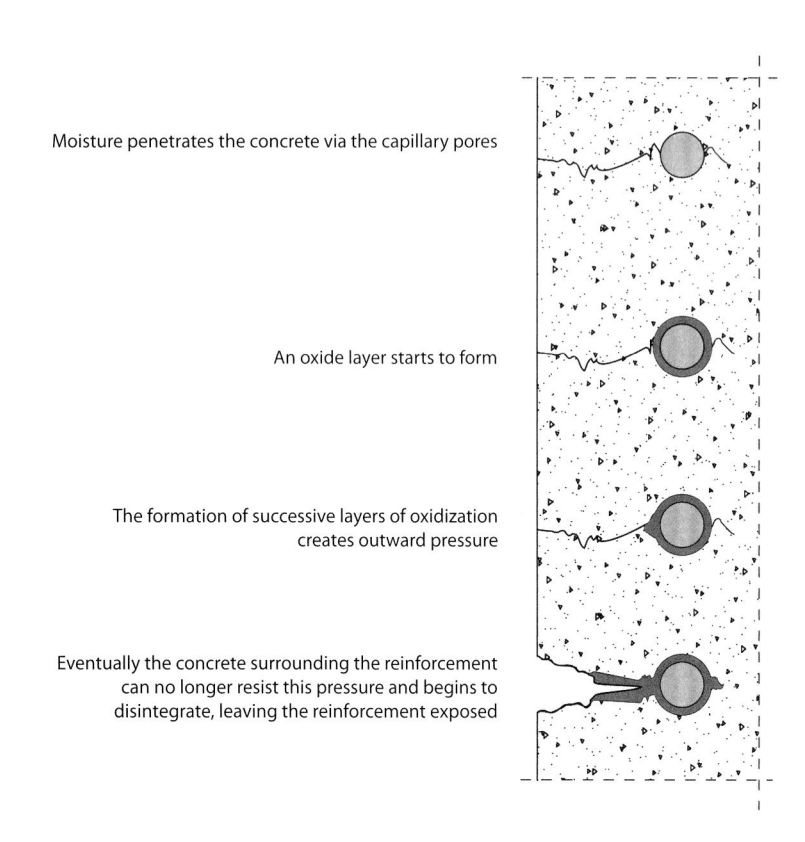

Effects of corrosion on non-galvanized steel reinforcing bars. In a relatively short time the steel can be significantly weakened. Galvanized steel bars do not suffer from this type of corrosion and maintain a good adherence to the concrete.

Moisture penetrates the concrete via the capillary pores

An oxide layer starts to form

The formation of successive layers of oxidization creates outward pressure

Eventually the concrete surrounding the reinforcement can no longer resist this pressure and begins to disintegrate, leaving the reinforcement exposed

Defects and deterioration of concrete

Aqueous saline solutions, alkalis or acids, and oxygen must all be present. If one of these is absent (if the concrete were completely submerged under water, or in a completely dry environment, for example) then corrosion would not occur.

Seeing as most natural environments possess elements that are chemically harmful to concrete, a reinforced concrete element that is exposed to the weather will begin to suffer degradation of its reinforcement after a few years.

Of course, the element would be much more durable in ideal conditions.

As corrosion has the effect of reducing the thickness and, therefore, the strength of the steel bars it is important for reinforced concrete structures to provide a covering of concrete around the bars that is of sufficient thickness.

The alkalinity of concrete has the effect of creating a passivating layer around the steel. This thin film of oxide has low permeability, which keeps the risk of electro-chemical corrosion at bay.

This film is very sensitive and can be easily destroyed if the concrete is permeable enough. This is because if carbon monoxide or carbon dioxide from the air penetrate the concrete they will react with the calcium, reducing the concrete's alkalinity. Soluble chlorides can also attack the passivating layer.

It is difficult to gauge how quickly corrosion can develop once the concrete has been cast and the reinforcement is no longer visible. It is therefore important to take particular care in achieving a properly dosed and mixed concrete because what occurs during the construction phase is what later determines the quality and durability of the protective layer.

What protects the reinforcement from the aggressive agents that cause corrosion is the concrete covering that surrounds it. In order for this covering layer to be effective it has to have a minimum thickness of 20 mm (3/4 in).

The cracks that appear in concrete has a result of corrosion of the reinforcement tend to be parallel to the main reinforcement bars or stirrups. The size of the cracks will vary with the state of the corrosion.

If corrosion is advanced enough, it can produce large cracks due to the significant outward pressure that the oxidization layer produces, which can cause the bar to be as much as 10 times its original thickness.

Factors that facilitate corrosion

If several key precautions are ignored in the construction of reinforced concrete then corrosion can develop and progress rapidly. If the mixing, pouring and curing stages are not carefully carried out then the result can be excessive quantities and sizes of pores in the concrete.

This has the effect of reducing the mechanical strength of the concrete, as large pores are more likely to join together and form cavities through which moisture can penetrate to the core of the element.

If this happens, the reinforcement is exposed more quickly to moisture, accelerating the process of oxidization.

The presence of pores is inevitable in cast concrete, but they should be kept as small as possible in order to reduce the risk of the pores interconnecting, as preventing it would help impede hydration.

A suitable water : cement ratio, in terms of weight, is 0.4: 1. Of this 40% of water, 25% crystallizes during hydration and 15% contributes to the plasticity of the wet concrete.

During hardening, this 40% is absorbed into the surrounding environment. Its evaporation is what creates pores in the concrete.

The proportion of water: cement of 0.4: 1 should not be exceeded because doing so would increase the size and quantity of pores created during evaporation. The negative consequences of high porosity have already been studied earlier but, to reiterate, the main result is an increase in capillary absorption of water and gases.

In environments that undergo low temperatures, there exists the risk of freezing, a process that considerably weakens concrete.

Tests have proven that in increasing the water: cement ratio from 0.4 to 0.75: 1, carbonation occurs four times faster and that the number of pores increases more than one hundred fold.

Two examples of incorrectly placed reinforcement. In the upper picture, the reinforcement in this cantilever was placed near the underside and not near the top, while in the lower picture the layer of concrete covering the reinforcement in this retaining wall is far too thin.

It is practically impossible to avoid cracks appearing in concrete. The width of cracks is what determines how serious they are in terms of furthering degradation. Wide cracks can be especially dangerous in aggressive environments. When the crack is less than 0.2 mm (1/144 in) wide, it is unlikely to cause oxidization of the reinforcement, as long as the environment is not too aggressive and provided the protective layer of concrete is thick enough to resist carbonation.

If the environment around the concrete is of a particularly corrosive nature, such as a marine or industrial location, oxidization should be considered as a risk with cracks as thin as 0.1 mm (1/288 in).

If the concrete is used in a water reservoir or dam, oxidization can occur even when the cracks are thinner than 0.1 mm (1/288 in).

The environment is the most deciding factor in the corrosion of steel reinforcement. Variations in climate determine the level of humidity which, when combined with chlorides and sulfates, is what determines the risk and scale of corrosion.

Chemical aggressiveness is common in industrial environments, where the combination of rain and sulfur dioxide results in sulfuric and sulfurous acid, the combination of which not only neutralizes the alkalinity of the concrete, but also reacts with the calcium carbonate.

This can result in the formation of gypsum or aluminum compounds, which create an increase in volume that later causes the concrete to disintegrate.

Carbonation

Carbonation is the process through which the covering layer of concrete loses its alkalinity, which is the property that provides chemical protection to the reinforcement. Carbon dioxide from the atmosphere reacts with the alkaline substances present throughout the concrete's pores and in those elements that have undergone hydration. This has the effect of lowering the pH of the concrete. Below a critical level of pH 9.5, protection of the reinforcement can no longer be guaranteed.

Carbonation in reinforced concrete first occurs at the surface and then works its way into the concrete. The area that the carbonation is able to affect will depend on time and depth. The thickness of the protective layer determines these two factors.

The depth to which carbonation penetrates will also depend on the quality of the concrete in question.

Needless to say, the speed at which carbonation can develop depends on the porosity of the concrete. Cements that are rich in lime provide improved protection to the reinforcement because they are more alkaline.

For this reason, cements that contain alkaline products, such as blastfurnace slag and pozzolana, are recommended when improved protection is required. This is also why Portland cement is so commonly used, because it possesses a good alkalinity as well as other favorable properties that mean it can produce good quality concrete.

Penetration of chlorides

Chlorides can attack concrete from the outside environment and from its interior. A block of concrete is a heterogeneous element that contains different substances. Aggregates are incorporated into the solid mass, and some of them can be harmful, which is one of the ways in which corrosion can spread out from the inside of the element. Another possibility is that calcium chloride is present because it was added as a hydration-accelerating additive. If one of these situations occurs, it is quite possible that the reinforcement was never properly passivated, in which case corrosion could rapidly develop.

If the chlorides originate from the environment, the protective concrete cover over the bars will only have a finite capacity to resist corrosion. As a result, it is the nature of the mechanism through which the chlorides are introduced that will determine how quickly and where corrosion begins. If the rates of capillary suction and/ or diffusion are low, this will have the effect of delaying the corrosion. These rates can be lowered by using concrete with a low water : cement ratio, a high cement content (which also favors compaction), and through proper curing.

If the concrete does not have any cracks, 'free' chlorides are the only means by which chlorides can penetrate. However, bound chlorides can be freed through reaction with sulfates and the process of carbonation.

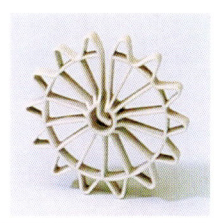

The use of spacers is vital when trying to ensure that the protective covering of concrete around the reinforcement is of sufficient thickness. From left to right: Universal, Ferropes Gancho and Ruver.

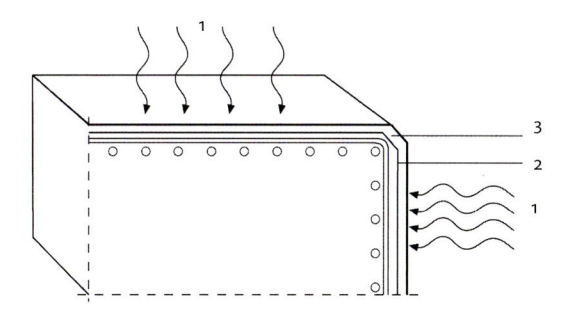

1. Penetration of aggressive substances
2. Critical layer of carbonated chlorides
3. A concentrated attack, a rapid deterioration of the concrete, a rapid corrosion of the reinforcement

The concentration of aggressive substances at the corners and edges of concrete elements

Concrete batching or mix design

Richness in cement (kg/m³)	Proportions			Liters			Uses
	cement	sand	gravel	cement	sand	gravel	
100	1	6	12	75	450	900	Fills, joints, hiegenic concrete
150	1	4	8	110	440	880	Trenches, foundations, unusually thick casts.
200	1	3	6	145	435	870	Retaining walls, foundation wells, slabs.
250	1	2,5	5	170	425	850	Pillars, supports, pavements
300	1	2	4	207	415	830	Reinforced concrete, footing, special walls.
350	1	2	3	240	480	720	Structural concrete, pillars, beams
400	1	1,5	3	263	395	790	Thin reinforced slabs, stress pieces, joists.
450	1	1,5	2,5	290	435	725	Special prefabricated items, pretensed items.
500	1	1	2	360	360	730	Highly specialized maximum control tasks.

Approx. water needed for 1m³: 150 - 250 liters.
Approx. weight of 1m³: 2.200 - 2.500 kg.
Weight of 1 bag of cement: - 50 kg
Volume of 1 bag of cement: - 33 liters

Denomination and uses of the various portland cements

Denomination	Classification		Uses
	type	class	
portland cement	I	I - 0	Prefabricated items and heavy duty concrete (special public works).
		I	
composite portland cement	II	II	General use concrete and mortar.
slag concrete		II - S	
pozzolanic portland cement		II - Z	
portland cement with ash		II - C	
blast furnace cement	III	III - 1	Special types of concrete for aggressive environments.
		III - 2	
pozzolanic cement	IV	IV	Concrete and mortar for moderate environments. Hydraulic works.
mixed cement	V	V	Stabilizations, bases for roads.
aluminous cement	VI	VI	Fire-resistant or refractory concrete. For use in aggressive environments.

Concrete batching or mix design

Richness in cement (lb/ft³)	Proportions			ft³			Uses
	cement	sand	gravel	cement	sand	gravel	
6.26	1	6	12	2.65	15.89	31.78	Fills, joints, hiegenic concrete
9.39	1	4	8	3.88	15.54	31.07	Trenches, foundations, unusually thick casts.
12.51	1	3	6	5.12	15.36	30.72	Retaining walls, foundation wells, slabs.
15.64	1	2,5	5	6	15	30.01	Pillars, supports, pavements
18.77	1	2	4	7.31	14.65	29.31	Reinforced concrete, footing, special walls.
21.9	1	2	3	8.47	16.95	25.42	Structural concrete, pillars, beams
25	1	1,5	3	9.29	13.95	27.89	Thin reinforced slabs, stress pieces, joists.
28.16	1	1,5	2,5	10.24	15.36	25.6	Special prefabricated items, pretensed items.
31.29	1	1	2	12.7116	12.71	25.78	Highly specialized maximum control tasks.

Approx. water needed for 35.31ft³: 150 - 250 liters.
Approx. weight of 35.31ft³: 4850.17 - 5511.5 lb.
Weight of 1 bag of cement: - 110.231 lb
Volume of 1 bag of cement: - 33 liters

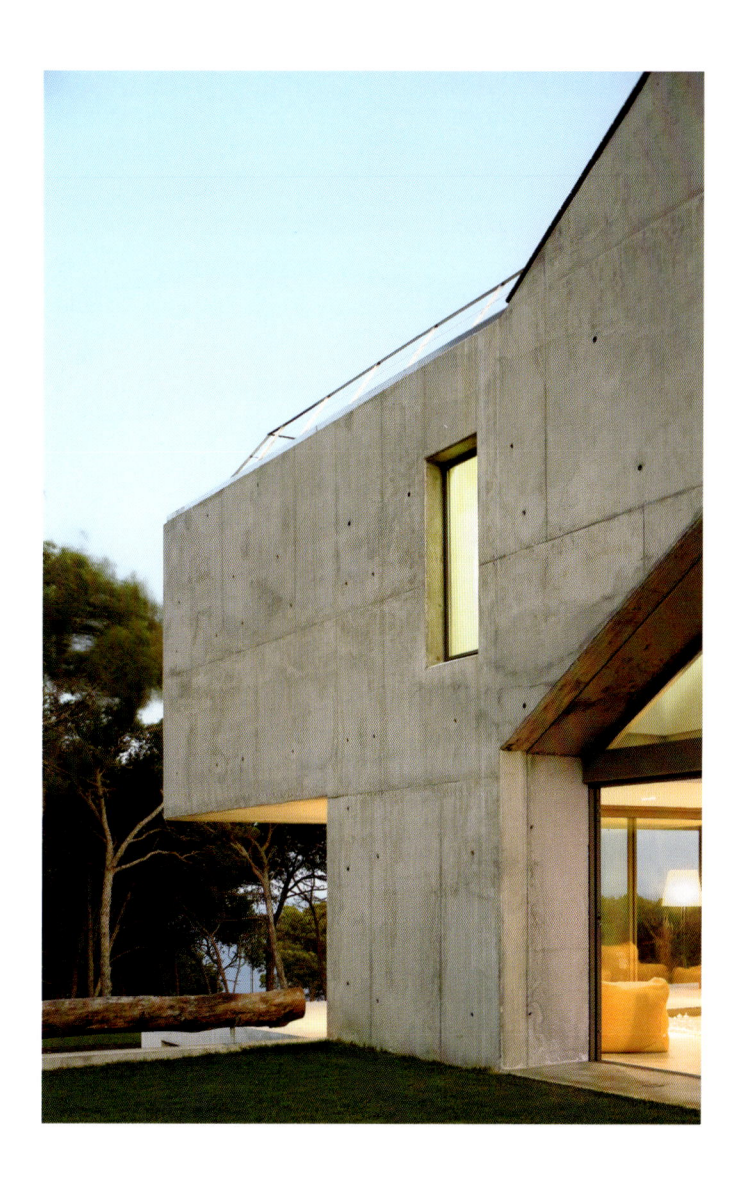

Concrete protection and repair

Concrete protection and repair

Surface treatments and maintenance of concrete structures

Concrete structures can be given additional chemical and physical resistance against attack from atmospheric and other agents through the application of coatings such as paints, varnishes, films and renders.

These coatings can be applied immediately onto new buildings or can be applied a-posteriori onto existing structures if their durability needs to be improved.

During the life of the building these coatings will have to undergo periodical maintenance to see if re-application is required.

In recent years the technology in the field of protective coatings has evolved greatly, both in terms of materials and methods of application.

Normally they are used to reduce the absorption of water, the penetration of harmful gases and salts and, occasionally, to protect the concrete against specific chemicals.

Methods of concrete surface protection

The methods for protecting concrete surfaces can be classified into two broad categories:

- Thick coatings
- Protective paints

Results of tests comparing different types of protective treatments for concrete

Protective treatment	Water absorbed 7 days after application (%)*	Permeability to chlorides 30 days after application (x 10 ppm)	Penetration of CO_2 (% of mass)
Untreated concrete (for reference)	9,5	5,5	2,1
Acrylic based	9,5	1,5	1,0
Polyurethane based	9,2 - 9,5	3,0 - 5,5	1,0 - 1,6
Chlorinated rubber	6,5	1,0	0,8
Silicone based	9,3	0,3	1,7
Silane based	2,6	0,1	1,0
Acrylic top coat	9,5	2,0	1,0
Two stage silane/siloxane & acrylic	2,2	0,1	0,1

* tested on concrete 28 days after pouring

Applications and properties of different protective paints

In general, bi-component products are more efficient than mono-component ones. When the solvent has a similar base as the solute the durability and penetration are improved compared to when water is used as the solvent.

Polyurethane based paints and varnishes are the most durable and provide excellent impermeability and protection against the risk of carbonation.

Epoxy based products are those that best adhere to the concrete and are themselves the most chemically and mechanically resistant. However they are susceptible to photodegradation from ultraviolet rays. For these reasons their ideal application is indoors, in particularly aggressive industrial environments, for example.

Acrylic based varnishes are more resistant to ultraviolet rays, do not yellow under exposure to sunlight and only slightly alter the appearance of the concrete.

Systems that involve a first coat of epoxy resin and a second coat of polyurethane dissolved in solvent have been proven to be very effective on outdoor surfaces in industrial environments because they provide good chemical resistance and do not suffer photodegradation.

The durability of the protection largely depends on an adequate preparation of the surface prior to application, the correct choice of product and the level of quality control enforced during its manufacture, storage and application on site.

It is recommended that the product be thoroughly tested before deciding on its use. As the quality of the paint depends on the quality of its constituents, two products that appear similar in composition might produce very different results. Laboratory tests have proven that the level of protection increases considerably with the number of coats, though above four coats the improvement is negligible.

Thick coatings are used in specific situations where the concrete is situated in a particularly harsh chemical or physical environment. For example, if the concrete is in constant contact with corrosive chemicals, liquids under pressure or harmful gases or if it is exposed to extreme abrasion or impacts. The chemical and physical properties of the coating will differ according to which of these problems it is meant to alleviate.

This category includes: bituminous, vinylic, asphaltic, neoprene, butyl rubber and coal tar epoxy based coatings; anticorrosive tiles and bricks; special cements and mortars (e.g. epoxy, phenolic, polyester, sulfur, silicate or furan based) and high temperature resistant paints that are reinforced with a synthetic film. It is recommended that any such products be tested first to ensure their suitability for the purpose required.

Protective paints

These methods are used to protect against the eroding agents most commonly present in industrial, urban and marine environments.

Their purpose is to reduce the risk of the concrete becoming contaminated or eroded and to preserve the concrete's appearance.

Two different systems exist:

- **Water repellant coatings** that have open pores
- **Impermeable film coatings**

As well as providing protection against the principal eroding agents, all of these products must also:

- Resist the effects of the weather
- **Avoid the growth of fungi and bacteria** on the concrete's surface
- **Be resistant to knocks and scratches**
- **Resist photodegradation** caused by the sun's ultraviolet rays
- **Be chemically stable when in contact with concrete** to avoid the risk of efflorescence or saponification due to the high alkalinity of the substrate.

In general, water repellant paints can be applied onto smooth and rough surfaces and can repel water from pores in the concrete's surface when these do not have an opening of more than 3 mm (1/8 in). Impermeable films require a smooth surface for proper adhesion and can block pores of up to 0,1 mm (1/288 in). The application of a render onto the concrete is normally necessary to attain such a continuous surface.

Clear varnishes, which are used to protect exposed concrete surfaces, could also be considered to be a type of protective paint.

Both paints and varnishes adhere to the surface of the concrete forming a continuous layer of low permeability.

Water repellant paints

These products make the concrete surface waterproof but do not impede the penetration of gases or water vapor. To explain this phenomenon it is first necessary to explain certain properties of concrete. Concrete is hydrophilic and thus absorbs water liquid and vapor via several processes. The main process is capillary action, but pressure gradients, diffusion, adsorption and condensation also contribute.

Capillary action can introduce large quantities of water into the concrete if the pores are large enough and continuously distributed.

After it rains a thin film of water remains on the surface of the façade and this water can be absorbed through capillary action. This can also happen anywhere where the concrete is in contact with water, such as the foundations.

Water repelling (also known as waterproofing) products alter the angle of contact between the wall of the capillary vessels within the concrete and the water surface.

For this reason they are not considered as paints but rather as impregnating coatings.

They are mainly organic silica based products, such as silicone dissolved in special solvents or water, or silane dissolved in special solvents.

Impermeable films
Impermeable films form a continuous, semi-flexible film on the surface of the concrete. They block the passage of water, water vapor and gases.

To be applied these membranes require a surface that is homogenous, smooth and with open pores of no more than 0.1 mm (1/288 in). Even though they are more flexible than the concrete that they protect, most products of this type can still crack (due to movement, impacts, temperature, etc) once dry.

Techniques for the preparation of the surface prior to application
Concrete generally forms a good surface on which to paint because its roughness and porosity make it rapidly absorb moisture from paints or varnishes. In order to achieve a good adherence the surface should be tough, and cleaned to ensure that it is free of dust and other contaminants.

Before the paint is applied onto the concrete any cracks should be repaired, any holes or gaps filled and any other necessary repairs carried out.

When the surface is too rough and uneven, it should be leveled out prior to painting.

If any other products have been applied earlier to the concrete, such as curing compounds or mold release agents, these should be removed before proceeding with painting.

Characteristics of water repelling paints

Properties	Limitations
They reduce the capacity of the concrete to absorb water from its surface.	They do not prevent the penetration of water vapor or gases, or water under pressure.
They permit the drying of humid concrete because they allow the escape of water from inside the concrete to the air in the form of vapor.	They do not fully prevent the risk of carbonation.
They reduce the level of absorption of soluble salts.	They do not fully prevent leaching, although they do reduce it.
They penetrate into the concrete's pores.	
Since they do not have the appearance of a film they do not alter how the concrete looks.	
They are highly resistant to ultraviolet rays and hence photodegradation.	
They do not require an especially smooth concrete surface for their application.	

Characteristics of impermeable films

Properties	Limitations
They significantly reduce the risk of carbonation.	They alter the appearance of the concrete, giving it a more glossy appearance (this also applies to transparent and opaque varnishes).
They reduce the permeability to the entry, and diffusion of, soluble salts.	
They significantly reduce the risk of leaching.	They do not allow moist concrete to dry out properly.
They inhibit the growth of fungi, bacteria and mold.	They require a smooth surface for their application and are thus unsuitable for use on concrete cast in rough formwork. In order to be used in such cases a smooth render needs to be applied onto the concrete before the membrane can be applied.

Methods of applying protective coatings

The correct application of a coating is just as important as the preparation of the surface and the correct choice of product in order to achieve a good, durable finish.

The first step is to ensure that the product is properly stirred before application as most products contain several constituents that separate because the heavier parts settle during storage.

It is thus often necessary to scrape the bottom of the container with a spatula in order to achieve a good mix.

If the product is particularly viscous, the stirring may have to be done mechanically.

The cautions to be observed during application will vary according to each product but the following points generally apply:

- **Ambient temperature should be between 10 and 50°C (122 degF) when painting.** Painting of surfaces while they are exposed to direct sunlight should be avoided.
- **Begin painting immediately after the concrete has been cleaned** in order to avoid new contaminants collecting.
- **Do not paint when the relative humidity of the air exceeds 90%**
- **The relative humidity of the concrete surface should be less than 5 or 6%** unless if the hardening process depends on a reaction with water or if the paint is water-soluble. Equipment is available that can immediately read this value.
- **Avoid spray application in windy situations.**
- **When applying with a spray, each consecutive coat should be 50% thicker than the previous one.**

Spraying

The method of applying a coating using a spray is potentially useful because it allows the easy treatment of large areas. The physical properties (consistency, for example) of the product are deciding factors as to whether or not it can be spray applied. Products that have medium viscosity and/or are thixotropic are suitable for spray application.

An airless method is the most suitable for applying waterproofing paints because the equipment needed is simpler than that needed for methods that use compressed air.

Spray application requires little manpower but is generally unsuitable for use on small surfaces.

Application using brushes and rollers

The application of the first coat using brushes and/or rollers ensures better absorption when the surface is porous or irregular.

Brushes are best used on relatively small areas and the brush size chosen should suit the size of the area to be painted.

Flat, nylon brushes are the type most commonly used, with 10 cm (4 in) considered to be the maximum recommended size.

Application using rollers is only recommended on regular, flat surfaces. They allow for faster work on walls and ceilings.

Main causes of deterioration of the protective coating

The main causes of damage to protective coatings are:

- **Incorrect product choice.**
- **The product has inadequate resistance against the effects of the weather.**
- **Incorrect treatment of the surface prior to application.**
- **Excessive dilution of the product prior to application.**
- **Insufficient number of coats.**

Quite often the product applied does not meet the demands of the situation. An example would be the use of an impermeable membrane when a water repelling paint with open pores would have worked better.

Painting should not be done when rain is forecast within the following days and it is necessary to wait for three days after the rainwater has naturally dried before continuing with painting. It is thus advisable to paint during the driest season of the year.

The concrete must be properly hardened before application because a dusty surface would be inadequate for painting on. Surfaces that have traces of mold release agent or grease are also unsuitable.

If the paint is too diluted it will not have enough adherence to the surface and the result will be too porous, allowing the penetration of harmful agents. This mistake occurs most often with those paints that are water-soluble.

The application of an insufficient number of coats will not provide enough protection. This often happens with varnishes because they are transparent and one way to reduce the likelihood of it occurring is with frequent checks of the work on site. Ideally two or three coats should always be specified.

In practice, the ideal situation is when the client is in charge of buying the protective products and then sub-contracts the painting work separately.

Maintenance

The maintenance of concrete can be classified into:

- Preventative measures
- Corrective measures

A program of preventative maintenance is one that is applied to facades and concrete surfaces before any sign of degradation appears. Protective coatings have a shorter lifespan than the concrete structures that they protect and should thus undergo regular inspection to ensure they continue functioning as effective barriers.

As a rule of thumb, protective coatings should be reapplied every 2 to 3 years in the case of water repellant and water based paints, every 4 years in the case of solvent based paints and every 6 to 7 years for multi-layered systems.

However, what often happens is that early signs of degradation go unnoticed with the result that maintenance ends up being more corrective than preventative. A diagnosis then has to be made and the correct method chosen for repairing and protecting the concrete. There are various, well known, methods of repair and these have to be carried out before a protective coat is applied.

Repairing concrete

If concrete loses alkalinity or is contaminated by chlorides this can have major repercussions for the building structure. The biggest danger is when corrosion of the concrete leaves the reinforcement exposed to chemical attack (by chloride ions, for example) as it can then corrode and weaken the whole structure.

These types of chemical attack produce visible symptoms such as cracks and hollows on the surface of the concrete and can even result in significant portions of concrete breaking off, leaving the corroded reinforcement visible.

To avoid reaching such a dire situation it is important to ensure that the reinforcement cannot become corroded during construction. When dealing with existing structures it is also possible to act before signs of corrosion can produce themselves, which is always more advisable because treating the problem is extremely difficult at more advanced stages of degradation.

The solution with existing structures involves first removing the layer of concrete around the damaged reinforcement until the corroded zone is entirely visible and then introducing a new protective element around the bars. It is a precise approach that would be impossible to carry out if the entire concrete element was corroded because doing so would weaken the structural integrity.

Therefore, although this is the most widespread technique currently in use, it cannot guarantee durability because there is a risk that not all of the corroded zones have been repaired. The fact that the new protection has different characteristics to those of the existing concrete is also a potential liability after repair has been carried out.

There are several other, more expensive and complicated, methods of repair currently available that can also slow down and, in some cases, completely stop, the corrosion of reinforcement without the need for the bars to be exposed. They are: cathodic protection, electrochemical chloride extraction and realkalization. They are all very effective at stopping the problem at the source and preventing future corrosion.

However, preventative methods are still the most advisable in situations where the first symptoms of corrosion have not yet appeared.

If the structure is already damaged, the conventional method of revealing the reinforcement is a vital first step but should always be followed by a process of realkalization or electrochemical chloride extraction.

Repair of damaged areas

The concrete is picked at until the whole carbonated area has been removed, leaving the reinforcement bars accessible. The technique involves the following stages:

- **Removal of the damaged concrete** and cleaning of the exposed surface
- **Protection of the reinforcement** to restore its structural capacity
- **Application of the new covering material**

Removal of the damaged concrete

This is done with machinery or by hand and involves the removal of all those pieces of concrete that have been broken by the outward pressure that the reinforcement's corrosion has produced.

All loose, carbonated pieces and those that contain chloride ions are removed until reaching the 'healthy' concrete. The reinforcement must be fully exposed on all sides, which requires the removal of a few centimeters of concrete behind the bar, so that the new protective layer can completely envelop the bar.

The steel should also be exposed in certain areas that do not display the symptoms of corrosion in order to check that the bars in that location are indeed in good condition.

This avoids the risk of ignoring areas where corrosion is just beginning and that would only develop the visible symptoms later. An expert opinion is needed to identify which areas should be removed. The concrete can be removed manually with a chisel, pneumatic needle scaler, or other similar devices.

This operation can require careful examination of its structural repercussions, especially if particularly large and/or deep areas of concrete are removed from an element.

Parts of the element may need to be temporarily supported with props. The work of removal should be divided into relatively small stages across different areas of the damaged zone to avoid overly weakening (and potentially breaking) one part of the structure.

The area of concrete to be removed must first be cleaned and the method used will depend on the type of concrete. All dust and dirt must be removed from the surface using compressed air, jets of water or by vacuuming.

The steel must also be completely cleaned to ensure that no traces of corrosion remain before the application of the new protective cover. If any rust is left over then corrosion could continue, at a rate that would depend on the quantity of electrolyte present.

Reinforcement at a change in section of a concrete beam

Cleaning of a concrete column after the damaged concrete has been removed and before the new protective layer is added

The reinforcement can be brushed, sanded or 'rinsed' with sand. The chosen method must completely remove rust so that the entirety of the steel under inspection is in good condition.

Even though these cleaning methods are not technically difficult, insufficient cleaning is the most common reason why a repair does not fully eliminate corrosion. Therefore this stage must be undertaken with the utmost care.

Protection and structural reparation of steel reinforcement
Once the steel has been properly cleaned, the protective layer is applied. This can be cement grout, various types of plastics, epoxy resins or specialized reinforcement corrosion inhibitors.

A coat of adhesive epoxy can also be applied to the steel and the concrete in order to improve the adherence and form a better seal between the additional protective layer and the existing element.

If the new protection is not going to be applied immediately after the reinforcement has been cleaned then adhesive epoxy, with a small amount of fine sand added, is applied to the steel in order to later improve the bond between the reinforcement and the protection.

In many cases new reinforcement is also incorporated into the element at this stage if too large an area has been removed or if it is deemed otherwise necessary to increase the structural capacity of the element.

A rule of thumb is that if more than 15% of the material is removed then it is necessary to recalculate the structure and, potentially, restore the initial strength of the steel in some way.

The restoration of the reinforcement is realized by cutting the weaken bars and replacing them for other bars overlapped and tied with wire or welded to the existing bars.

If new reinforcement has to be incorporated then the damaged bars must be cut and replaced. The new sections of steel will overlap a little with the existing ones and can be welded or tied into place by wire.

If the steel is to be welded then it is necessary to check first whether or not the new and existing types of steel are compatible for welding together.

Specialist splice sleeves for connecting the two bars are also available and are easy to use. When the splice is going to be done using wire then the bars should overlap by a length that is equal to forty times the diameter of the bar.

Normally, when the amount of material removed is less than 15%, the reparation will not pose a structural risk and no new reinforcement is needed.

Application of the new covering material
Before the new covering material is put in place the concrete surfaces that have been left exposed due to the removal of material must be carefully examined in order to check that no cracks are present. If there are cracks then a diagnosis must be made as to their origins to be sure that they are not symptoms of the corrosion that the repair is trying to avoid. Epoxy resin has been proven to be effective in blocking all types of cracks, by both forming a strong bond that restores structural integrity and by creating an effective seal.

The type of epoxy recommended depends on the width of the crack and can be classified as follows:

- **Cracks less than 0.2 mm (1/144 in) wide:** Bicomponent epoxy adhesives that have a viscosity of 100cP at 20°C (68 degF)
- **Between 0.2 mm and 0.6 mm (1/144 and 1/48 in):** Bicomponent epoxy adhesives that have a viscosity of less than 500cP at 20°C (68degF)
- **Between 0.6 and 3 mm (1/48 and 1/12 in):** Bicomponent epoxy adhesives, that can be pure or combined with cuartz or glass dusting, and have a viscosity of less than 1500cP at 20°C (68 degF)
- **Cracks more than 3 mm (1/12 in) wide:** Loaded epoxy adhesives can be used. The added particles can be sand with a grain size under 1 mm (1/24 in) or 0.6 times the narrowest width of the crack, normally added in a proportion 1:1, adhesive: sand.

In order to close a gap with adhesive in a way that also restores the unity and structural integrity of the element, a temporary outer seal must first be made with tubes inserted through the seal that allow for later injection of adhesive into the full depth of the crack.

The spacing of these tubes along the length of the crack will depend on the width and depth of the crack and a tube should be inserted at every junction where two or more cracks converge. The outer seal must have completely hardened before injection can begin. This usually takes 24 hours.

The repair, layer by layer, of a heavily corroded column

The adhesive is then injected, under pressure using a caulking gun or mechanical jack, through the tubes. Efficient equipment is also available that automatically measures, mixes and injects the adhesive.

Once any internal cracks have been fully sealed the repair of the concrete can continue. The volume of concrete removed must be replaced with new concrete in order to consolidate the structure and provide covering for the reinforcement.

The mortar used for this purpose must have the following essential characteristics:

- Sufficient strength
- Offer good adherence to the existing concrete and reinforcement
- Suffer as little shrinkage as possible
- Resistance against the different corroding agents inherent in the surrounding environment
- Have an elastic modulus and coefficient of thermal expansion that are compatible with those of the existing element

The mortar can be mixed on-site as long as the above requirements can all be guaranteed or it can be prepared off-site by the manufacturer for a more precise dosage.

If the mortar used is conventional (i.e. made with hydraulic cement, with or without additives) its properties will be very similar to those of the existing element and the cost of repair will also be reduced.

One type of mortar that is commonly used for this purpose is the family of polymer cement mortars as they provide better adherence, impermeability and strength. Organic based epoxy resin mortars and polyester mortars are particularly effective in situations where only a shallow layer is required. Many different repair mortars are available and the decision as to which one to choose depends on the depth of the area to be replaced, the surface with which it has to bond, the total volume needed and the characteristics of the existing element.

Before the repair mortar is applied a film of cement, acrylic or epoxy adhesive must be applied across the whole surface of exposed material with which it will be in contact. The application of the mortar can be done manually and without the need for formwork.

Whichever method of repair is chosen, it must be carried out steadily, in successive phases that leave enough time for each layer to dry and thus avoid the risk of damage from shrinkage. The specific timing and considerations will depend on the type of repair material chosen and when using a commercially available product the manufacturers' instructions must always be followed.

The final surface finish must ensure good impermeability against water and chlorides.

Materials used for the repair of damaged concrete

The materials for repair currently available commercially can be classified into three groups:

- Non-organic based
- Organic based
- Mixed base

Non-organic based materials include all cements, whether they are Portland cement or not, and can be further divided into traditional and non-traditional types.

The traditional types include grout, mortar, micro-concrete and concrete. The non-traditional types include expansive Portland cement, magnesium phosphate and aluminum phosphate cement, ettringite cement and aluminate cement.

Organic based materials used for repairing concrete are synthetic resins containing a thermally stable polymer binder. The resins are made of two or three components that are mixed prior to application. Mixing sets off the chemical process of polymerization, which is what causes the resin to eventually harden. The most commonly used types are unsaturated **epoxy, polyurethane and polyester resins.**

Mixed base materials are made by adding certain types of polymers to the water used for mixing the concrete. They give additional properties to the concrete without reducing its alkalinity, which is the passivating quality that protects the steel. As the polymer is a liquid latex, it can be mixed with the cement.

When the water has disappeared, it increases the binding effect of the cement, resulting in a mortar that is more compact, more impermeable, with a lower Young's modulus and a coefficient of thermal expansion similar to that of a hydraulic mortar without additives. There are various types of polymers that achieve these qualities when mixed with Portland cement.

Stopping or reducing the corrosion of metal reinforcement

Cathodic protection

The technique of cathodic protection aims to give the reinforcement a value of electrical potential that can prevent corrosion. There are two systems: galvanic cathodic protection and impressed current cathodic protection.

In the first system the reinforcement is converted into the cathode of an electromagnetic battery and a galvanic, or 'sacrificial' anode is attached to the surface of the reinforced concrete element. The galvanic anode is made of zinc or magnesium, both of which have a lower electrochemical potential than steel and thus cause the flow of ions to reverse and flow away from the reinforcement. This causes the galvanic anode to suffer the effects of the corrosion, leaving the reinforcement intact.

The system of impressed current cathodic protection works by introducing a continuous controlled electrical current. The negative anode is connected to a DC power source and attached to the steel reinforcement and the positive electrode is made of a semi-inert or non-corrosive material.

The anode can be made of any conductive material that has a service life of at least 20 years. The most commonly used materials are: graphite, platinum plated titanium, tantalum, niobium, silver and lead alloys, etc.

The problem that both systems face is that the reinforcement must be continuous. Achieving this in a new structure is much easier than in an existing one and so it helps if the decision to use cathodic protection is made at the design stage.

The anode can have various shapes and is normally a mesh or grid that is fixed to the concrete or embedded in sheets of polyethylene.

Electrochemical chloride extraction

The extraction of chlorides is achieved by creating an electric field between the reinforcement and a metallic mesh that is submerged in an electrolyte medium placed on the surface of the concrete.

The process is similar to that of cathodic protection in that the chloride ions are forced to flow towards the positive electrode that is situated outside the concrete element.

Damaged areas of the structure have to be repaired before the process of extraction can begin. If the steel corrosion has caused expansion and subsequent cracks in the concrete, the concrete in the affected area must be removed and the corroded bars replaced. Then the electrical connections can be made to the steel. The layout of the connections will depend on the continuity and size of the bars, but there must be a minimum of one every 20m^2 (215 sqft).

Finally, a metallic mesh is attached to the surface of the element and embedded in an electrolyte such as water-saturated felt or cellulose fiber. The electrolyte must remain humid throughout the process. Once the equipment has been set up it is connected to an electrical circuit of 1 A/m^2, with the negative pole being the cables connected to the reinforcement and the positive pole being the metallic mesh. It is important for the electric current to be stable.

The extraction of chlorides can take between one and three months to finish. In the first few weeks,

Comparison of the properties of different mortars

Properties	Resin based mortars	Hydraulic mortars
Compressive strength (N/mm², psi)	55-110	20-70
Elastic modulus (N/cm², psi)	500-25.000	20.000-30.000
Flexural strength (N/cm², psi)	25-50	2-5
Tensile strength (N/cm², psi)	9-20	1,5-3,5
Change in length at breaking point (%)	0-15	0
Coefficient of thermal expansion (mm ºC)	25-30 × 10-6	9-14 × 10-6
Density (kg/dm³, slugs/ft³)	0,7-2,1	2-2,3
Maximum service temperature (ºC, degF)	40-80	300
Time needed to reach 80% strength	48 horas	2-4 semanas

samples must be taken from the concrete in order to check that the process is developing normally. If the results are good then a decision can be made as to when the extraction can stop. Once the process is finished, the electrical current is switched off and the metallic mesh and electrolyte are removed. The concrete surface is then cleaned, any areas that were removed are replaced and a protective finish is applied to the surface.

Even if this system has many benefits, it is extremely costly and is a very delicate process. As it is a relatively unexplored method, the exact side effects and the maximum amount of chlorides that it can remove are not yet known.

Realkalization
This system activates alkalis (OH- ions) by moving them from areas of high pH to others that are more acidic.

This can be achieved by applying cement rich mortars to the surface of the concrete while keeping the area wet. In this way alkalis can penetrate to a depth of one or two centimeters.

The most efficient way to do this is by using an industrial method that is based on the same principle as the techniques mentioned above. A mesh is placed on the surface of the concrete that is then given a coating of cellulose binder impregnated with an alkali (sodium carbonate). An electric field is then generated that converts the reinforcement into a cathode and the mesh into an anode. The alkaline solution on the metallic mesh then rapidly penetrates deep into the concrete via electro-osmosis.

The operation can take between 15 days and one month and it can make the carbonated concrete reach a pH of between 9 and 10.5. Once it is finished, a protective layer should be applied to the concrete in order to avoid further carbonation.

This system, like the ones mentioned above, is expensive and is much more complicated to implement and less effective on existing structures.

Concrete specifications

Type of stress	Formula	\multicolumn{4}{c}{Specified strength, f_c, lb/in²}
		2,500	3,000	3,500	4,000
Shear (f_v)					
Beams with no web reinforcement	$1.1\,(f_c)^{0.5}$	100	110	126	141
Joists with no web reinforcement	$1.2\,(f_c)^{0.5}$	61	66	77	86
Members with stirrups	$5\,(f_c)^{0.5}$	250	274	316	354
Slabs and footings	$2\,(f_c)^{0.5}$	100	110	126	141
Bearing (f_b)					
On full area	$0.25\,f_c$	625	750	1,000	1,250
On 1/3 area or less	$0.37\,f_c$	938	1,125	1,500	1,875
Bending (f_c)					
Compression	$0.45\,f_c$	1,125	1,350	1,800	2,250
Tension	$1.60\,(f_c)^{0.5}$	80	88	102	113

Concrete and agglomerate products

In recent years concrete has made a comeback in the public perception as being a potentially versatile material, after having earned itself the reputation of only being useful for the production of repetitive, gray blocks. Of course concrete does not have to be gray, nor is it only capable of making rectangular buildings. It is an industrial material that has undergone an important evolvution. For example, glass fiber reinforcement has given us extremely durable concrete, and there are many other new types that have improved ductility and elasticity. Even such a basic property as its opacity has been challenged. There already exist various, commercially available, translucent concretes made with transparent, fiber optic aggregate. There has also been a proliferation of surface finishing techniques, and designs, even photographs, can now be printed onto concrete surfaces.

Advances have also been made in terms of environmental impact, the most obvious of which is the use of recycled aggregates. Another such improvement is possible with the incorporation of photocatalysts, such as titanium oxide additive, that help the concrete to reduce air pollution.

Agglomerates that use polymer-based binders instead of cement are similar in many ways to standard concrete. Their most common application is in floors because almost any kind of aggregate can be used in them, so that an almost infinite variety of colors and finishes are possible.

fibre C

Rieder

Concrete panels with glassfibre reinforcement

FibreC is an innovative concrete panel strengthend by glassfibre components. FibreC is high-strength, thin, flexible and malleable and can be used in special forms flat as well as rounded. Rough edges as well as roundings and curves can be achieved within a single flowing material without adhesives. Various visual effects can be achieved by using covered or uncovered fixing solutions.

Available standard measures for fibreC panels are 1.20 x 3.60 m but can be stretched to a length of 5.00 m with a minimum thickness of 13 mm. The material has excellent thermal resistance for absolute safety in terms of temperature stability (standing up to 350°) and therefore provides optimum fire protection for multi-storey buildings up to a height of 100 m.

Another dimension for playing with the endless varieties marks the possibilities for color selection and defining of different surface structures. The color palette ranges from any grayscale tone to natural tones such as teracotta, green or brown. Different structures, matt polished or brushed emphasizes the modern face of glass fibre concrete.

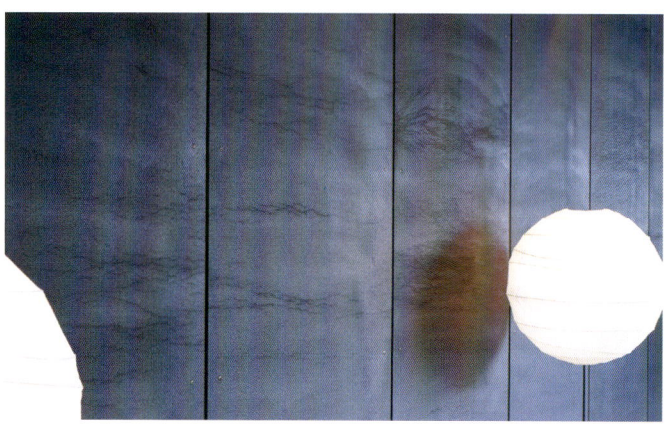

www.rieder.cc
Tel.: +49 (0) 803-190-1670
Fax: +49 / (0)80-319-0167-169
E-mail: office@rieder.cc

ecoX

Meld

Concrete from post-industrial recycled materials

Made with nearly 70% post-industrial recycled materials, ecoX retains the verve of extremeconcrete® and adds an earth-friendly dimension. ecoX challenges the notion that recycled is somehow less than original. This ecologically sensitive material offers potential LEED credits, prevents items from filling up landfills and presents a whole much greater than the sum of its parts. And all this while providing an attractive aesthetic.

www.meldusa.com
Tel: +1 919-790-1749
Fax: +1 919-790-1750
E-mail: info@meldusa.com

CarbonCast
AltusGroup
Precast concrete with carbon fiber grid reinforcement

CarbonCast® is precast concrete that uses carbon fiber grid reinforcement for face reinforcing or shear transfer depending on the application. Because the carbon fiber reinforcing resists corrosion, CarbonCast precast products require less concrete cover, resulting in added durability, lighter weight and improved sustainability over conventional precast concrete and competitive building systems. In addition, the reduction of concrete enables the integration of insulation, which can increase R-values in cladding panels. CarbonCast Architectural Cladding Panels can weigh up to 50 percent less than conventional precast panels. This permits engineers to reduce substructure or specify smaller cranes for lifting the panels into place. When used in the flanges of CarbonCast Pretopped Double Tees, carbon fiber grid can reduce weight by 12 percent and eliminate the need for sealers and sacrificial barrier coatings. When used as a shear truss connector in CarbonCast High Performance Insulated Wall Panels, carbon fiber grid helps provide thermal performance up to steady state R-37 or more, given its relatively low thermal conductivity, and provides for full composite action for load-bearing applications. CarbonCast products and materials have undergone extensive material characterization of carbon fiber grids (modified ASTM D3039) and full-scale product testing including ASTM E119 fire tests.

www.altusprecast.com
Tel: +1 866-462-5887
E-mail: info@altusprecast.com

Panel Omega Zeta
CIRCA S.A.
Lightweight façade panel

Omega Zeta panels are produced on an industrial scale and can be customized in size, texture, color and mechanic perforations. Because of its versatility regarding its design and the properties that it presents as an effecitve thermal and acoustic insulator this is the ideal solution for modern architecture. It can be assembled three times faster than conventional systems, is ecological and recylcable as well as being highly resistant to weather conditions and earthquakes.
The panels for façades are composed of high resistance mortar and metal covering bidirectionally pretensed. This panel is waterproof and fire resistant.
The panels are very light-weight and are 3 cm thick. This modular wall element, assemble from the exterior, comes in different sizes up to 220 × 300 cm.

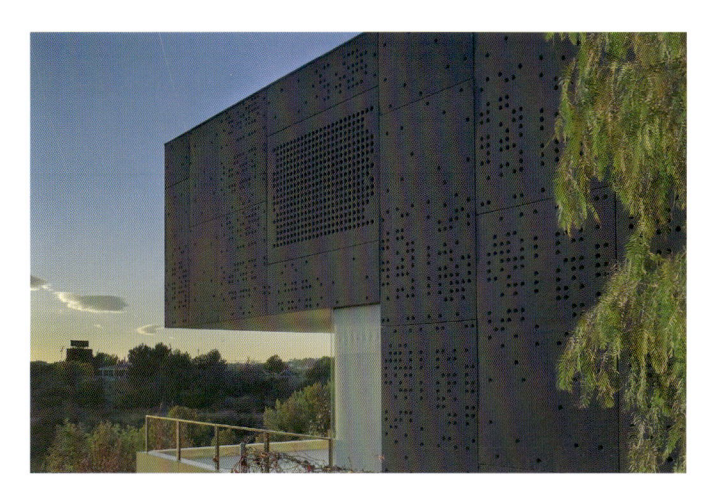

www.choosecolumbia.com
Tel: +1 800-637-1609

Graphic Concrete
Graphic Concrete Ltd
Concrete surface treatment

Graphic Concrete™ includes patented technology and products that enable the prefabrication concrete industry to produce stylish new concrete surfaces cost effectively and safely.

The technology is based on applying a surface retarder to a special membrane that is spread over the mould table. The designed pattern is created by the contrast between the fairface and the exposed fine aggregate finish.

The membrane's high level of rigidity makes it ideal for the production of large concrete surfaces. The membrane can also be used without the surface retarder for the production of fairface surfaces. The surface retarder applied to the membrane slows the setting of the concrete to the desired depth in specific areas. The unset surface part is usually washed away from the cast the next day, revealing the aggregate contained in the concrete. The washed surface stands out from the surrounding unwashed concrete surface due to its roughness and the contrasting color of the exposed aggregate. Altering the application area of the surface retarder makes it possible to create the desired patterns on the concrete.

The normal depth of the pattern is so-called fine exposure, i.e. about 1 mm. The cement can also be pigmented, which provides the color of the fairface surface. The aggregates can be a variety of different colors, which are then highlighted in the exposed areas.

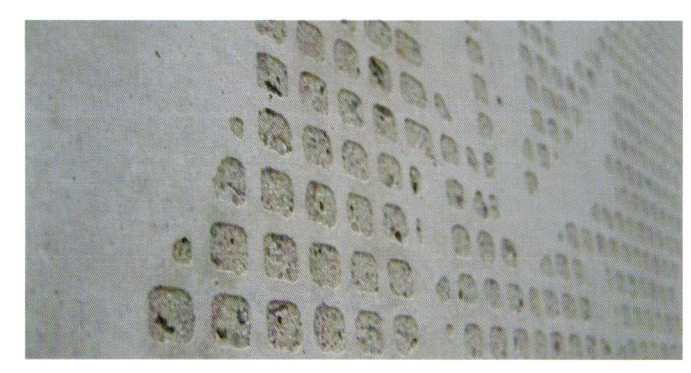

www.graphicconcrete.com
Tel: +35-896-842-0093
Fax: +35-896-842-0091
E-mail: info@graphicconcrete.com

Photo-engraving Formliners
Reckli
Concrete from post-industrial recycled materials

The use of elastic RECKLI®-Formliners for texturing the exposed face of concrete surfaces has attained a high degree of acceptance in terms of quality, ease of use and economic efficiency. The new generation of RECKLI® Photo-Engraving Formliners expands these possibilities. The combination of the RECKLI®-System and the Photo-Engraving Technology creates a surface pattern which can vary from fine to course depending on the resolution of the image used. This image can then be incorporated onto the finished concrete surface by using the RECKLI® Formliner system.

The Photo-Engraving Process is a computer-based method for transferring image data onto sheet materials by means of milling technology. First an image template is scanned and converted into 256-grayscale. In order to transfer the image onto the sheet material, a machining file is generated from the identified grey values, whereby the file includes milling commands for a special CNC milling machine.

The milled model is used as a master for casting the elastic RECKLI®-Formliners. Their elasticity, quality and reusability contribute to the aesthetics and the economic efficiency of the whole process and make it possible to recreate the image onto the concrete surface.

www.reckli.de
Tel: +39 (0)232-317-060
Fax: +39 (0)232-317-0650
E-mail: info@reckli.de

Litracon

Litracon

Light-transmiting concrete

Litracon™ is a combination of optical fibers and fine concrete. It can be produced as prefabricated building blocks and panels. Due to the small size of the fibers, they blend into concrete becoming a component of the material like small pieces of aggregate. In this manner, the result is not only two materials - glass in concrete - mixed, but a third, new material, which is homogeneous in its inner structure and on its main surfaces as well.

The glass fibers lead light by points between the two sides of the blocks. Because of their parallel position, the light-information on the brighter side of such a wall appears unchanged on the darker side. The most interesting form of this phenomenon is probably the sharp display of shadows on the opposing side of the wall. Moreover, the color of the light also remains the same.

The proportion of the fibers is very small (4%) compared to the total volume of the blocks. Moreover, these fibers mingle in the concrete because of their insignificant size, and they become a structural component as a kind of modest aggregate. Therefore, the surface of the blocks remains homogeneous concrete. In theory, a wall structure built from light-transmitting concrete can be several meters thick, because the fibers work without almost any loss in light up until 20 meters. Load-bearing structures can be also built of these blocks, since glass fibres do not have a negative effect on the well-known high compressive strength value of concrete. The blocks can be produced in various sizes and with embedded heat-isolation.

www.litracon.hu
Tel: +36 30-255-1648
E-mail: info@litracon.hu

Luccon

Luccon-Lichtbeton GmbH

Concrete with embedded fiber optic cables

Luccon Lightconcrete is a combination of modern concrete and embedded fiber optic cables. Fiber upon fiber light is projected through the construction element – for example images beyond a wall appear pointwise or digitized on the opposite side, regardless of whether they are shadows, light, colors, projections or displays. The dimensions of the construction element are basically irrelevant with one exception: With increasing thickness the experienced image on the hidden side appears increasingly peculiar and strange. Moving images are displayed in a fascinating manner and make the stone surface look iridescently lucent. The transparency of the stone lets one suspect more than is shown and suggests a curious airiness in spite of the heavy compactness.

Luccon characteristically transforms back into stone when it changes from dark to light – or when a wall wanders from day into night. An innovative method has made it possible to produce thermally separated elements with the same transparency as the "standard" product. On both sides – outside and inside – Luccotherm shows the attractive Luccon look in spite of an insulating layer.

www.luccon.com
Tel: +49 2331-340-29-40
Fax: +49 2331-340-29-41
E-mail: udo.ellerbrake@luccon.com

Impreton

Edfan

Printed concrete pavement

The printed concrete pavement Impreton is an in situ set slab whose surface is colored with non-metallic hardeners, so that the material acquires the surface hardness and strength of stone. It is stamped with a mold in order to obtain the selected pattern and texture. Pavements may also be imprinted with non-slip designs.
Printed pavements Impreton combine the strength, durability and flexibility of designs in concrete with the aesthetic characteristics of paving stones, bricks, slates and other materials.
One of the advantages of these pavements is their design flexibility. Given the product's application technique, different patterns, designs, colors and textures may be combined, with no limits to the possible options. Another advantage is its rapid application: both the pavement and the substrate are set in a single operation, at an approximate rate of 80 sqm per day.

www.microcemento.com
Tel: +34 93-320-9092
Fax: +34 93-320-9093
E-mail: info@microcemento.com

Thincrete

Edfan

Textured cement colored coating

Thincrete is a cementitious coating that can be aplied to floors and walls of both interiors and exteriors. It has a broad range of textures that immitate natural stones like slate, granite and others.
Thincrete can be aplied over existing surfaces without the need to remove any material. It is protected with sealants and easy to maintain.

www.microcemento.com
Tel: +34 93-320-9092
Fax: +34 93-320-9093
E-mail: info@microcemento.com

Microcement

Edfan

Micro polished pavement

Microcement is a layer between 1 and 2 mm thick, applicable to floors, walls and furniture. Previous uses include environments such as: commercial stores, rural settings and city houses, apartments, and private garages and has attained optimum results. It has been used for exteriors as well as interiors with equally impressive results.

Placement versatility and the wide range of possible colors make Microcement an ideal material for interior architecture.

The advantages of Microcement are:

- Quick Placement: up to 50 sqm per day with just two people working on it.
- Quick transit release: in just a few hours.
- Colors: There are 34 available colors and special colors are also available on request.
- No need to remove floor: In most cases the Microcement can be placed over existent floors and walls.
- It does not require joints: which allows for continuous coating without cuts.
- Minimum Thickness: between 1 and 2 mm thick, thus avoiding level differences with surroundings.

www.microcemento.com
Tel: +34 93-320-9092
Fax: +34 93-320-9093
E-mail: info@microcemento.com

ArmourColor

ArmourCoat

Decorative surface finishes

The ArmourColor range can create the perfect interior for all functional and design requirements, and make ideal wall coverings for private and public use, particularly in high traffic areas. Highly versatile and robust, the finishes are scrub resistant, breathable and comply with both UK and American fire classification requirements. Producing impressive interiors which combine color and durability, they add personality to any space.

The range, which includes BaseColors and protective Clearseal coatings, can be applied to a wide range of substrates including concrete, plaster and brick.

Perlata: Perlata is an elegant finish with a subtle sparkle or shimmer, creating visual texture and directional effect. The finish is dependent on the hand of the applicator, creating a unique and visually striking wall coating at close quarters, yet subtle when viewed from a distance.

Tactite: a high performance solution for demanding interiors, Tactite creates a tough, durable and hygienic wall coating. The finish is exceptionally hardwearing, easy to clean and includes anti-bacterial properties to prevent mould and bacterial growth. Tactite is highly suitable for commercial interiors such as hospitals, schools, offices and high traffic public areas where cleanliness is essential. Also ideal for domestic use, Tactite features a 'soft touch' feel to create a warm, inviting interior with a suede or textured finish.

www.armourcoat.com
Tel: +44 (0) 173-246-0668
Fax: +44 (0) 173-245-0930
E-mail: sales@armourcoat.co.uk

Cristallino, Rocksolid
Trend
Agglomerate floors from recycled materials

Trend's agglomerates are made from up to 80% industrial and post-consumer recycled materials. Their value doesn't lie in their resistance, versatility and aesthetic appeal alone: used glass and production excess, destined to become waste, gives the agglomerate surfaces their shine.

The Cristallino agglomerate is made from scrap products such as washing machines doors, rearview mirrors, carlights and from recycled glass bottles and containers. It is obtained by mixing the granules of glass with a pigmented polymer which gives it its color. The transparency of the glass gives the slabs an attractive depth.

Rocksolid is made from remains of quarry extractions. By combining quartz and granite in different percentages infinite combinations of colors can be obtained.

Sculptural
ArmourCoat
3d seamless wall designs

Sculptural™ walls are constructed from a series of pre-cast panels that are bonded to the substrate. The panel joints are then filled and sanded and a final decoration is applied to the surface. Sculptural™ designs are created by combining computer-aided design with traditional hand sculpting to create designs that fit together with total accuracy.

Some of the designs are based on a single panel that creates a repeating pattern; others are made from a sequence of different panels that can be integrated together in many different ways to create totally unique sculpted walls.

Sculptural™ panels are mineral based and incorporate up to 30% post-consumer recycled content (depending on design), are non-toxic and are completely non-combustible. The panels are extremely dense and hard with a smooth ceramic-like surface. Once the panels are installed each design can be finished in a range of decorative surface finishes.

www.trend-vi.com
Tel: +39 044-433-8711
Fax: +39 044-473-8747
E-mail: info@trend-vi.com

www.armourcoat.com
Tel: +44 (0) 173-246-0668
Fax: +44 (0) 173-245-0930
E-mail: sales@armourcoat.co.uk

StoLotusan Color
Sto
Façade paint featuring the Lotus effect

The Lotus effect is a natural phenomenon discovered on the Asian lotus plant. After each rainfall this plant's leaves are immaculately clean and dry, as they are not wettable with water; dirt runs off with the raindrops. This self-cleaning capacity is based on a microstructure which minimizes the contact area between the leaf on the one hand and dirt and water on the other. As the leaf surface is also highly water-repellent, droplets of water roll off the surface immediately, taking loose dirt particles with them.

The StoLotusan Color façade paint is the first technical product to incorporate this phenomenon, which was christened the Lotus Effect® by its discoverer, the botanist Dr. Wilhelm Barthlott. Façades treated with this product remain dry and attractive for longer. The new surface technology also reduces the risk of attack by microorganisms. Algae and fungal spores are either washed off or are unable to survive on a dry and dirt-free façade.

Lotusan is a façade paint with a matt, mineral look which can be finished in many colors of the StoColor System. StoLotusan Color enables simple, seamless application and offers good permeability for water vapor and carbon dioxide. The StoLotusan Color G variant is additionally provided with film conservation to combat algae and fungi. Designed especially for difficult locations (shaded, on the edge of woodland ...), this variant is even more effective in delaying colonisation by microorganisms. The combination of film conservation and natural protection employing the properties of the lotus leaf thus offers maximum protection from "uninvited guests" on façades.

www.sto.de
Tel: +39 (0) 774-457-1020
Fax: +39 (0) 774-457-2020
E-mail: infoservice@stoeu.com

COL.9
BASF
Anti-aging for façades

COL.9®, a novel nanobinder from BASF for facade coatings, emulates the example of biominerals like bone and dental enamel. COL.9® is a dispersion of organic plastic polymer particles in which nanoscale particles of silica, the basic constituent of glass and quartz, are incorporated and evenly distributed. Thanks to this combination of elastic organic material and hard mineral, COL.9® based coatings combine the different advantages of conventional coating types. For example, unlike brittle, mineral based coatings, the widely used synthetic resin based dispersion paints are highly crack-resistant. But in summer, when dark house walls reach temperatures of 80° C and above in the sun, these coatings betray their weakness: on exposure to heat the synthetic resin begins to soften, and particles of soot and other contaminants stick to their surface. Because of its high silica content, however, the nanocomposite of COL.9® doesn't have this thermoplastic tackiness. At the same time, the mineral particles provide the coating with a hydrophilic i.e. water attracting surface on which raindrops are immediately dispersed. As regards cleanliness, this offers a dual benefit: in heavy rain, particles of dirt are washed off extensively from the façade surface. Also, the thin film of water remaining when the rain has stopped dries extremely quickly, which prevents mold formation. In contrast, the rain rolling off unevenly in thick droplets from water-repellent surfaces of fully synthetic resin coatings often leaves behind unattractive streaks of dirt.

www.basf.com
Tel: +49 (0)621-600
Fax: +49 (0)621-604-2525

Zaha Hadid Architects
Phaeno Science Center Wolfsburg

Designed to present the visitor with a degree of complexity and strangeness ruled by a specific system, the phaeno Science Centre awakens curiosity and discovery.
The building is located at the end of a row of culturally significant buildings by Aalto, Scharoun and Schweger; performing as an urban barrier along the Bahnhofsstrasse, it encloses the northern edge of the inner city, while it simultaneously links into the new Volkswagen Autostadt.
The inner city's multiple lines of movement continue through the building at ground level. The axis of Wolfsburg's significant buildings enters the Science Center like a view through a kaleidoscope, and scatter towards the Volkswagen Autostadt.
The large space is supported and distributed by funnel-shaped cones, some of which give access to the space, others flood the inside with natural light, and still others house the service functions.
The conical forms derive from the surrounding urban axis. These directions organically shape the building and its functions. One funnel becomes the main entrance, another becomes the lecture hall, and three more fuse into a big exhibition space under the main meeting hall: an alien, but oddly coherent crater landscape is the result.
The choice of materials continues the strategy of strangeness and fusion, based on the aesthetic effect of smooth, porous, sound-absorbing materials and different surface treatments.
Lighting used as an architectural asset establishes visual landmarks and allows for flexibility when changing exhibitions.
Exhibition designers can identify the "hidden pattern" of the service grid easily when installing a new show. The ceiling is simplified and a coherently organized service system allows vast open spaces as well as the installation of temporary walls. Light and shadow are the visual guidelines through the building, creating focal points and paths of light. The overall interior brightness requires to be tempered, to contrast with the highlighted exhibits. Visitors will intuitively follow the path of illuminated focal points. A smooth carpet of light provided underneath the building reflects light onto the underside of the sculptural forms. Increased illumination draws visitors to the entrances. The flow of visitors will determine other technical lighting requirements, including the creation of different zones.

Architect:
Zaha Hadid Architects
Location:
Wolfsburg, Germany
Photographs:
Michael Rasche / Artur,
Roland Halbe / Artur,
Werner Huthmacher / Artur

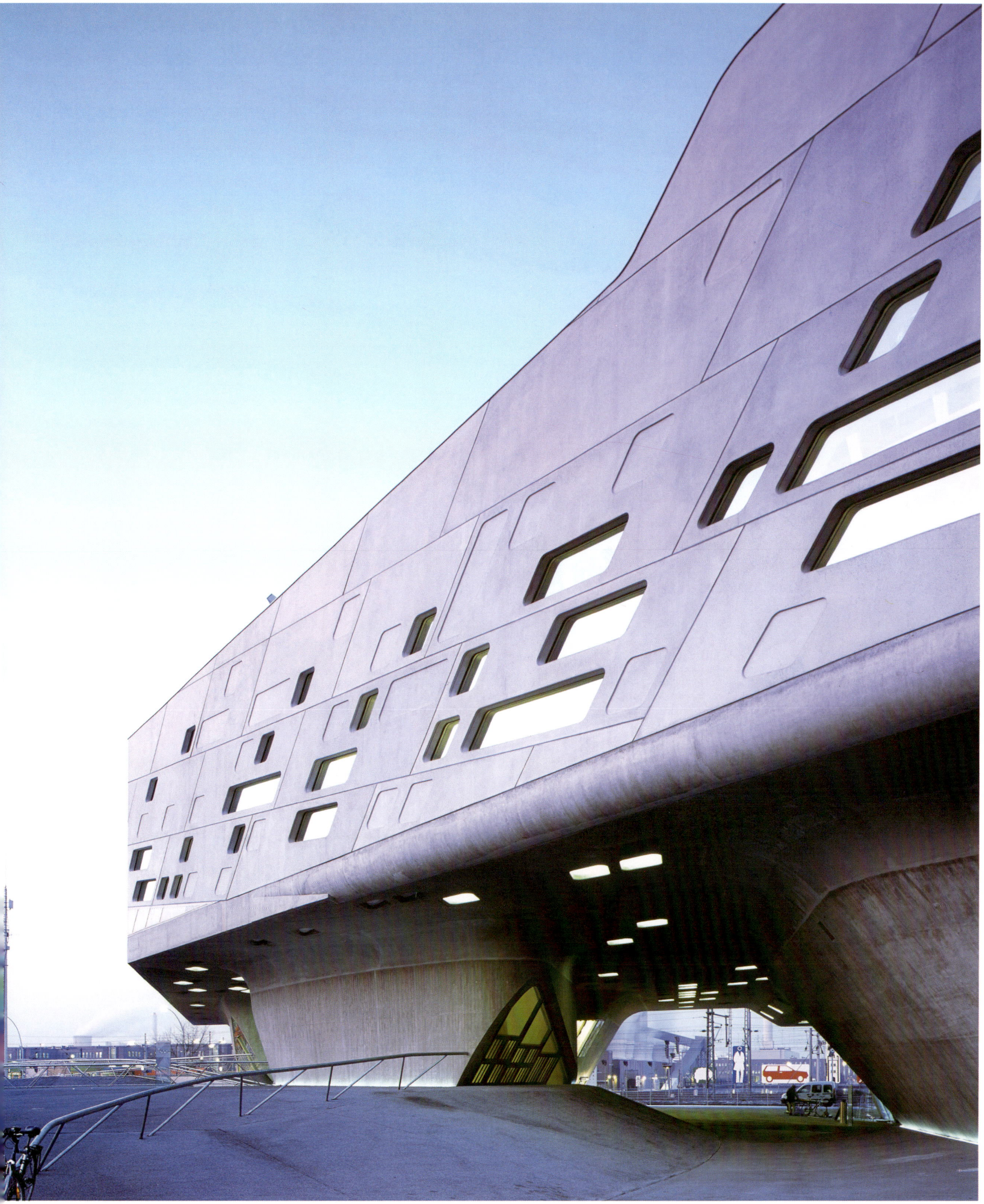

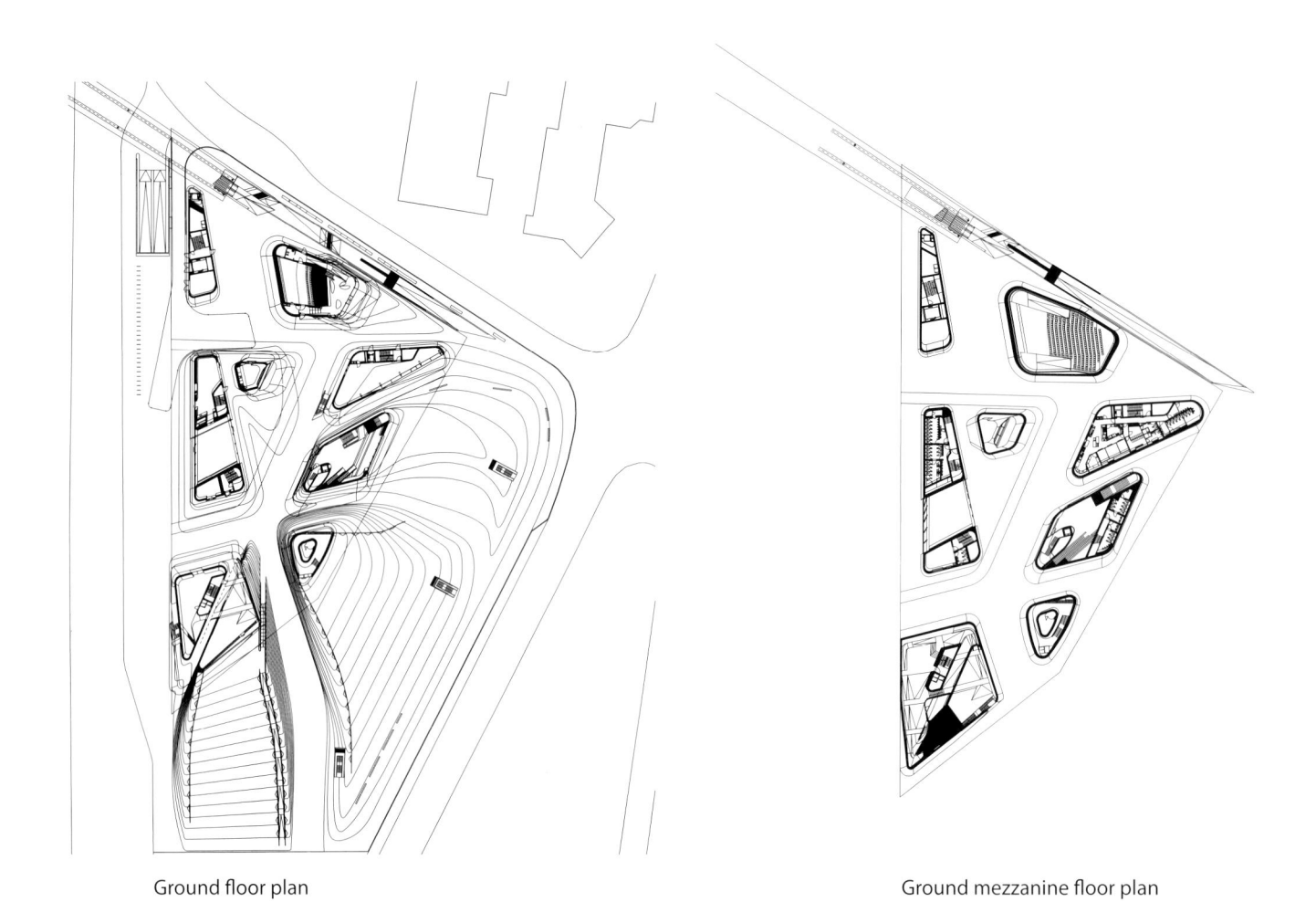

Ground floor plan

Ground mezzanine floor plan

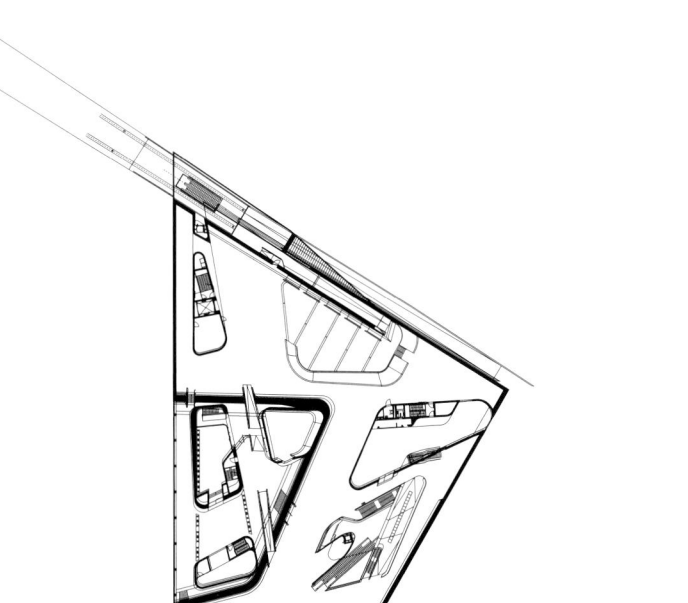

Concourse floor plan

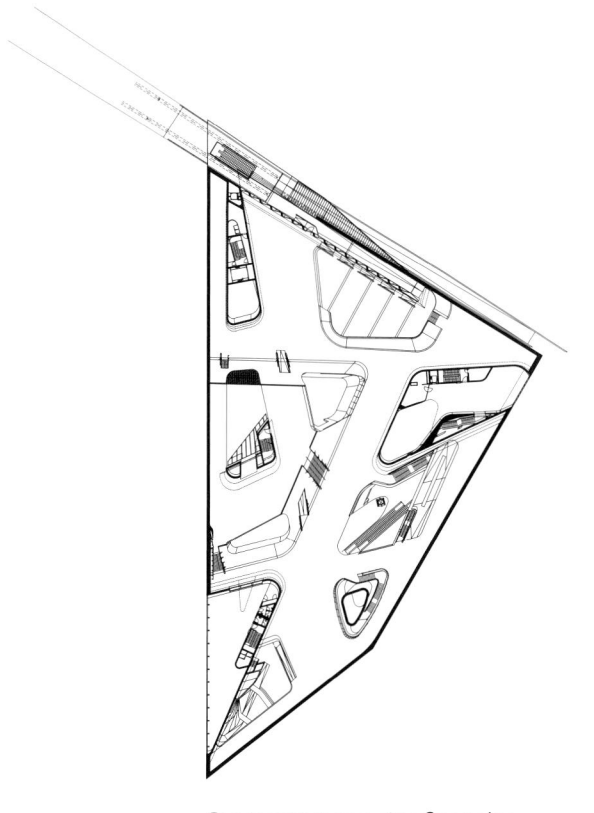

Concourse mezzanine floor plan

Zaha Hadid Architects

© Werner Huthmacher / Artur

© Werner Huthmacher / Artur

Zaha Hadid Architects 69

Zaha Hadid Architects

The conical forms derive from the surrounding urban axis. These directions organically shape the building and its functions. One funnel becomes the main entrance, another becomes the lecture hall, and three more fuse into a big exhibition space under the main meeting hall: an alien, but oddly coherent crater landscape is the result.

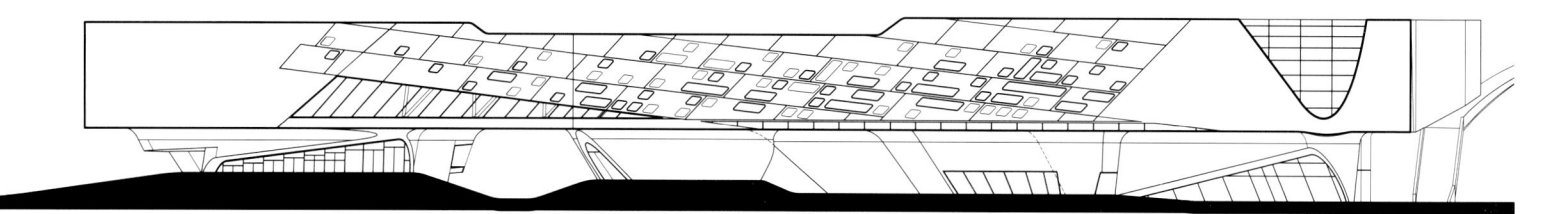

South elevation

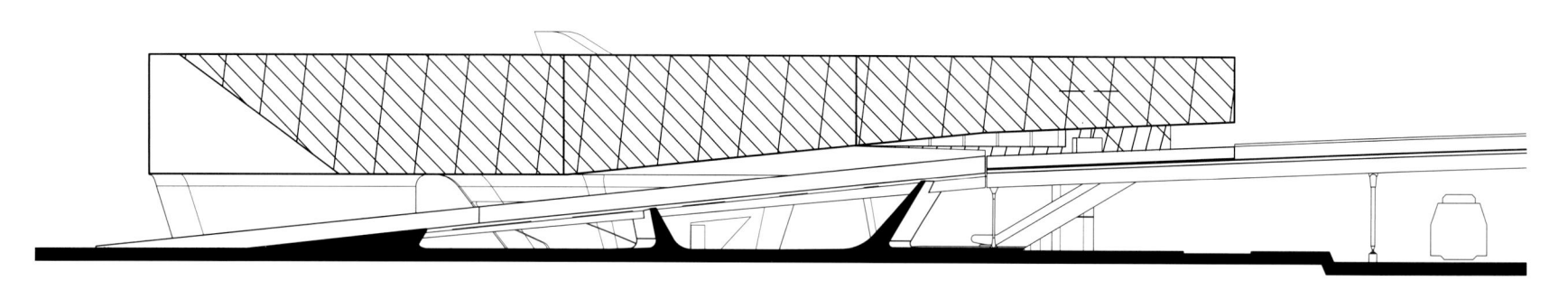

East elevation

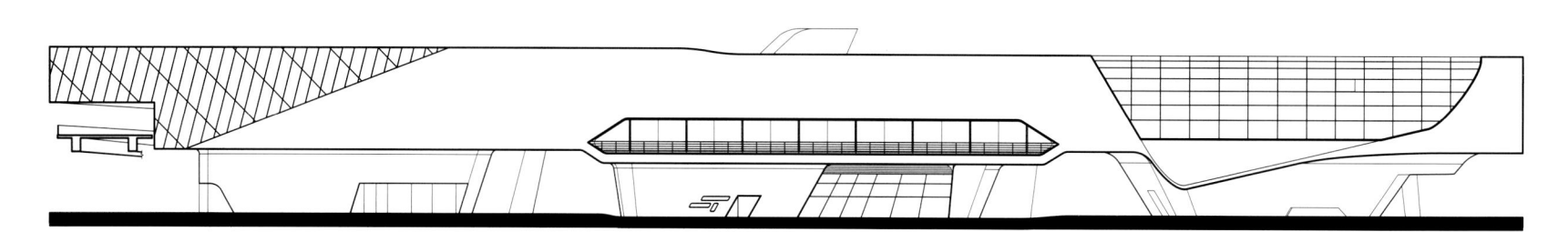

North elevation

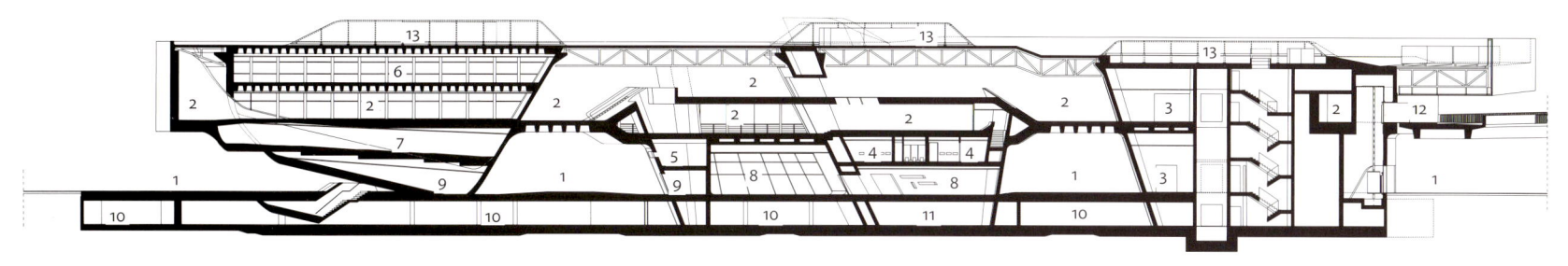

Section

1. Landscape
2. Exhibition room
3. Laboratory
4. Toilets
5. Staff room
6. Administration
7. Shop
8. Event space
9. Workshop
10. Parking
11. Toilets / plant room
12. Bridge to autostadt
13. Plant room

Zaha Hadid Architects

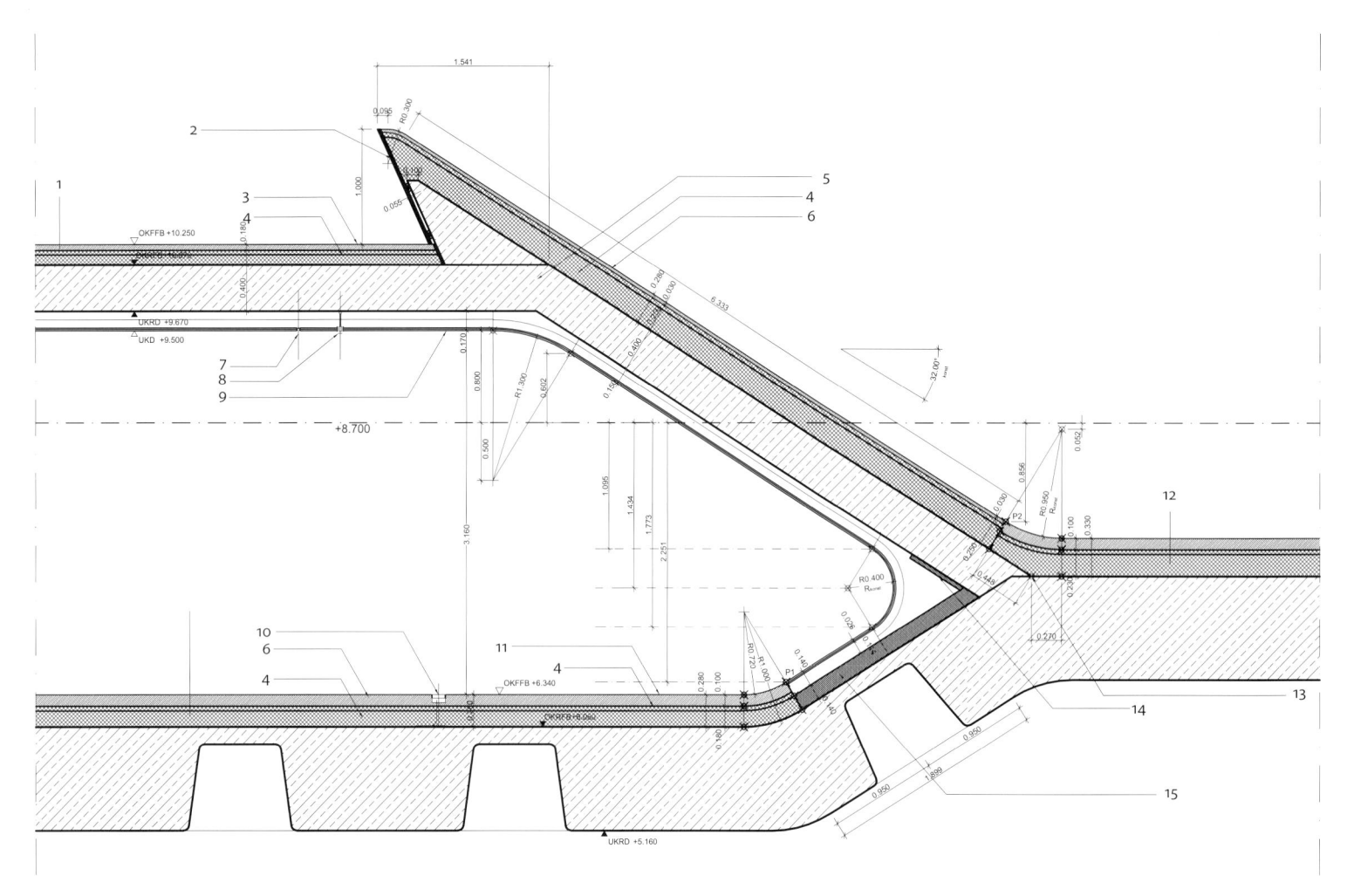

1. Thermozell 250 t = 87 mm
   Thermozell 500 t = 40 mm
   Insulating membrane, t = 0.2 mm
   Concrete, t = 50 mm
   Rubber seal, t = 3 mm
2. Metal cladding, t = 26 mm
3. Cement
4. Thermocell
5. Reinforced concrete
6. Concrete render
7. Steel 'E'-section
8. Sprinklers
9. Suspended ceiling
10. Concrete
11. Guiderail embedded in paving
12. Thermozell 250 t = 190 mm
    Thermozell 500 t = 40 mm
    Vapor barrier, t = 2 mm
    Insulating membrane, t = 0.2 mm
    Reinforced concrete, t = 95 mm
    Mortar, t = 3 mm
13. Roof joint
14. Glass, t = 40 mm
15. Glass, t = 140 mm

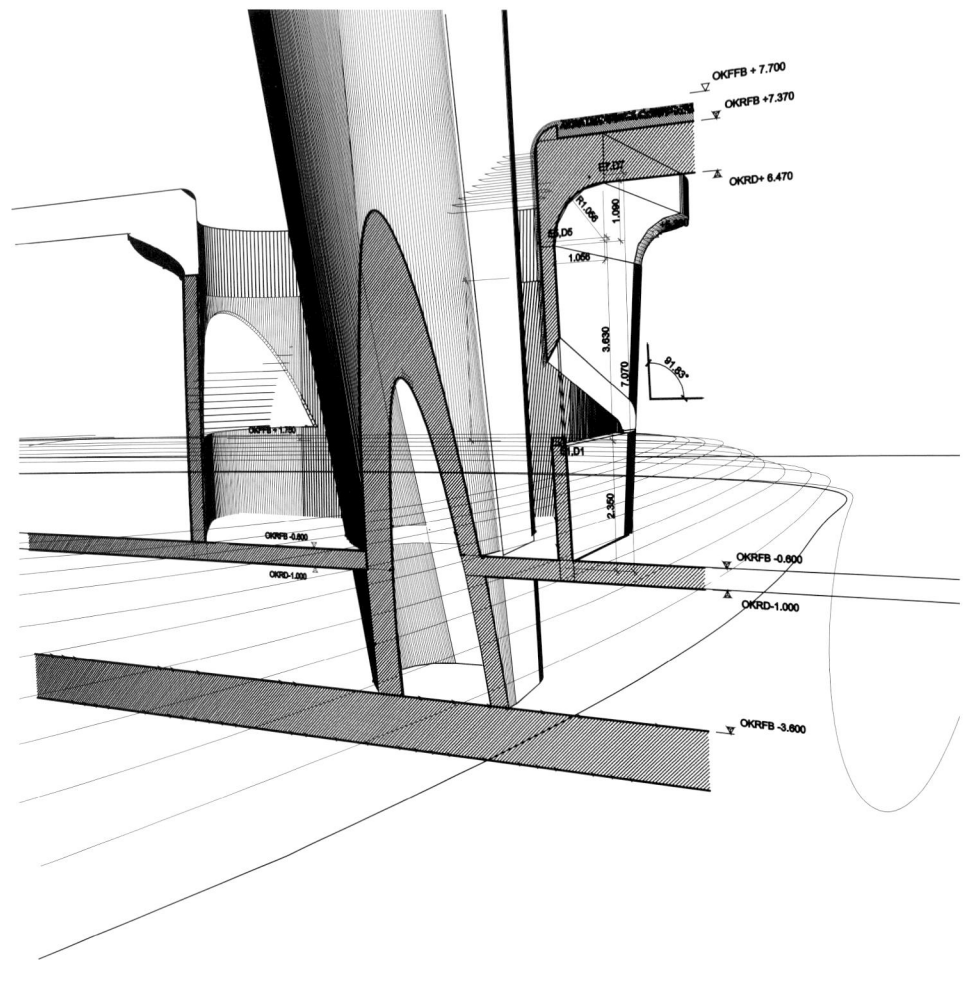

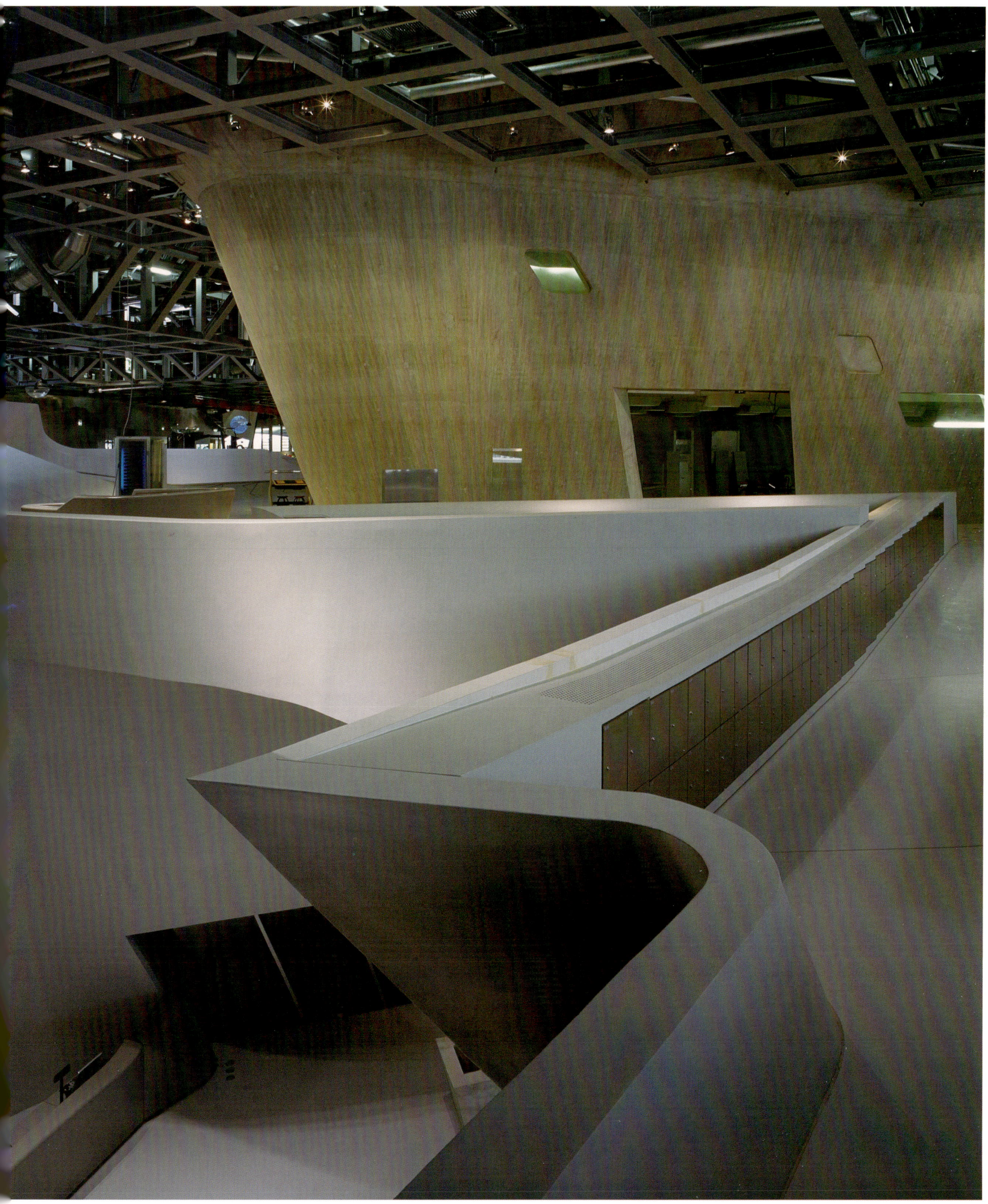

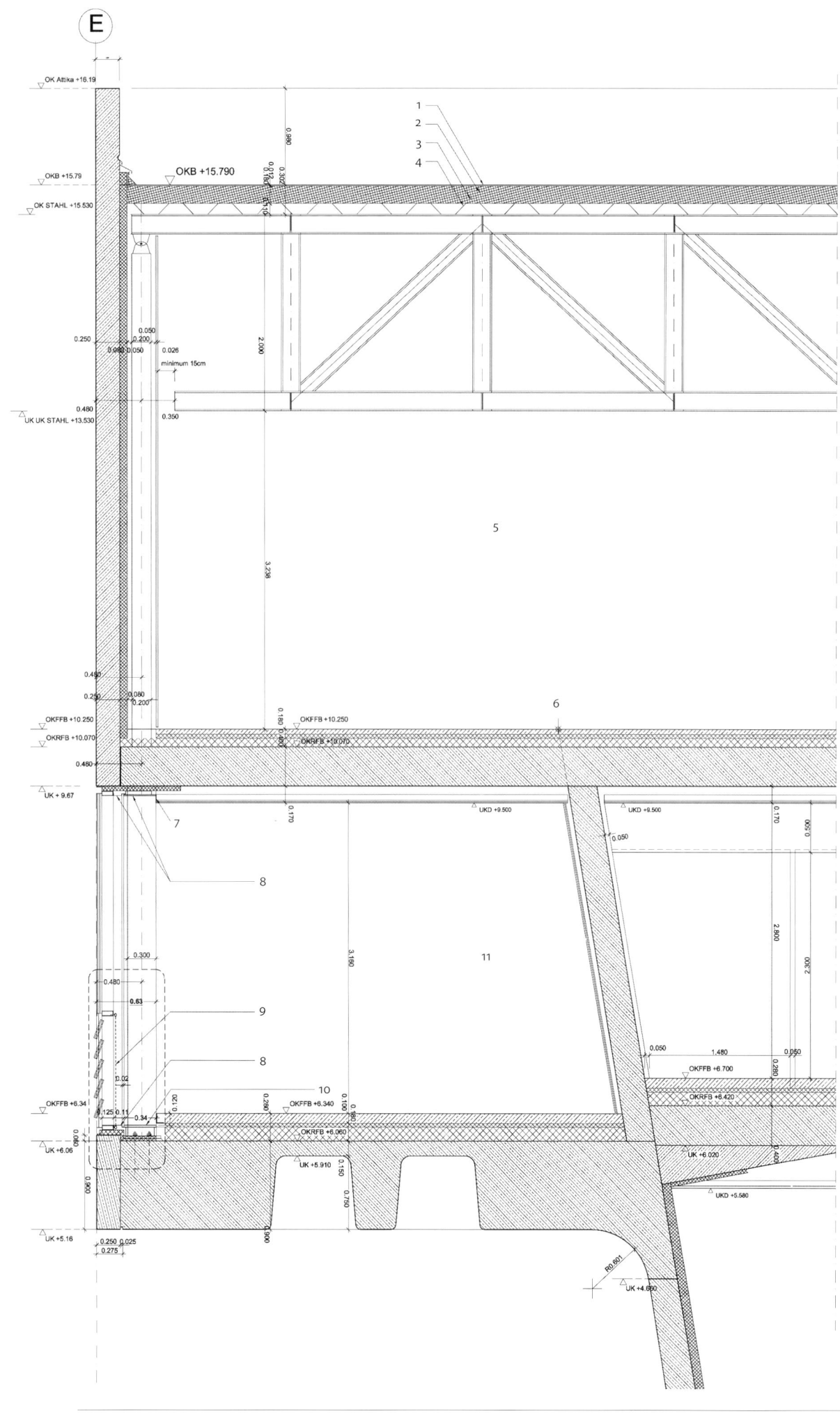

1. Roofing membrane
2. Mineral wool, t = 150 mm
3. Insulation
4. Trapezoidal metal sheet
5. Circulation hub
6. Floor slab
7. Metal cladding sheets
8. Joint between metal sheets
9. Parapet, h = 1 m
10. Convector fan integrated in the floor build-up, h=112 mm
11. Ground floor

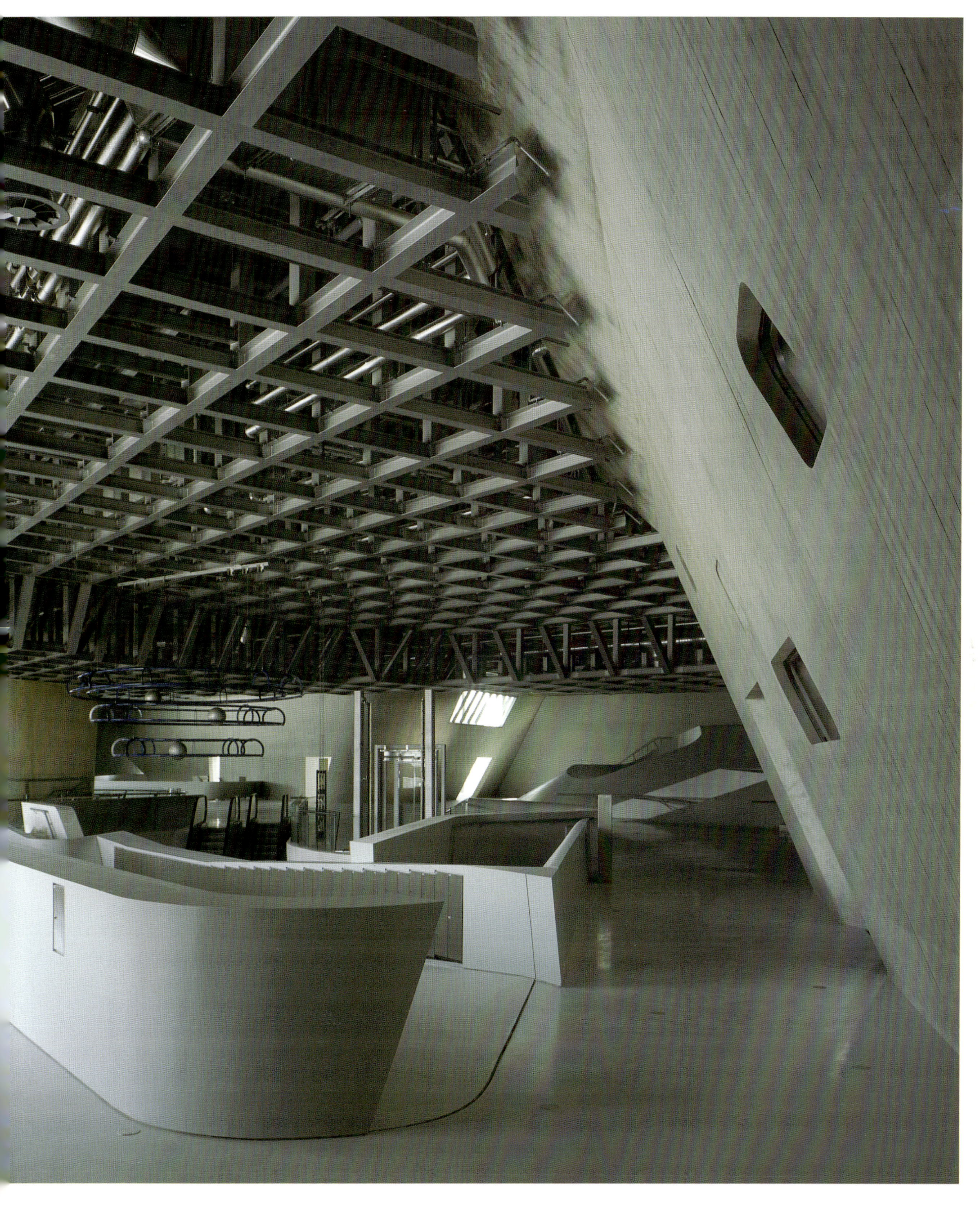

Zaha Hadid
Bergisel Ski Jump

In December 1999, Zaha Hadid Architects won an international competition to design a new ski jump on Bergisel Mountain in Innsbruck, a city with a long tradition as a venue for winter sport competitions. The new ski jump is part of a larger renovation project for the Olympic arena and replaces the old ski jump, which no longer met international standards.

The project is unusual because it went beyond the relatively one-dimensional task of designing a technical building for a single purpose. The striking silhouette is what made Hadid's design stand out from the others: suggesting an almost animal-like presence, the ski jump has all the hallmarks to become a local landmark. About 90 meters high and almost 50 meters long, the building is a combination of a tower and a bridge. Structurally, it is divided into a vertical concrete tower and a spatial green structure, which integrates the ramp and the cafe. Two lifts take visitors up to the cafe 40 meters above the peak of Bergisel, where spectators enjoy views over a spectacular alpine panorama, and watch the athletes below flying across the Innsbruck skyline.

The construction process was complicated because of the need to work similtuneously below grade, on the surface and at considerable height. To coordinate the construction process, the architects roganized the logistical control of the site ot the last detail, taking into consideration the difficult topographical conditions of the mountain and the high technical demands of the building, while working within a short construction schedule.

Conceptually, the structural elements are not different systems, just part of an overall construction that came together to form a uniform, fluid building. To support this image of fluidity, the building was covered with metal sheets marked with fine vertical grooves that follow the curves and reflect light differently according to the time of day, while at night, lights trace the cafe and the track of the ramp. The inside of the ramp, which has a U-shaped cross section, and the inside of the cafe are lit by strips of light that change color.

Architect:
Zaha Hadid
Location:
Innsbruck, Austria
Photographs:
Hélène Binet

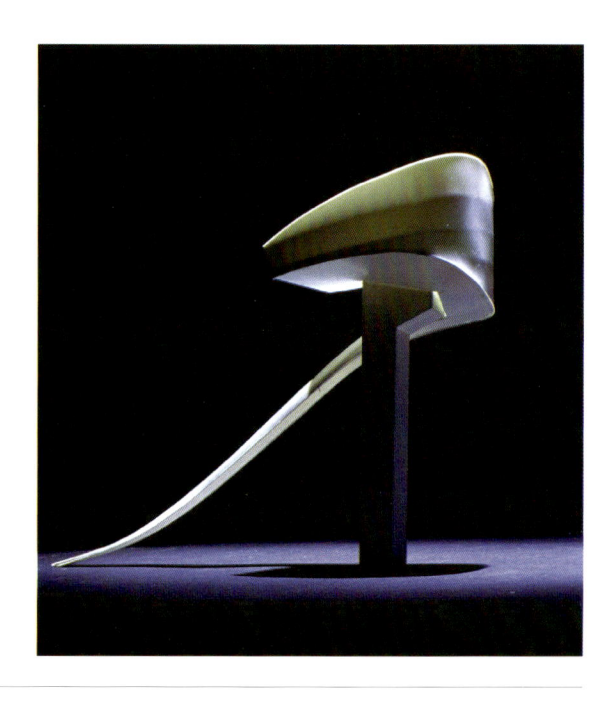

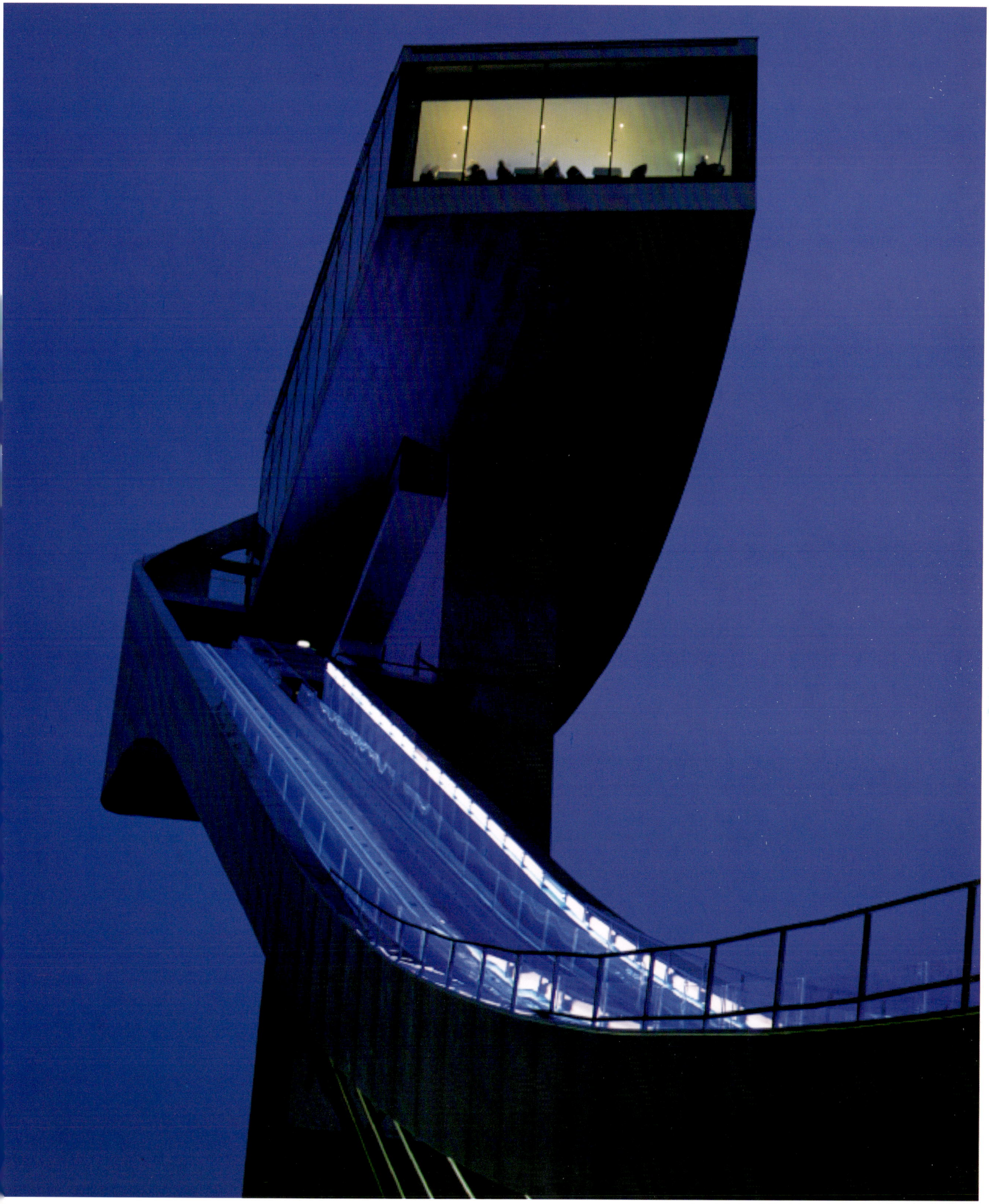

Ground plan

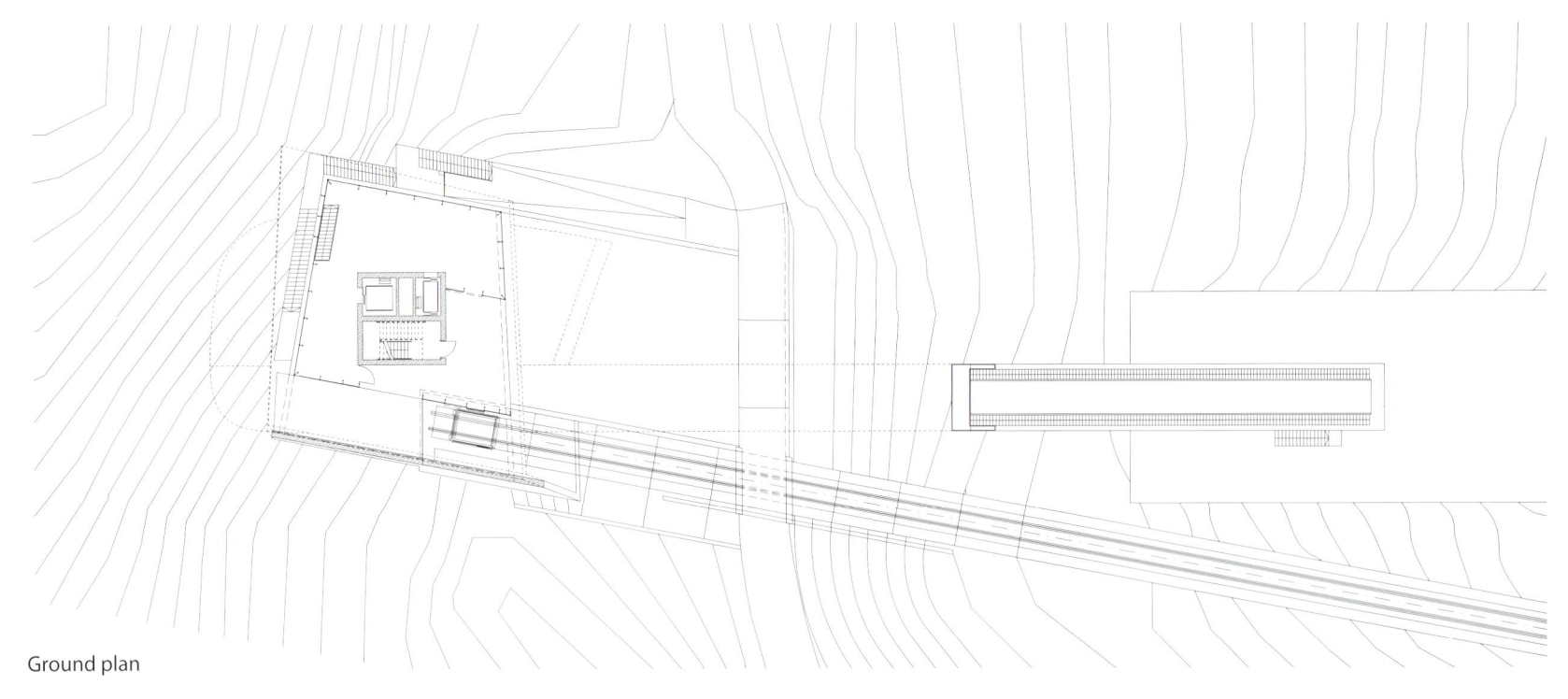

80 Zaha Hadid

The new Bergisel Ski Jump is a sweeping, geometric run that fits perfectly against the background of the towering Alps.

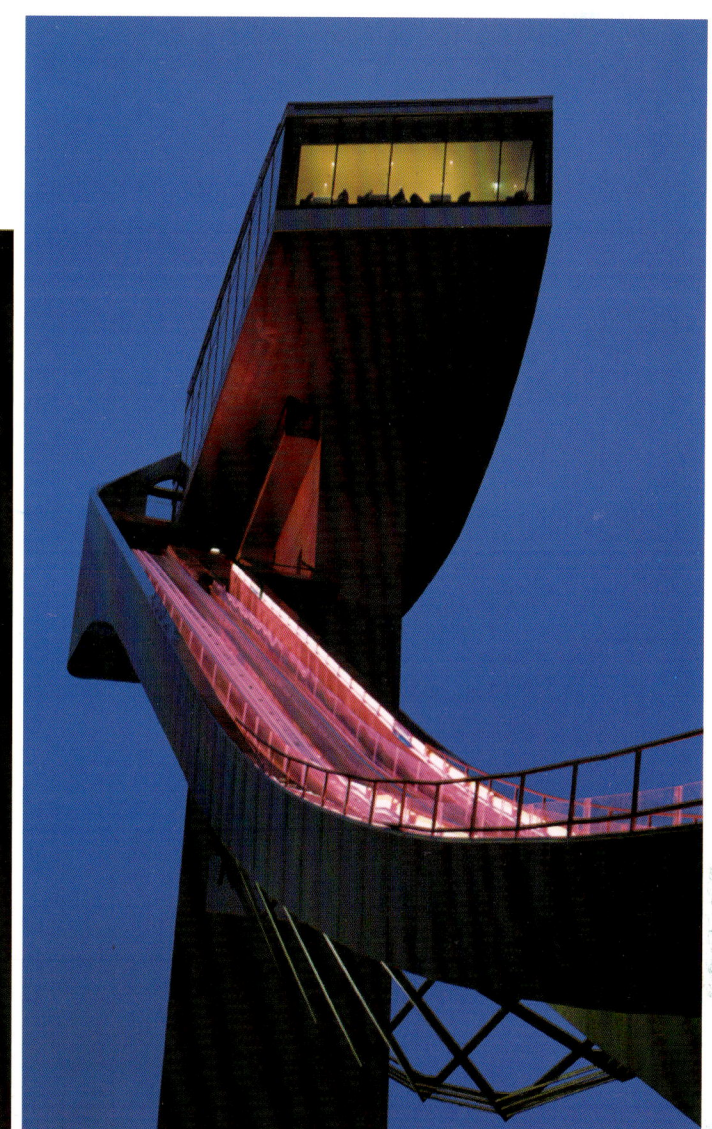

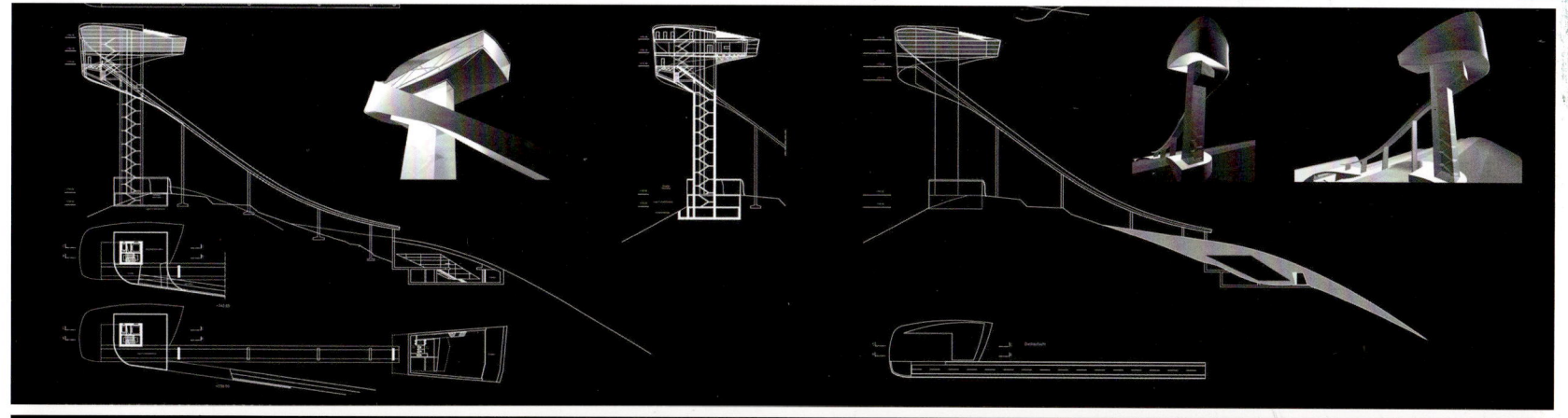

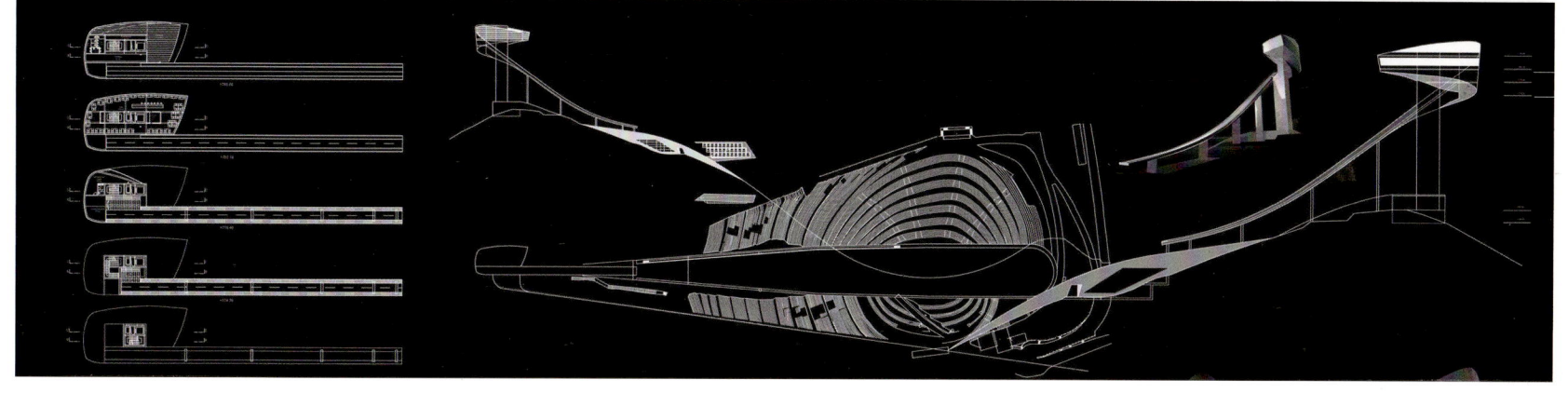

Zaha Hadid

Level +35

Level +39

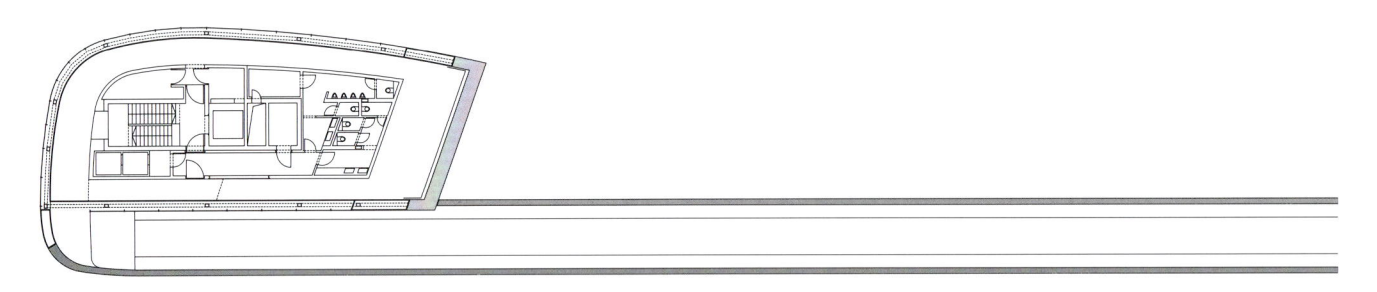

Level +43

The brief called for a hybrid between specialized sports facility and public areas including a cafe and a viewing terrace, expressed by the architects as a single new shape that extends the topography of the slope into the sky.

Zaha Hadid

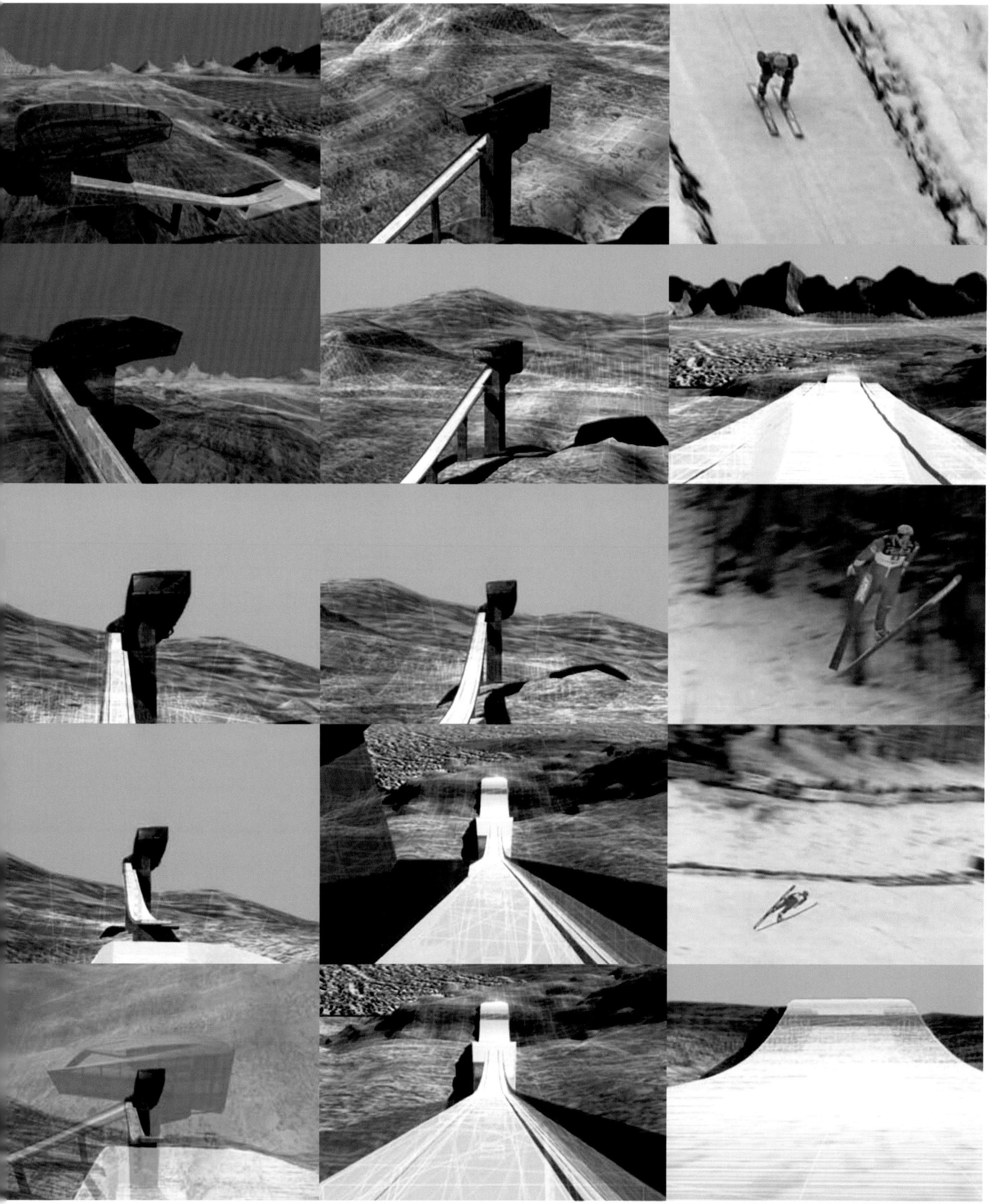

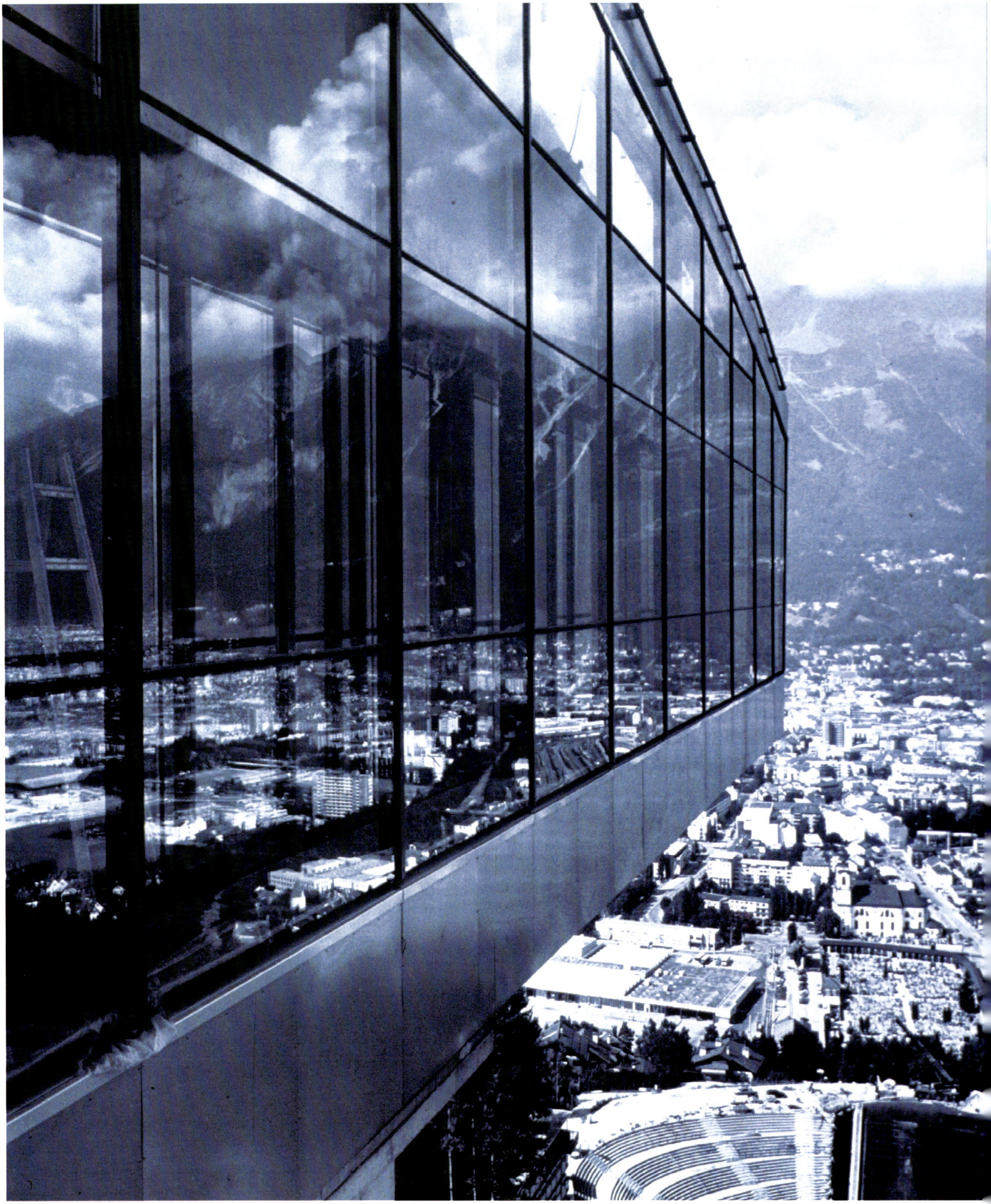

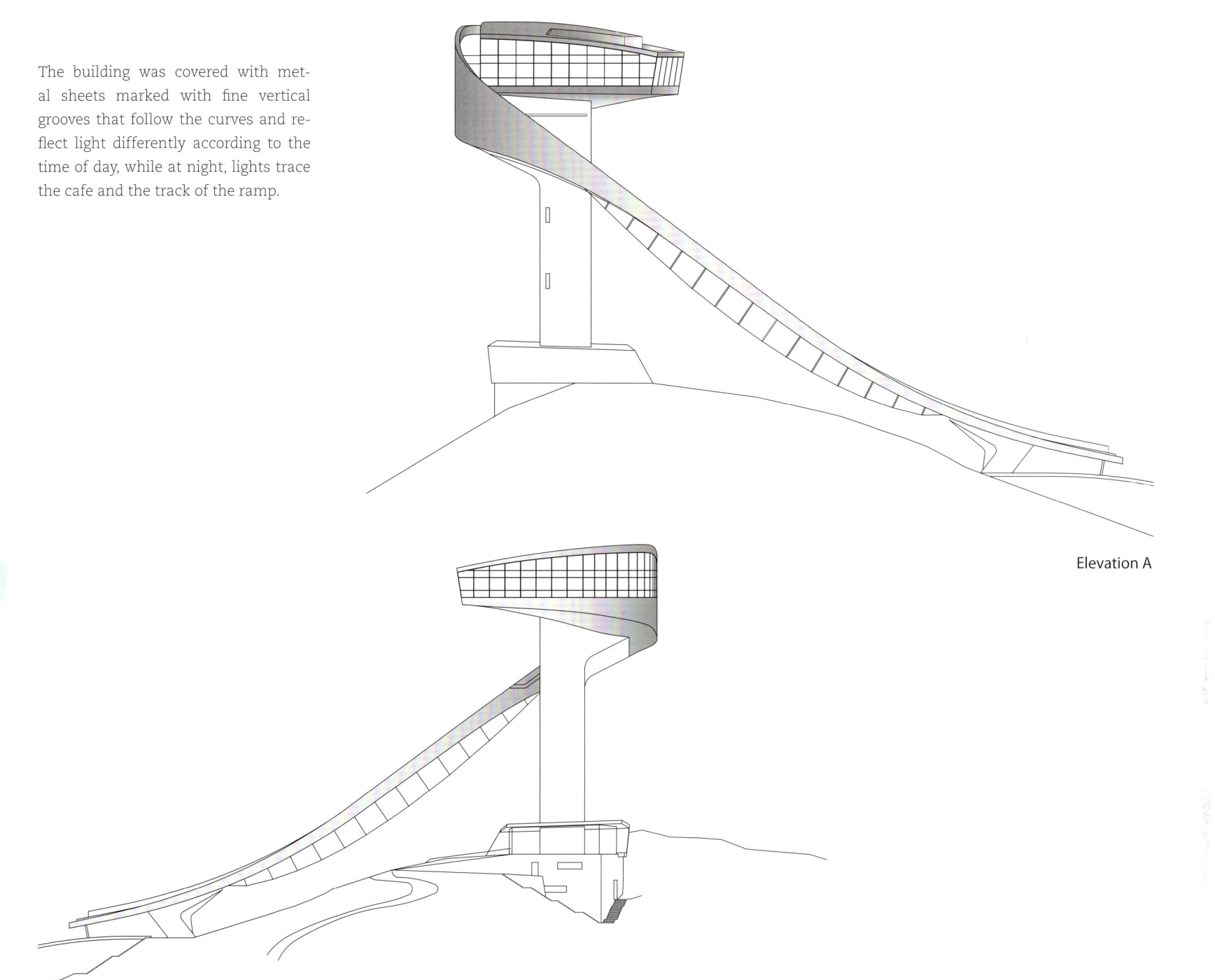

The building was covered with metal sheets marked with fine vertical grooves that follow the curves and reflect light differently according to the time of day, while at night, lights trace the cafe and the track of the ramp.

Elevation A

Elevation B

Zaha Hadid

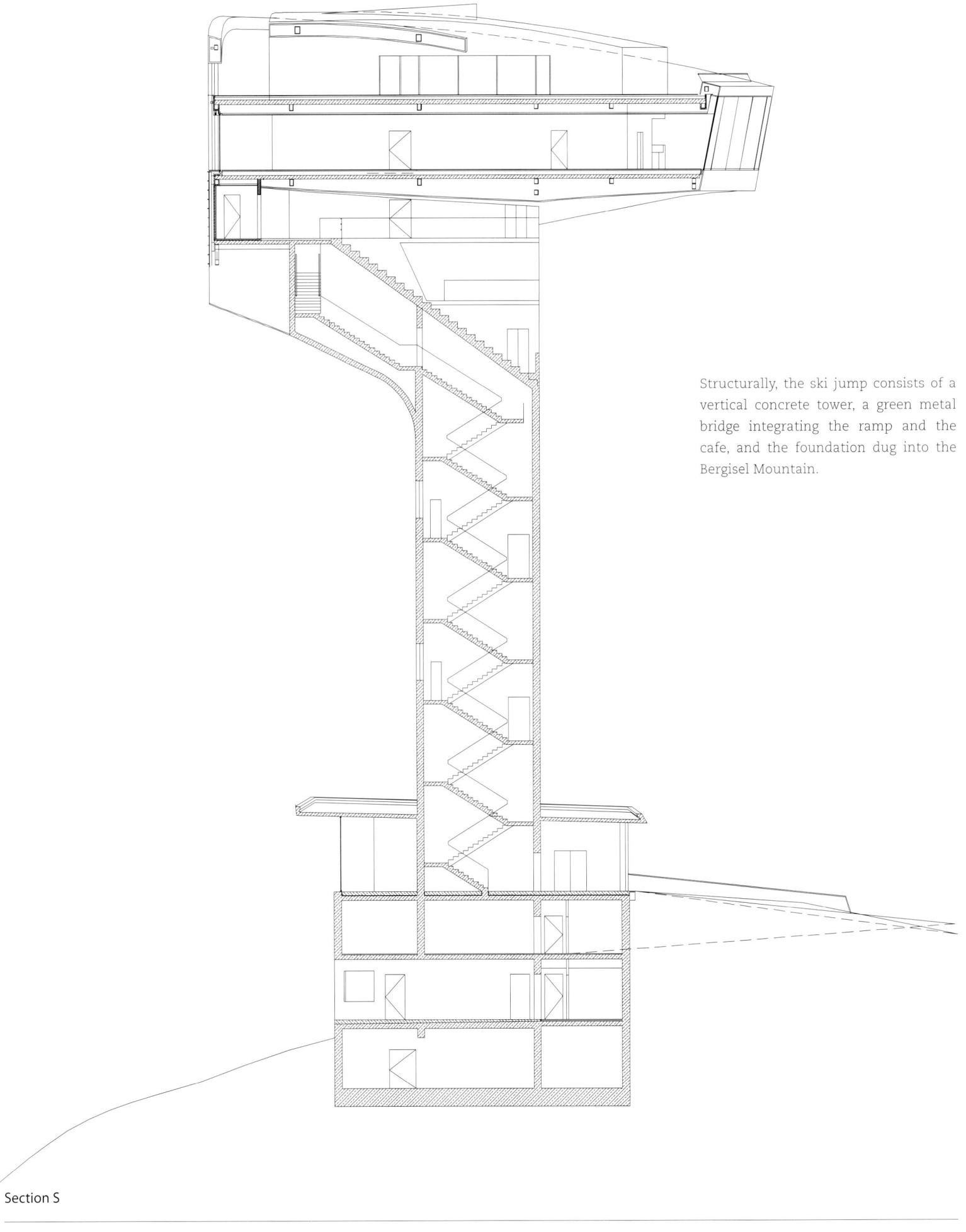

Structurally, the ski jump consists of a vertical concrete tower, a green metal bridge integrating the ramp and the cafe, and the foundation dug into the Bergisel Mountain.

Section S

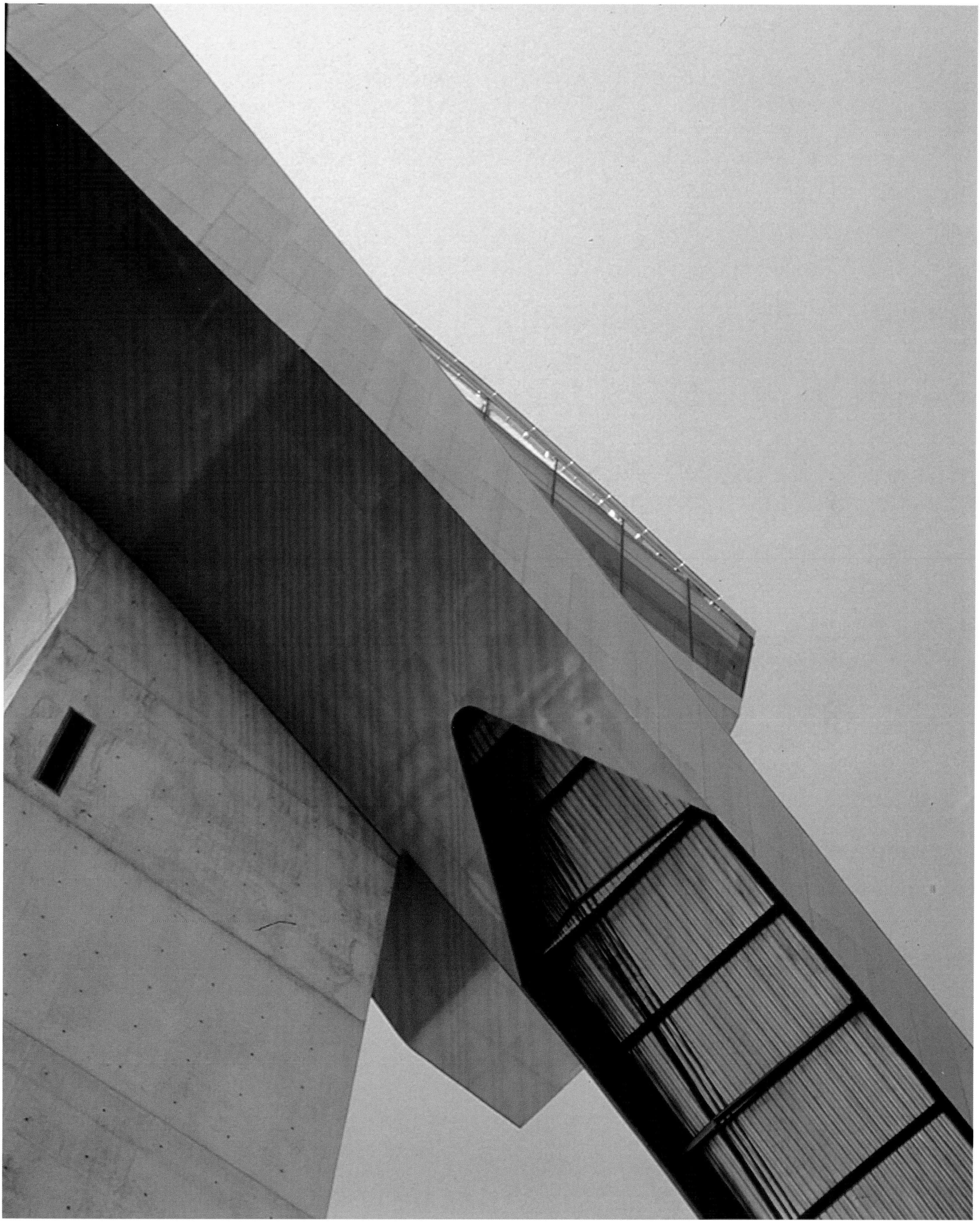

Alberto Campo Baeza
Blas House

This house, located on the top of a hill looking north towards the mountains near Madrid, represents Campo Baeza's response to the site.
The design addresses both the mountain and the distant views by integrating two volumes, one more earthy and designed for living, the other airy and fragile, meant for contemplating the natural surroundings and enjoying the views.
The first volume is a concrete box, and also acts as a platform on which the upper volume is built, a transparent glass box with a delicate white-painted steel structure. The concrete box, rooted in the ground like a cave, contains the living areas. The layout is clear and simple, with service areas in a row towards the back, and the spaces they serve placed towards the front of the house.
Stairs lead from this lower level to the glass box above the platform, which consists of an outdoor area and covered lookout with views to the mountain.
Light was a central concept in the design, continuing the tension between the two sections. In the upper part of the house, the architect worked with horizontal light crossing the horizontal space, and the ideas of transparency and continuous space. Standing in the shaded lookout, the observer can contemplate the mountain landscape, which is illuminated by the sun and emphasized, so that it seems to come towards him or her. In the lower section, the windows frame the views of the mountain landscape.

Architect:
Alberto Campo Baeza
Location:
Madrid, Spain
Photographs:
Hisao Suzuki

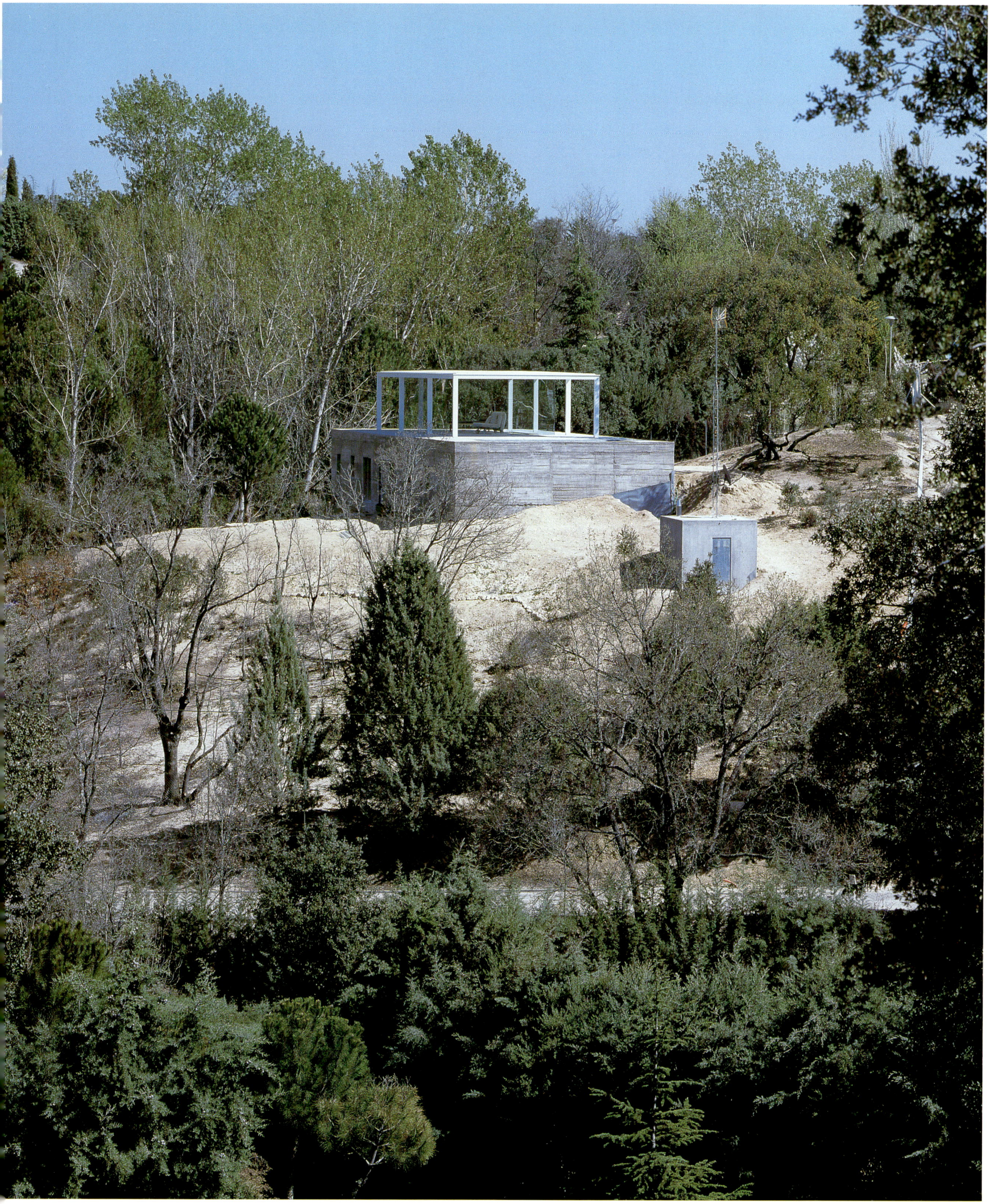

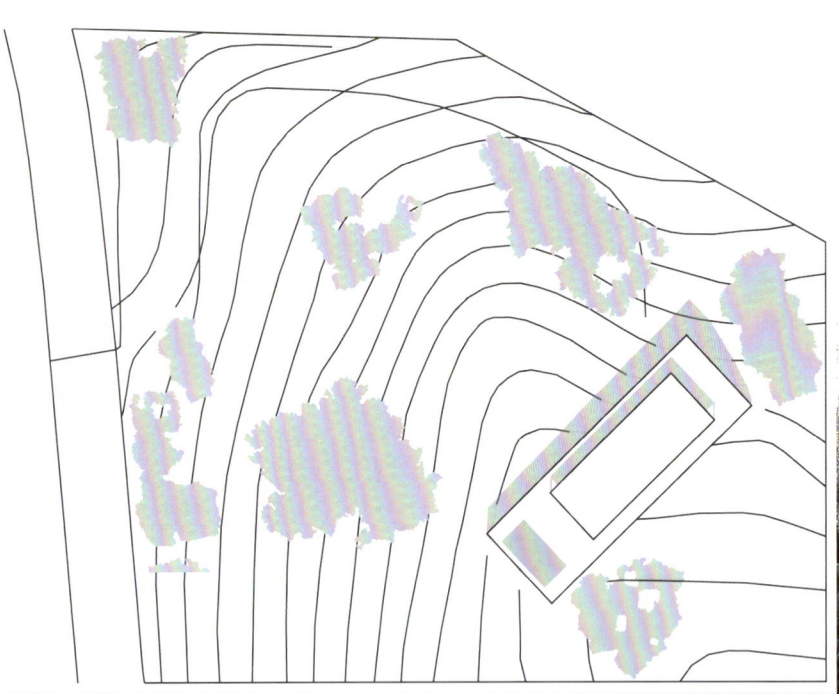

Alberto Campo Baeza

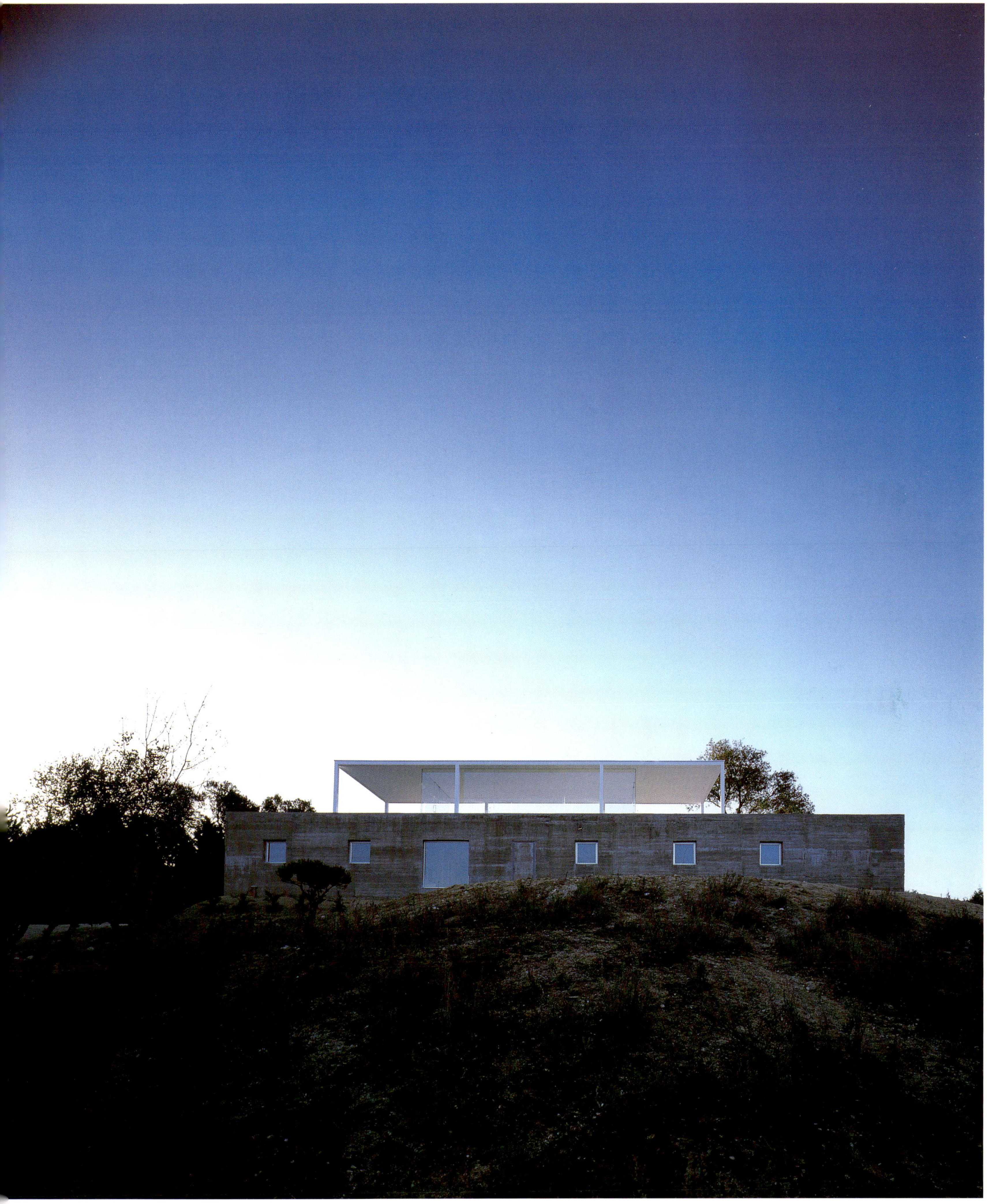

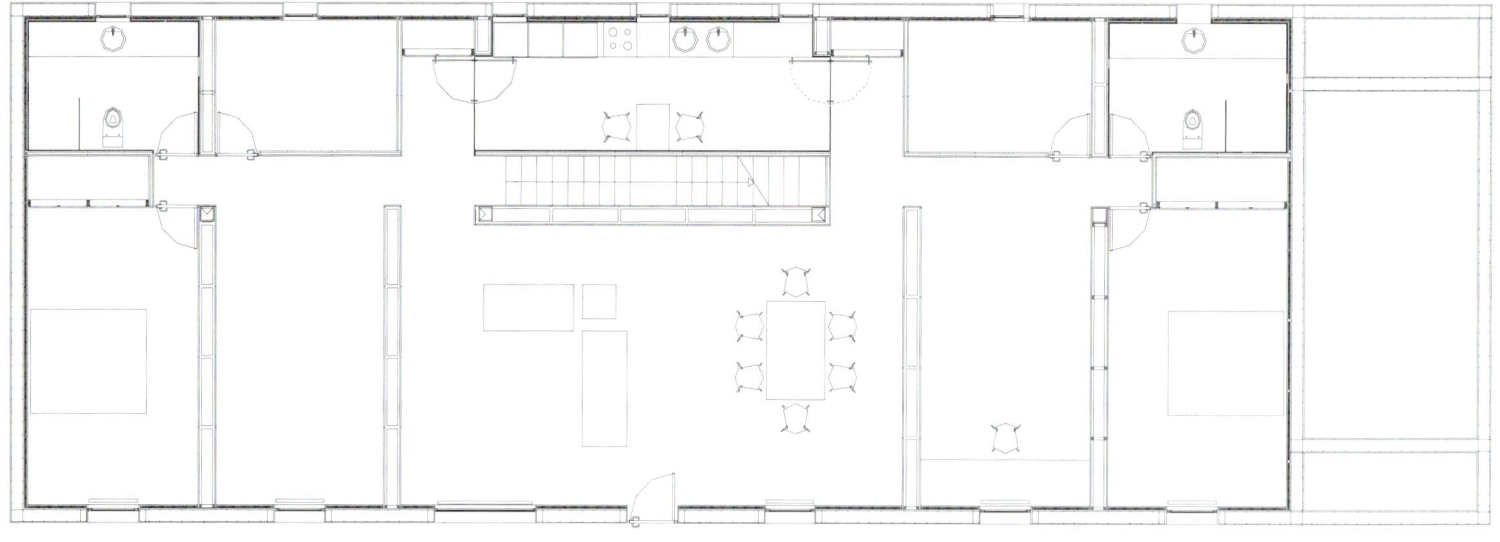

Ground floor plan

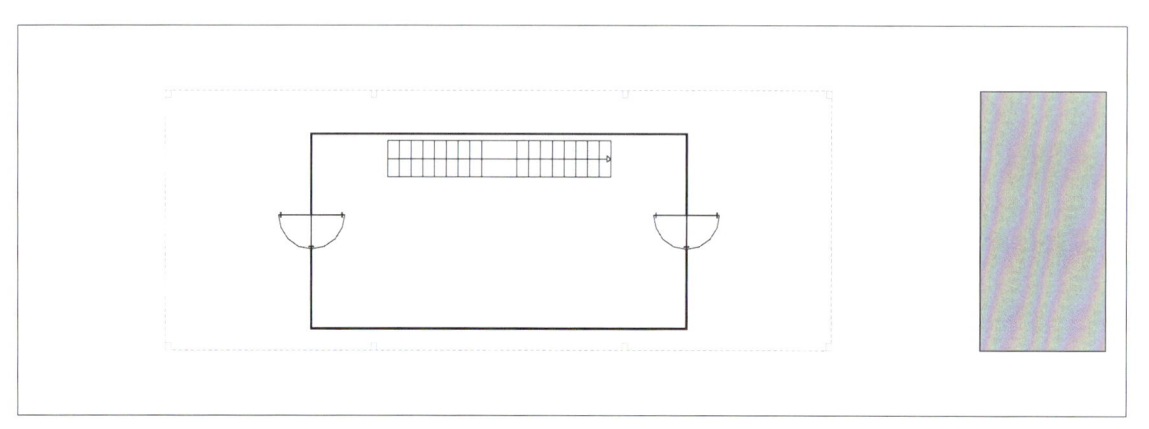

Podium

The base is a cave-like space that provides refuge. Above, a glass hut provides a space for contemplating nature. The measurements are exact and the proportions carefully calculated, creating a feeling of purity and peace.
The simple interiors in the lower volume frame the view, while in the upper section the glass walls make the house appear to be part of the landscape.

Alberto Campo Baeza

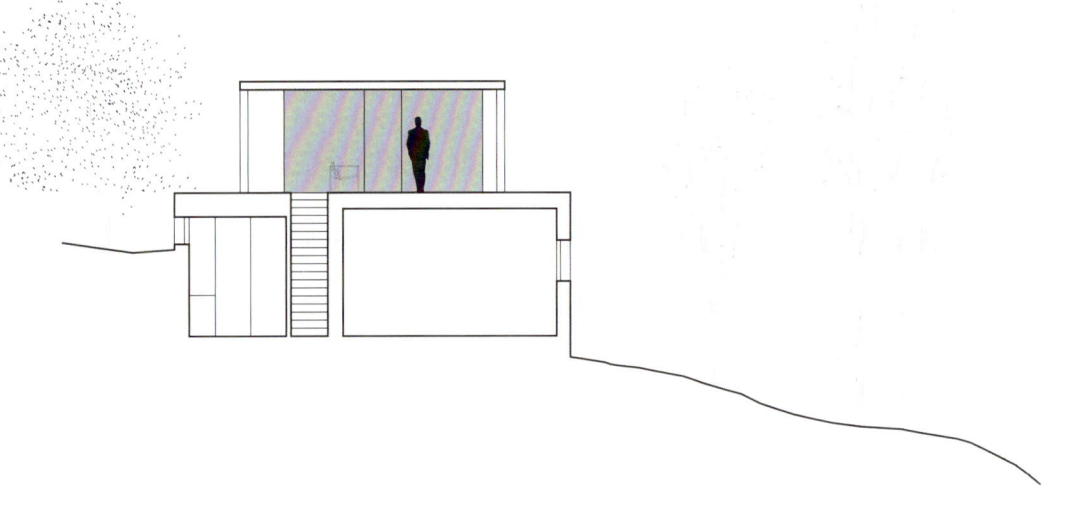

South-north section

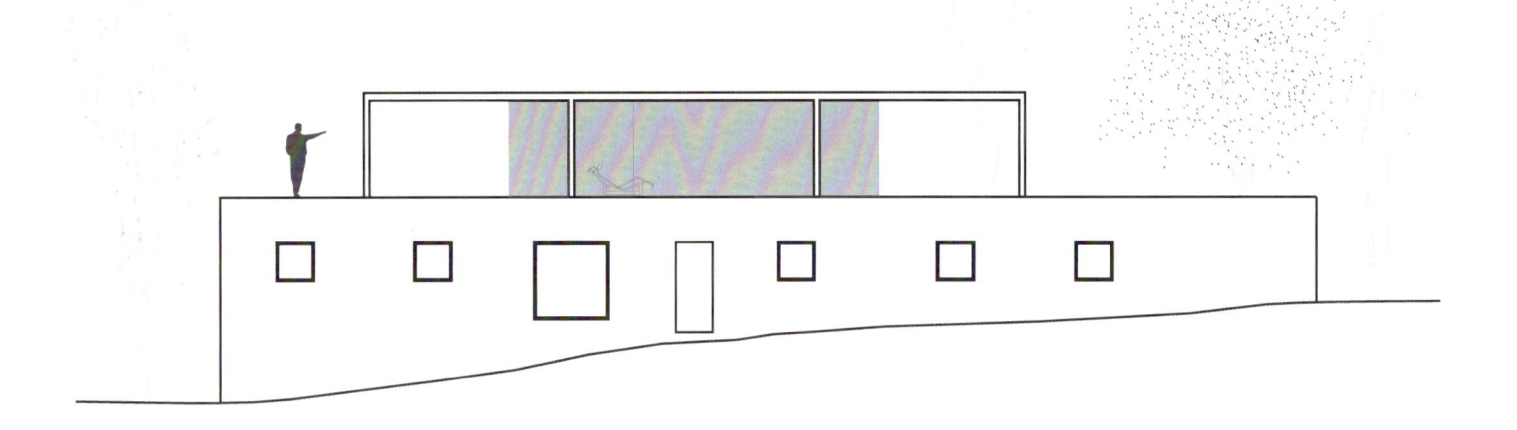

North elevation

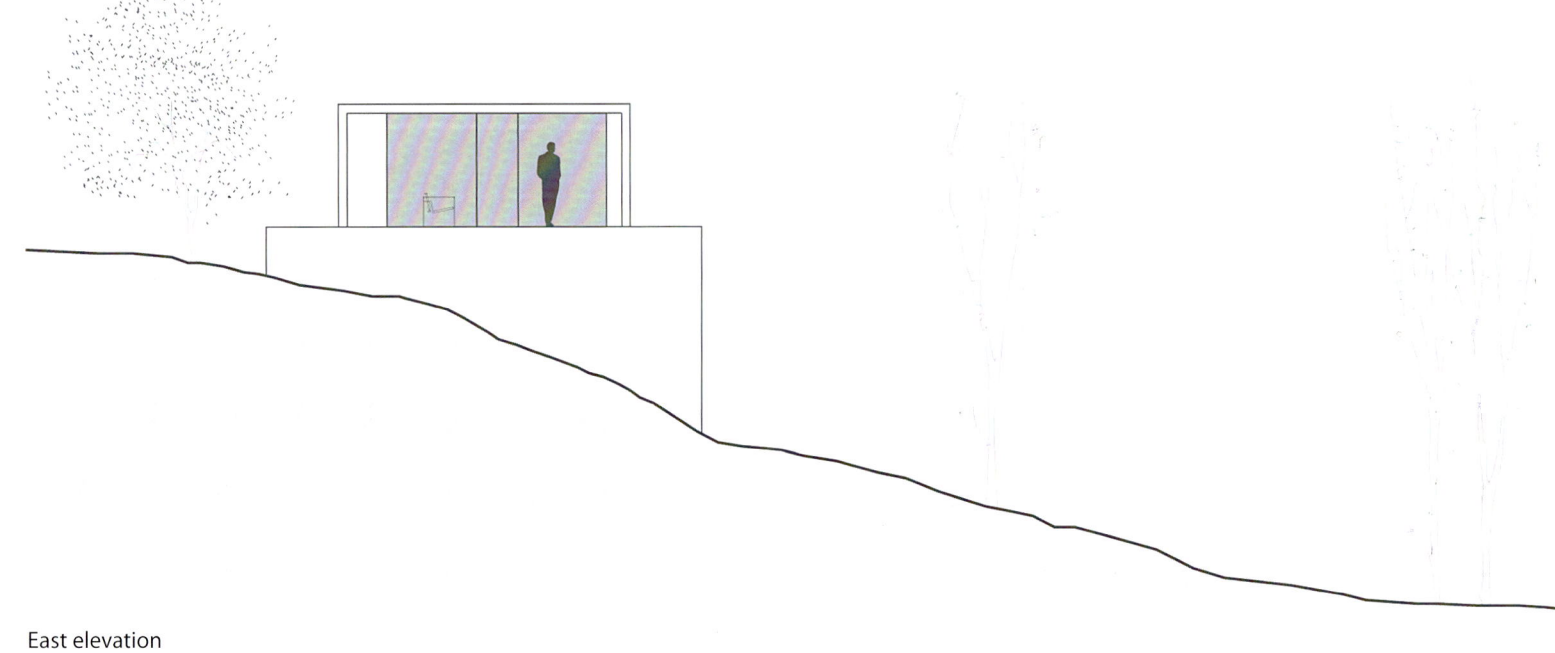

East elevation

94 Alberto Campo Baeza

Alberto Campo Baeza

1. 5 + 5 fixed Stadip glazing
2. 84 × 226 cm folding door with 10 mm safety glass
3. Continuous concrete, waterproof finish
4. Sloped damp-resistant concrete compression layer
5. Separating layer
6. 3 cm extruded polystyrene insulation
7. Waterproof membrane
8. Separating layer
9. 5 cm compression layer
10. False ceiling
11. 0.5 % slope
12. 80 × 210 cm folding door with 10 mm safety glass
13. 12 mm double plasterboard panel painted white
14. High-density polyurethane foam insulation
15. 25 cm thick reinforced concrete wall
16. 60 × 40 × 3 cm stone paving
17. Bond coat (2 cm)
18. Sand (3 cm)
19. Compression layer (3 cm)
20. PVC
21. "Isover" insulation (4 cm)
22. Compression layer (5 cm)
23. 20 × 120 cm Macrofur
24. Perforated brick
25. Reinforced concrete foundation pad
26. H-50 concrete
27. Profile finishing
28. Reinforced concrete beam
29. Fastening strip
30. 12 mm double panel of pladur/plaster painted white
31. Step with 3 cm stone
32. 7 cm stone skirting board
33. Natural ground
34. 1-2 mm "Rhenofol CV" waterproofing
35. Fiberglass felt protection
36. Polystyrene Roofmate SL insulation, 1250 × 600 × 30 mm
37. 0.25 polyethylene "Rhenofol PE" barrier
38. HEB 180 profile painted white
39. Perimeter finish, Roofmate
40. HEB 180 profile painted white
41. Trim
42. 15 × 120 cm Macrufor
43. 14 mm finish
44. 4 × 1.4 cm fastening
45. Metal pillar painted white
46. 5 + 5 fixed Stadip glazing
47. 20 × 20 cm anchor plate
48. Continuous concrete, waterproof finish
49. 20 × 120 cm Macrufor plate
50. High-density polyurethane foam insulation
51. 12 mm double panel of pladur/plaster painted white
52. PVC trim
53. 180 × 180 window with double glazing and aluminum carpentry
54. 0.5 % slope
55. 25 cm thick reinforced concrete wall

Alberto Campo Baeza

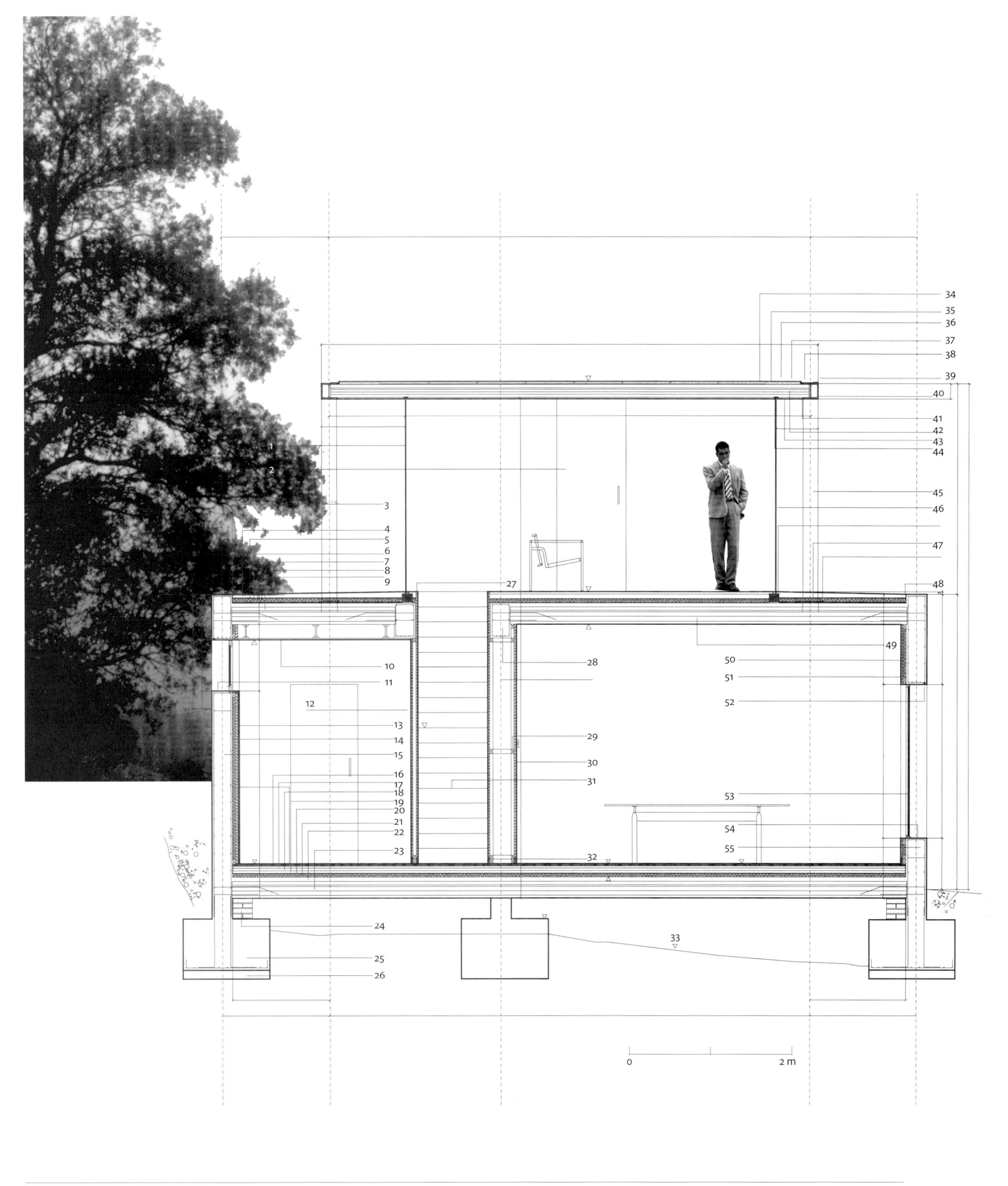

Besonias - Almeida -Kruk

Casa Mar Azul

Mar Azul is a seaside town situated 400 km (250 miles) south of Buenos Aires, with an extensive beach of virgin sand dunes and a dense conifer forest. The owners, members of the architectural studio and regular visitors to the area, chose this splendid forest backdrop to build this small summer house.

The environmental and scenic characteristics of the site, and the unusual position of the architects as both clients and designers of the project allowed the them to approach the project as an opportunity to experiment.

The search for alternatives had just three limitations: minimal impact on the landscape, a low budget, and a practically no-maintenance objective. With these premises in mind, it was decided to build the house as a prism of minimum height, defined by an envelope of exposed concrete, which harmonizes in texture and color with the forest, and by large window panes, which reflect the surroundings and allow the house to integrate completely with its setting. The complementary functions (spare bathroom, water tank and deposit) are housed in a vertical, wooden prism, hidden among the trees.

The simple volume that accommodates the main functions was divided into two very different areas: one totally glazed, surrounded by a wide, wooden terrace, designed for reunions and totally integrated with the forest, and the other more protected, with more modest openings and used for the bedrooms, the bathroom and a space for cooking. The house has no official entranceway: it can be accessed via the glazed section, through sliding doors located on two of the facades. This way of entering, together with the spatial vagueness of the lounge area, allows for widely diverse uses. Two metal sliding doors can be shut, when required, separating this area from the other rooms.

Being regular visitors to the forest, the architects understood the need for ensuring a generous entry of light. An L-shaped light entry point was incorporated into the center of the floor plan, coinciding with two sides of the bathroom. The effect, in the bathroom and lounge area alike, is lighting that changes through the course of the day.

Architect:
María Victoria Besonías,
Guillermo de Almeida, Luciano Kruk
Location:
Mar Azul, Buenos Aires, Argentina
Photographs:
Mariana Rapaport

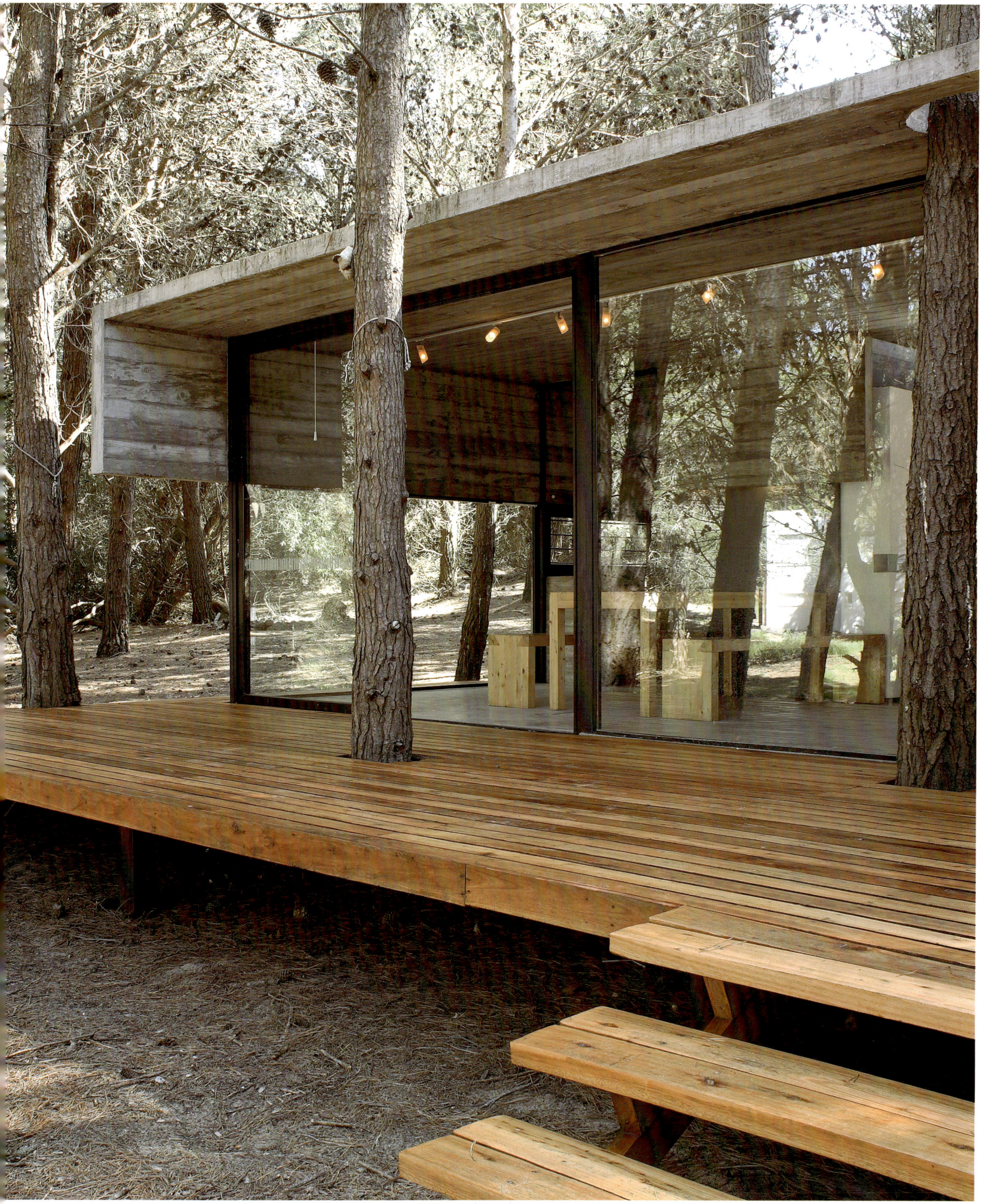

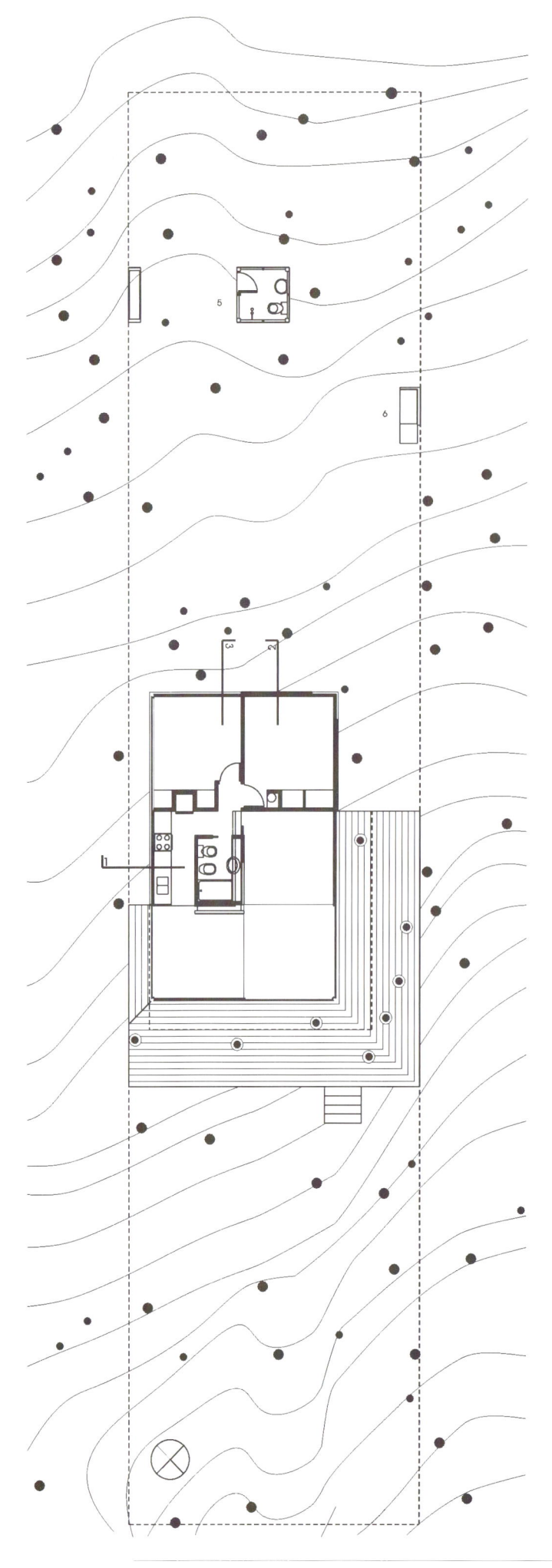

The microclimate of this seaside forest and the house's frequent use in mild or warm seasons permitted a low-cost constructive solution, which could be quickly realized, based on an envelope of exposed concrete with no complements needed to improve the thermal insulation. Furthermore, the expressive qualities of exposed concrete, together with its properties of resistance and impermeability, made any surface finish unnecessary.

Besonias - Almeida -Kruk

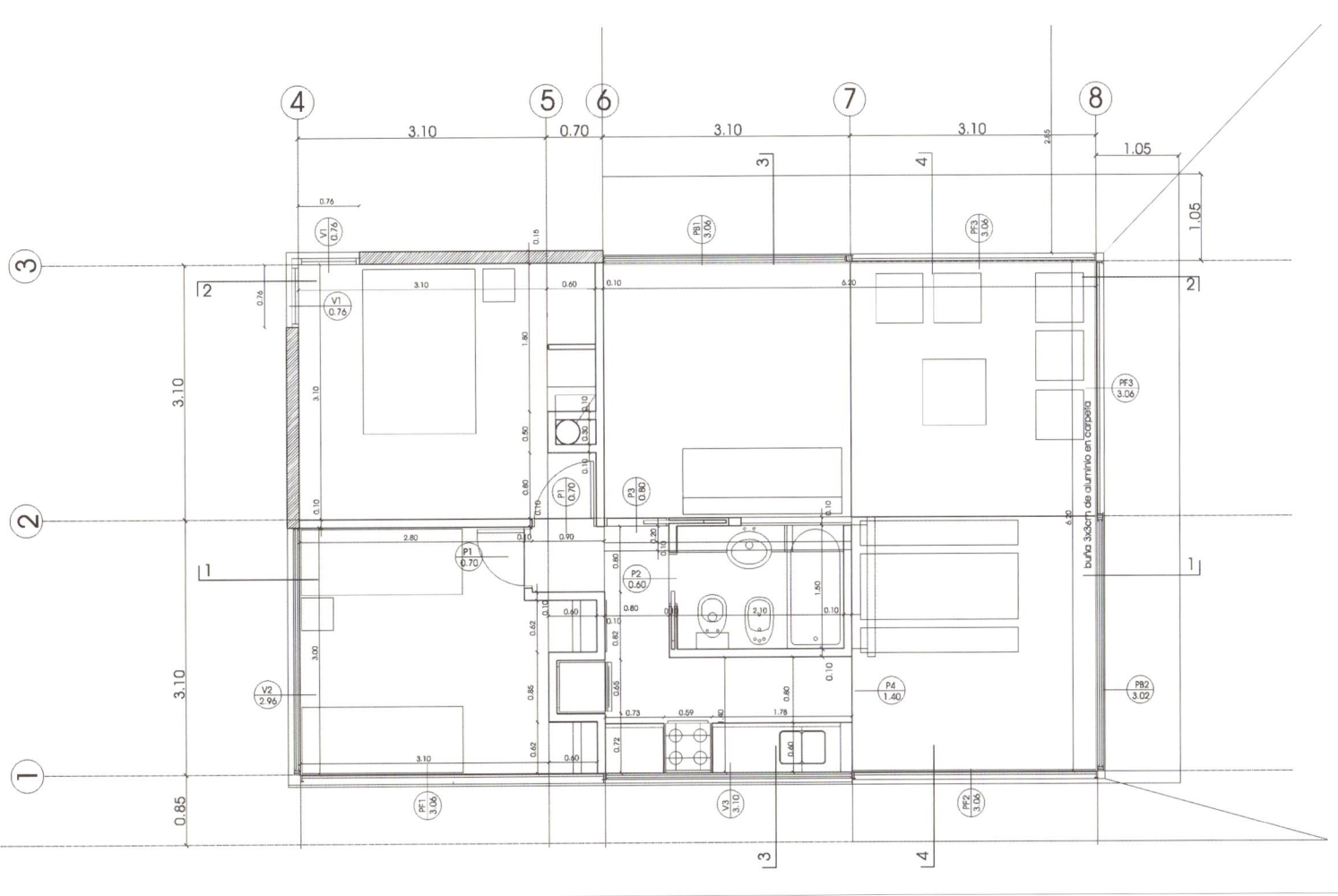

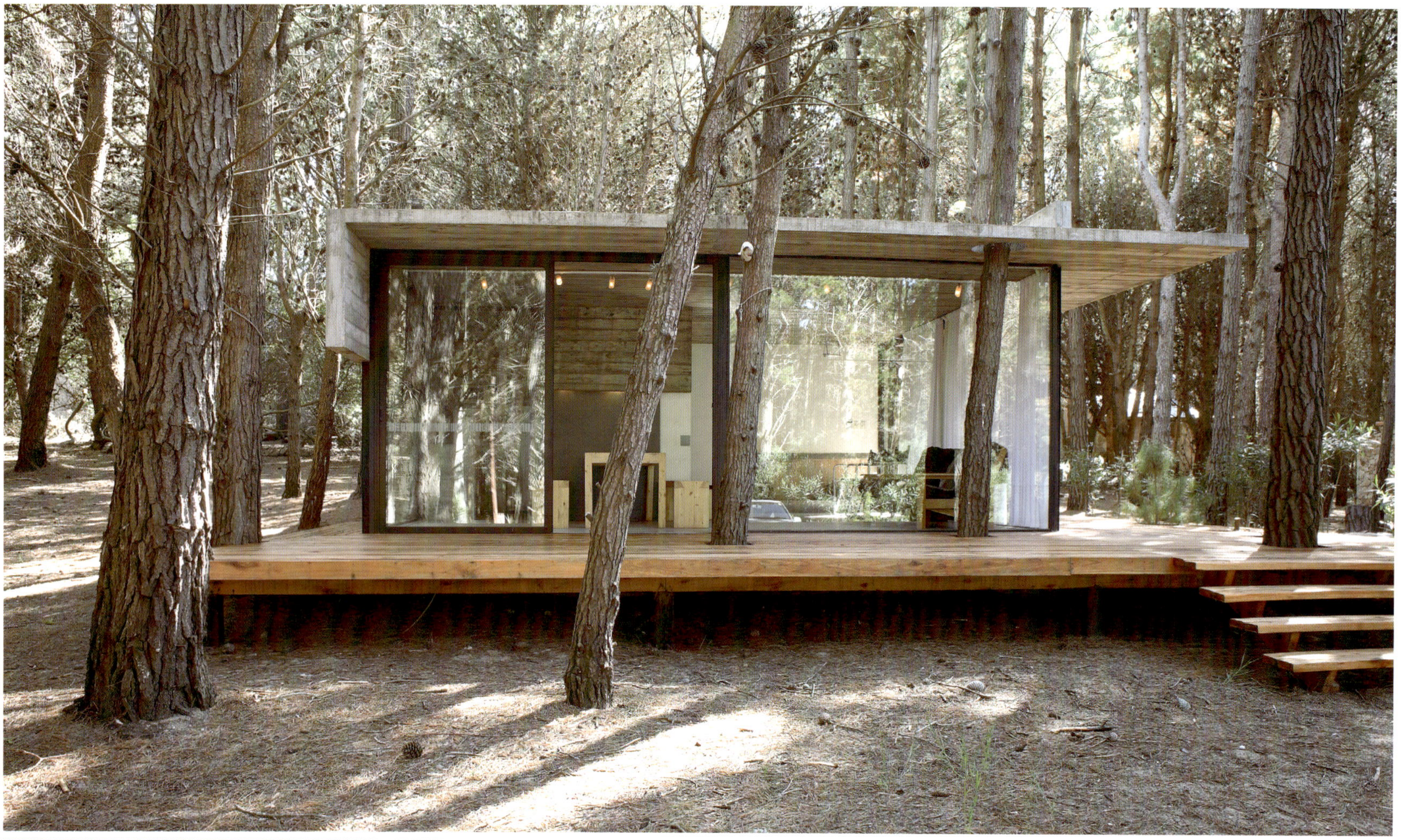

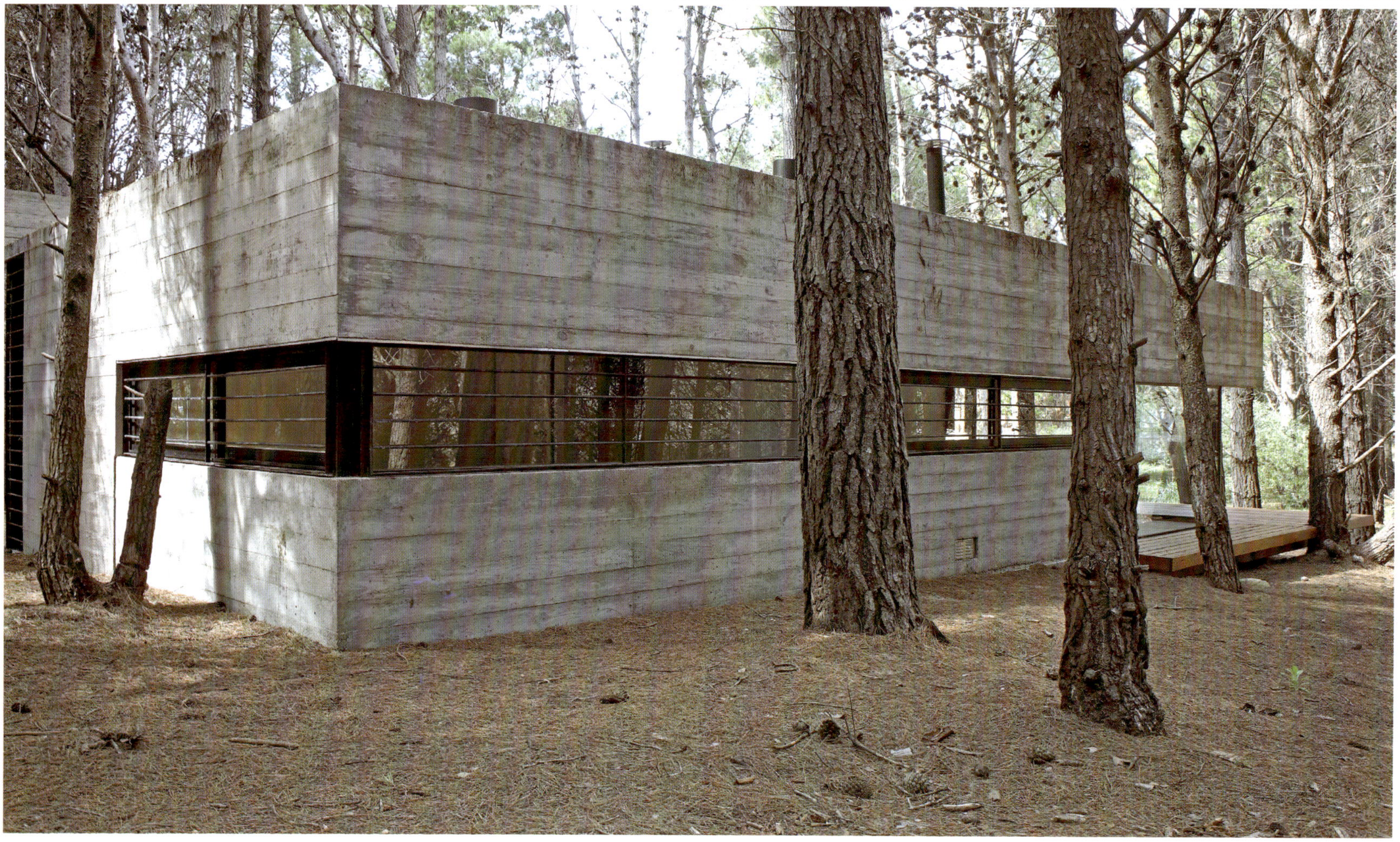

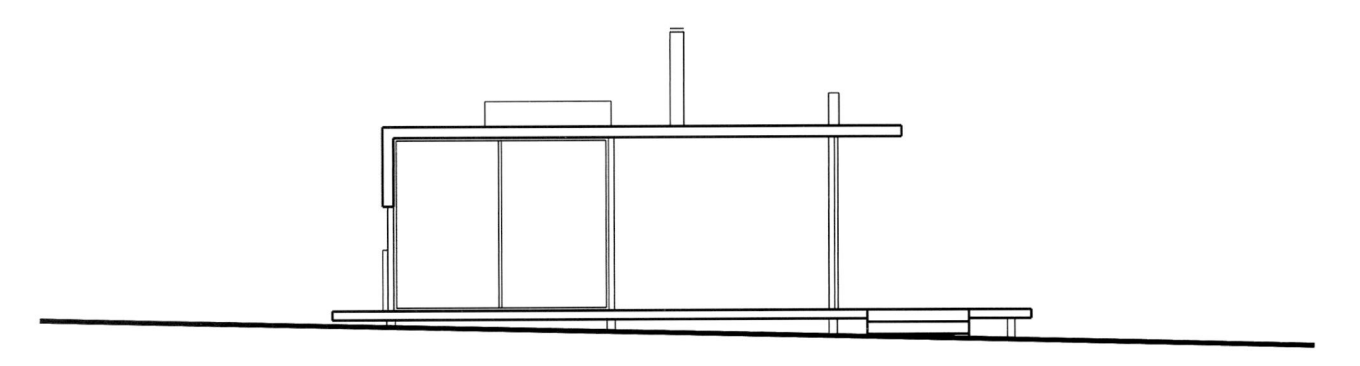

Northeast elevation

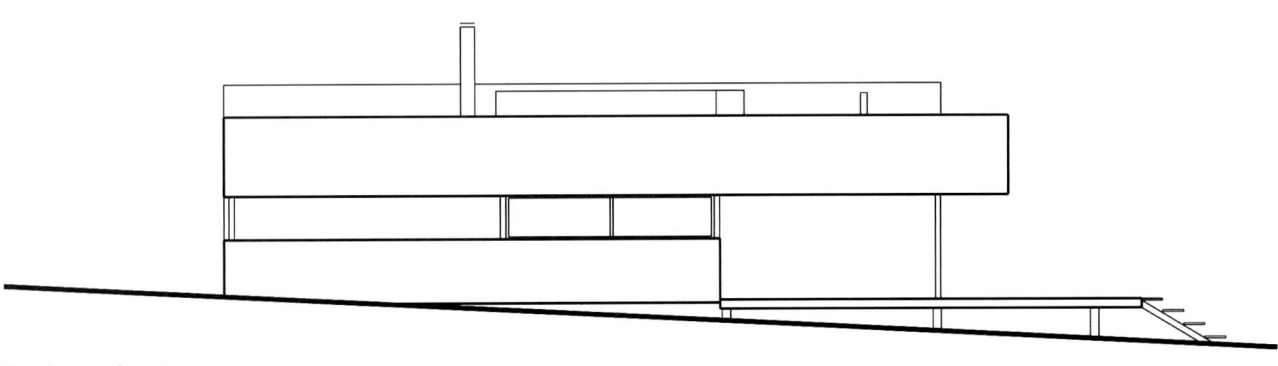

Southeast elevation

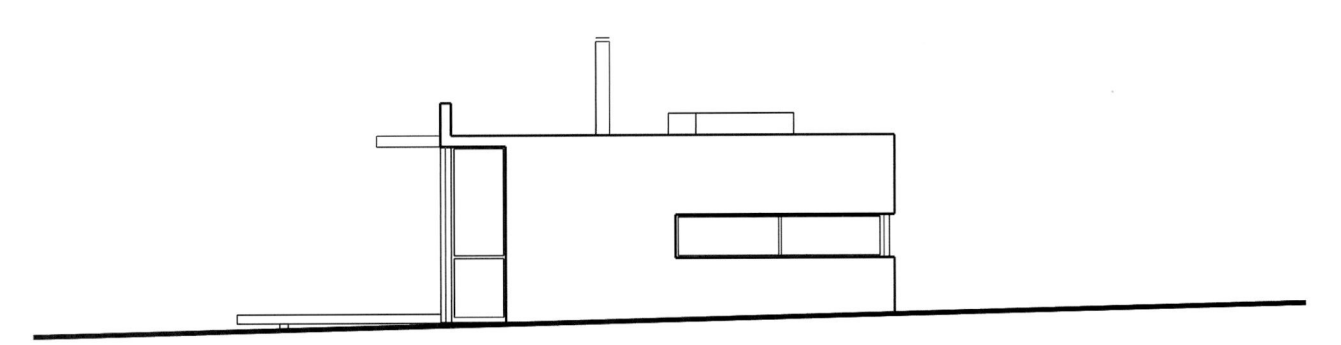

Southwest elevation

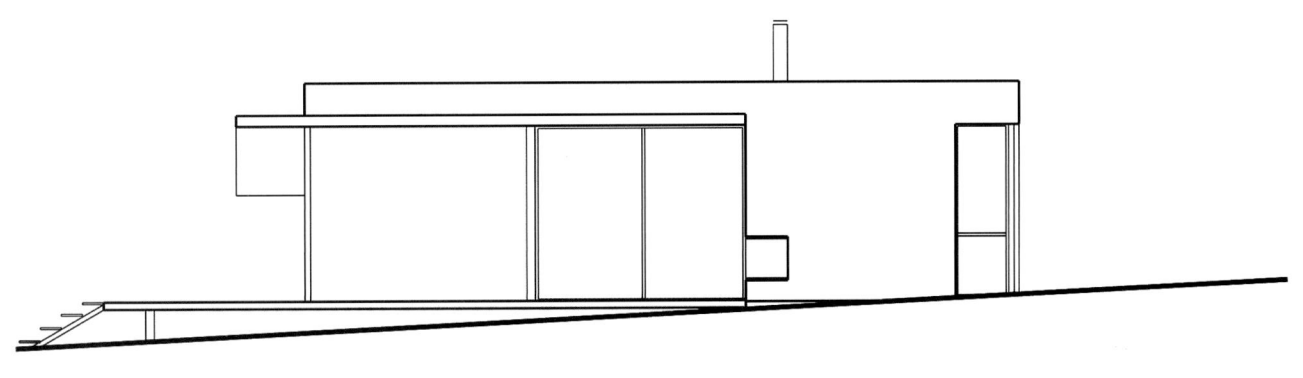

Northwest elevation

Besonias - Almeida - Kruk

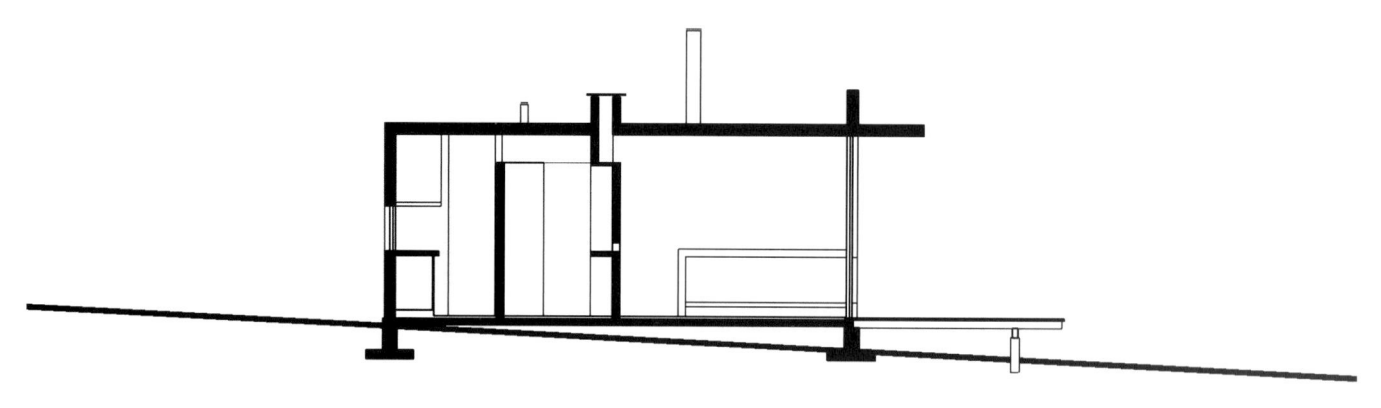

Section 1

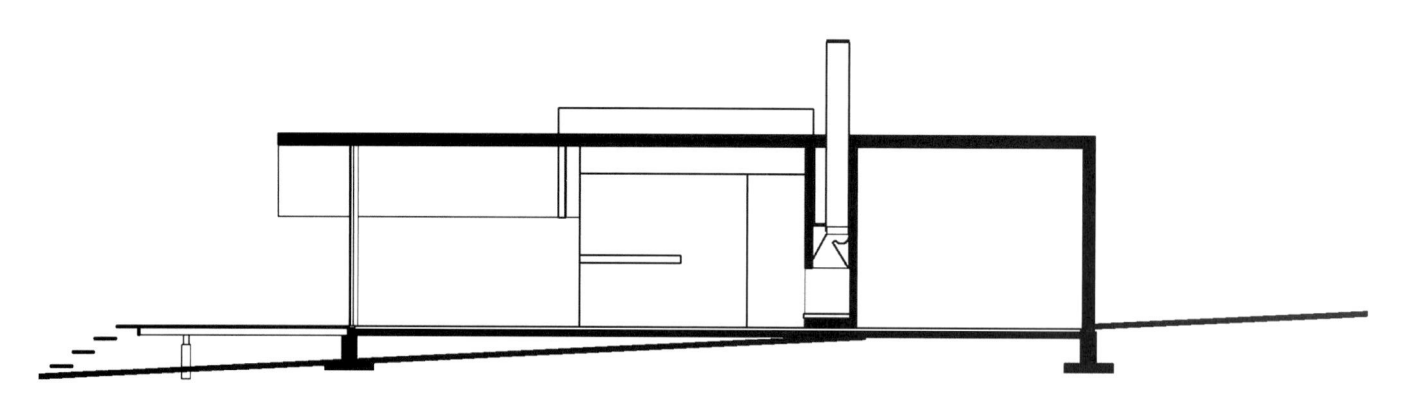

Section 2

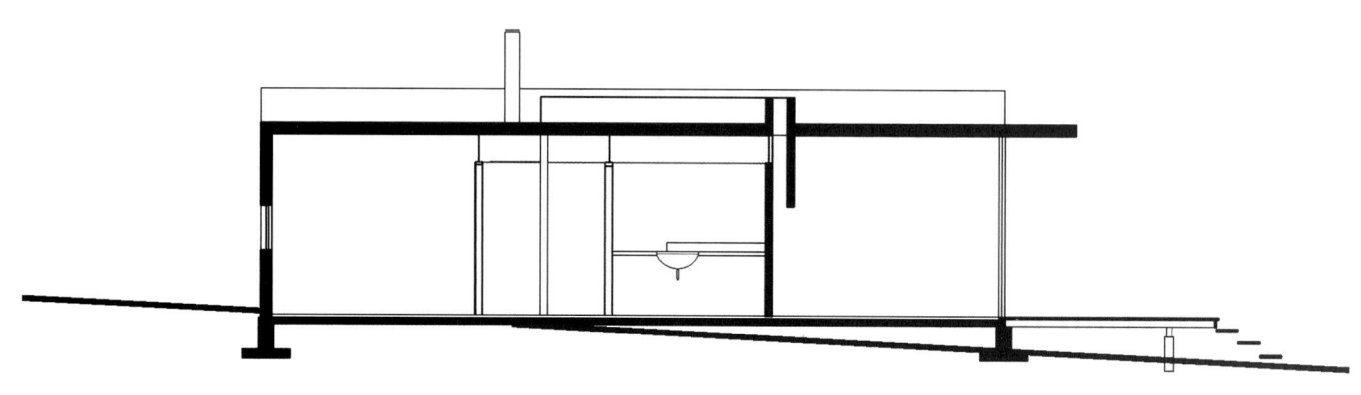

Section 3

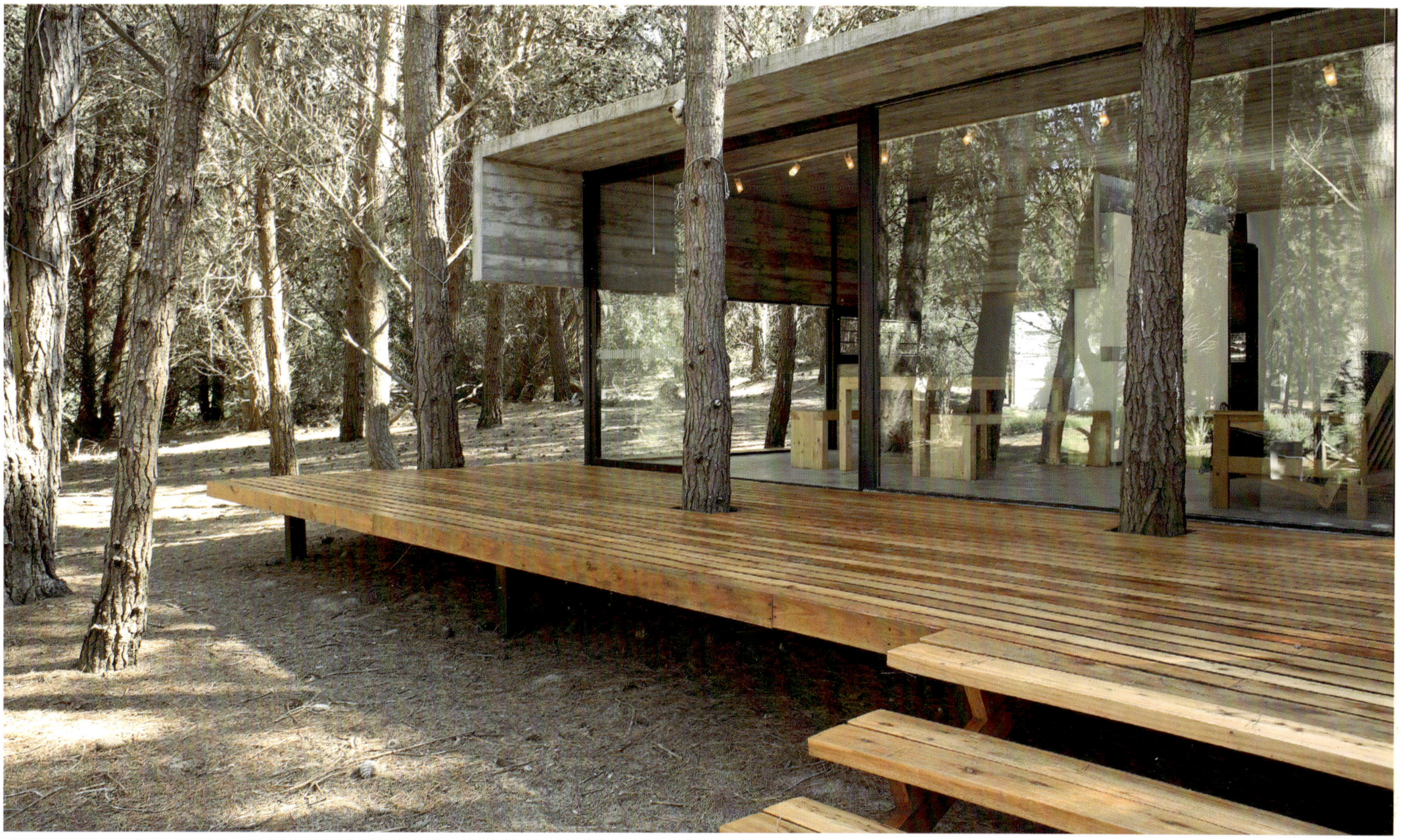

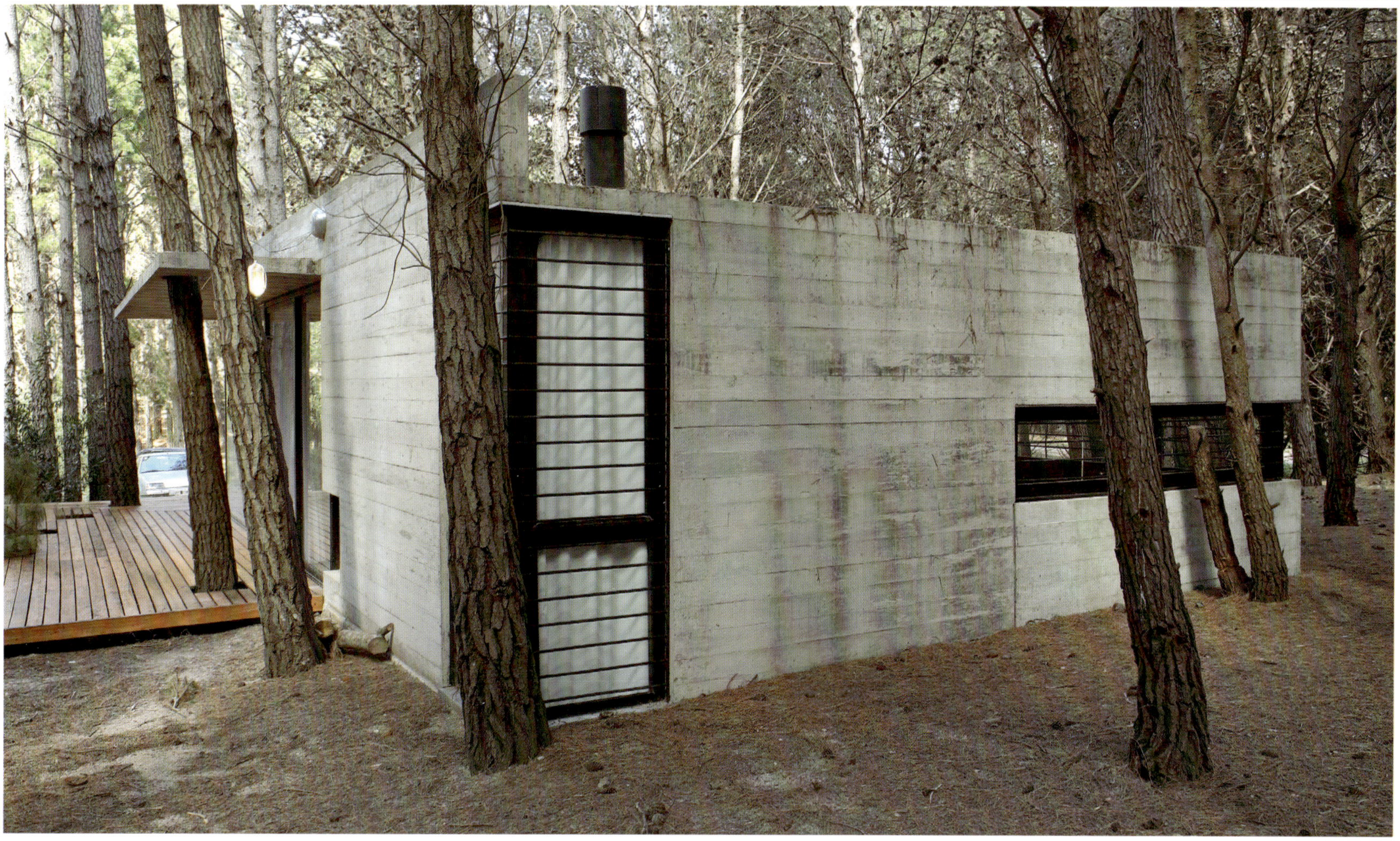

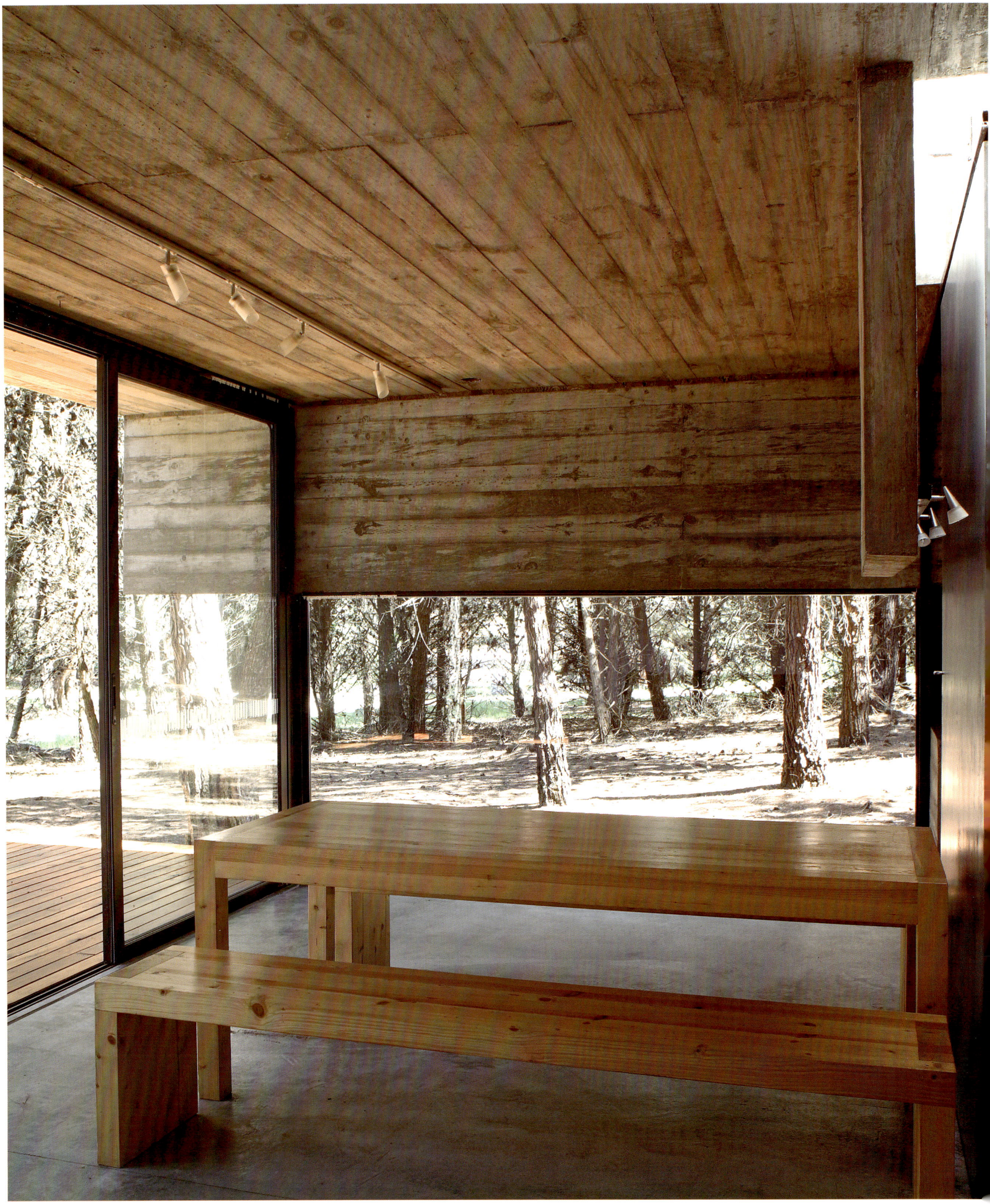

The furniture, especially designed for this house, was made from Canadian pine salvaged from packaging crates for engines.

The control of the light and exterior views was resolved through black out curtains in the bedrooms and boile curtains in the glazed section.

1. Supplementary block
2. Galvanized sheet metal No. 18
3. Batten fixture block
4. Rafters 2 × 4 in
5. Columns 5 × 5 in
6. Planks 6 ft × 4 in × ½ in
7. Batten 2 × 2 in
8. 2 × 4 in diagonal ties
9. Insert columns 5 × 5 in
10. Rafters 2 × 6 in
11. Boarding ½ in
12. Roof frame diam. 1/4 in C/ 6/8 in
13. Supplementary strips
14. Rafter 2 × 4 in (permanent formwork)
15. Roof frame diam. 1/4 in (quantity. 3 bars)
16. Column section painted with coal tar
17. Reinforced concrete pile
18. Finishing angle
19. Nail with hermetic head
20. Folded sheet metal
21. Polycarbonate

V4

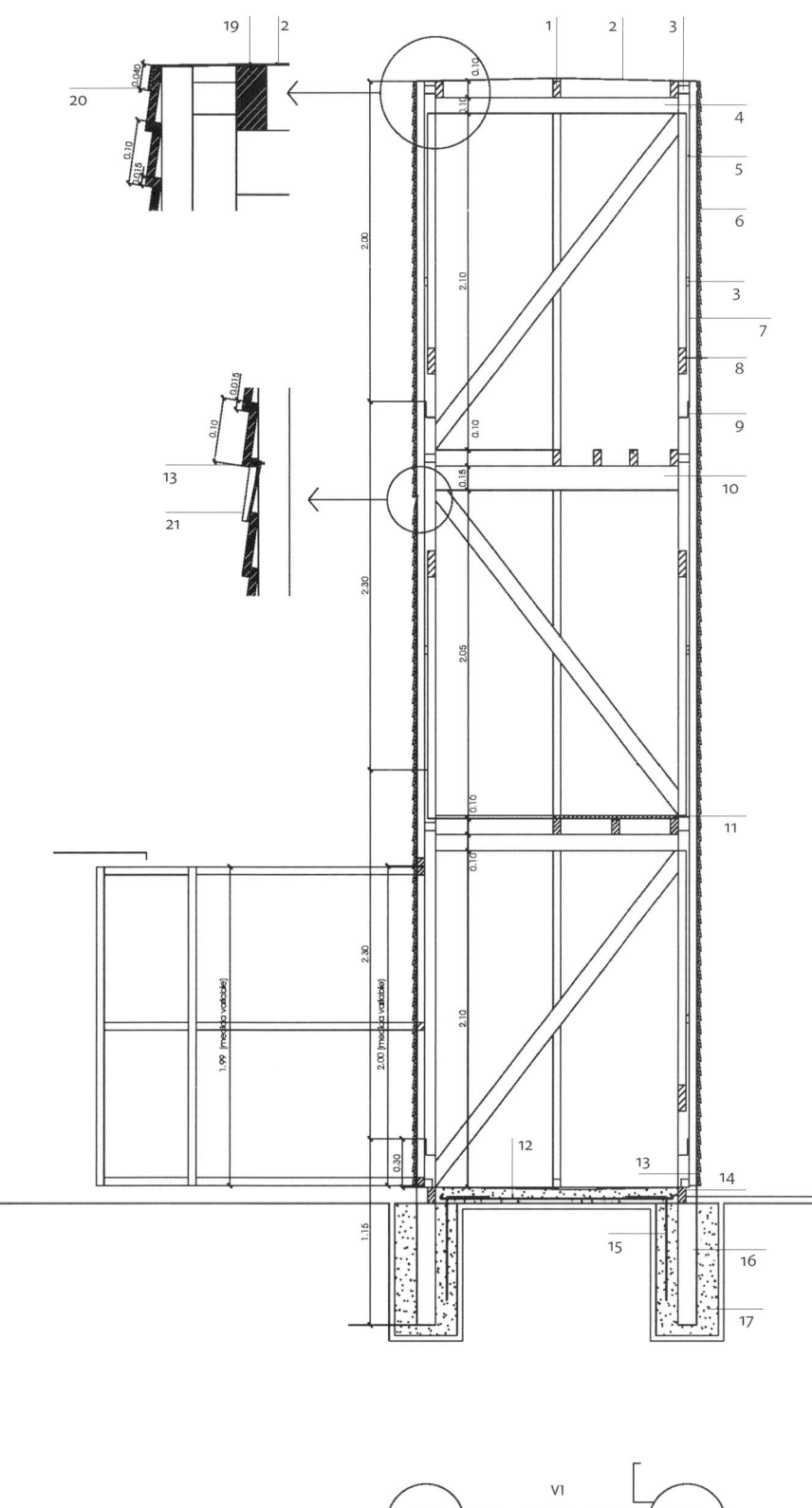

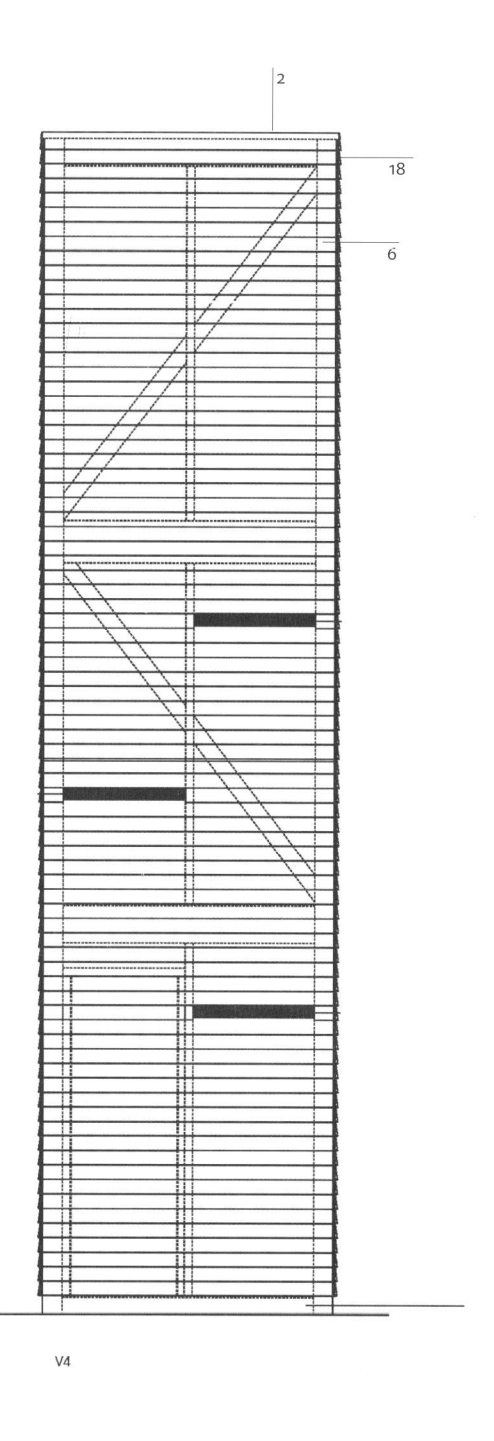

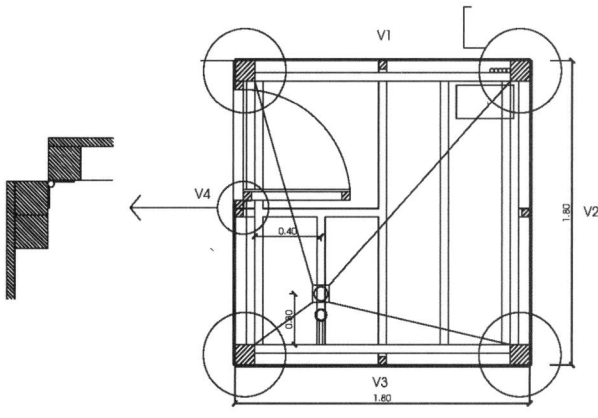

Besonias - Almeida - Kruk

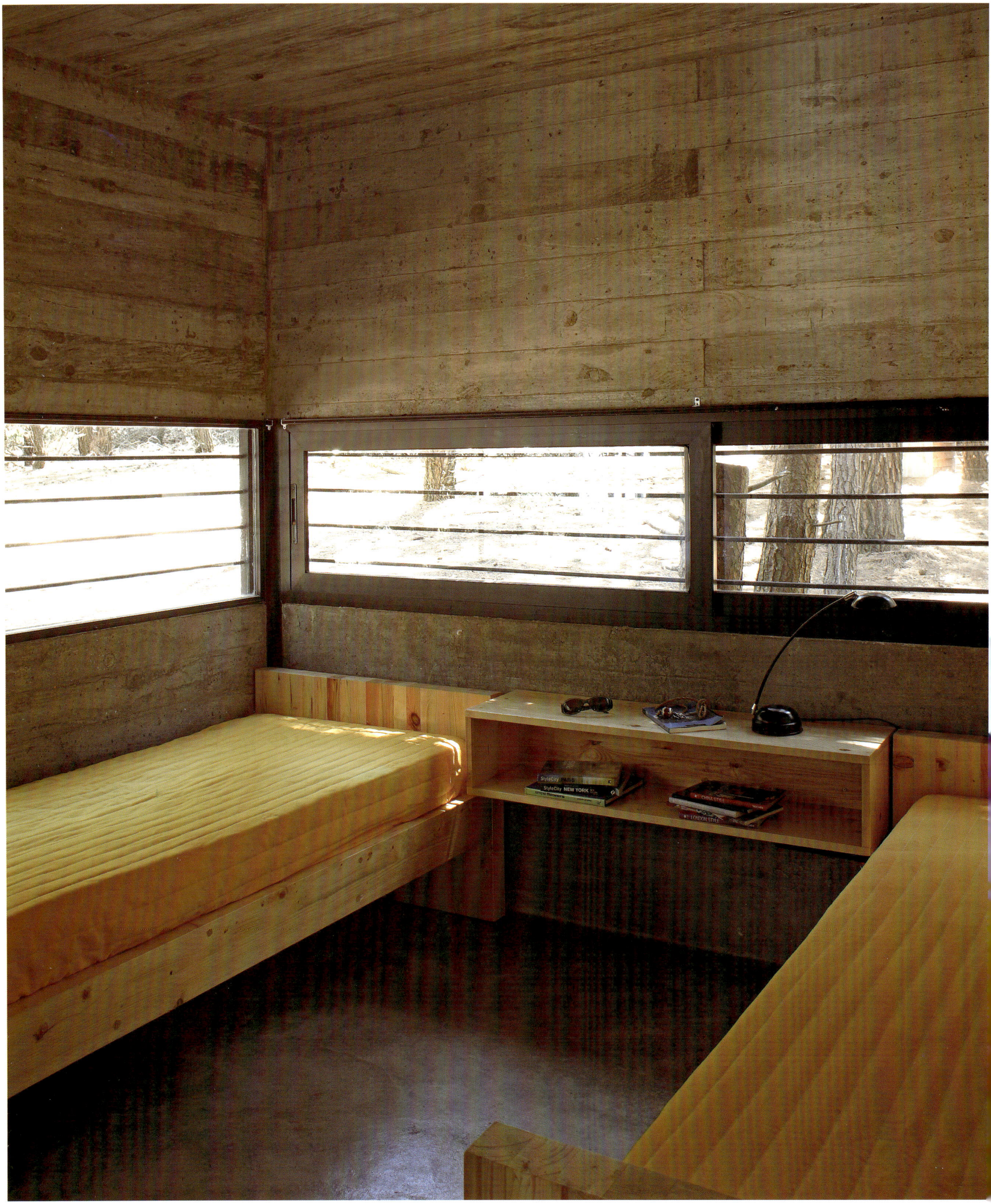

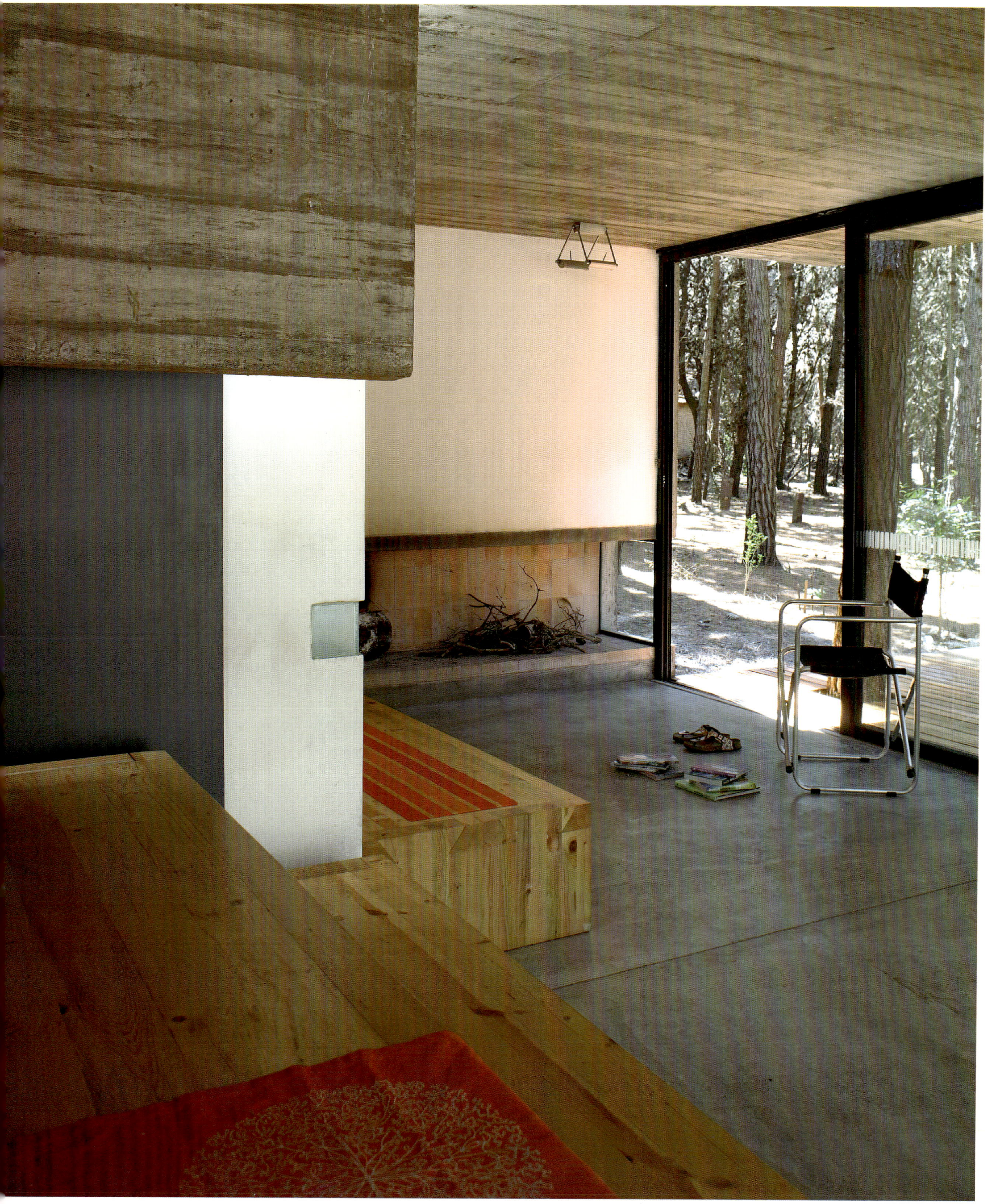

Cloud 9
Villa Bio

Villa Bio is the name given to this home located in the suburbs of Llers in the Spanish province of Girona. The architect Enric Ruiz-Geli defines this as a "bio" structure as the reflection of a contemporary construction style that he envisages as a platform for today's art and culture. For the architect, "inhabiting" takes place on an existing platform that can become art: the art of habitation.

This platform was conceived as a linear landscape of "events" that buckles away from the terrain to double back on itself. It is a linear concrete structure with a continuous C-shaped section.

The definition of the exterior enclosures was based on the idea of the concrete solidifying to create a "liquid" topography. The design began with a 3D model of the desired topography, like a Virilian landscape in relief. The designers used CadCam, with 3-axis milling, to create a 3D image measuring 24 x 3 meters. The mold became the formwork for the north and south façades.

The platform took on its mutant, liquid form with a green roof and interior landscape of glass blocks by Emiliana Design stamped with digital rendering. The roof features a hydroponic garden that acts as insulation and includes green LED lighting that highlights the vegetation.

The interior lighting system is varied and automatically controlled with a dynamic system that changes the color and intensity of the light according to the exterior natural light conditions.

Architect:
Enric Ruiz-Geli
Location:
Llers, Girona, España
Photographs:
Lluís Ros

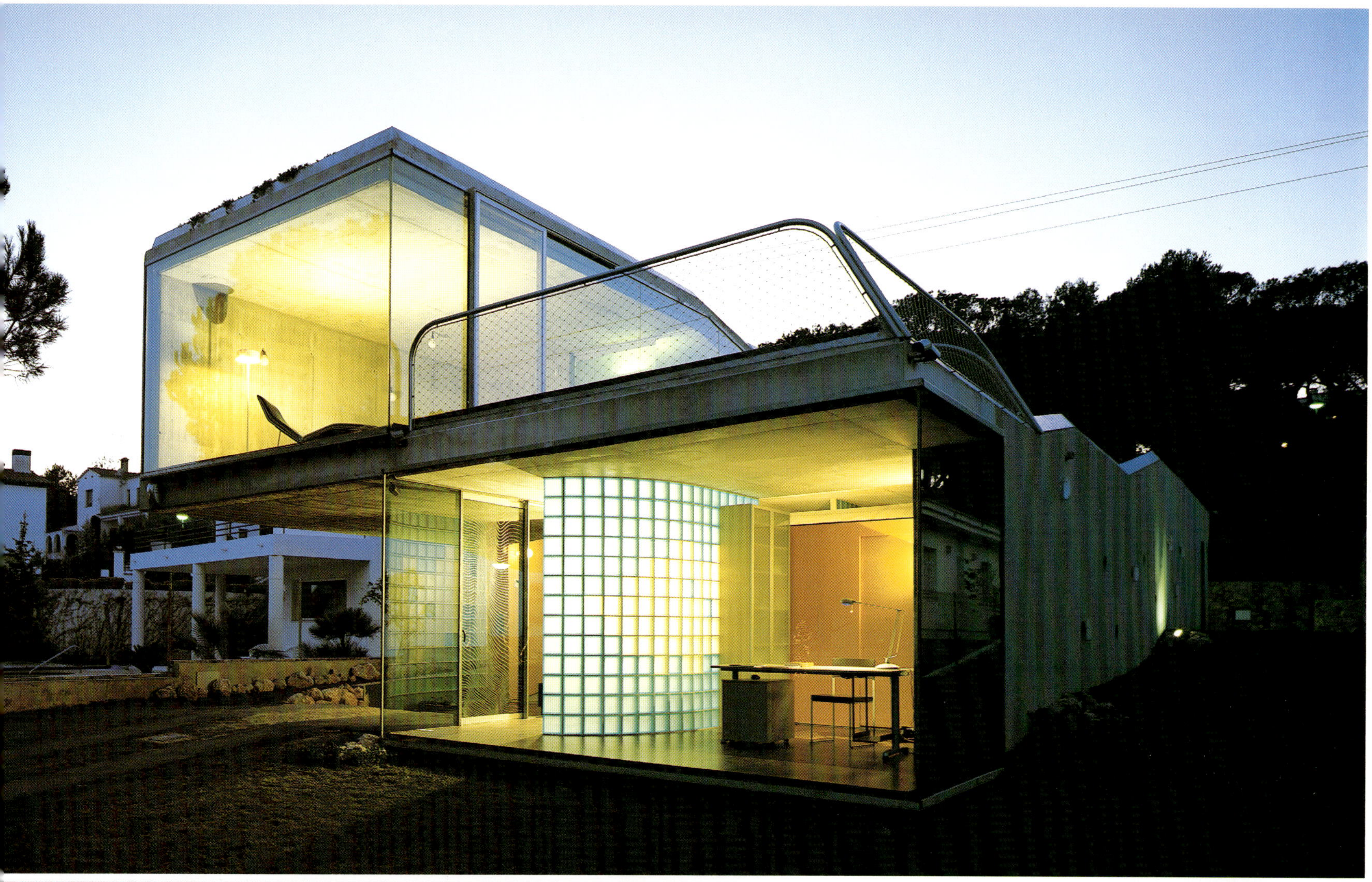
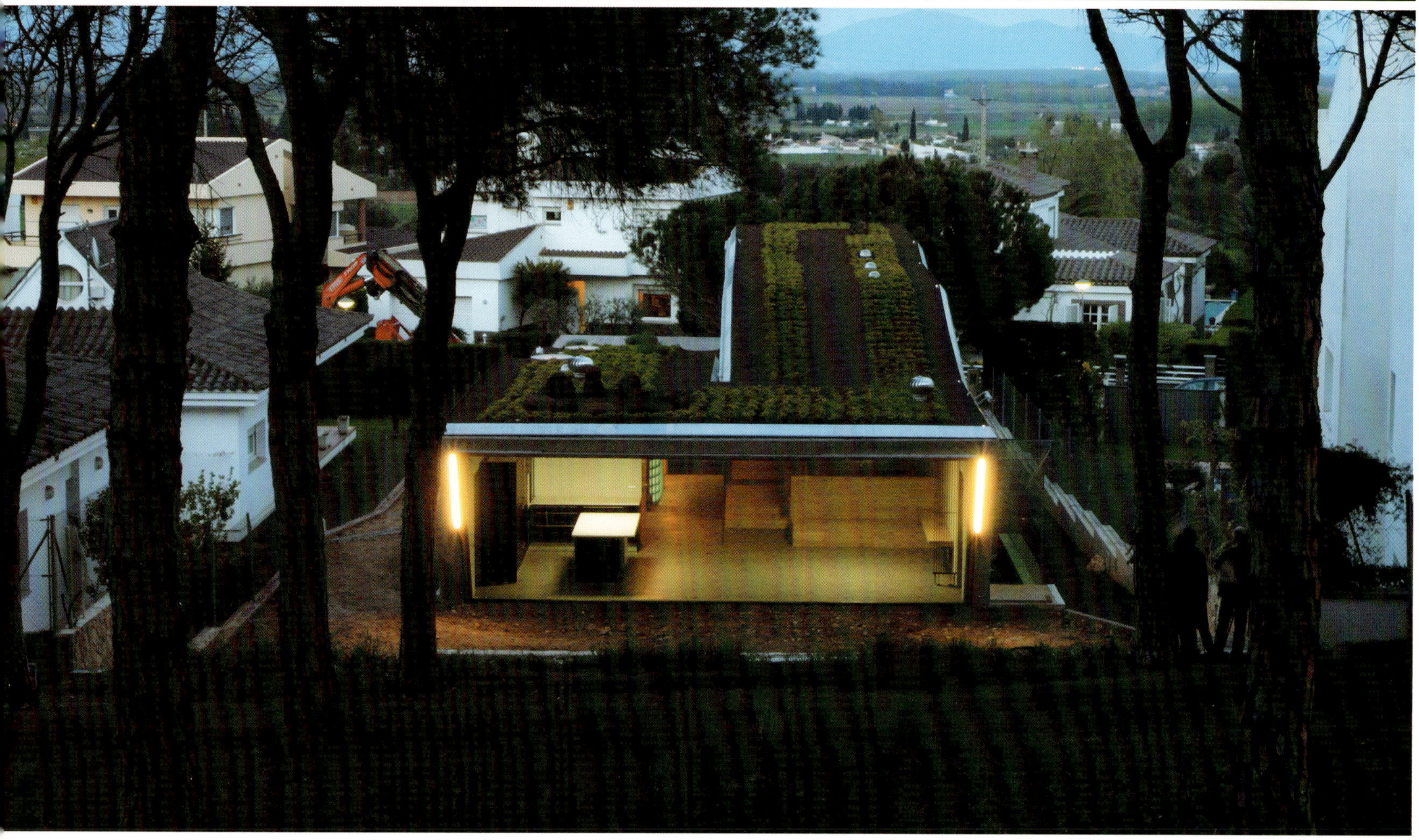

emplaçament

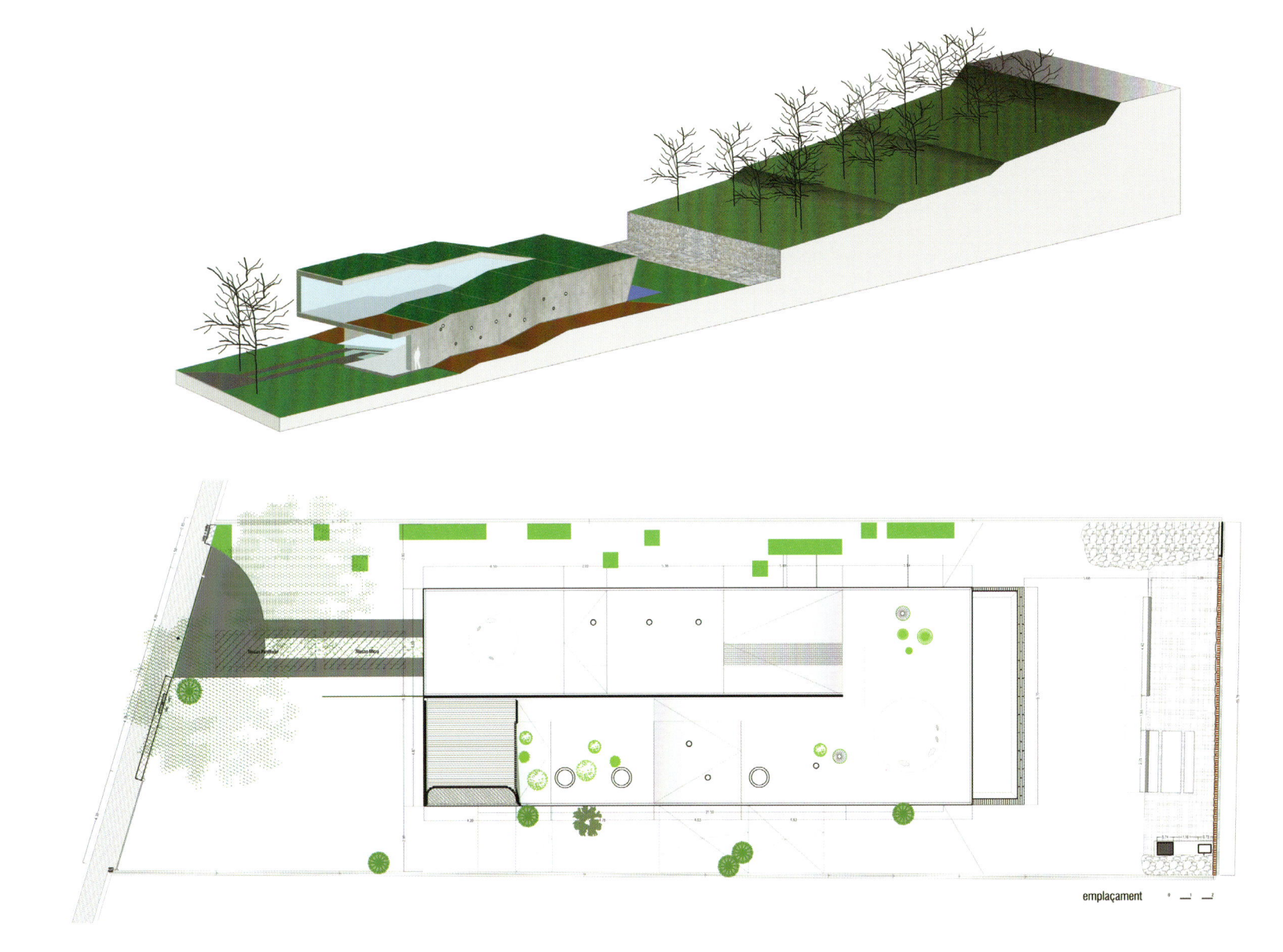

Cloud 9

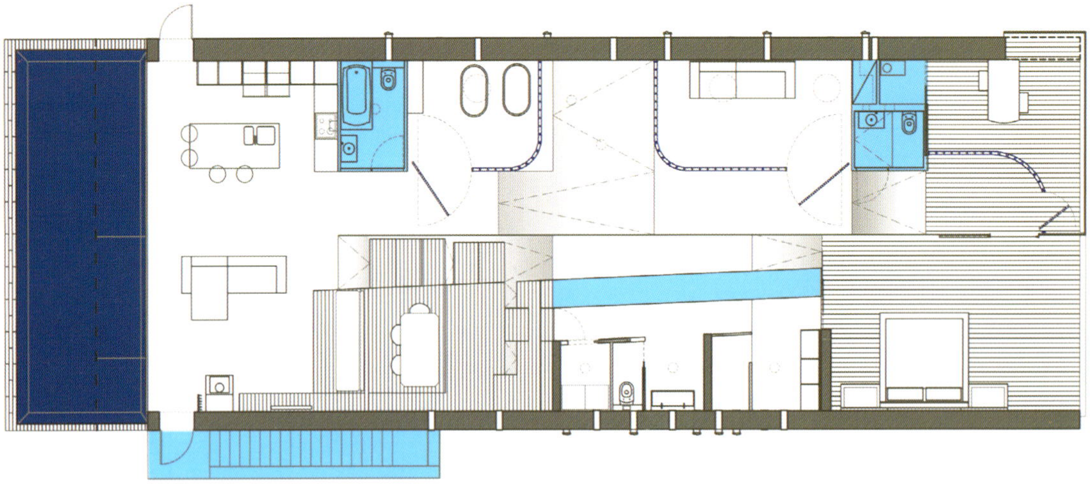

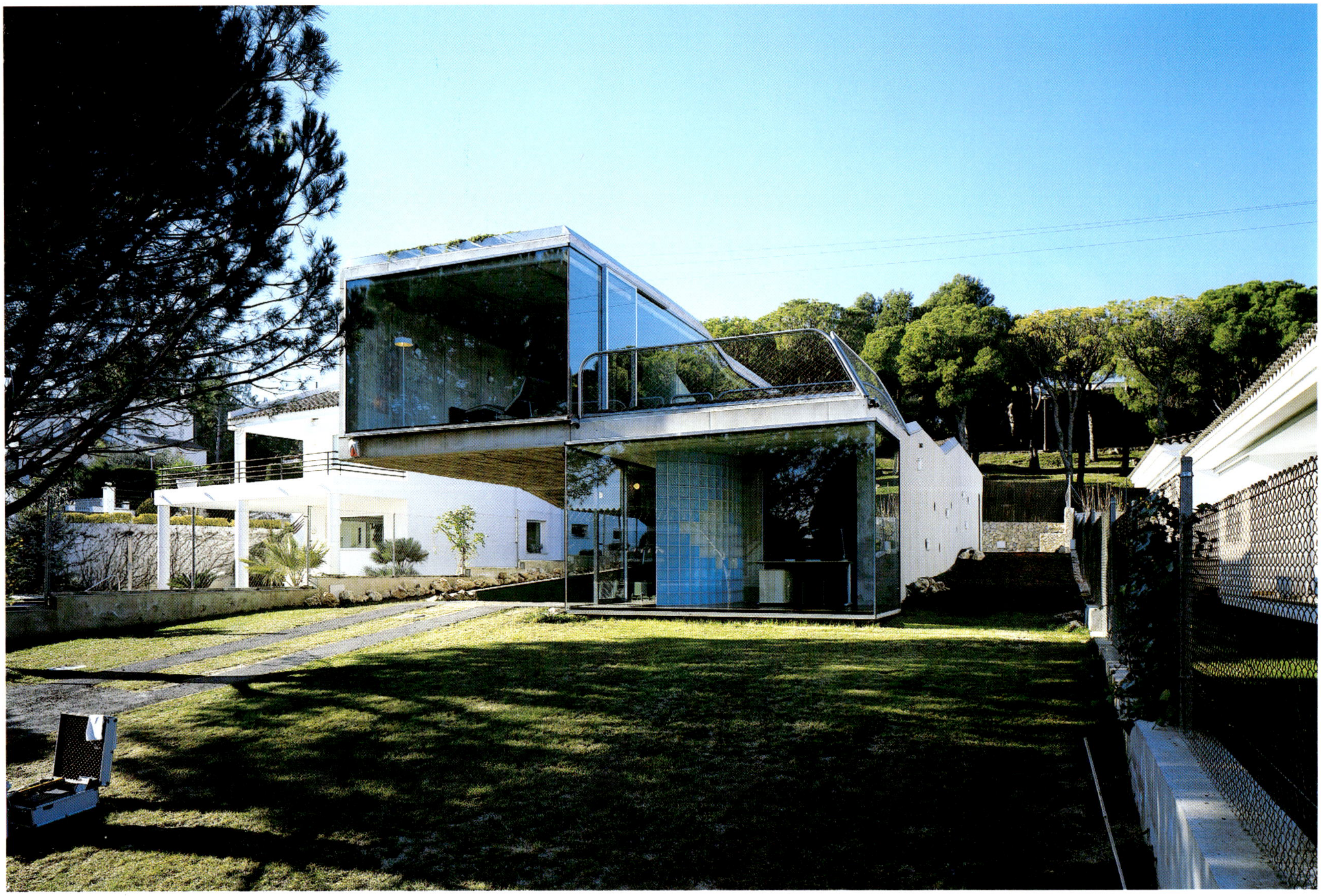

South elevation

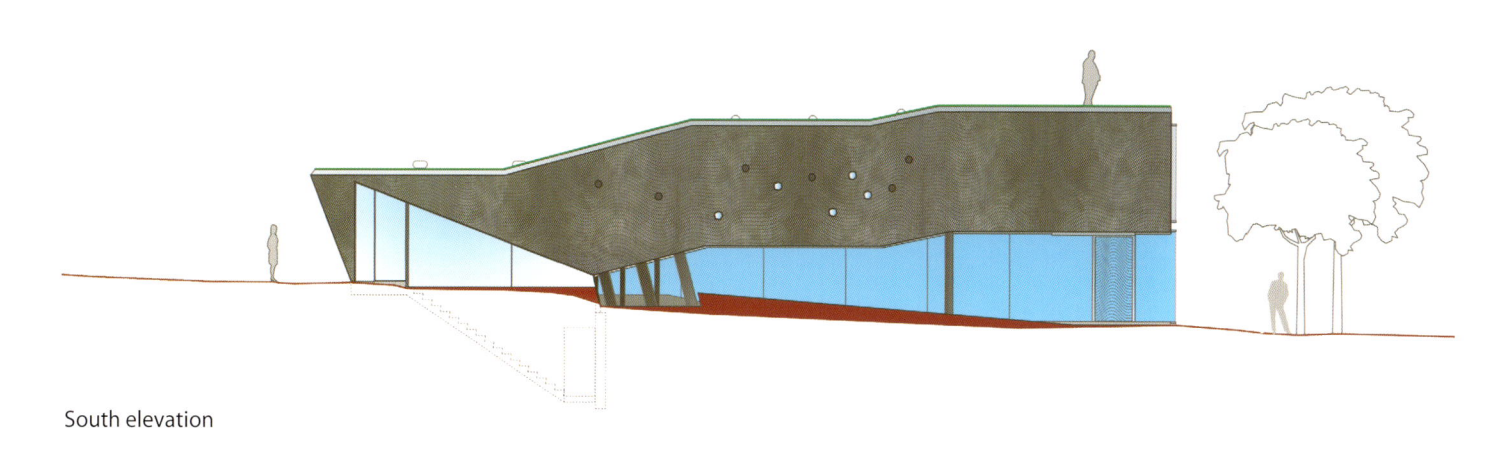

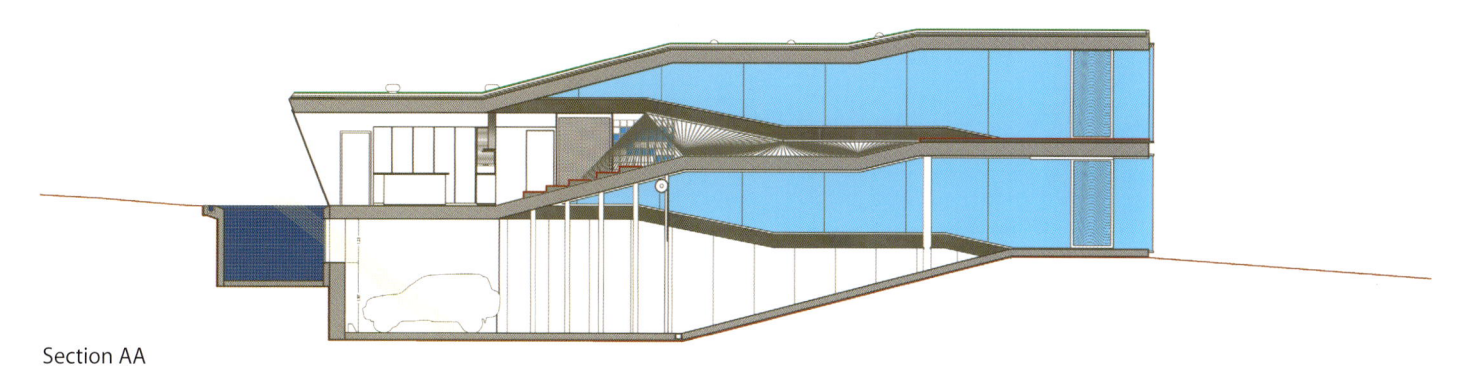

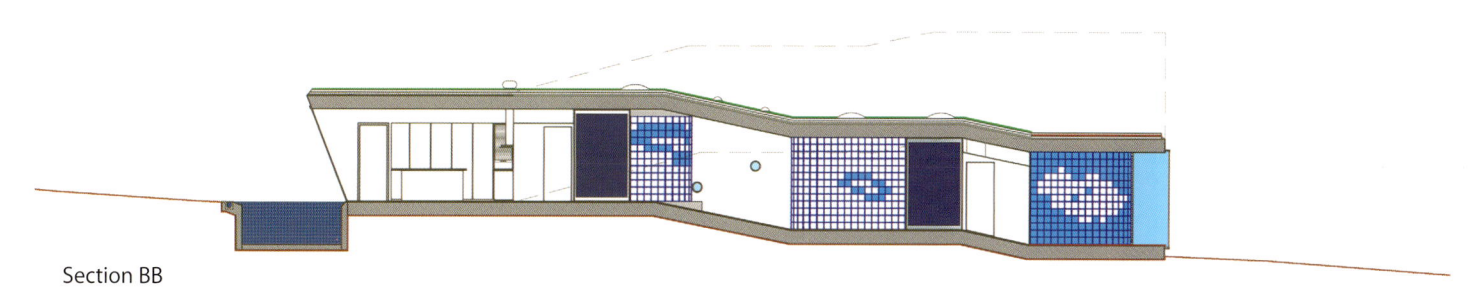

Section AA

Section BB

Cloud 9

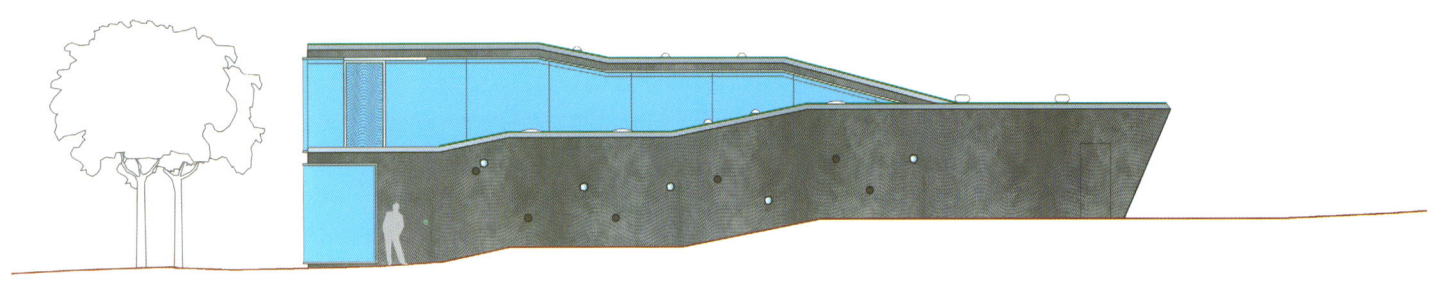

North elevation

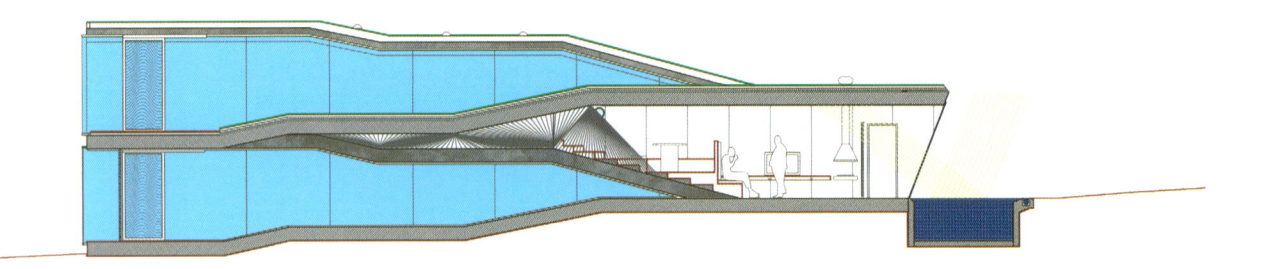

Section CC

Section DD

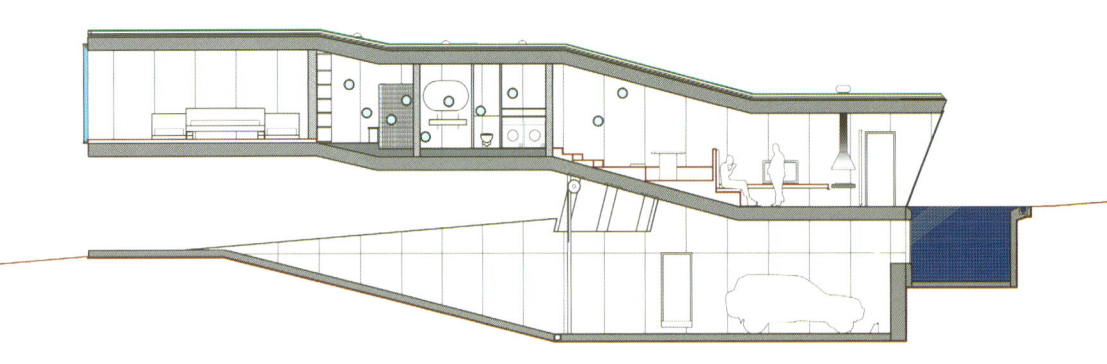

118   Cloud 9

Cloud 9 119

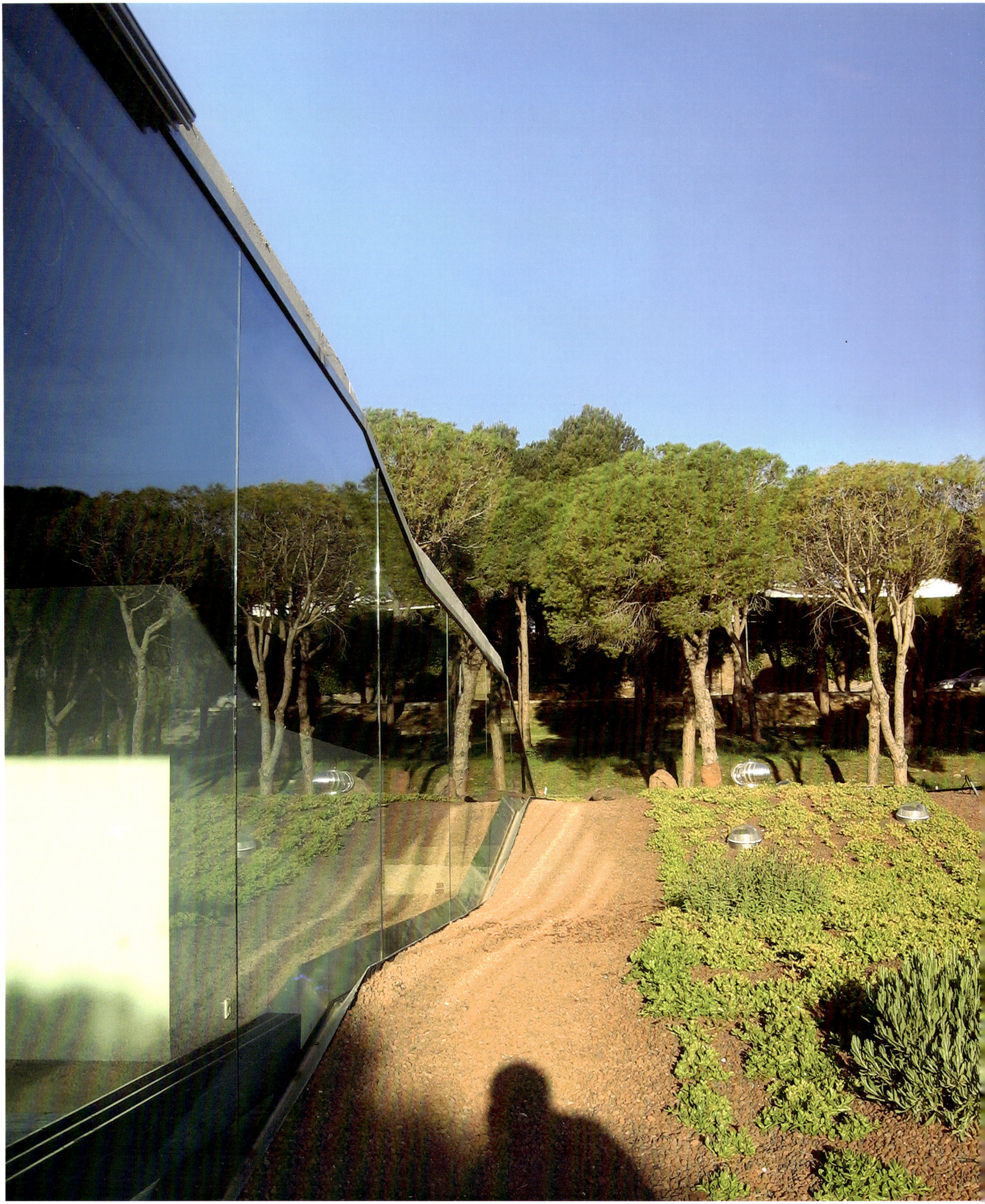

Cloud 9

121

1. Hydroponic green roof, by Burés or similar, with volcanic planting substrate, serving as thermal insulation layer.
2. Fair finished cast concrete façade with topographic relief achieved through shuttering boards carved using CADCAM technology, © Valchromat, patent pending.
3. Reinforced concrete wall, t = 450mm (1 ft 6 in), height = 3400 mm (11 ft 2 in). Forms part of RC box beam which 16 m (52 ft 6 in) cantilever.
4. Structural RC wall, t = 500mm (1 ft 7 in), height = 3400mm (11 ft 2 in).
5. RC roof slab, t = 70 mm (1 ft 3 in), cantilevers 4.5 m (15 ft).
6. RC floor slab, t =370 mm (1 ft 3 in), cantilevers 4.5 m (15 ft).
7. Ventilation openings.
8. Glass 'rocks', by de Emiliana design.
9. Laminated glass glazing 10+10mm (3/8 + 3/8 in).
10. Rooflight.
11. Solar light tube, Solatube S.A.
12. Domotic lighting system with light color and intensity variation, Sivra system by Iguzzini.
13. Entrance door, laminated vinyl finish, with vectorial topographical printed image.
14. Garden access door, made from recycled water-repellant MDF shuttering boards, varnished.
15. Lighting feature with pixilated landscape images, Superficies de Luz by Pavés, design by Laia Jutglá.
16. Industrial high impact resistant poured concrete floor, in self-compacting concrete, Pavindus S.A.
17. Access ramp to garage, low acoustic impact asphalt surface, by Joaquim Quirante.
18. Vegetation, by Burés S.A.
19. Volcanic rock in side yard, Burés S.A.
20. Non-slip glass, 140 mm (5 in), to transmit ambient light to garage below.
21. Volcanic rocks, Burés S.A.
22. External lighting, Linealuce by Iguzzini.
23. LED lighting in roof edge, green.
24. Aromatic plants.

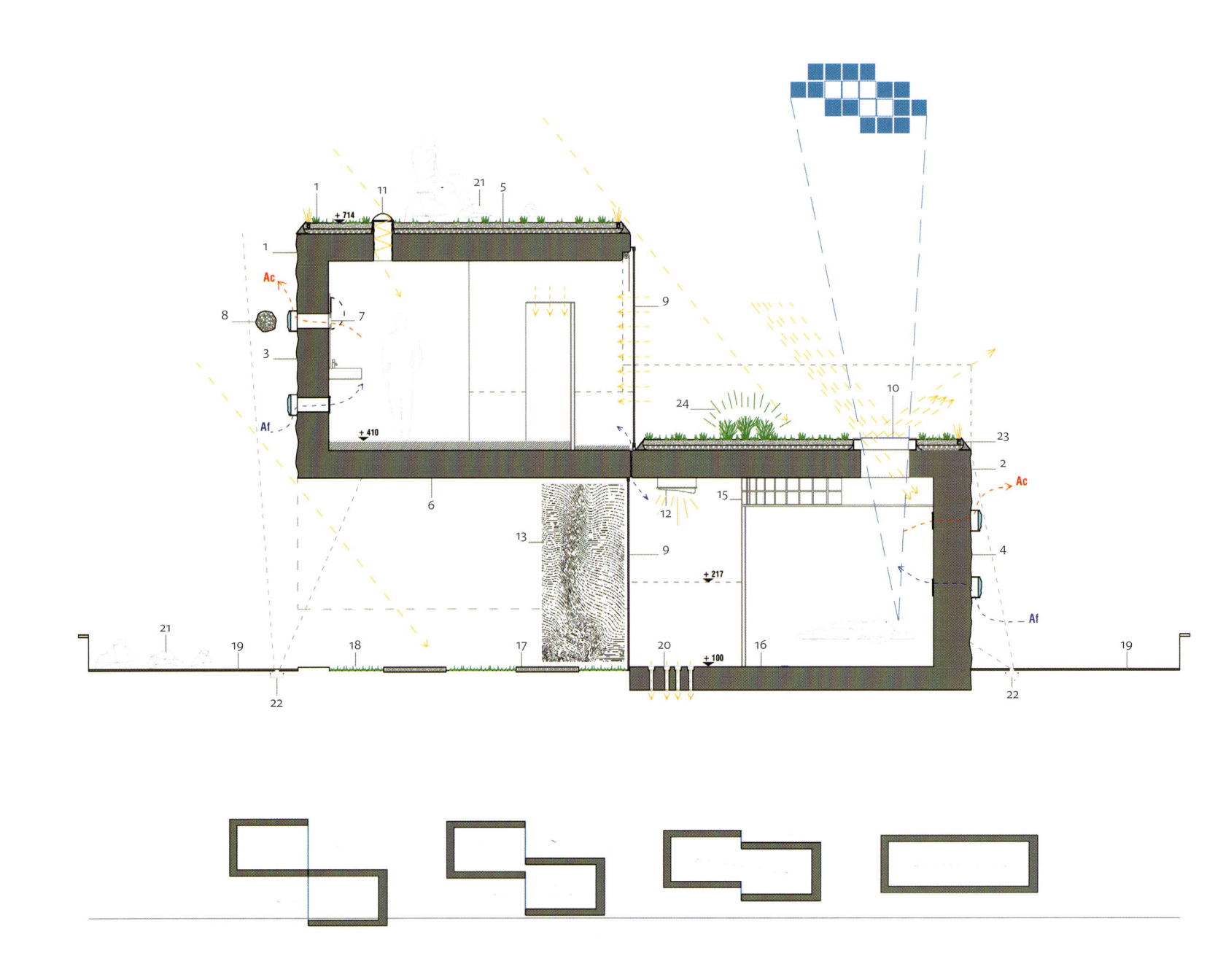

Cloud 9 123

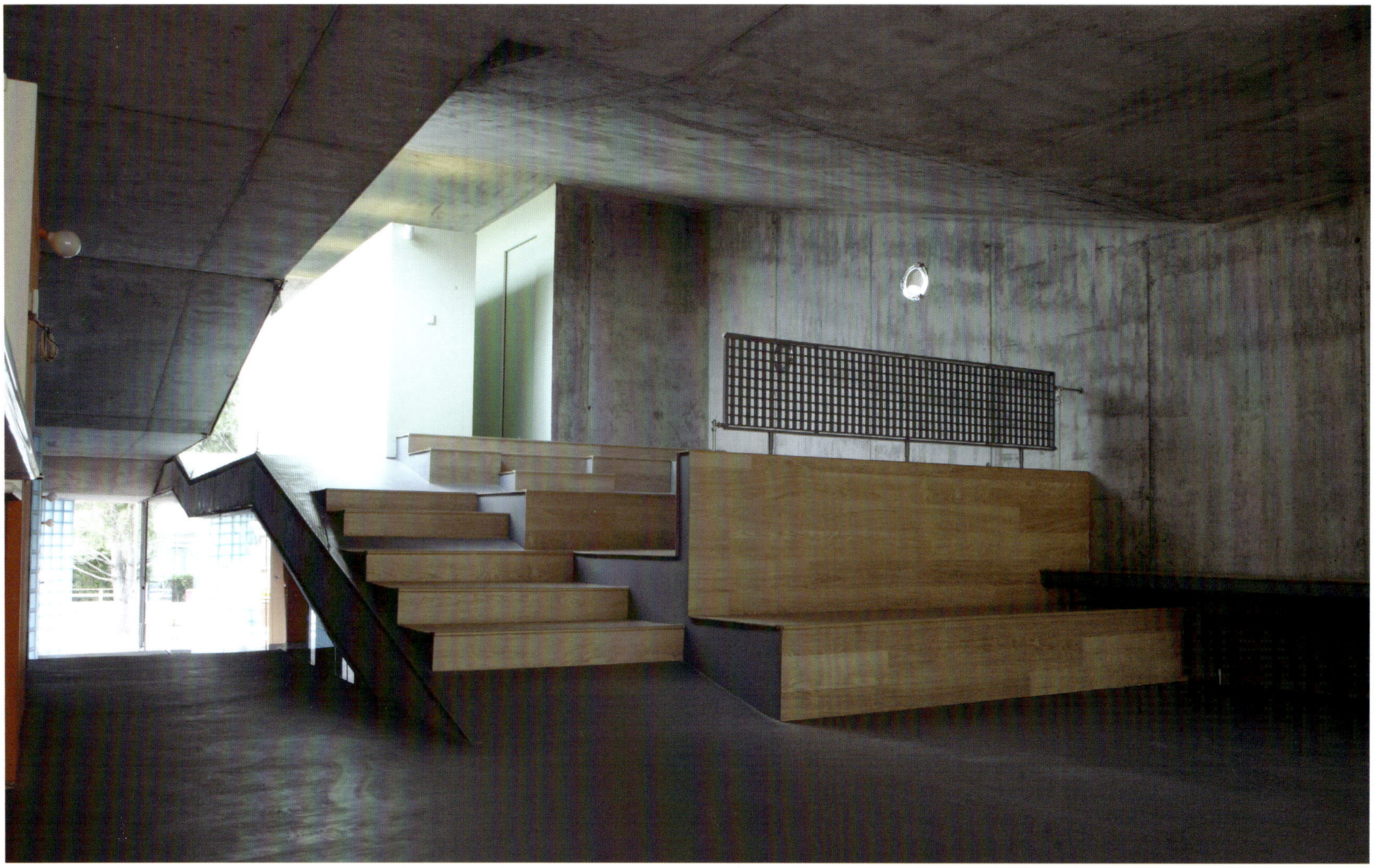

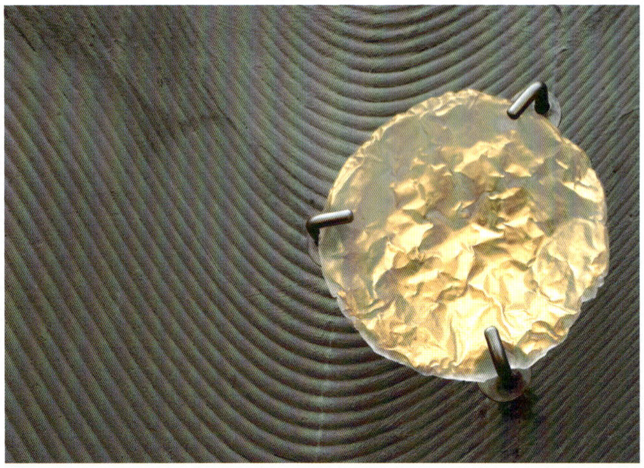

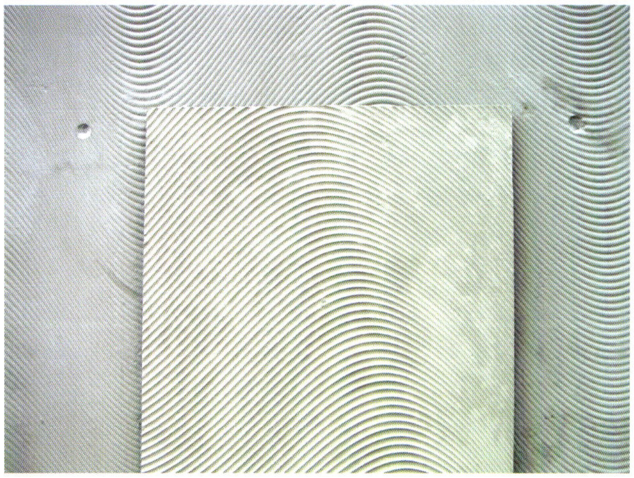

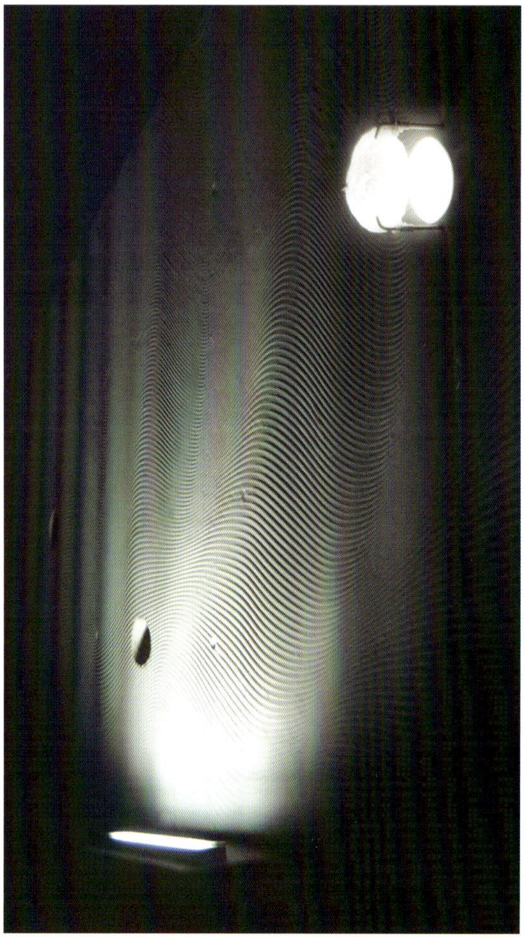

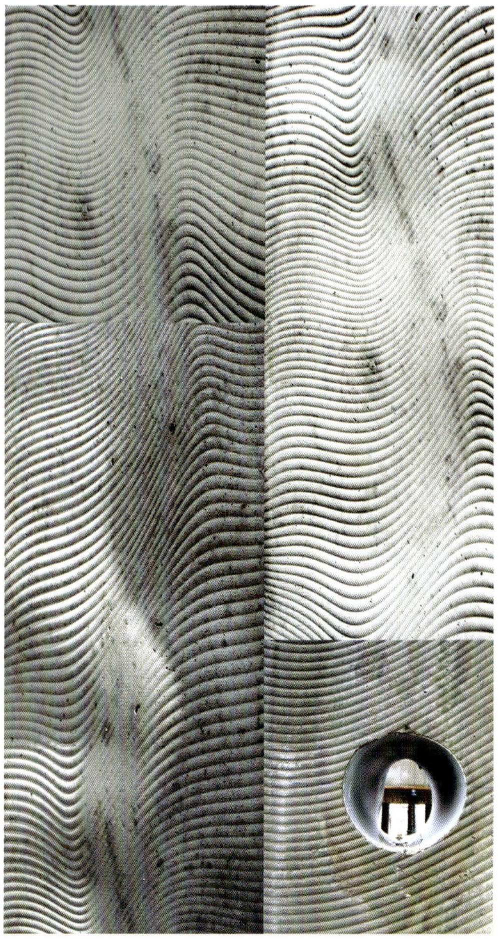

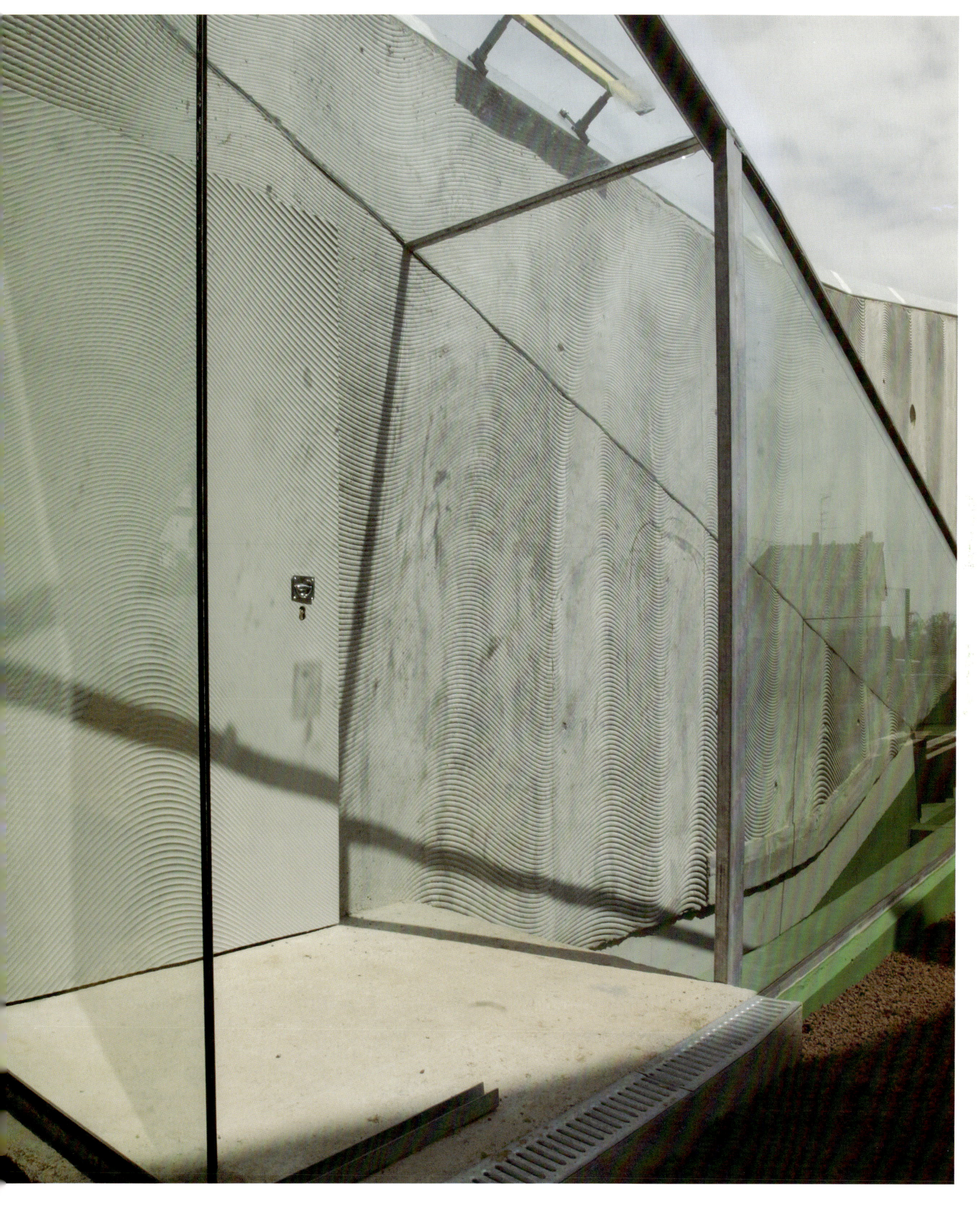

Ken Architekten
Kindergartens Zentral I and II

At the back of the Central School building in Dietikon, a strip of land between the school and the small-scale residential neighborhood was selected for the construction of two nursery school buildings. The City of Dietikon employed the firm Ken Architekten after they won the competition for the project in 2002. The two kindergartens were completed in 2005 within the budget of 1.4 Million CHF (Swiss francs).

The remains of a 247-foot long fortification wall, dating back to World War II, divide the strip longitudinally. The architects used this singular circumstance as the premise around which to develop the whole design concept. The fortification wall has a vertical and an oblique side. This two-sidedness became the theme of a threshold, articulating the difference between the entrance and the interior of the kindergarten. The fortification wall also determines the simple concept of the structure. Two reinforced concrete slabs rest on the wall and fold down to the ground to create two enclosures. The old rampart thus became the support on which the inverted concrete angles rest, delimiting the two volumes that face each other across a small stretch of lawn. The concrete slabs overhang the oblique side of the defensive wall to generate roofed entrance areas. A level change in the terrain generates a raised base for the two volumes. Glazed sliding doors are set back under the open sides of the concrete angles. The ribbon windows in the long façades are set flush with the exterior surface; inside, a row of brightly colored deep window surrounds at child height animate the wall.

Mirrored surfaces cover the ceilings and interior walls, unifying the space; in each classroom a rust-colored floor to ceiling wooden unit contains cloakrooms, toilets, the kitchen and storage room, marking the functional division of the space into the play space, group space, and cloakroom.

Architect:
Ken Architekten
Location:
Dietikon, Switzerland
Photographs:
Hannes Henz

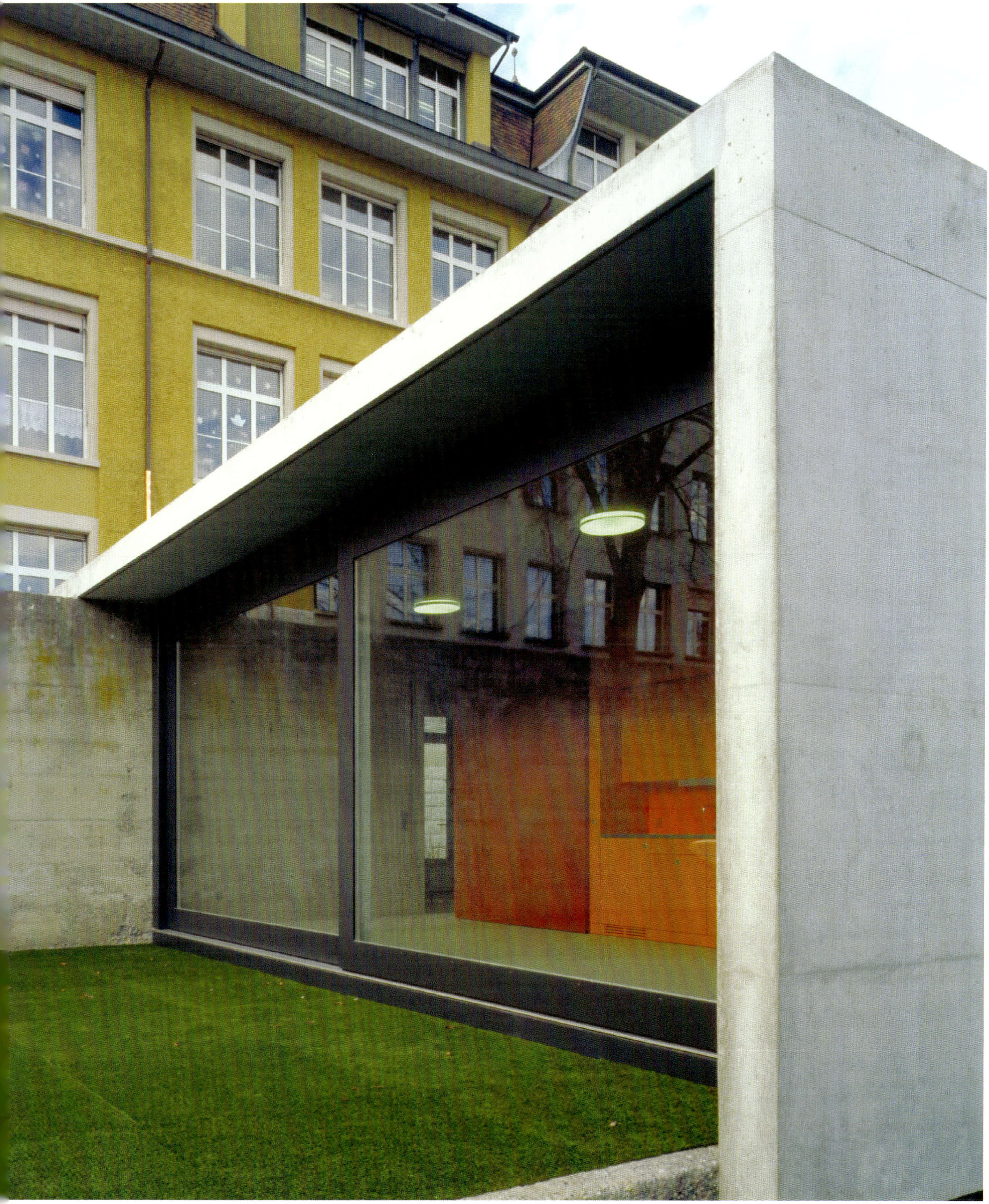

Site plan and photographs of the site before the construction.

128 Ken Architekten

0 10m

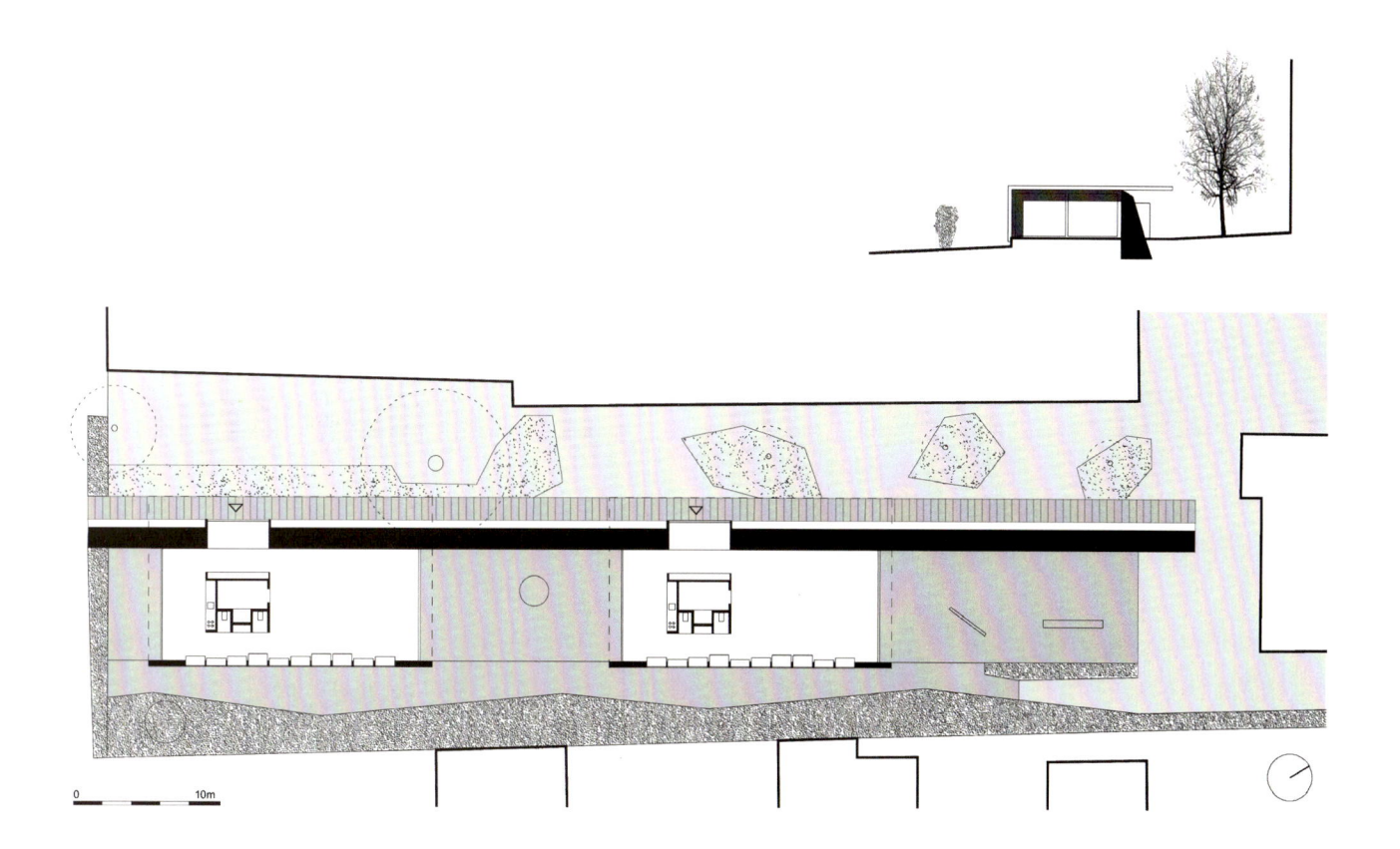

Ken Architekten

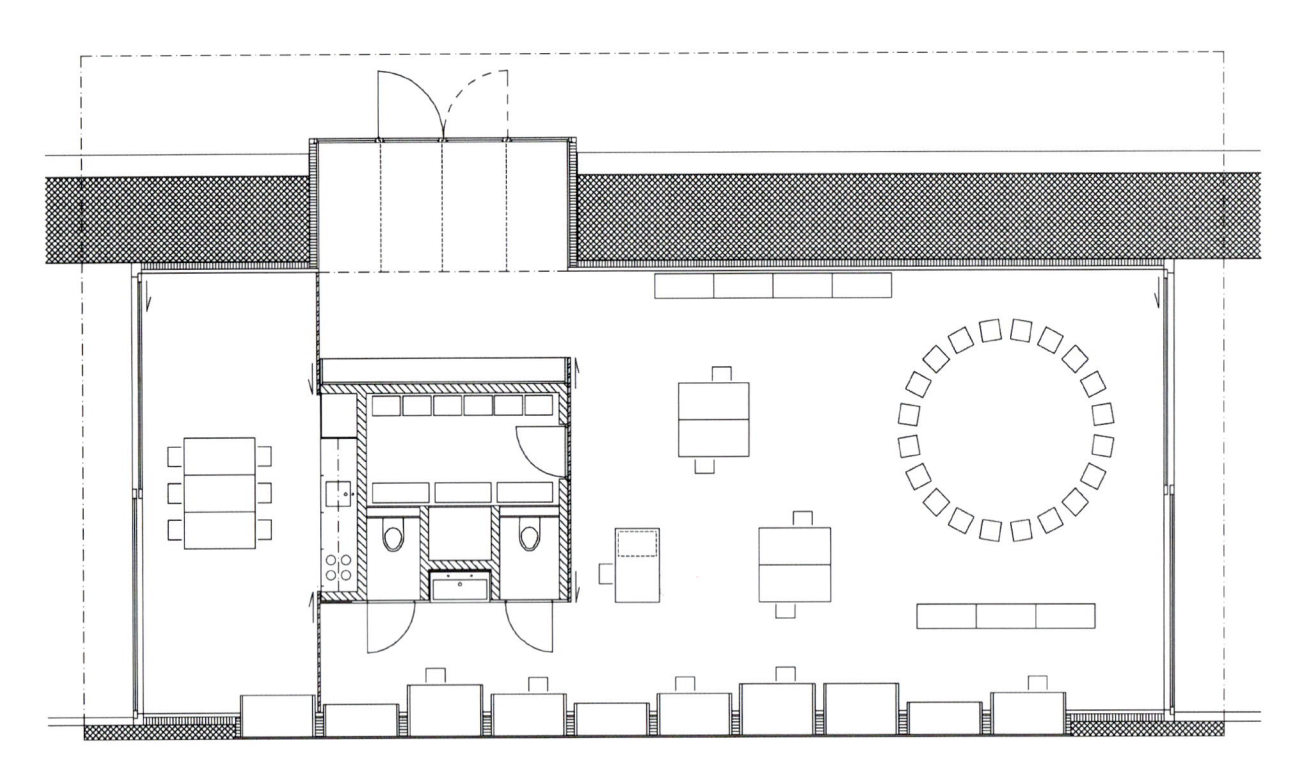

Sudden variations in scale make the simple space visually ambivalent; bright colors are visible from the outside, giving the interior of the kindergarten a kind of 'Wonderland' appearance.

Ken Architekten

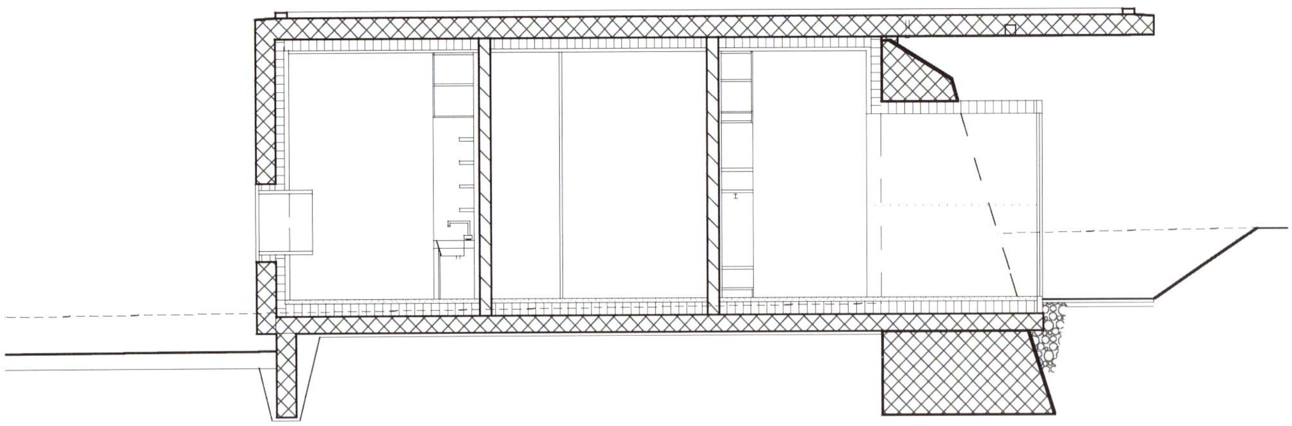

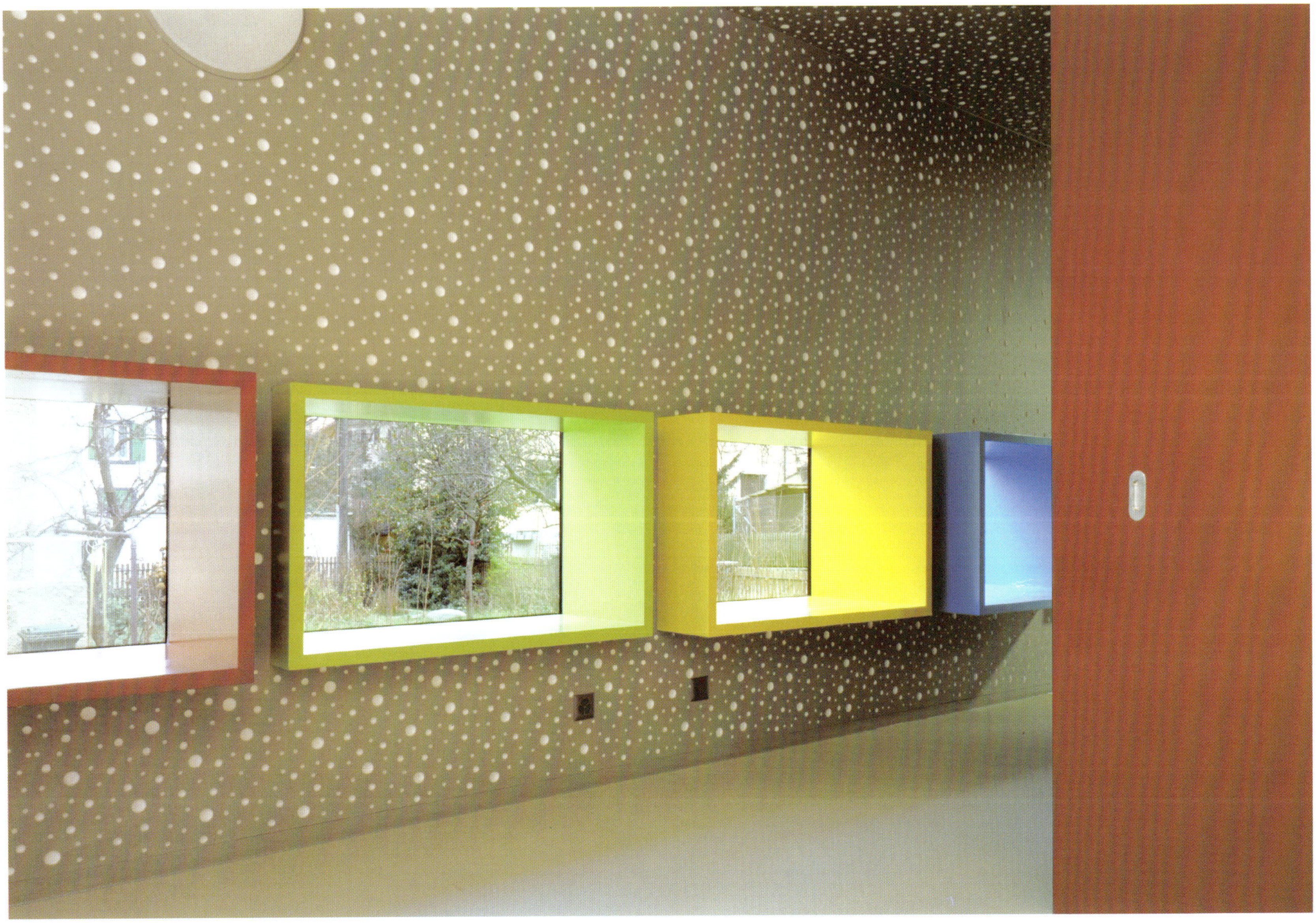

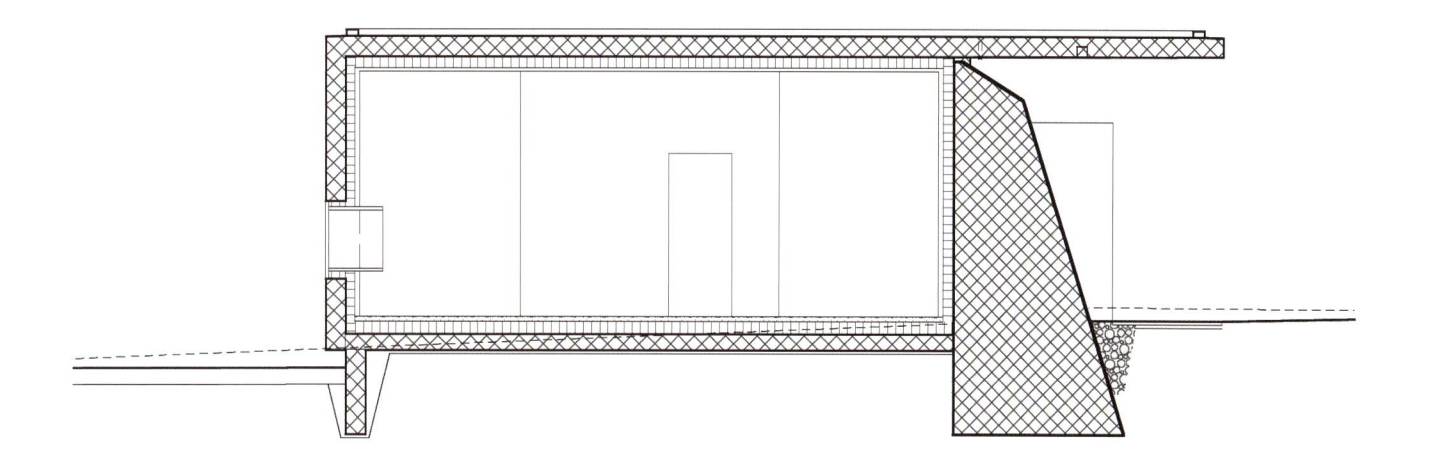

Ken Architekten

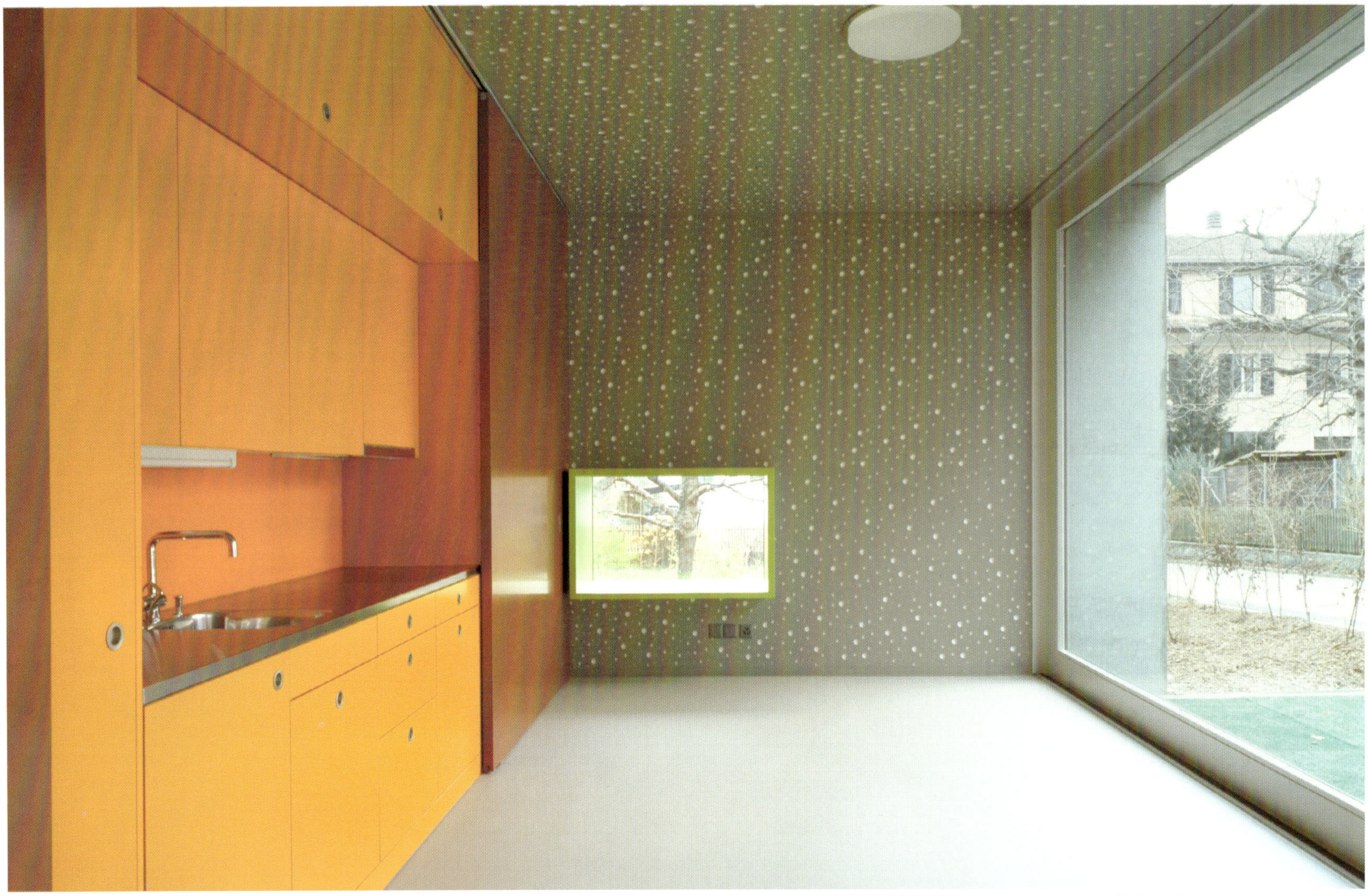

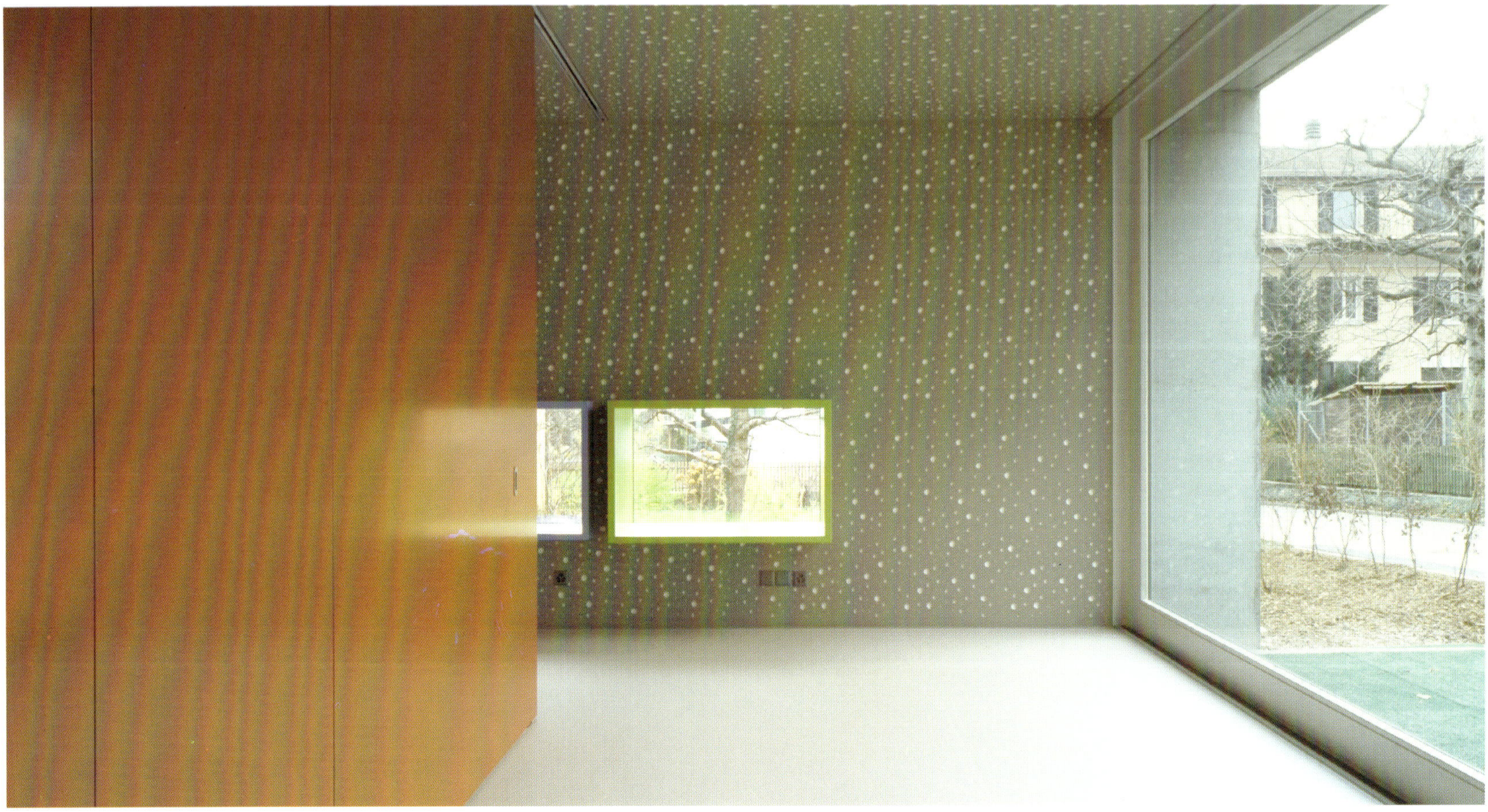

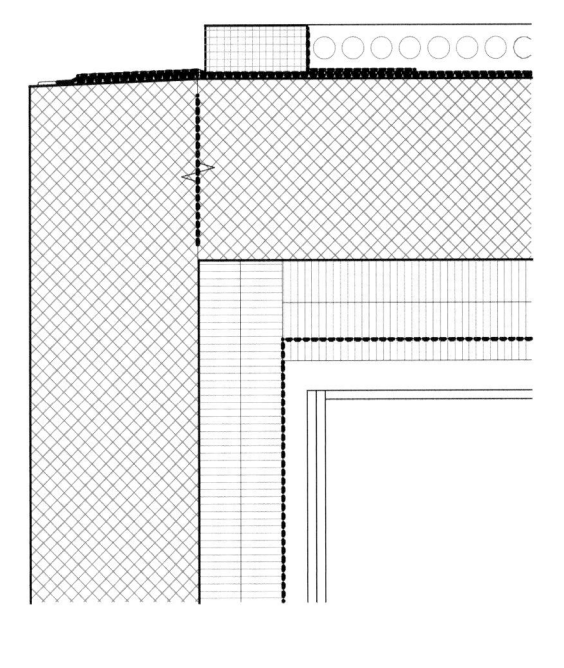

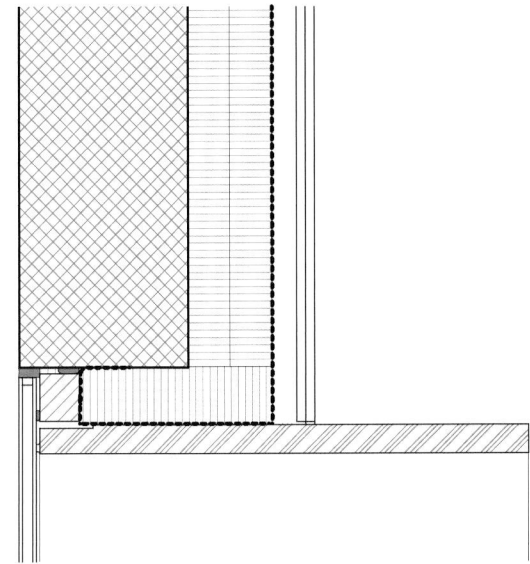

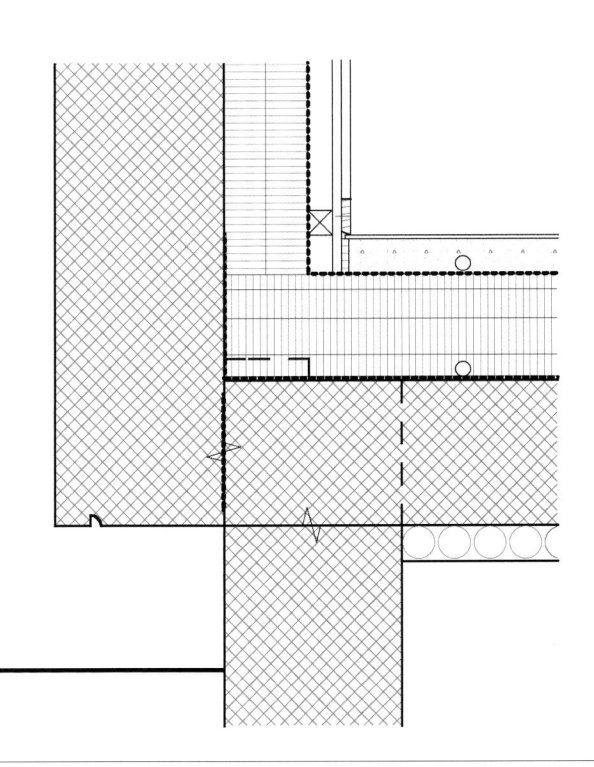

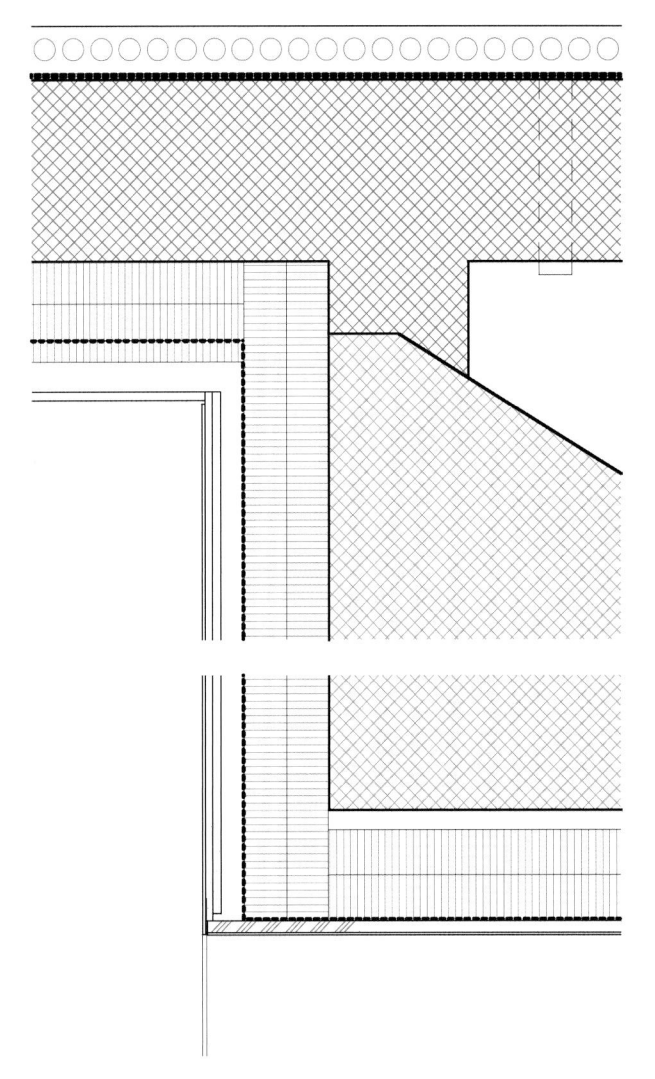

Green roof build-up
- 60 mm soil
- 5 mm polypropylene reinforced rot-proof roofing felt, as humidity storage
- 5 mm EP5 WF S elastomeric reinforced asphalt sheet with anti-root layer
- 5 mm EP5 WF, flashing attached to the concrete with epoxy resin

Roof structure
- 250 mm concrete
- 60 + 50 mm mineral fiber insulation 32 kg/m³
- Humidity barrier, Flamex
- 40 mm mineral fiber 32 kg/m³
- Approx. 30 mm electrical wiring
- 12.5 mm GKP sound proofing 12 / 20 / 35 R

Exterior wall composition
- 240 mm concrete
- 2 × 60 mm mineral fiber insulation 32 kg/m³
- Humidity barrier, Flamex
- 35 mm electrical wiring
- 12.5 mm GKP
- 12.5 mm GKP sound proofing 12 / 20 / 35 R

Wall build-up
- Various, especially the old fortification wall
- 2 × 60 mm mineral fiber 32 kg/m³
- Humidity barrier, Flamex
- ca. 33 mm electrical wiring
- 12.5 mm GKP
- 9.5 mm GKP
- Approx. 4.5 mm linoleum-cork

Floor build-up
- Approx. 5 mm linoleum-cork, polyurethane finish
- 50 mm layer of self-levelling waterproof floor base
- Supports for the heating pipes in the radiant floor heating
- 20 mm thermal insulation swisspor EPS 30, type 3
- 40 + 50 mm ALPUR/ROXAN-aluminum
- 30 mm EPS 30
- Electrical wiring adhered on site
- Approx. 5 mm humidity barrier BIKUVAP VA4
- 200 mm slab
- 50 mm meager concrete

Ken Architekten

Eisenman Architects
The Memorial to the Murdered Jews of Europe

This memorial, designed by New York architect Peter Eisenman, is dedicated to the Jewish victims of the Holcaust. It occupies a 19,000 sqm (205,000 sqft) site between Berlin's Brandenburg Gate and Potsdamer Platz, on what used to be the no-man's-land between East and West Berlin and what is now part of the newly created parliament and government district. Due to its location the site had to be cleared of existing foundations, World War II bombs, mines and ammunition before the project could get underway.

A total of 2711 gunmetal gray reinforced concrete stelae are each uniquely positioned on a uniform grid to form a wave like composition that sweeps across an undulating topography. In places the slabs drop to as much as 2.4 m (7 ft 9 in) below surrounding street level. All of the stelae have an identical plan dimension of 2.38 × 0.95 m (7 ft 9 in × 3 ft 2 in), although they vary in height from 0 to 5 m (16 ft 2 in), progressing from the field's boundary to the central areas. Precision positioned to a narrow spacing of just 0.95m (3 ft in), the stelae create parallel and orthogonal footpaths, which run throughout the memorial.

Visitors, who find themselves winding their way through the forest of stelae, are struck by how distant the busy city center seems, and how quiet and reflective the atmosphere is. The stelae are designed to produce an uneasy, confusing atmosphere, and the whole sculpture aims to represent a supposedly ordered system that has lost touch with human reason. The overwhelming sense of disorientation is increased by the askance tilt of each stele.

Collectively, these leaning monoliths create a lilting wave motion across the field from east to west and from north to south. The absence of any obvious entry or exit point, or any prescribed route through the stelae adds to the feeling of insecurity that this place has been designed to generate.

The architect has firmly stated that no measures should be taken to protect the site from graffiti or vandals so that people can wander freely through its corridors and reflect on what it represents without being observed. Furthermore, Eisenmann has stated that 'Like a prison or concentration camp the monument should survive attacks unscathed, as the stelae are all made out of concrete.'

Architect:
Eisenman Architects
Location:
Berlin, Germany
Photographs:
contributed by Eisenman Architects

Eisenman Architects

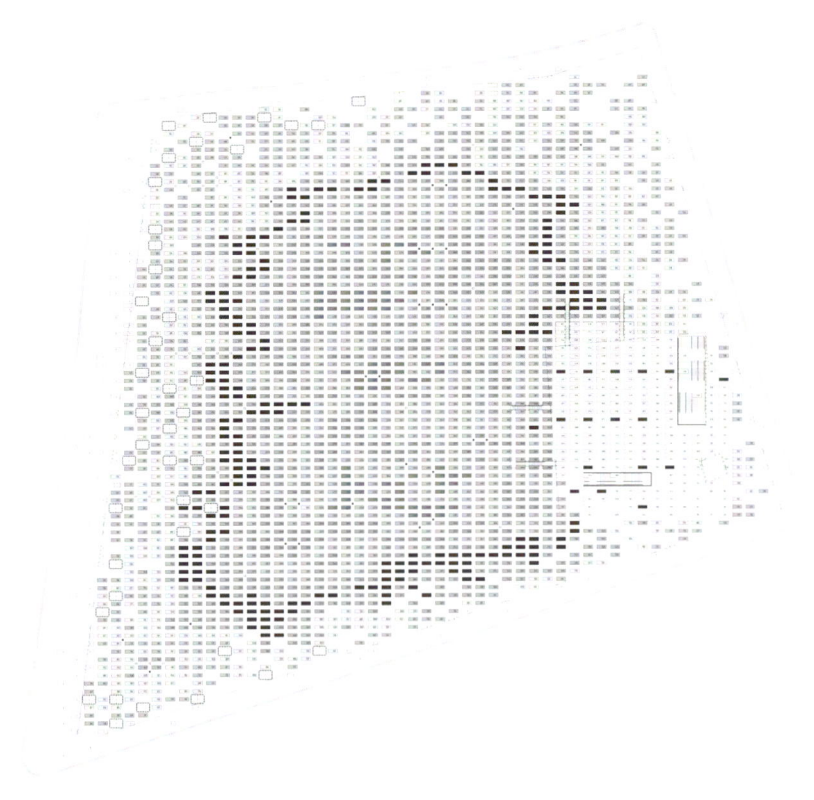

Color code plan

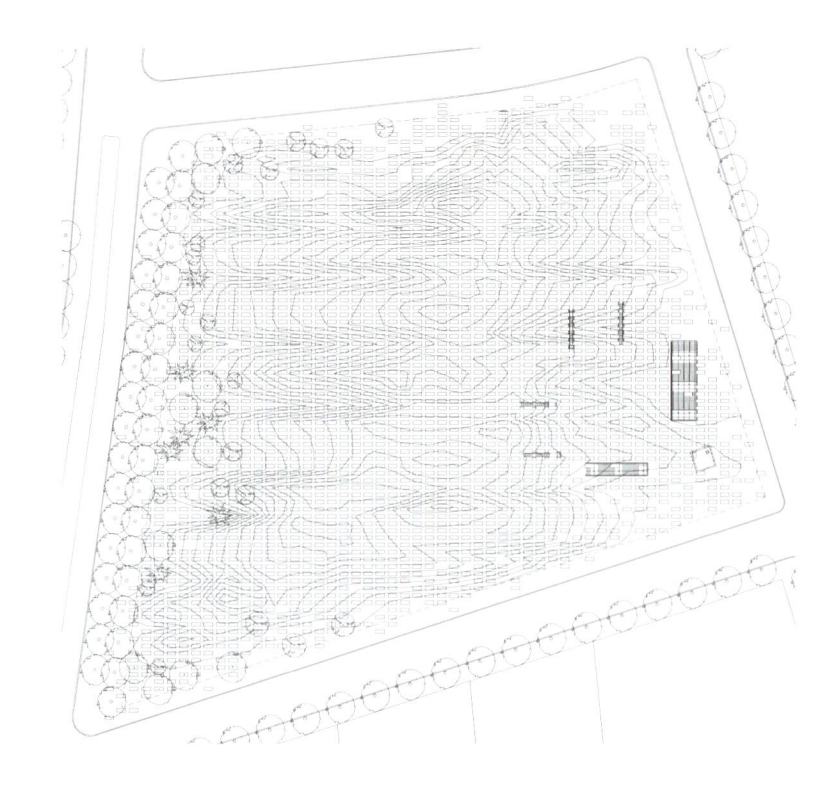

Site topography with context

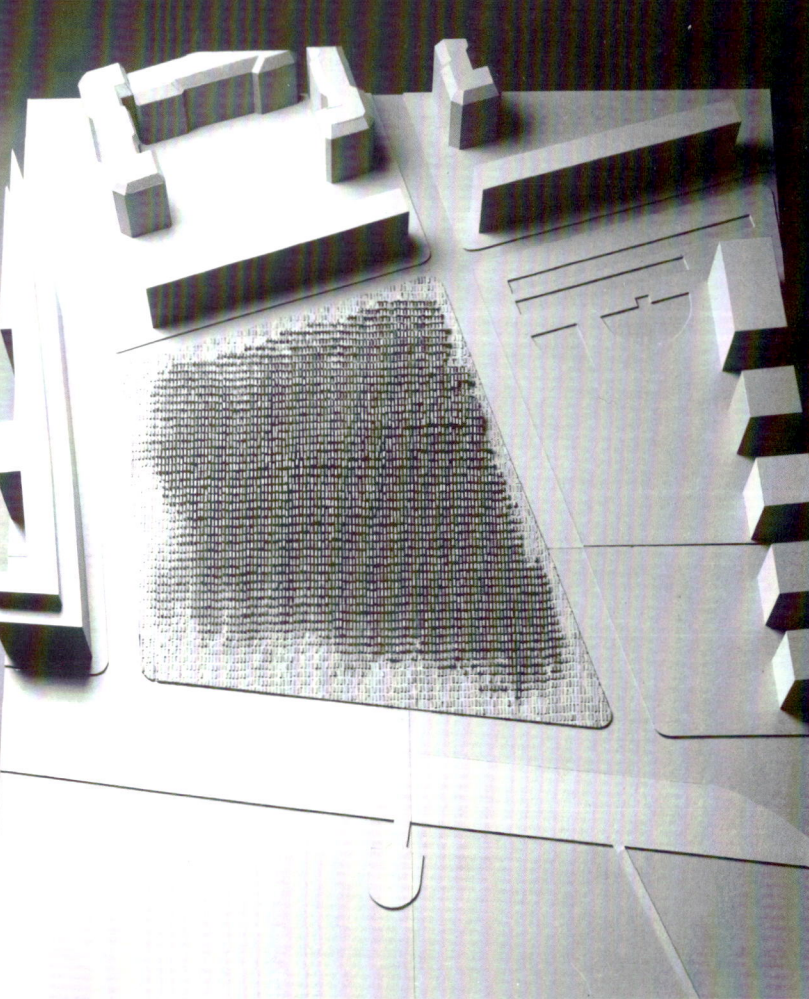

138 Eisenman Architects

Eisenman Architects				139

140 Eisenman Architects

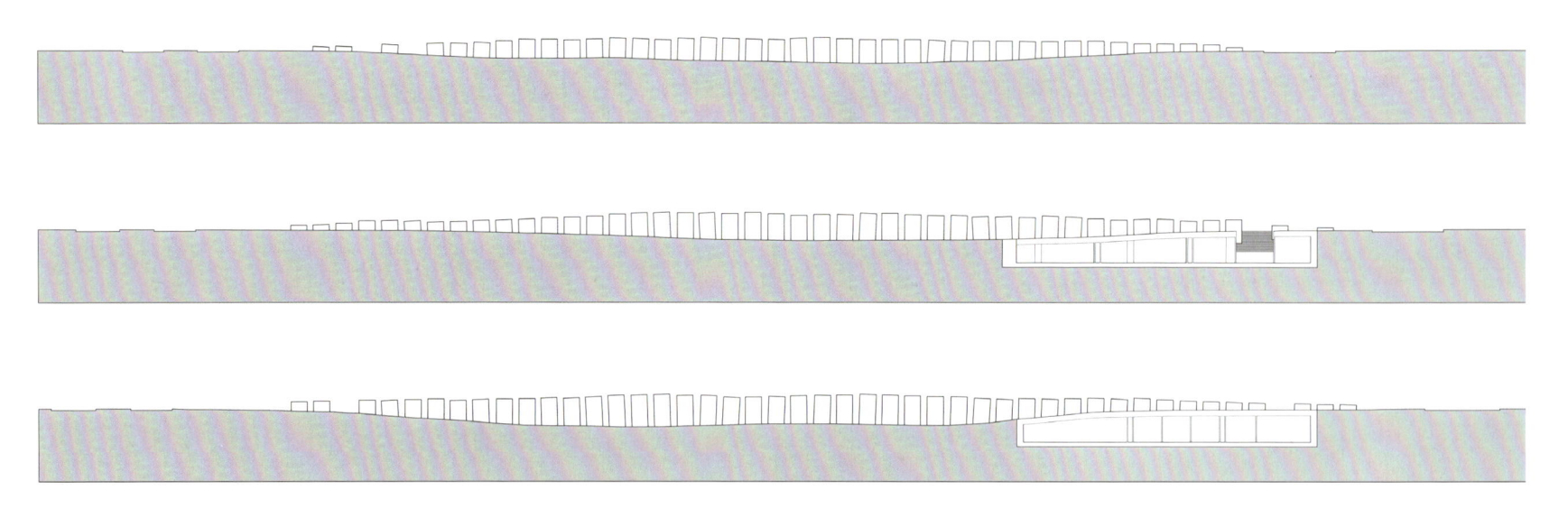

Eisenman Architects 141

Alan Dempsey & Alvin Huang
[C]space DRL10 Pavilion

[C]space is the winning entry in the AA DRL10 Pavilion competition, which was held to celebrate the tenth anniversary of the AA Design Research Lab in conjunction with an exhibition and publication of a book that comprehensively documents the work of the course.

The competition was open to all 354 graduates and the winning entry was designed and developed by Alan Dempsey and Alvin Huang. It was selected by the jury for its radical use of material, it's expression of form as a continuous transformation of furniture to floor, walls and roof structure; and it's constructability within a tight schedule and budget. The design was proposed to be entirely constructed from Fibre-C, a thin fiber-reinforced cement panel that is normally used as a cladding material.

The striking presence of the pavilion invites inspection from a distance and upon closer interaction reveals its ambiguity through the merging of sinuous curves, structural performance, and programmatic functions into a single continuous form. As you move around, the surface varies from opaque to transparent, producing a stunning threedimensional moiré. The surface encloses while also providing a route through for passing pedestrians blurring the distinction between inside and outside. The jointing system in the pavilion exploits uses a simple interlocking cross joint which is tightened by a set of locking neoprene gaskets. Close consultation with the Fibre-C technical department in Austria and extensive material testing were required to develop the design. Sixteen iterations of the design were modelled and tested over a period of six weeks. In parallel to the digital modelling, numerous rapid prototypes, scale models and full scale physical mock-ups were built to develop the design of individual elements and test the tolerance and fit of the assembly.

Architects:
Alan Dempsey & Alvin Huang
Client:
Architectural Association, Design Research Lab
Location:
Bedford Square, London, UK
Photographs:
Contributed by the architects

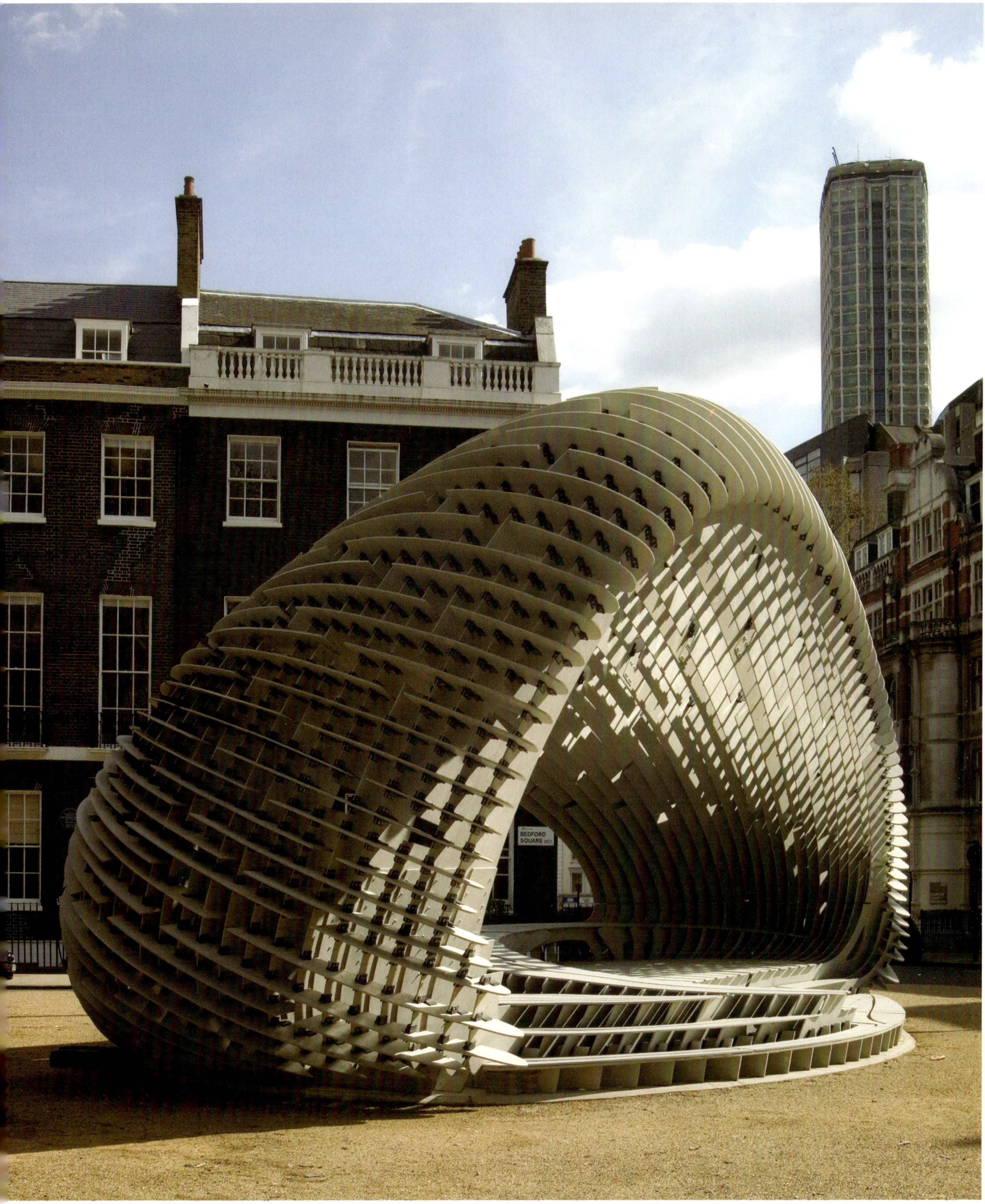
BEDFORD
SQUARE WC1

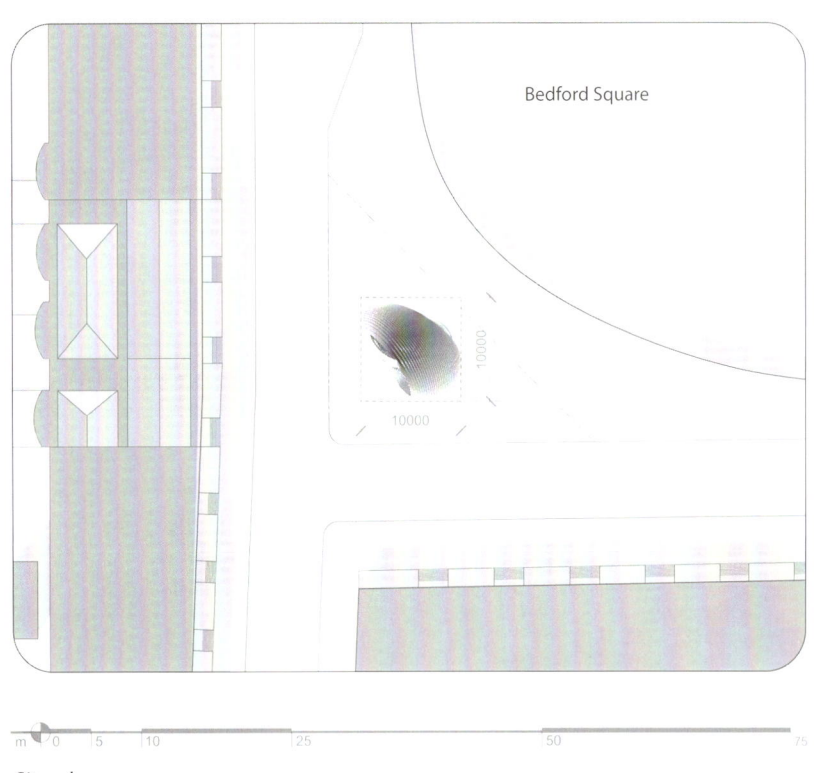

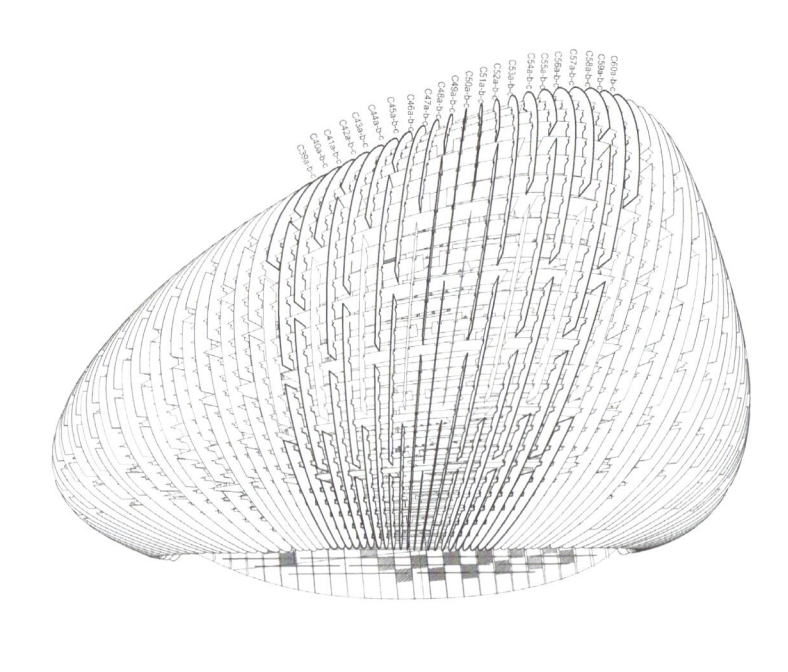

Site plan

Plan

Alan Dempsey & Alvin Huang

Alan Dempsey & Alvin Huang

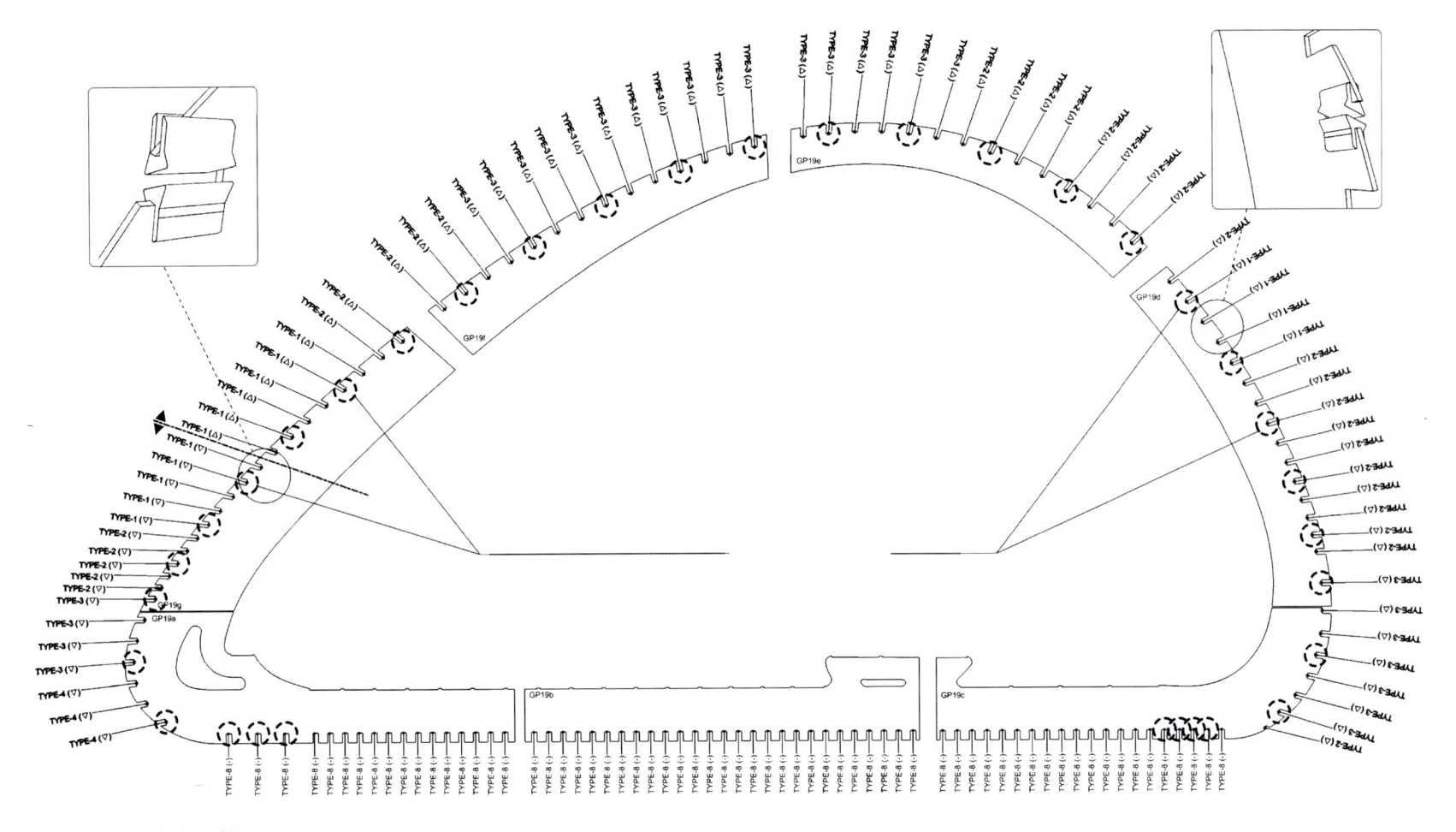

Global profile 19

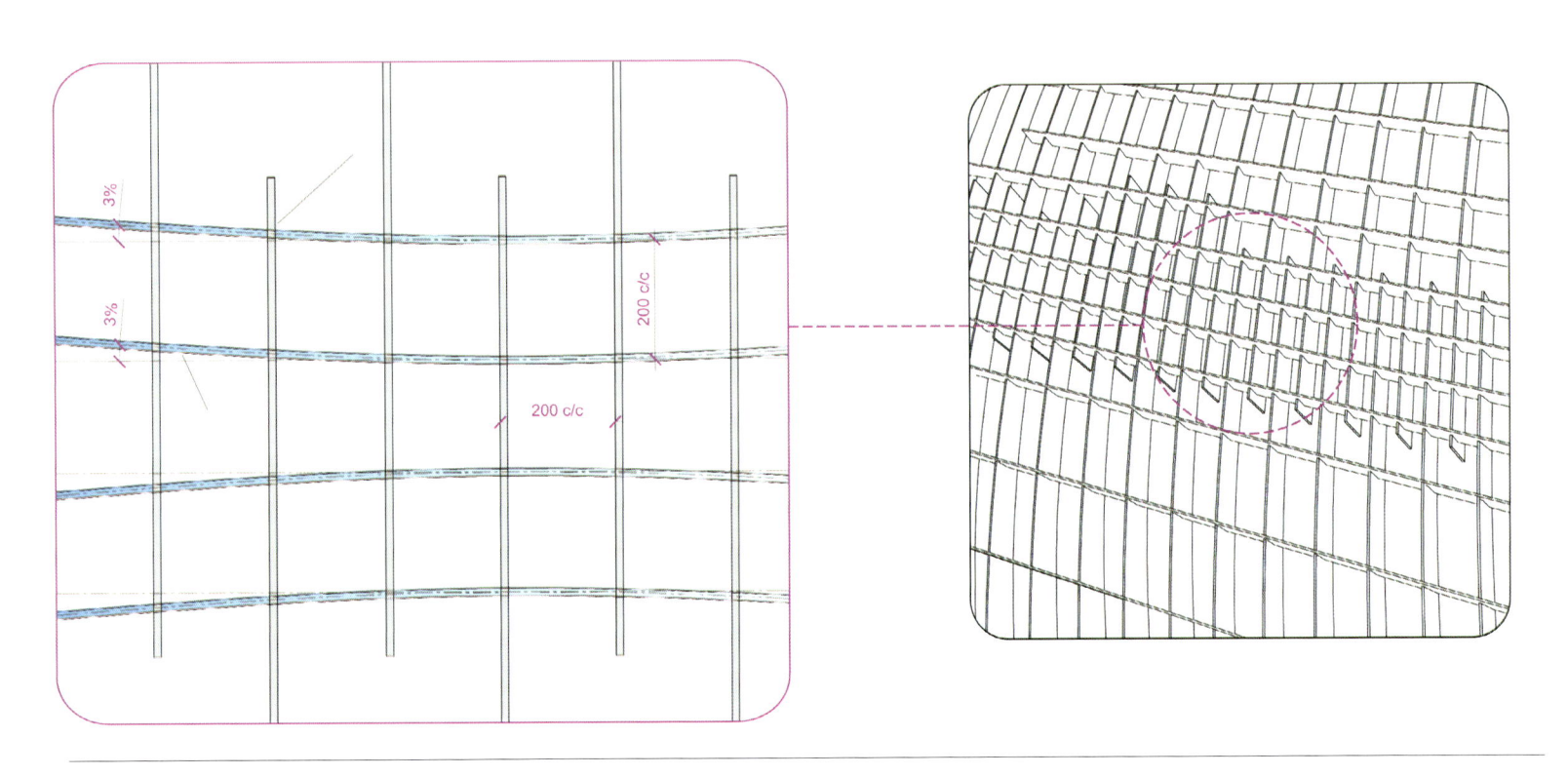

146 Alan Dempsey & Alvin Huang

Each piece is joined to the next with at least three cross members set at 200 mm centers. The notches are located so that the fins must be slightly flexed to lock into place thus creating a tight joint.

The pavilion is constructed from 850 different pieces that have been cut with a CNC mil from standard 13mm fiber-reinforced cement sheets. After the pieces were delivered to the site, the entire pavilion was assembled over a period of 3 weeks by a dedicated team of staff and students. Over 70 drawing sheets were produced by the design team to describe in detail each step of the assembly sequence and locate each piece within the overall structure.

Gasket assembly

A. Pre-glue gaskets to notches on concrete global profiles prior to assembly.
B. Slot concrete cross-profile into glued gasket assembly from above.
C. Insert punched gaskets on to cross profile notches from below
D. Fasten bolts to fix second set of gaskets to cross profile.

1. Un-punched gasket
2. Concrete global profile
3. 50 mm notch
4. Glued gasket
5. Concrete cross-profile
6. Pre-drilled 8 mm holes
7. Punched gaskets
8. M6 bolts and washers

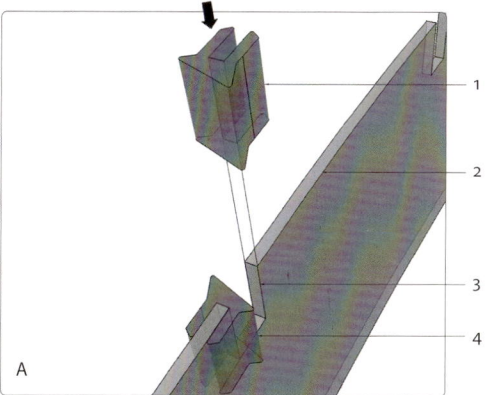

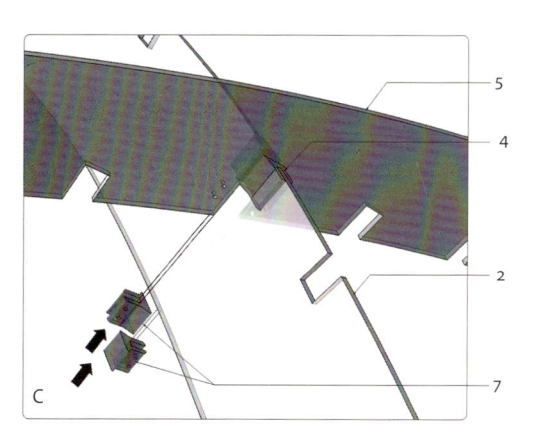

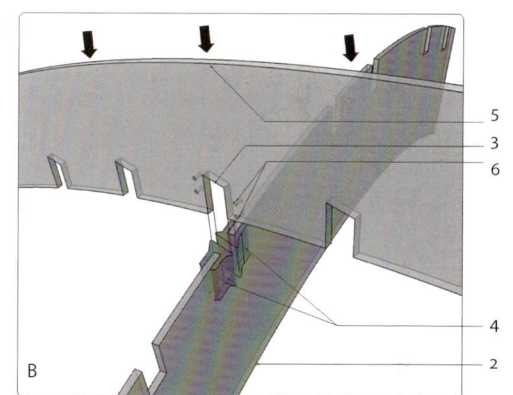

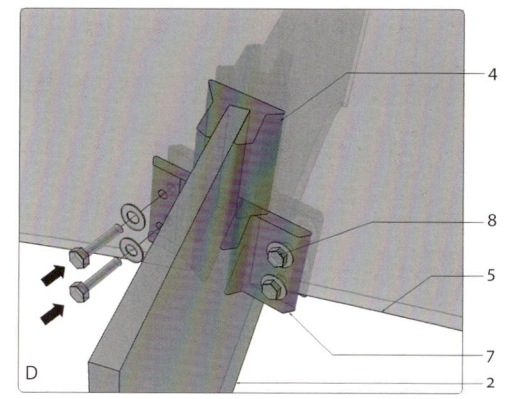

Alan Dempsey & Alvin Huang

Aranguren + Gallegos & Herrada + Maiz

Housing at Encinar de los Reyes

This development of 76 apartments and garages in a large landscaped plot is located in the Encinar de los Reyes, less than 10 km from the Center of Madrid.
The insertion of residential buildings with large landscaped surfaces beside the M-40 motorway led to the design of five built volumes arranged transverse to the motorway, thus creating two clearly differentiated fronts on the longest sides.
The north-facing façades are conceived as closed, defensive bodies, placed like the advertising hoardings that run along the sides of the road, protecting the dwellings from the aggression of the motorway.
In contrast, the south-facing façades are decomposed and fragmented, with terraces that look out over the landscaped areas of the plot.
To obtain such radically different façades, the service elements of the apartments (kitchens, drying areas, toilets, etc.), are located in a single compact body on the north façade, while all the living areas and bedrooms are on the façade overlooking the landscaped area.
Through the large window and "terrace-gardens", the space of the dwellings is prolonged toward the exterior, so nature and architecture are merged in a single expression. Thus, the existing trees and views become defining elements of the architecture.
Economy was sought in the construction and in the architectural expression of the project. Two materials were combined: concrete and wood. All the external walls of the blocks are built with prefabricated concrete elements of the same dimensions, which reduced the number of different pieces and thus the cost of construction.
The horizontal lines of the façades are reinforced with, on the southern side, wide bands clad in wood or reinforced concrete and, on the northern side, a permeable screen formed of narrow wooden and concrete strips. This light screen on the northern side has the effect of dissolving the mass of the building and affording the tranquillity that is desirable for a residential area.

Architect:
Aranguren + Gallegos & Herrada + Maiz
Location:
Madrid, Spain
Photographs:
Hisao Suzuki

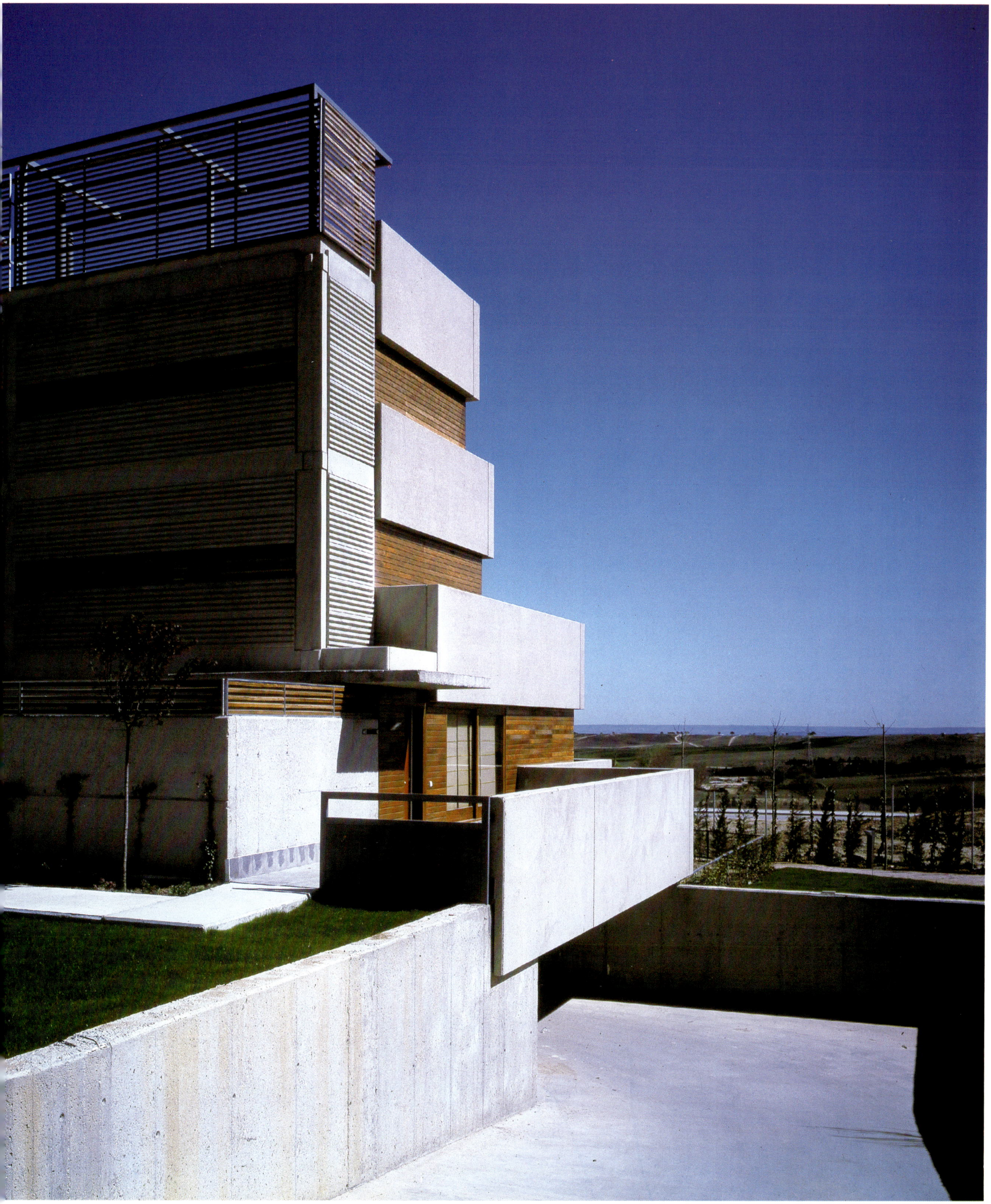

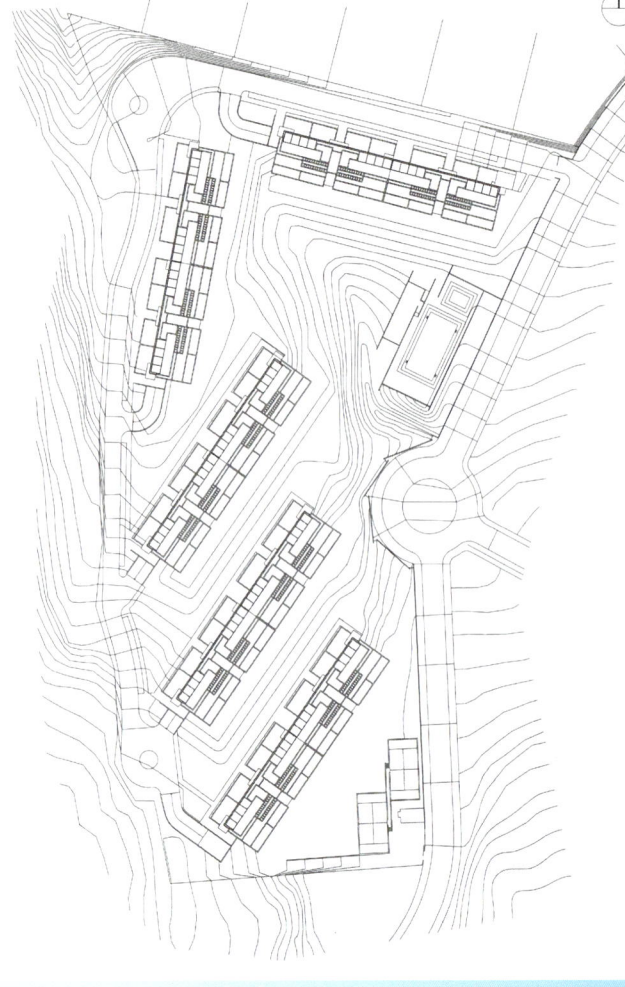

The challenge of creating 76 apartments and garages in a large landscaped plot at the edge of a freeway was solved imaginatively by the architects by means of north-facing façades that act as screens protecting the residential complex.

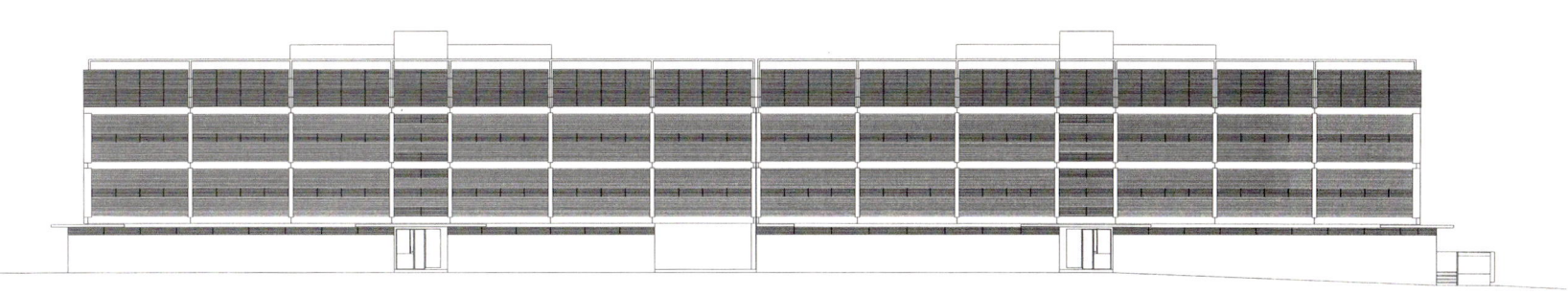

North elevation

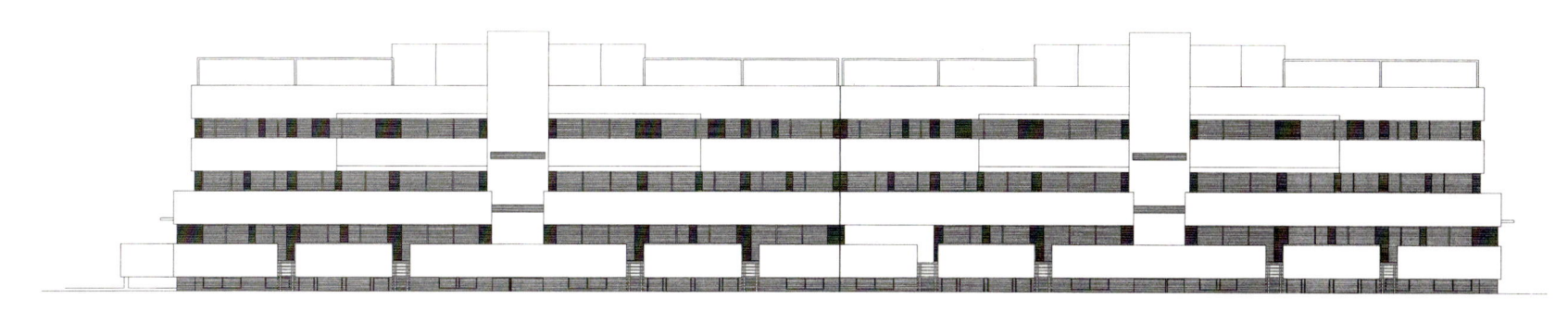

South elevation

Aranguren + Gallegos & Herrada + Maiz

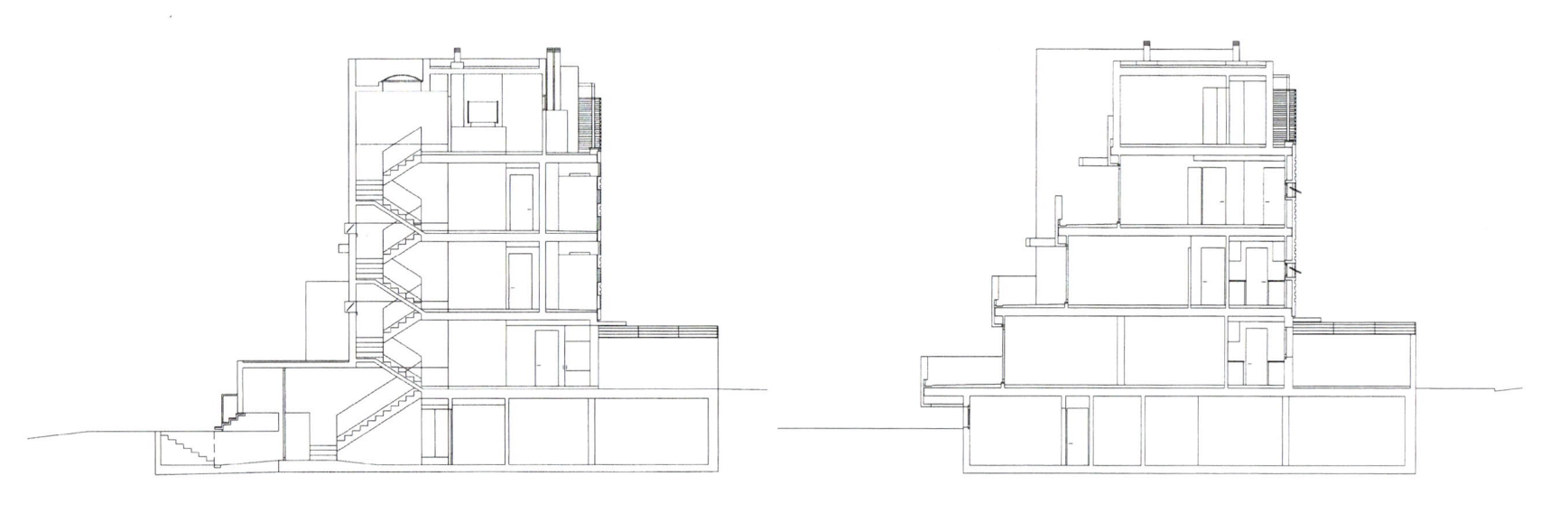

Section through stairs

Section through living room

154 Aranguren + Gallegos & Herrada + Maiz

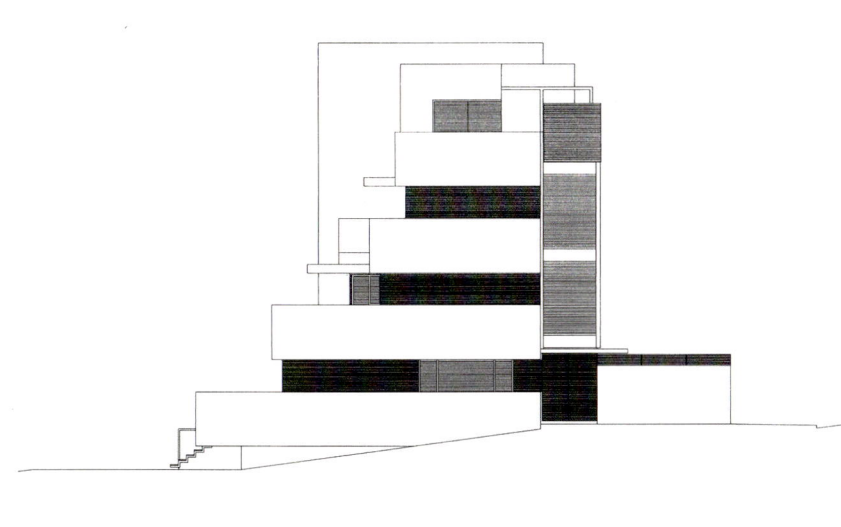

Side elevation

Aranguren + Gallegos & Herrada + Maiz

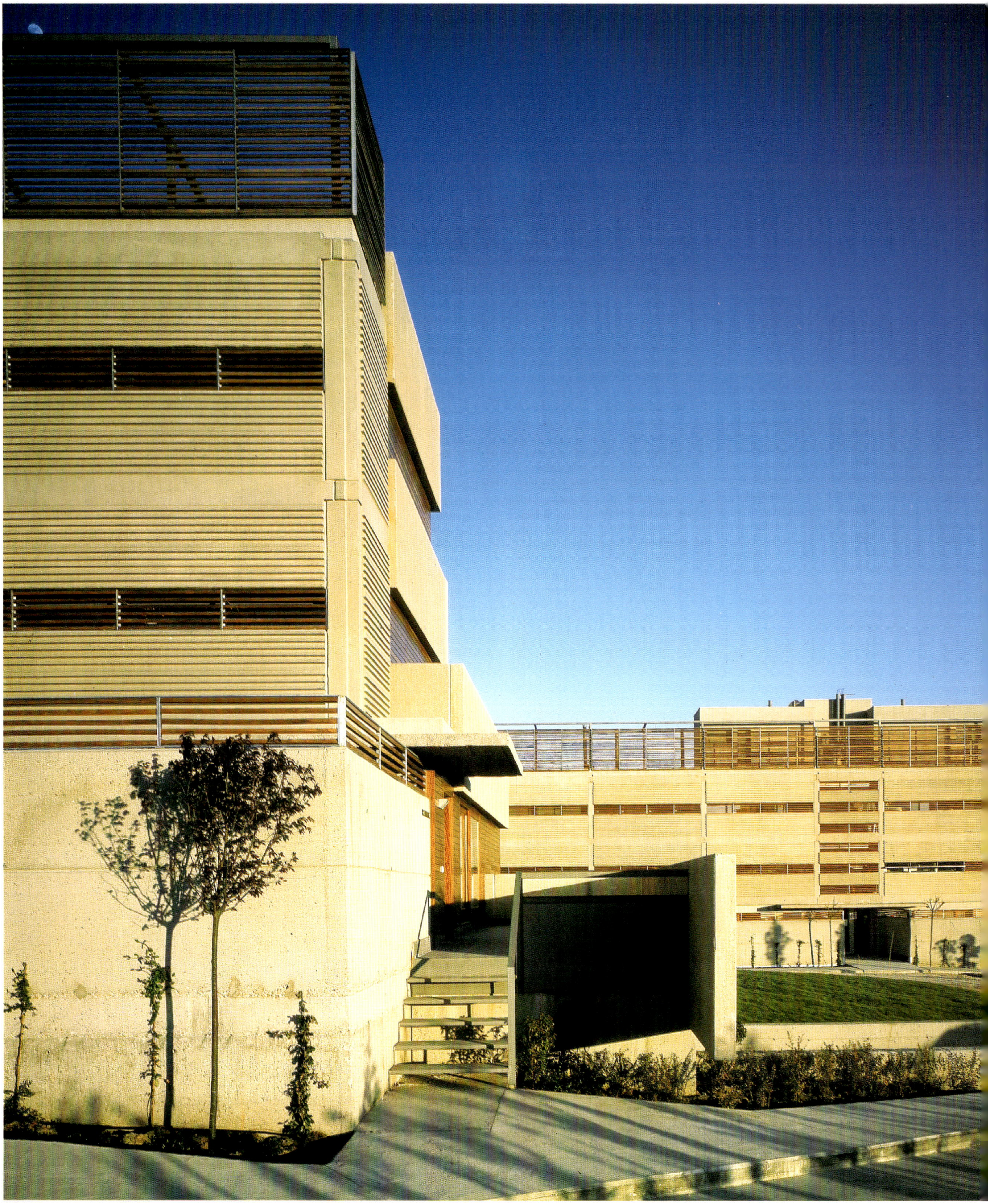

1. Pergola, metallic square sections 100 x 100 x 5 mm (4 x 4 x 3/16 in)
2. Wooden screen, teak battens 45 x 45 mm (2 x 2 in)
3. Metal frame, made of steel angles 40 x 40 x 3 mm (1 ½ x 1 ½ x 1/8 in).
4. Metal substructure to screen, T-sections 80 x 40 x 5 mm (3 x 1 ½ x 3/16 in)
5. Metal substructure to screen, T-sections 80 x 40 x 5 mm
6. Wooden skirting board.
7. Wooden door frame
8. Step, formed with 3 bricks.
9. Artificial stone
10. Cement tile paving.
11. Cement mortar, 20 mm (3/4 in)
12. Geotextile
13. Impermeable membrane, double
14. Geotextile
15. Cellular concrete gradients layer
16. Geotextile
17. Thermal insulation, 40mm (1 ½ in)
18. Geotextile

The main materials used for the construction of the complex are wood and concrete. The combination of these materials creates an effect of color and texture that gives dynamism to the pure, simple geometry.

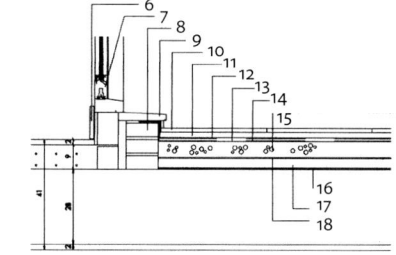

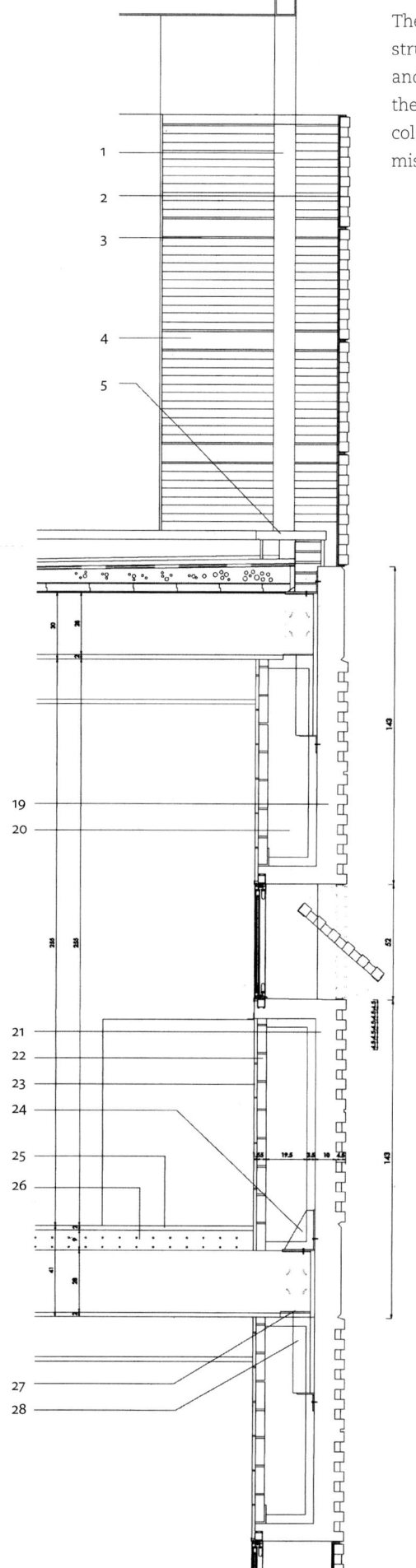

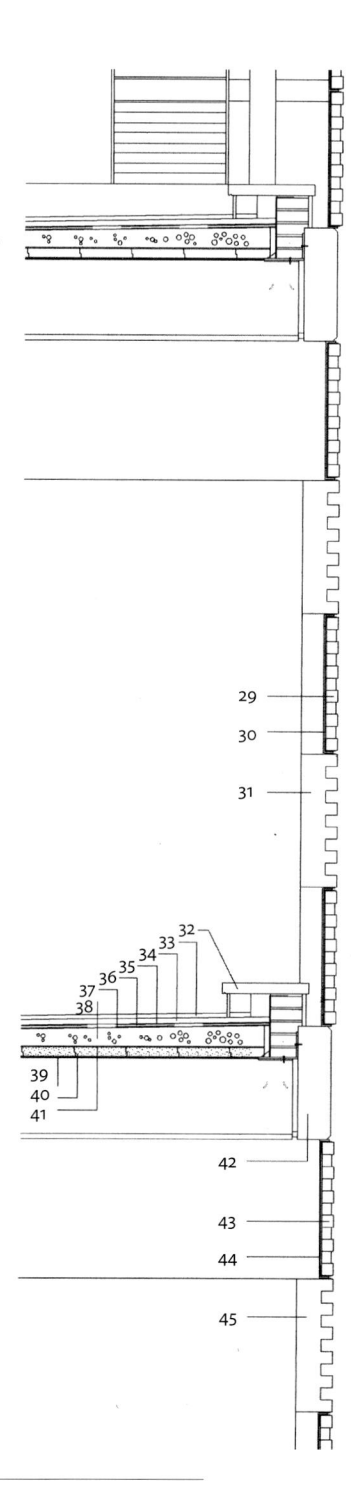

19. Prefabricated panel, type 1
20. Air gap, 195 mm, with projected polyurethane foam insulation, 35 mm (1 3/8 in)
21. Prefabricated panel, type 2
22. Brick partition wall
23. Interior cladding, marble
24. Metallic adjustable fixing element for prefabricated façade panels, screwed to plate cast into floor slab. Panels screwed to fixing
25. Floating parquet
26. Underfloor heating
27. Metal plate 200 x 300 x 10 mm (7 in x 1 ft x 3/8 in) fixed to floor slab
28. Metal tube, 80 x 80 mm (3 x 3 in), soldered to upper surface of slab
29. Wooden screen, teak battens 45 x 45 mm (2 x 2 in)
30. Metal frame, made of steel angles 40 x 40 x 3 mm (1 ½ x 1 ½ x 1/8 in)
31. Prefabricated panel, type 4
32. Coping, artificial stone
33. Cement tile paving
34. Tile Cement mortar, 20 mm (3/4 in)
35. Geotextile
36. Impermeable membrane, double
37. Geotextile
38. Cellular concrete gradients layer
39. Geotextile
40. Thermal insulation, 40 mm (1 ½ in)
41. Geotextile
42. Prefabricated panel, type 5
43. Wooden screen, teak battens 45 x 45 mm
44. Metal frame, made of steel angles 40 x 40 x 3 mm
45. Prefabricated panel, type 4

Construction details

1. Prefabricated panel, type 9
2. Projected insulation, 35 mm (1 3/8 in)
3. Air gap, 75 mm (3 in), with projected polyurethane foam insulation, 35 mm
4. Brick partition wall
5. Prefabricated panel, type 9
6. Artificial stone, 40 mm (1 ½ in)
7. Brick upstand, rendered on both sides
8. Artificial stone trim
9. Expansion joint, with flexible sealant
10. Gypsum plaster, 20 mm (3/4 in)
11. Monocapa render
12. Brick wall
13. Air gap, 75 mm (3 in), with projected polyurethane foam insulation, 35 mm (1 3/8 in)
14. Brick partition wall
15. Gypsum plaster, 15 mm (1/16 in)
16. Cement tile paving
17. Cement mortar, 20 mm (3/4 in)
18. Geotextile
19. Impermeable membrane, double
20. Geotextile
21. Cellular concrete gradients layer, gradient 1.5%
22. Geotextile
23. Thermal insulation, 40 mm (1 ½ in)
24. Geotextile
25. Prefabricated panel, type 9
26. Brick partition wall
27. Gypsum plaster, 15 mm (1/16 in)
28. Floating parquet
29. Metallic adjustable fixing element for prefabricated façade panels, screwed to plate cast into floor slab. Panels screwed to fixing
30. Underfloor heating
31. Pergola, prefabricated RC elements
32. Metallic adjustable fixing element for prefabricated façade panels, screwed to plate cast into floor slab. Panels screwed to fixing
33. Metal plate 200 x 300 x 10 mm (7 in x 1 ft x 3/8 in)
34. RC slab
35. Pergola, prefabricated RC elements
36. Ceramic tiles
37. Tile adhesive, 20 mm (3/4 in)
38. Geotextile
39. Impermeable membrane, double
40. Geotextile
41. Cellular concrete gradients layer, gradient 1.5%
42. Geotextile
43. Rigid thermal insulation, 40 mm (1 ½ in)
44. Geotextile

The north and western façades, closed with a wooden and concrete screen, houses the service area, while the south and eastern façades opens onto the landscaped areas and houses the living areas and bedrooms.

Construction detail

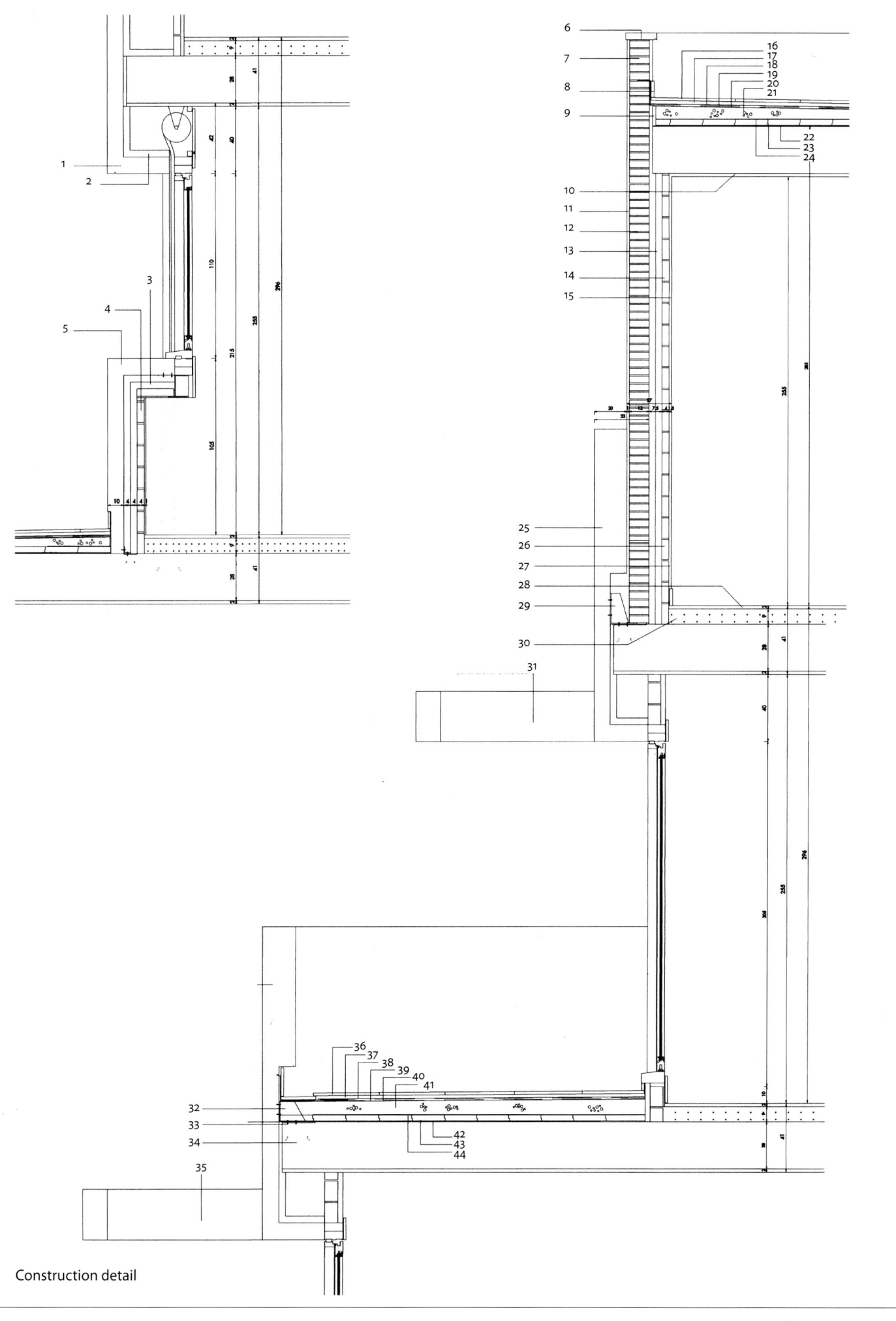

Bevk Perovic Architects
House H

The existing house is a typical northern-European single-family house from the 1960s, comfortable but lacking in personality. A building conceived as a shell separating the residents from the exterior environment, with its aggressive temperatures, winds and rain. As the various rooms in their existing home were occupied by the growing family and an increasing number of professional and academic activities became part of home life, the clients needed more room. The existing living area had become reduced to a corner of the dining room, so the clients' request was to add a longed-for living area outside.

The new extension contrasts with the rest of the house. Whereas everything in the existing building is conventionally orthogonal, the extension has an irregular floorplan; where the rest of the house is a self-contained volume, the extension is open to the garden. Within the context of a fully functional living room, with appropriately insulated walls and roof, and the double glazing necessary for comfort in the winter months, the extension is in direct visual touch with the environment. The time of day, the seasons and the variations in the weather make the rhythms of nature a permanent spectacle for the inhabitants of house H.

The body of the new extension is connected to the main building by a short passage that functions like the stick across the middle of a letter H, besides being the initial letter of the client's name. The small distance that separates the extension from the existing house is echoed in the separation between the extension and the garden, a distance articulated by a few steps which allow it independence form the gently sloping terrain. Though there is nothing makeshift about the materials used and the finishes achieved, it has an ephemeral air, as if it is poised, ready to depart at a moment's notice.

Architect:
Bevk Perovic Architects,
Matija Bevk, Vasa Perovic, Ana Čeligoj
Client:
Maja Hawlina
Location:
Ljubljana, Slovenia
Photographs:
Miran Kambič

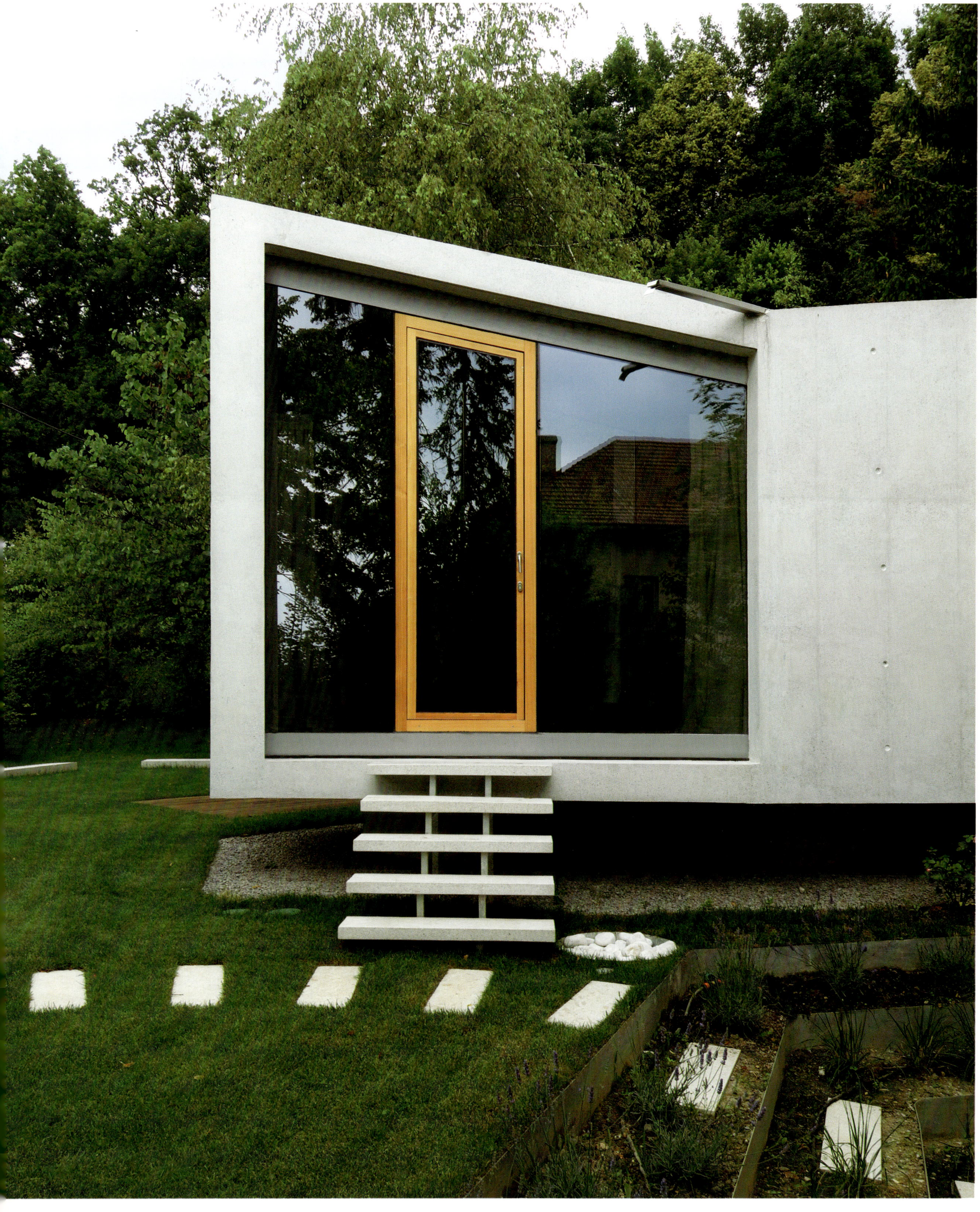

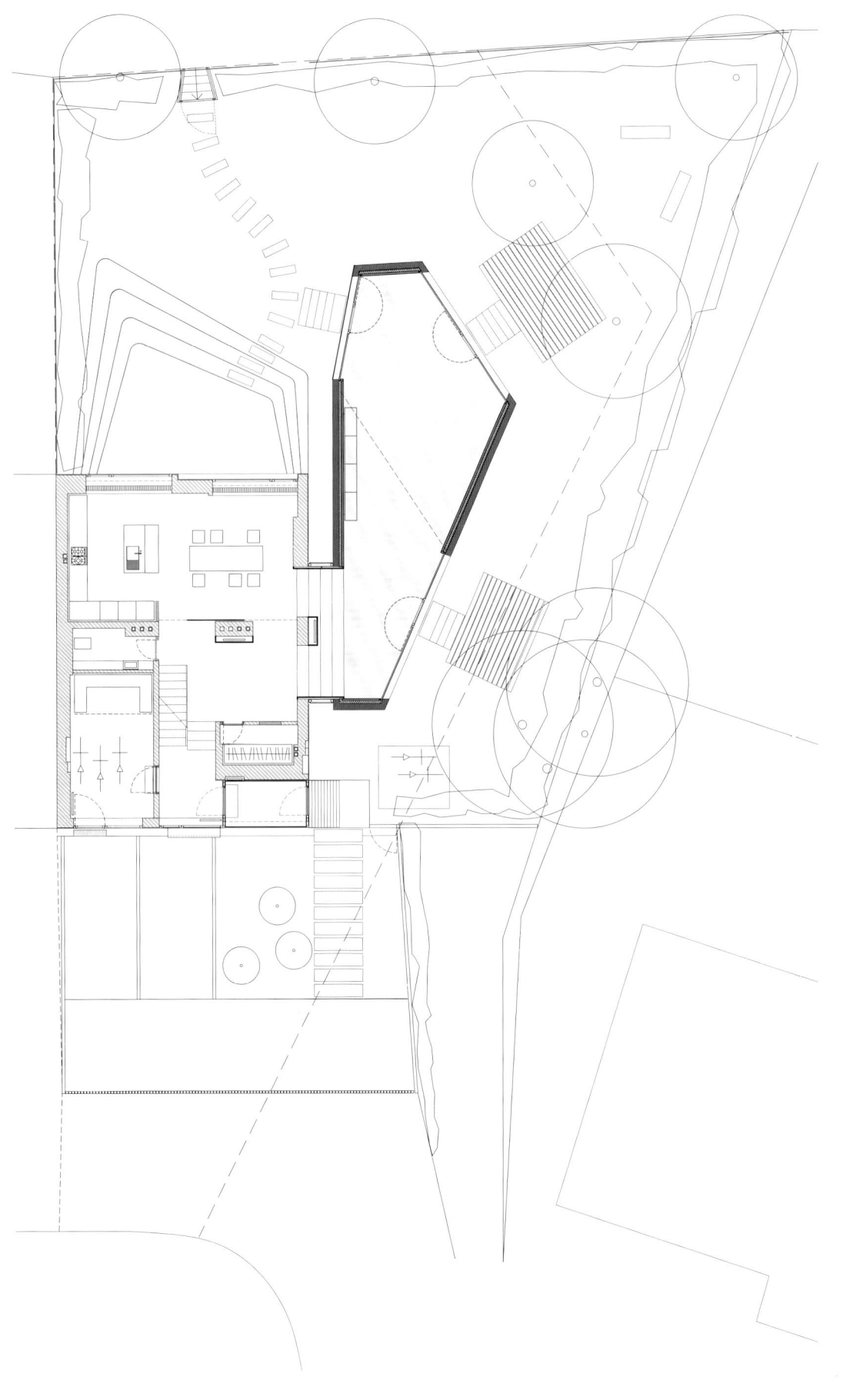

The body of the new extension is connected to the main building by a short passage that functions like the stick across the middle of a letter H, besides being the initial letter of the client's name. The small distance that separates the extension from the existing house is echoed in the separation between the extension and the garden, a distance articulated by a few steps which allow it independence form the gently sloping terrain.

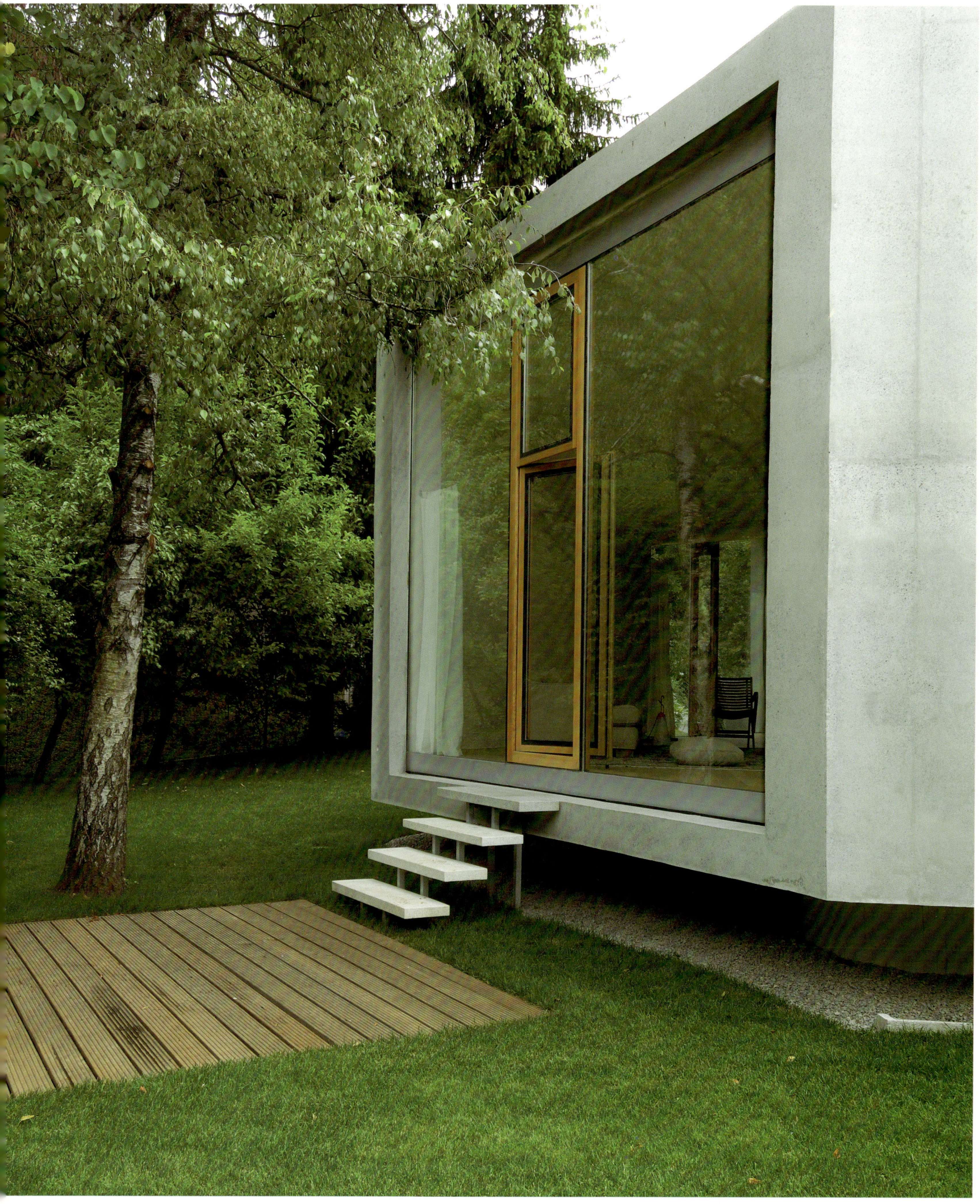

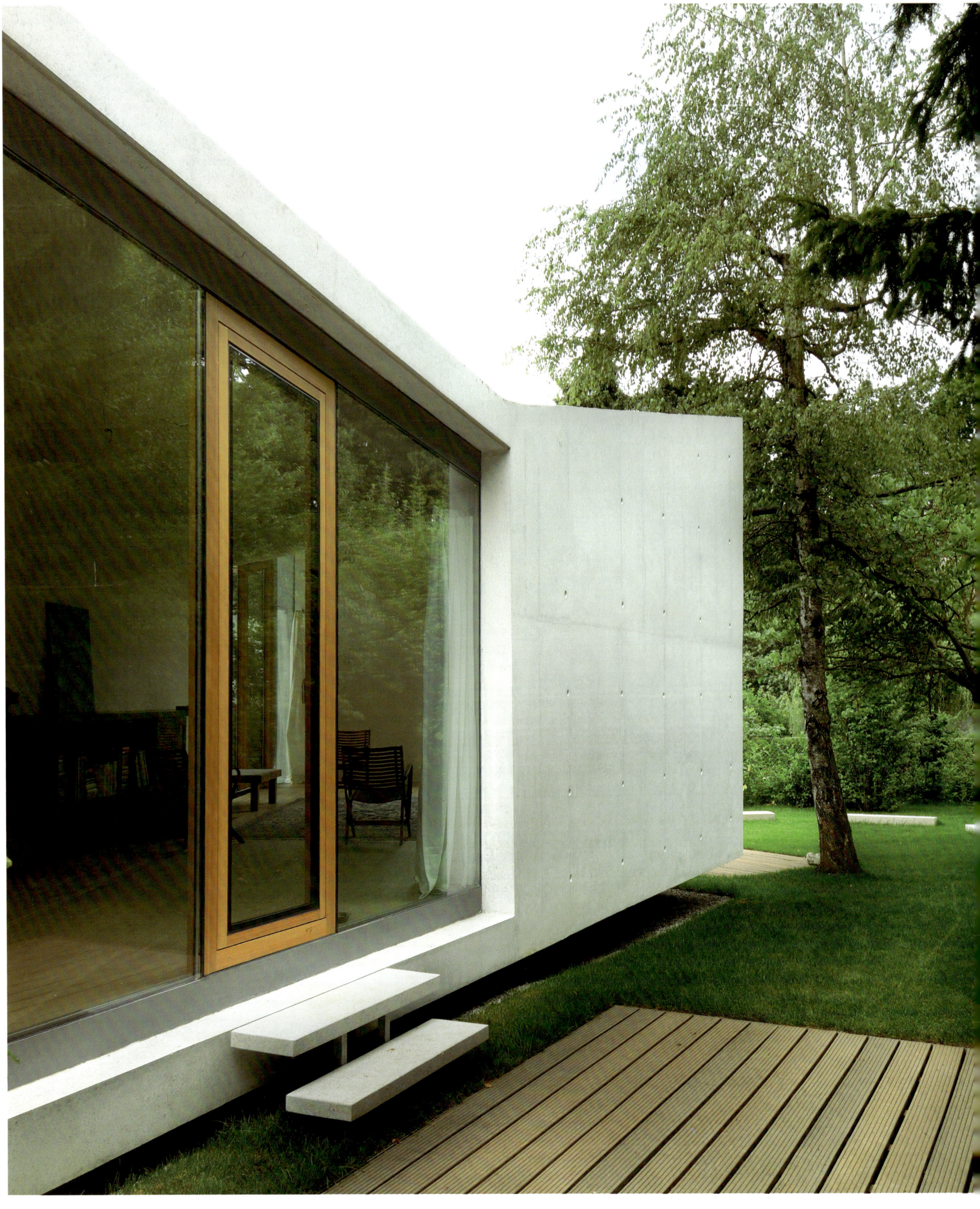

Bevk Perovic Architects

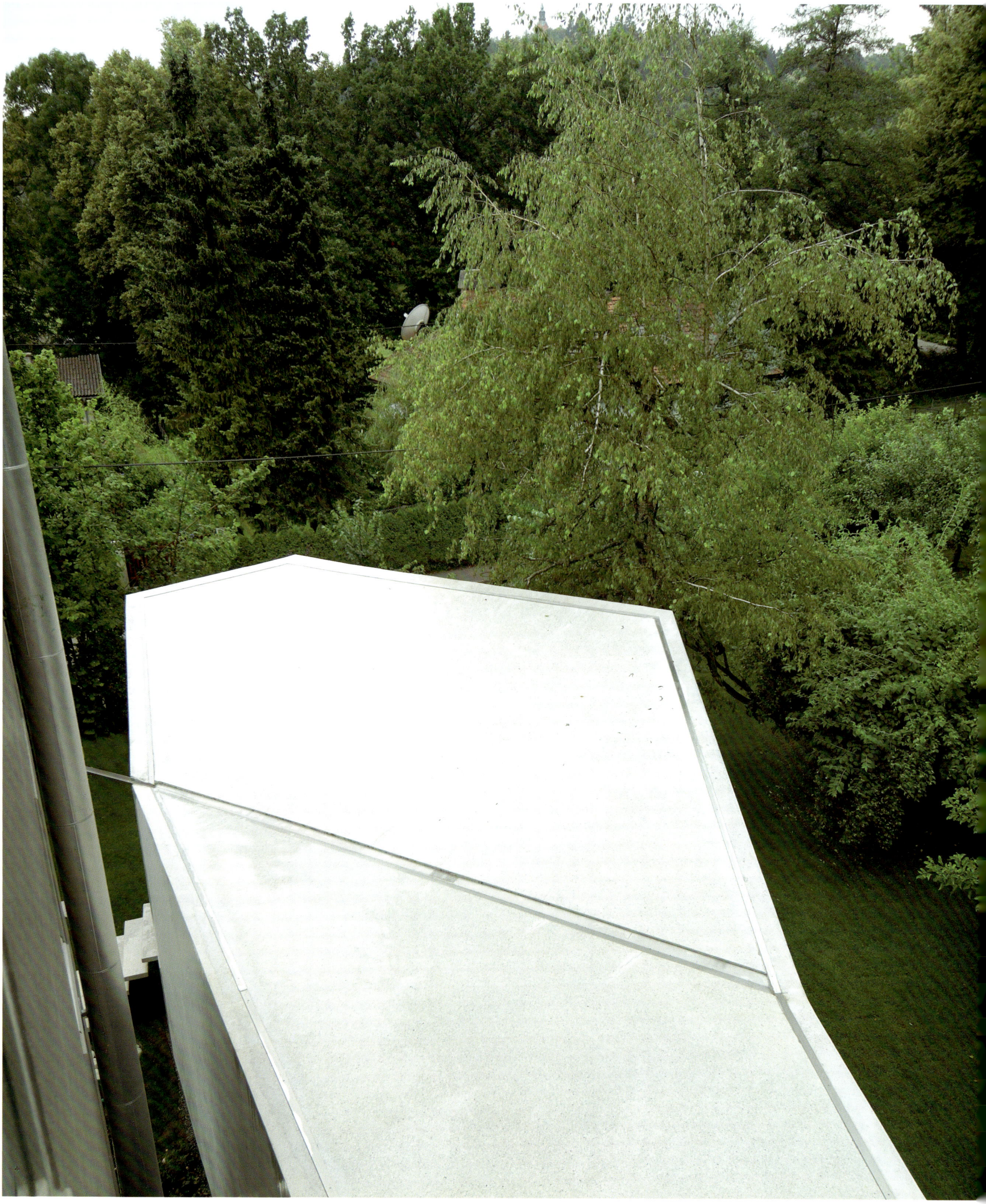

The new extension contrasts with the rest of the house. Whereas everything in the existing building is conventionally orthogonal, the extension has an irregular floorplan; where the rest of the house is a self-contained volume, the extension is open to the garden.

Miralles Tagliabue - EMBT
Vigo University Campus

The vitality of each faculty of Vigo University made it necessary to redefine what the qualities of this place should be and how they would be projected in the future. The task required coordination between the different operations already under way: a new access ring road, car parks, extensions to each faculty, integrated services, reforestation and a global proposal for the waste water collector.

The proposal was based on two apparently opposing lines of thought. The first was to emphasize the natural surroundings of the site while the second intended the new constructions to define a community spirit for students. The site is set in a magnificent location in Galicia, northern Spain, surrounded by green valleys. The project allows students to connect with this landscape and thus use it to help create the ideal atmosphere for study and concentration.

Trees have been planted in the large sports area transforming it into a forested space, defined by a large lake, which blurs the access infrastructure. The access road, in fact, will take on the characteristics of a tree-lined country road. The new series of buildings include services for students, shopping areas, a swimming pool and a gymnasium, among others. The project lends these spaces a sense of community through the use of squares inserted adjacent to some of the existing buildings. Slight modifications to the topography allow new constructions to be more open with a public feel to them. There are three such squares: by the rectory, the shopping area and the service space for students. They connect the new entrance with the new student residences. This section of the project has redefined the upper level of the university campus.

The walkway has been mounted on stilts allowing views from within the squares of the surrounding landscape and thus giving the interior of the compound a strong sense of open space. Stairs at regular intervals lead up to the construction, which banks around to form a long curve. From inside, large windows allow ample natural light to enter and again offer excellent views over the landscape and the inside of the campus. The concrete used for most of the space inside the new upper section contrasts sharply with the areas of lawn inserted between the parking spaces and the rest of the campus buildings. Both colors, the green from the grass and the gray from the concrete, recall the local landscape: rolling grass-covered hills and rocky mountains.

Architect:
Miralles Tagliabue - EMBT
Location:
Vigo, Spain
Photographs:
Duccio Malagamba

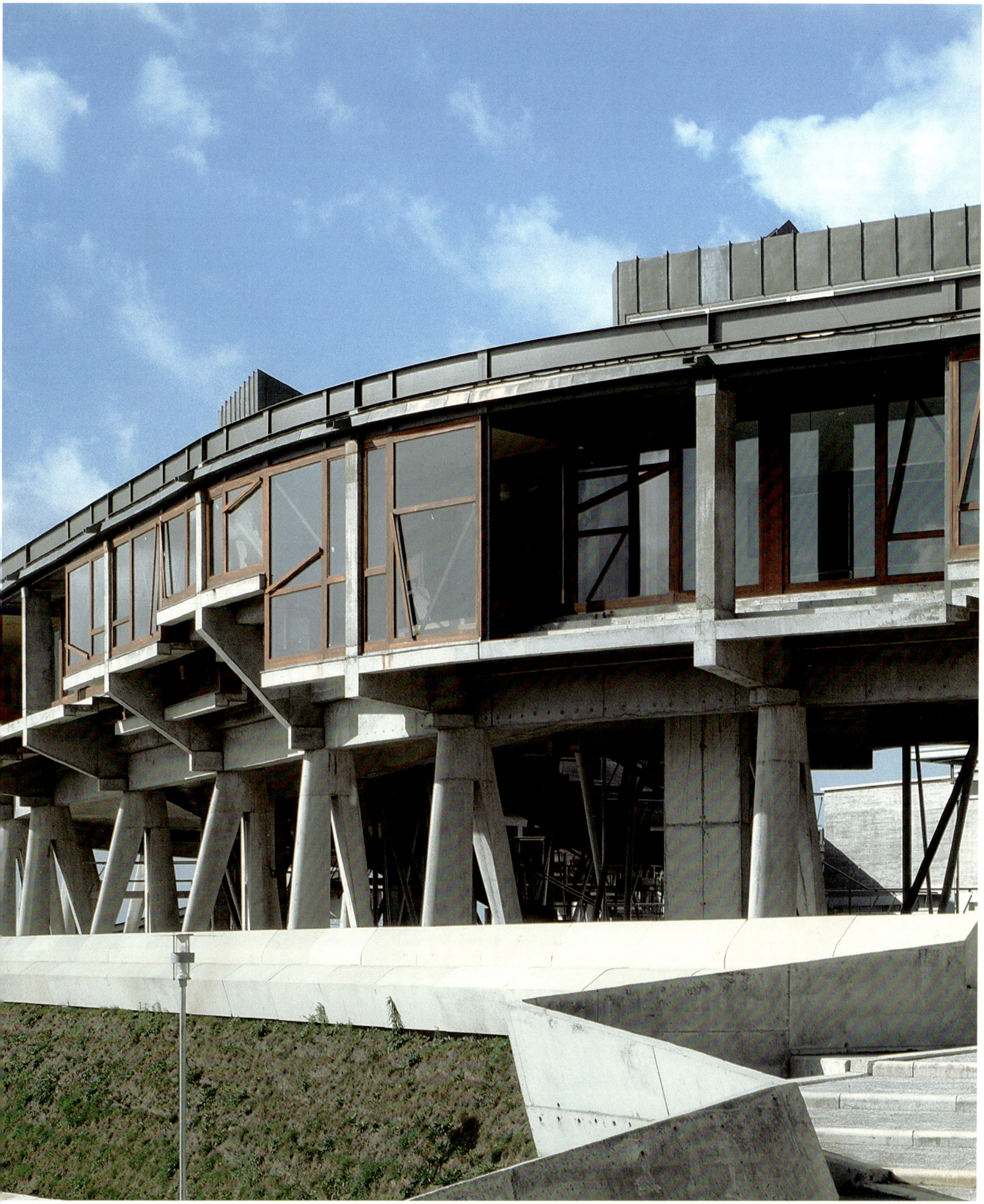

VIGO NOVO CAMPO

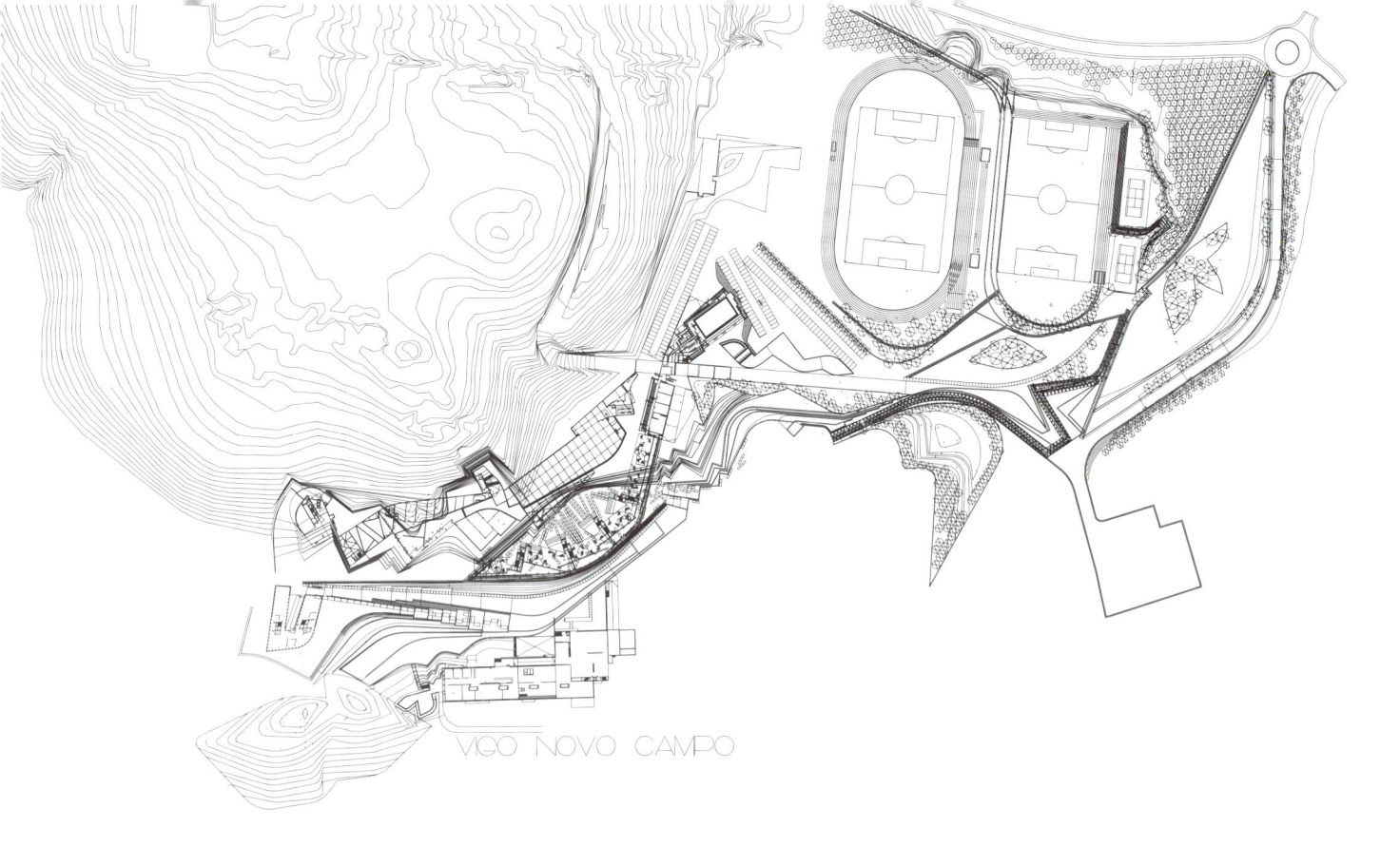

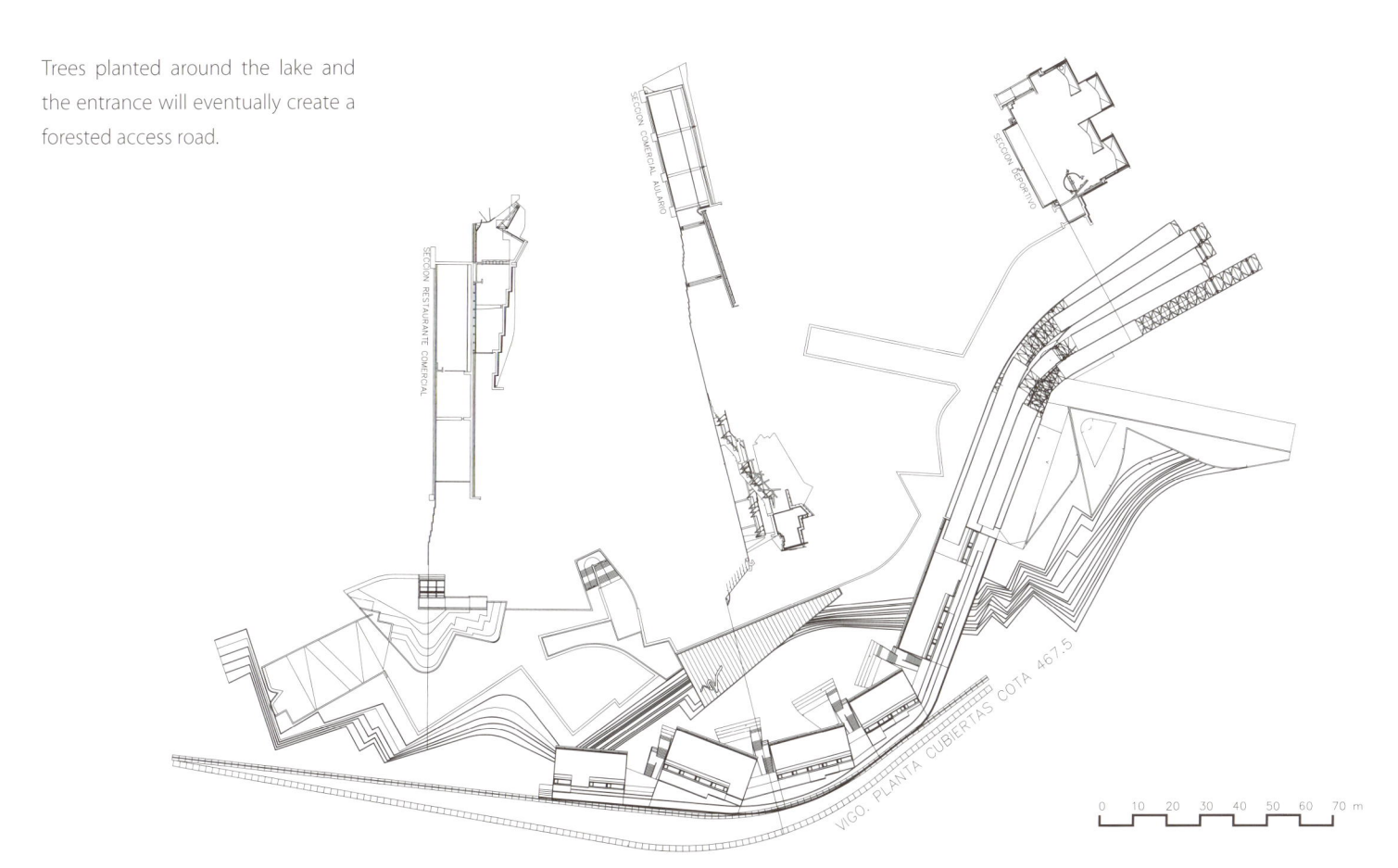

Trees planted around the lake and the entrance will eventually create a forested access road.

Side view

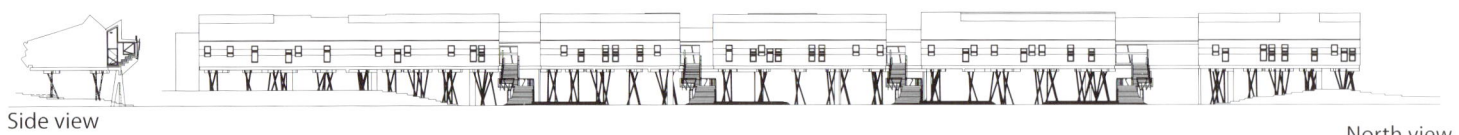

North view

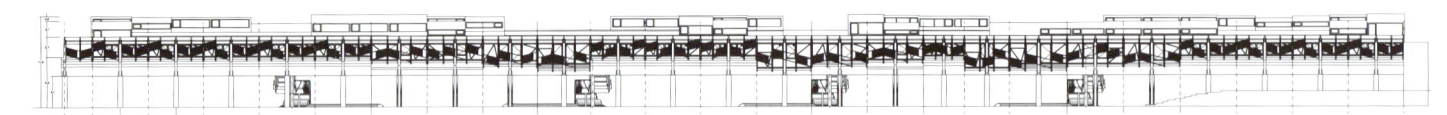

South view

172 Miralles Tagliabue - EMBT

Frontal view from square

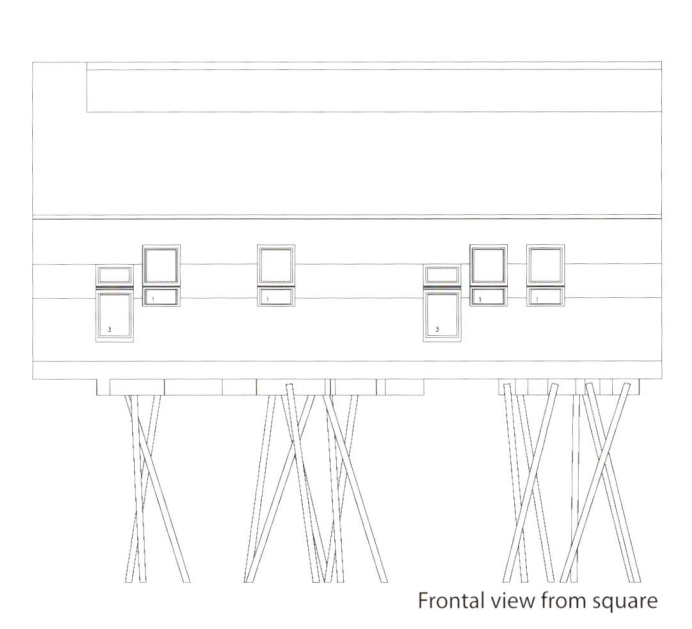

Miralles Tagliabue - EMBT

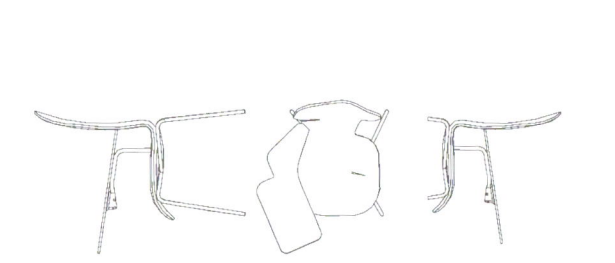

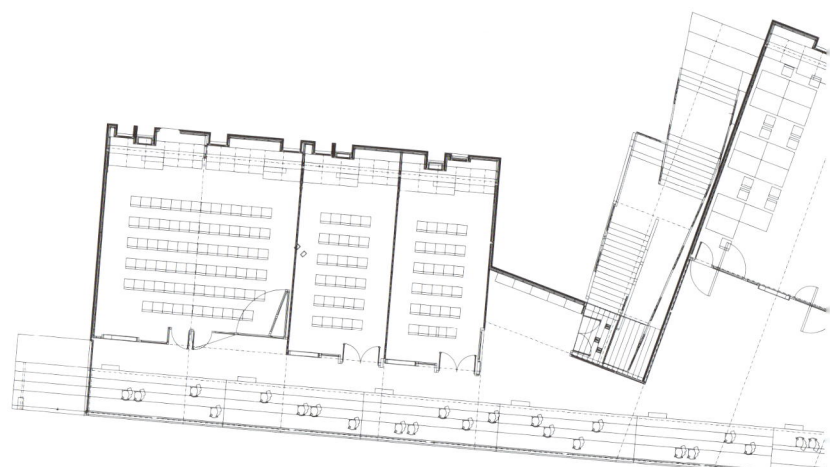

174 Miralles Tagliabue - EMBT

Façade detail

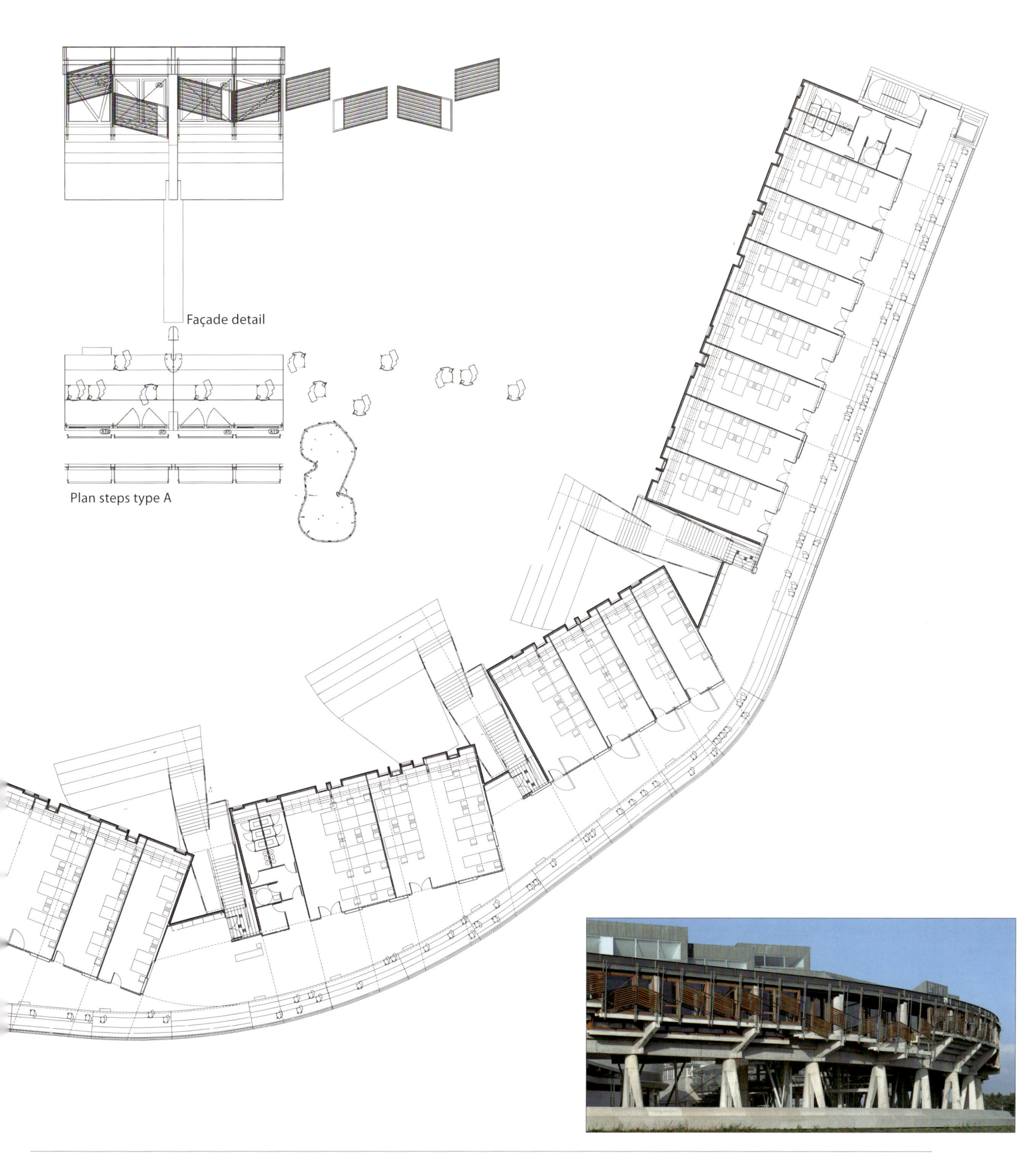

Plan steps type A

Miralles Tagliabue - EMBT

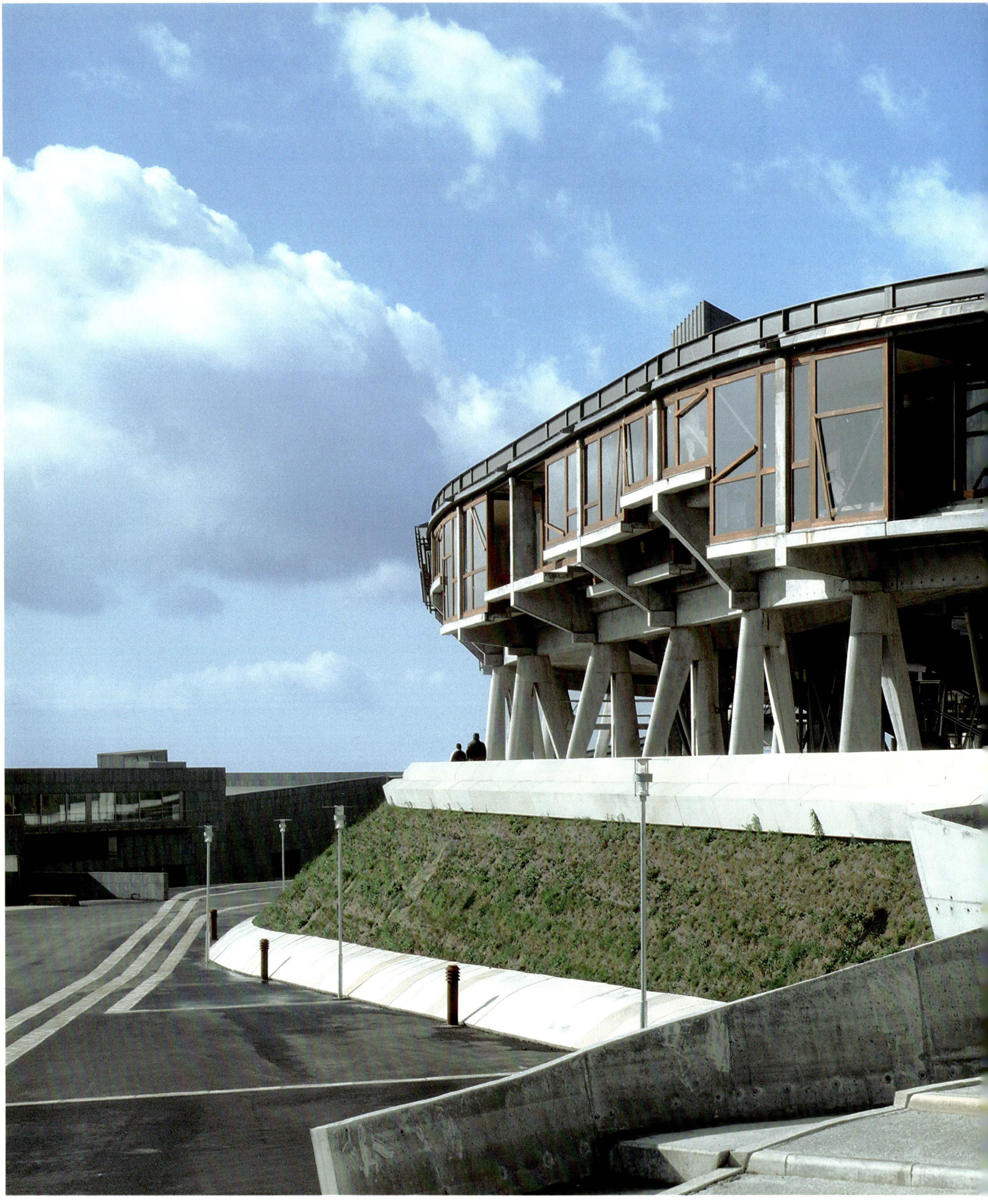

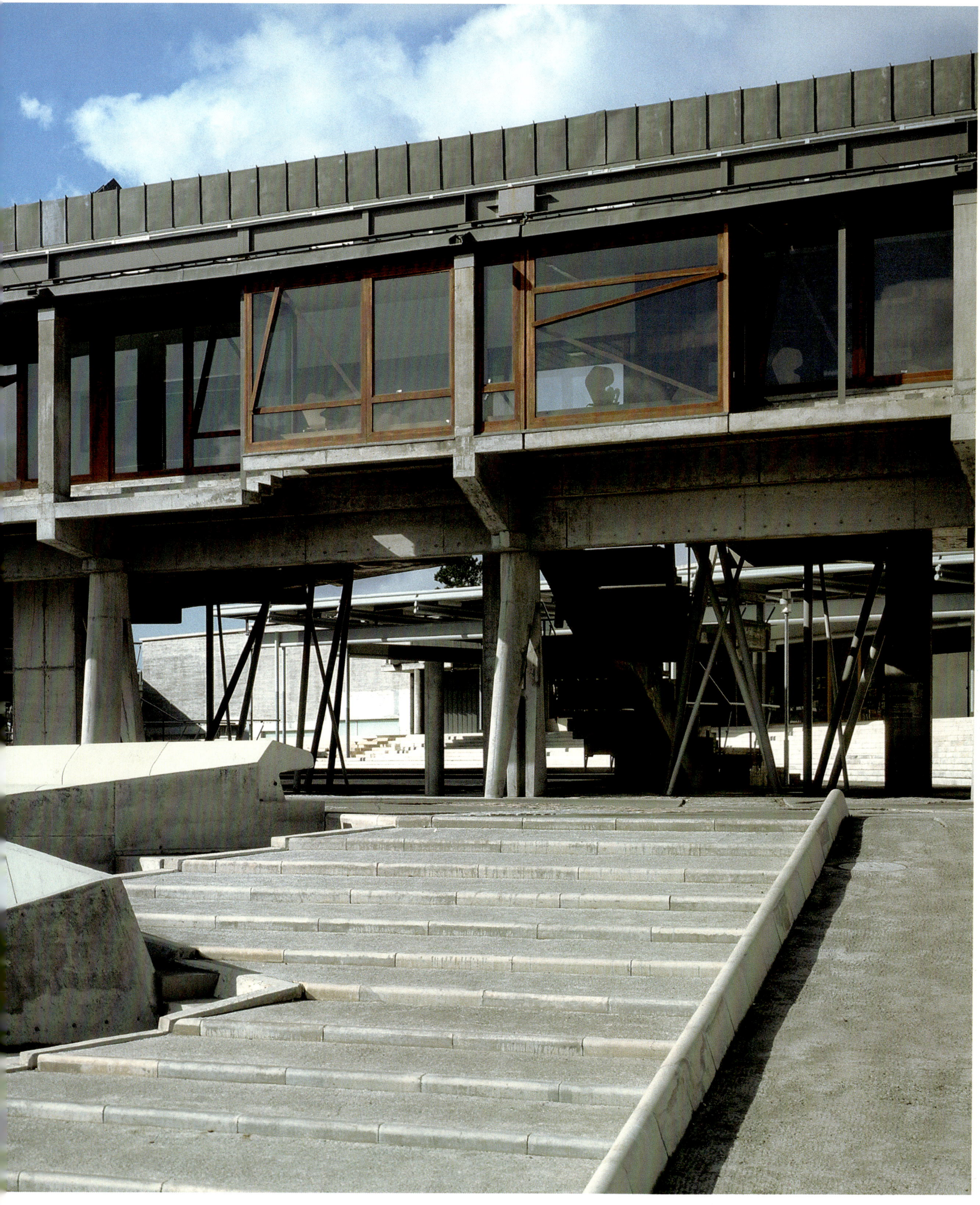

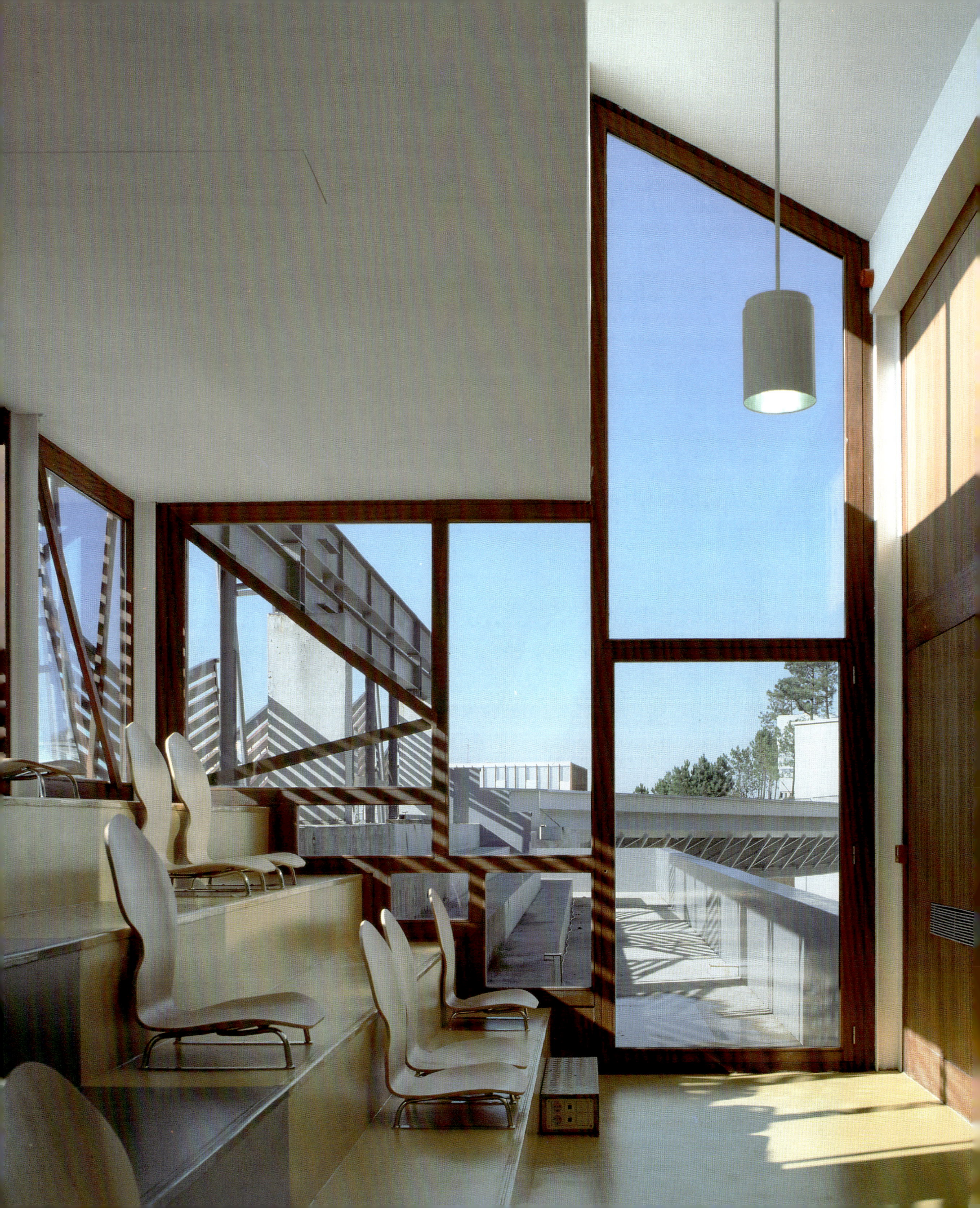

From inside, large windows allow ample natural light to enter and offer excellent views over the landscape and the inside of the campus.

Miralles Tagliabue - EMBT

Stilts prop up the new walkway, thus allowing those inside the campus to be able to see outside and generating a sense of openness.

Window detail
01. Circular tube section
02. T-shaped plate that gives form to the frame
03. Wooden frame

Window detail

Façade

Floor

Cross-section

Plan of paving and bas-reliefs

01. Wooden frame
02. Wooden panel
03. Titanium zinc
04. Painted panel
05. Plate with silicone

180   Miralles Tagliabue - EMBT

Typical section

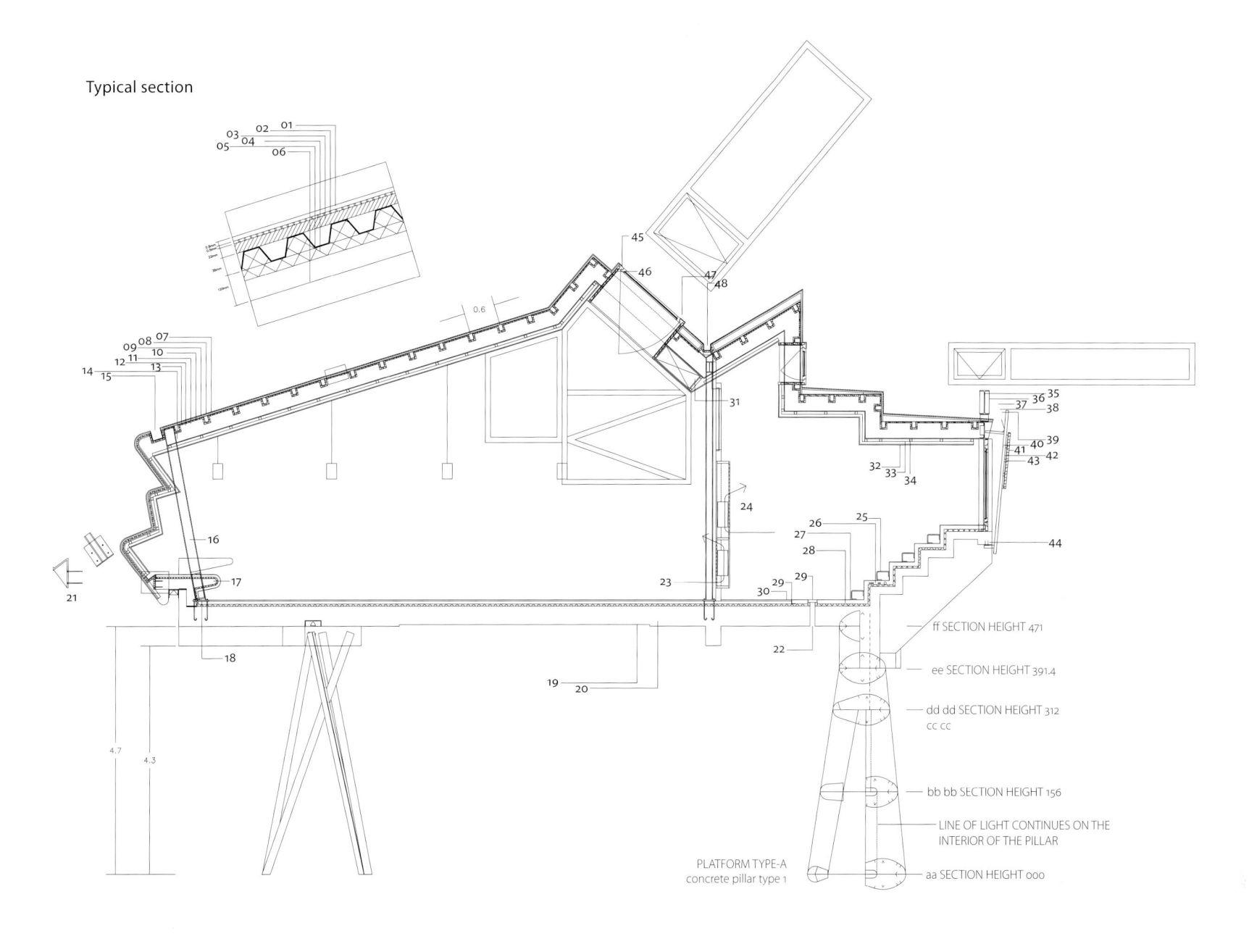

01. Zinc titanium plate 0.80 mm, coils 500 X 31000 mm
02. Stapled numa butyl laminate 0.5 mm
03. Waterproof MDF board 19 mm
04. Extruded polystyrene 40 mm
05. Galvanized ribbed steel plate
06. Steel I-beam 120 X 80 X 4 mm

DETAIL A
07. Zinc titanium plate 0.80 mm, coils 500 X 31000 mm
08. Stapled numa butyl laminate 0.5 mm
09. Waterproof MDF board 19 mm
10. Extruded polystyrene 40 mm
11. Metal bracing 120 x 50 x 600 mm
12. Galvanized ribbed steel plate
13. Steel I-beam 120 X 80 X 4 mm
14. IPE 330 mm
15. Zincified steel gutter
16. HEB 160
17. Prefabricated steel bench
18. Base plate for steel column
19. Bas relief 30 mm
20. Reinforced concrete slab 380 mm

DETAIL B
21. Anchor plates 8/10 mm welded to formwork
22. Hollow slab 100 x 100 mm
23. HEB 140
24. Wooden fan-coil housing
25. Maintenance access
26. Wiring duct
27. 3 mm Self-levelling mortar with epoxy resin
28. 60-80 mm screed, lightly reinforced, finished staightedged, 40 mm extruded polystyrene 35Kg/cm3
29. Slabs 195 x 195 x 50 mm, stainless steel plate flooring joint
30. Linoleum 3 mm
31. Maintenance access
32. Plasterboard 15 mm
33. Rockwool 50 mm
34. Plasterboard guide 50 mm
35. IPE 4 mm
36. Steel haunch
37. HEB connector 140 mm
38. IPE 450 mm
39. L-shaped steel frame 45 mm
40. Rounded hollow frame 50 mm, t=4 mm
41. L-shaped steel frame 45 mm
42. Plate connector t=4 mm
43. Bolondo wood board, trapezoidal section 40 x 40 x 50 x 70 mm
44. Concrete atachment plate, t=10 mm
     L-shaped steel frame 45 mm
45. Roll-up tarpaulin for solar protection
46. Metal framed covered skylight
47. Jamb interior finish with 19 mm board
48. MDF board for painting
     Metal window frame
49. Zincified steel gutter

Miralles Tagliabue - EMBT

Carme Pinós
Cube Tower

The design for this striking tower, situated on a 2,520 sqm (27,125 sqft) site grew from the objective of creating an office building that was ventilated using entirely passive means and lit naturally. By dispensing with the mechanical air-conditioning systems, lifetime energy consumption was considerably reduced and the air quality in the workspaces was improved.

The number of square meters of the building was pre-established but its height was not. Due to this condition, the architects took the decision of projecting a high building based around three concrete cores, which would contain all the installations and vertical circulation. These nuclei constitute the vertical structure of the tower. Variable section girders cantilever out from these pillars to form the different floors. The prestressed floor slabs are supported by these girders without the need for any columns. This facilitated the layout of the 10,000 sqm (107,600 sqft) parking area and generated open-plan office modules.

The building's center, i.e. the space between the three cores of vertical circulation, forms an open shaft which is lit laterally due to the alternate removal of three floors of office modules. This also makes them into windows for this central space allowing air to circulate freely and offering the possibility of doing without air-conditioning.

Given the exclusiveness of the area where the tower is located and the consequent value of its office space, one of the requirements of the clients was the creation of a distinctive building. This singularity is reflected in the spatial characteristics in the tower's interior, but is also evident in the building's external form and the use of materials in the façade. The tower's exterior texture is characterized by a wooden lattice skin with sliding doors that acts as a brise-soleil.

Architect:
Carme Pinós Desplat
Location:
Guadalajara, Mexico
Photographs:
Duccio Malagamba

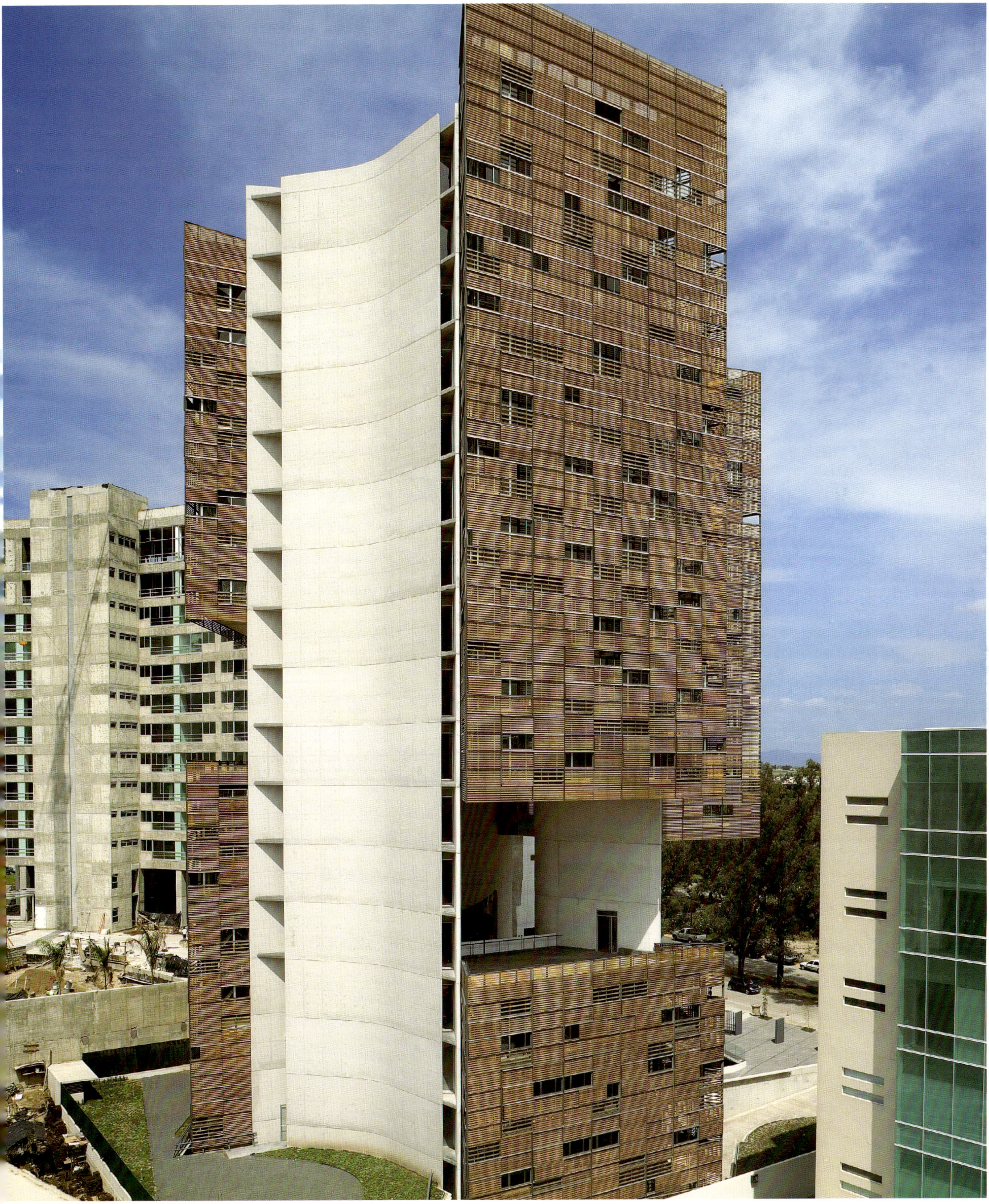

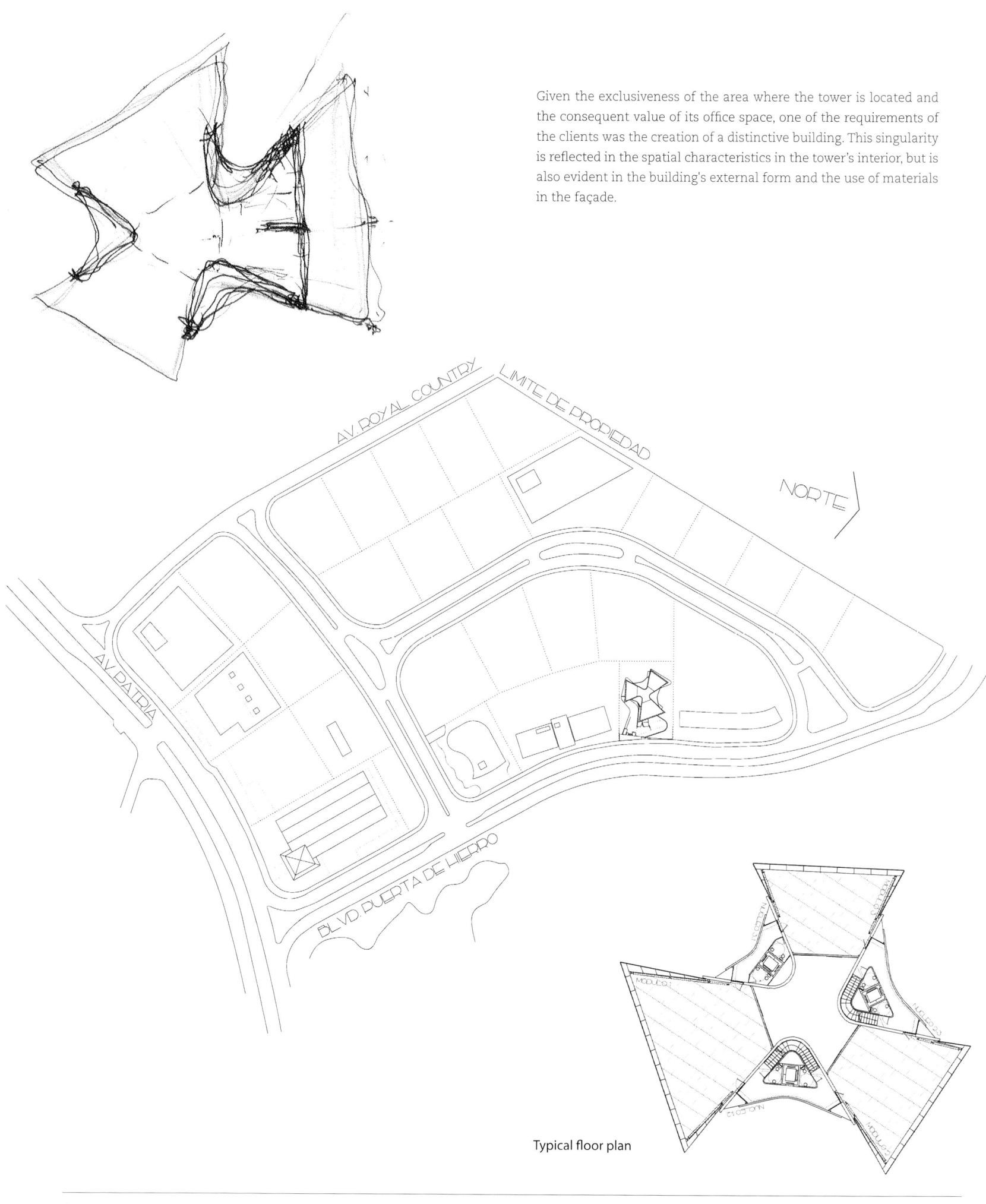

Given the exclusiveness of the area where the tower is located and the consequent value of its office space, one of the requirements of the clients was the creation of a distinctive building. This singularity is reflected in the spatial characteristics in the tower's interior, but is also evident in the building's external form and the use of materials in the façade.

Typical floor plan

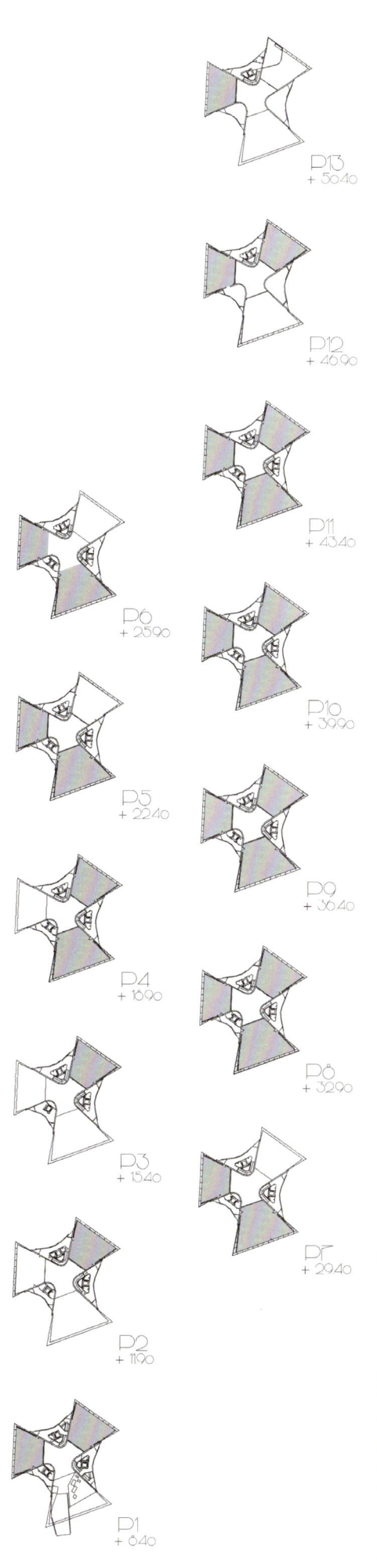

P13 +50.40
P12 +46.90
P11 +43.40
P6 +25.90
P10 +39.90
P5 +22.40
P9 +36.40
P4 +18.90
P8 +32.90
P3 +15.40
P7 +29.40
P2 +11.90
P1 +8.40

Carme Pinós

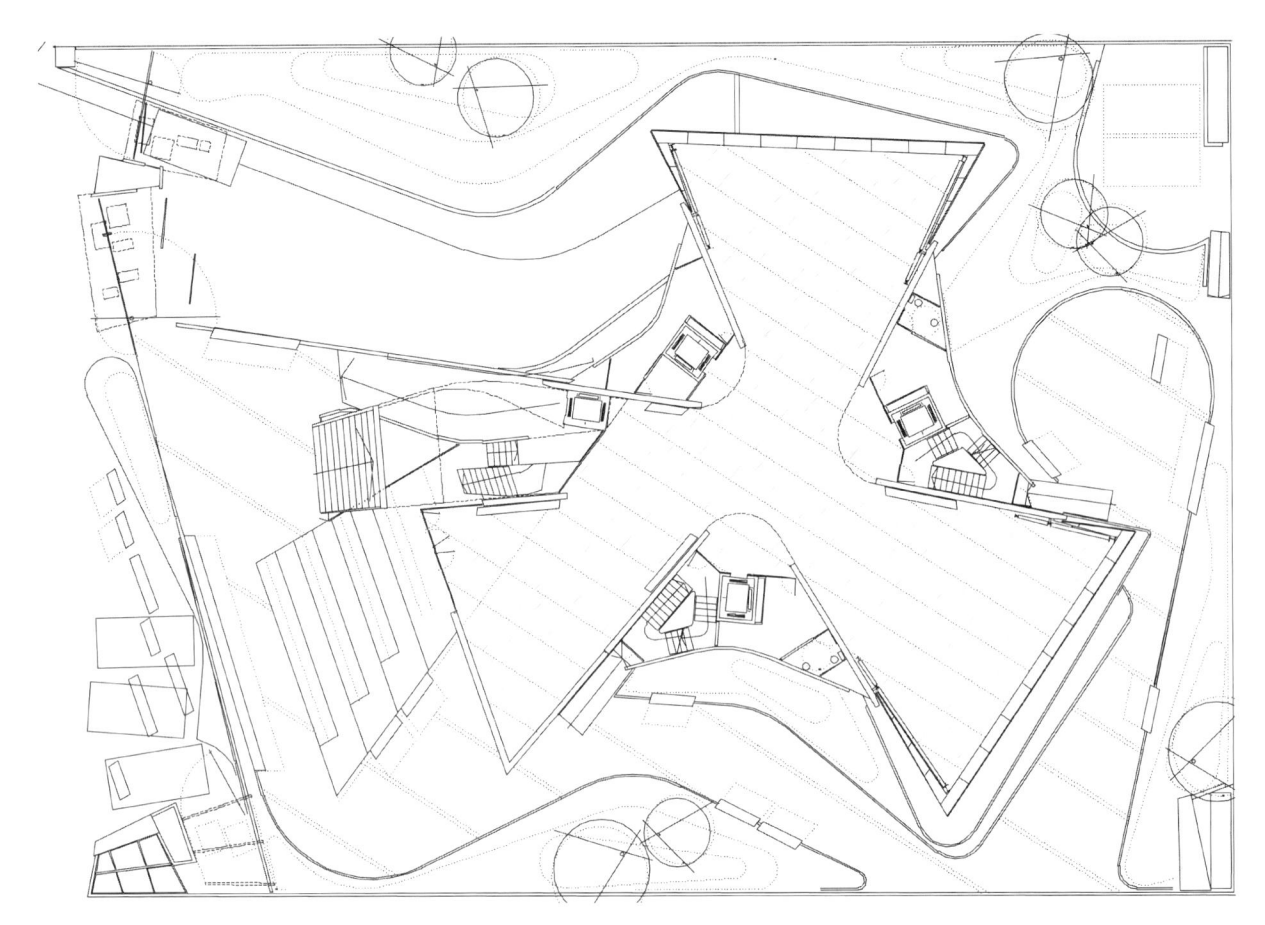

Ground floor plan

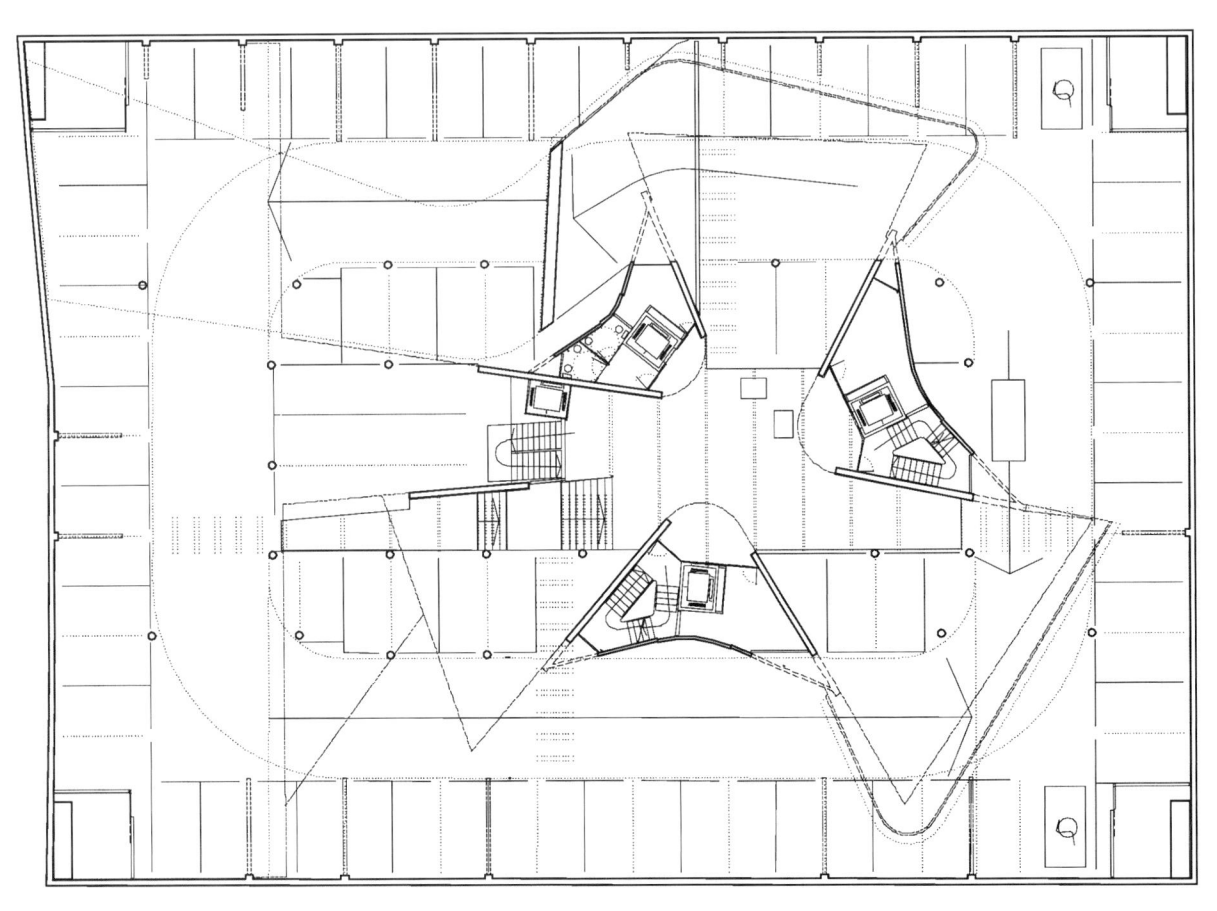

Parking plan

The number of square meters of the building was pre-established but its height was not. Due to this condition, the architects took the decision of projecting a high building based around three concrete cores, which would contain all the installations and vertical circulation. These nuclei constitute the vertical structure of the tower. Variable section girders cantilever out from these pillars to form the different floors.

Entrance level plan

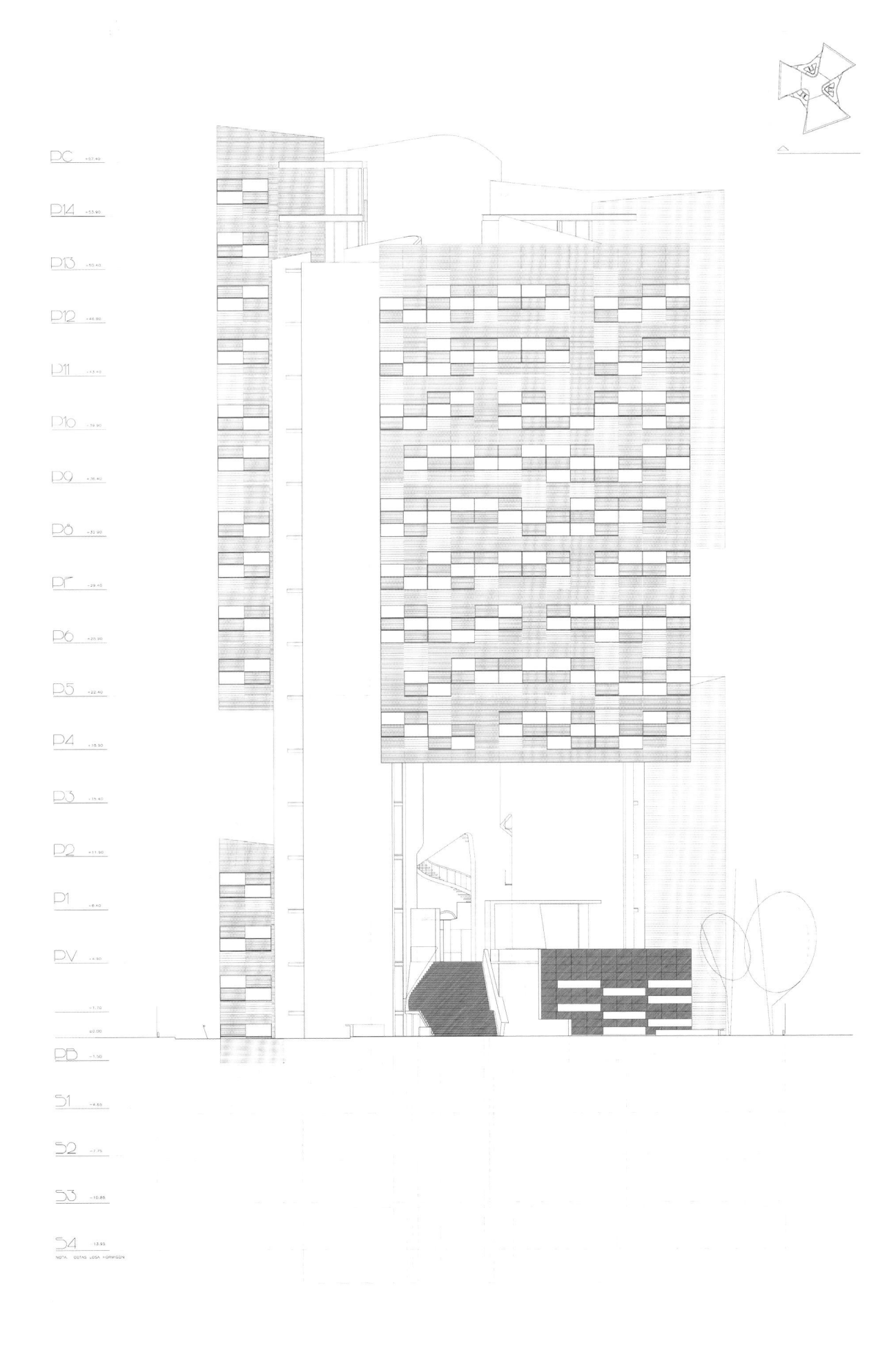

Carme Pinós

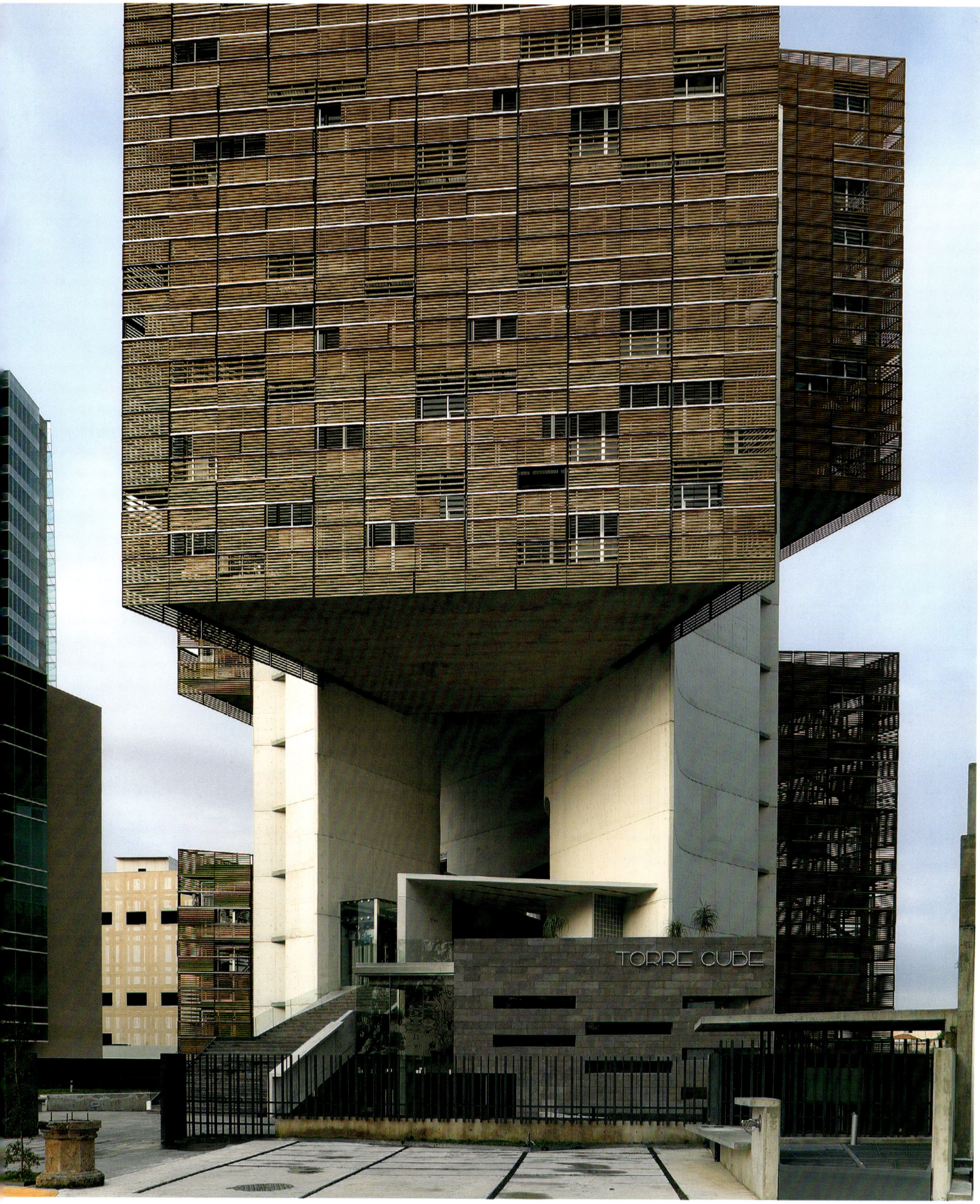
TORRE CUBE

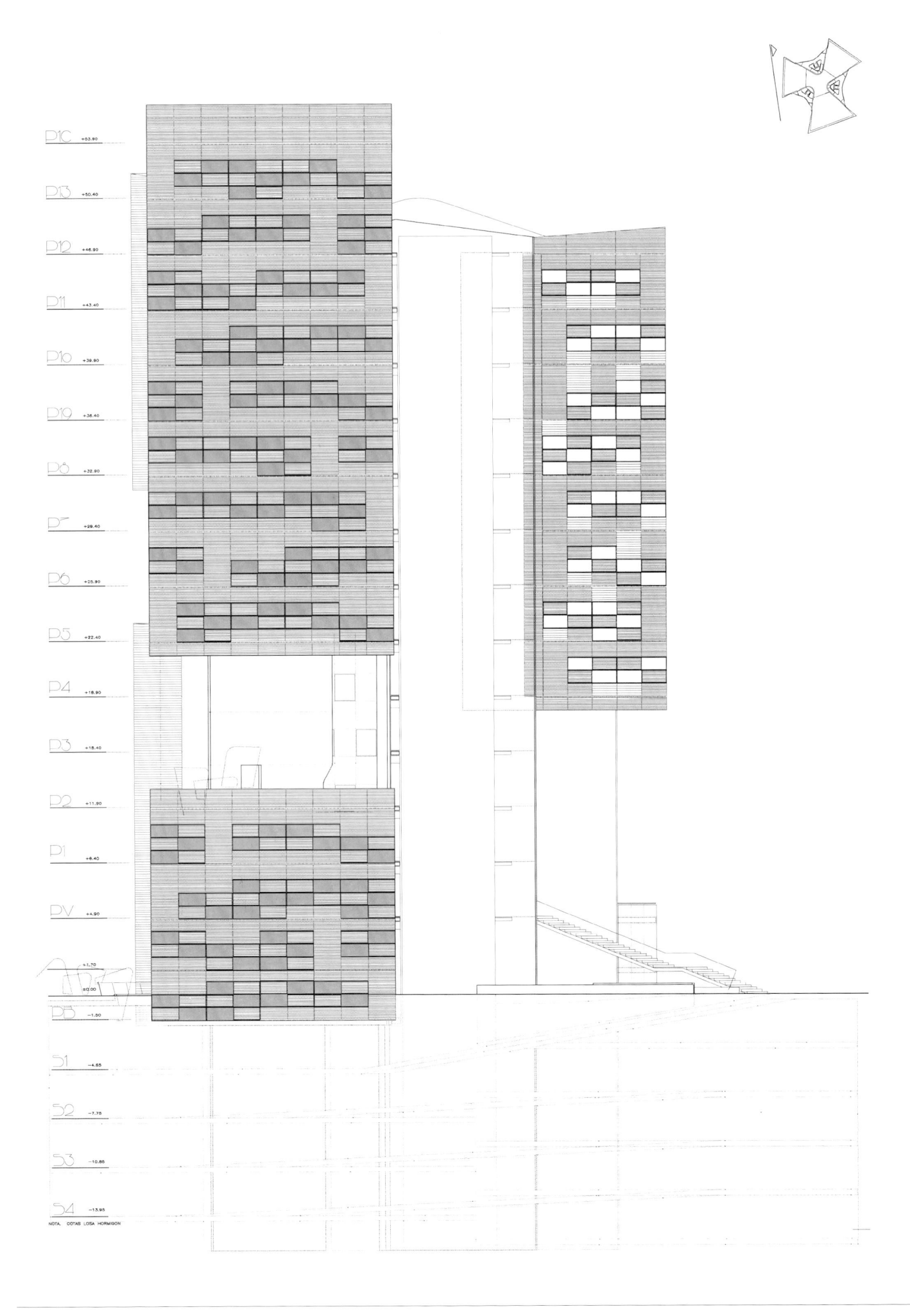

Carme Pinós

The building's center, i.e. the space between the three cores of vertical circulation, forms an open shaft which is lit laterally due to the alternate removal of three floors of office modules. This also makes them into windows for this central space allowing air to circulate freely and offering the possibility of doing without air-conditioning.

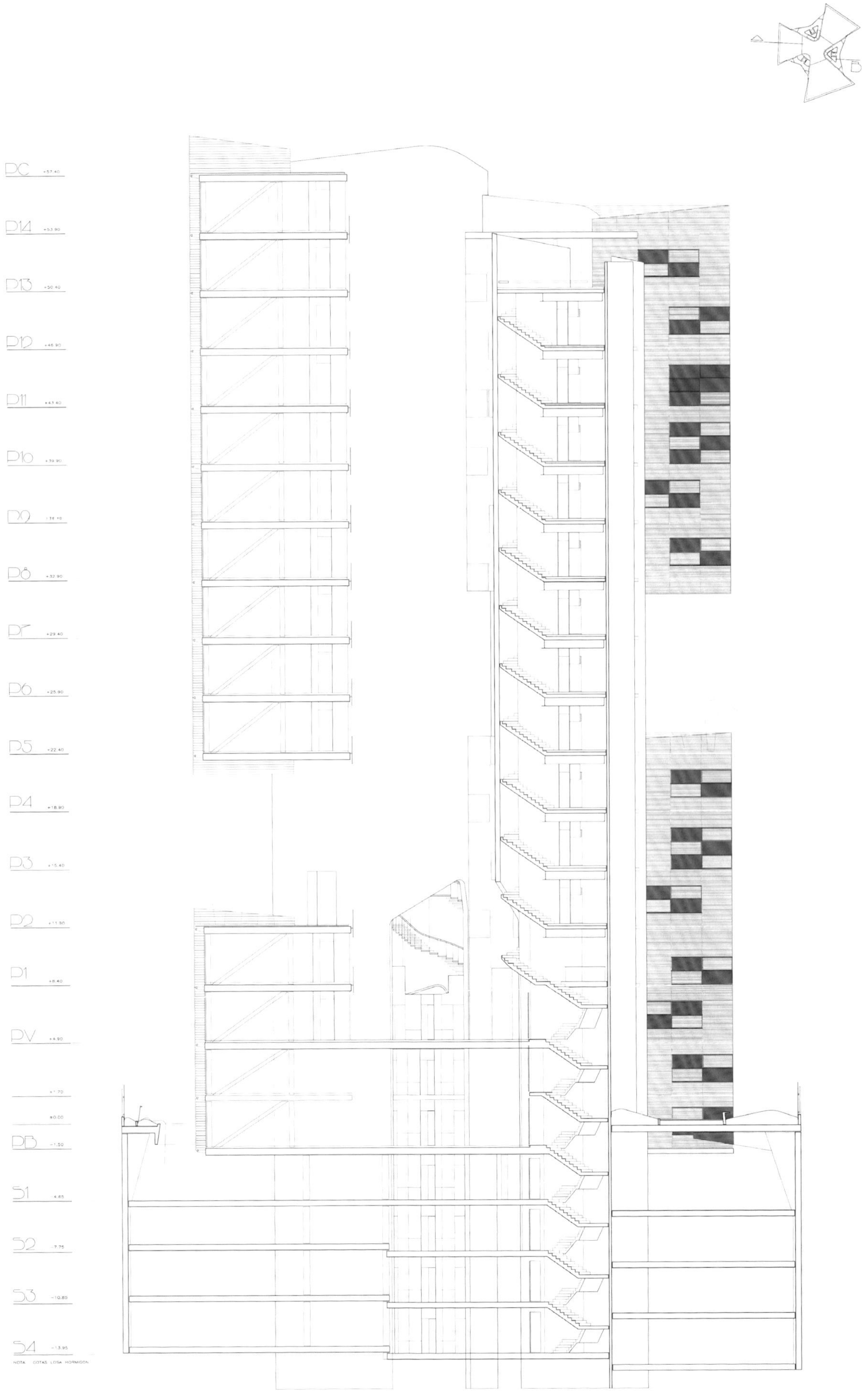
PC +57.40
P14 +53.90
P13 +50.40
P12 +46.90
P11 +43.40
P10 +39.90
P9
P8 +32.90
P7 +29.40
P6 +25.90
P5 +22.40
P4 +18.90
P3 +15.40
P2 +11.90
P1 +8.40
PV +4.90
+1.70
±0.00
PB −1.50
S1 −4.85
S2 −7.75
S3 −10.85
S4 −13.95
NOTA COTAS LOSA HORMIGON

Carme Pinós

Michael Shamiyeh / BAU|KULTUR
Seifert House

A sixty-three year old art gallery curator commissioned this house after fire destroyed her previous home, a building about 150 years old. For her new home she requested daily awareness of the rhythms of nature and its seasonal changes.
Sheltered under the building's single roof plane, and sustaining it at the same time, are two independent "boulders", irregular volumes that determine the only two enclosed parts of the space beneath the roof, which the glass curtain wall encloses. All the interior surfaces are of sand-blasted concrete, except the pastel-colored glazed concrete surfaces inside the "boulders", and the glazed concrete floor throughout, that emphasizes the integrated open plan.
As no columns stabilize the freestanding glass façade, the roof is an entirely cantilevered plane. Although some parts cantilever more than seven meters, the thickness of the roof was reduced by careful design of the reinforcement. Despite its openness and transparency, the general conception, location and shape of the house make it hard to glimpse the interior. The house – which is made of nothing but concrete and glass – was constructed in less than seven months with an incredibly low budget. The photographs were taken before the final garden design.
Regarding thermal performance, it is conceived as a passive energy house (3 layered glazing, high efficiency ventilation system, etc.). The ratio of surface to volume was critical as the ratio of glass to exterior surface could cause overheating in summer. The challenge was to improve the performance to achieve a well-balanced low-energy house with optimal thermal comfort. A simulation tool helped to reach the best interaction between solar gains, thermal mass, heating system and insulation. As the site is partly shaded by trees, a special weather profile was needed to accurately determine the best solution. The targeted air tightness of the building is 0.6 air exchange at 50 Pascal of pressure difference. The heating is by a radiant floor, supported by a high performance heat storage system.

Architect:
Michael Shamiyeh / BAU|KULTUR,
Bureau for Architecture, Urbanism and Culture
Location:
Volkersdorf, Enns, Austria
Photographs:
Paul Ott

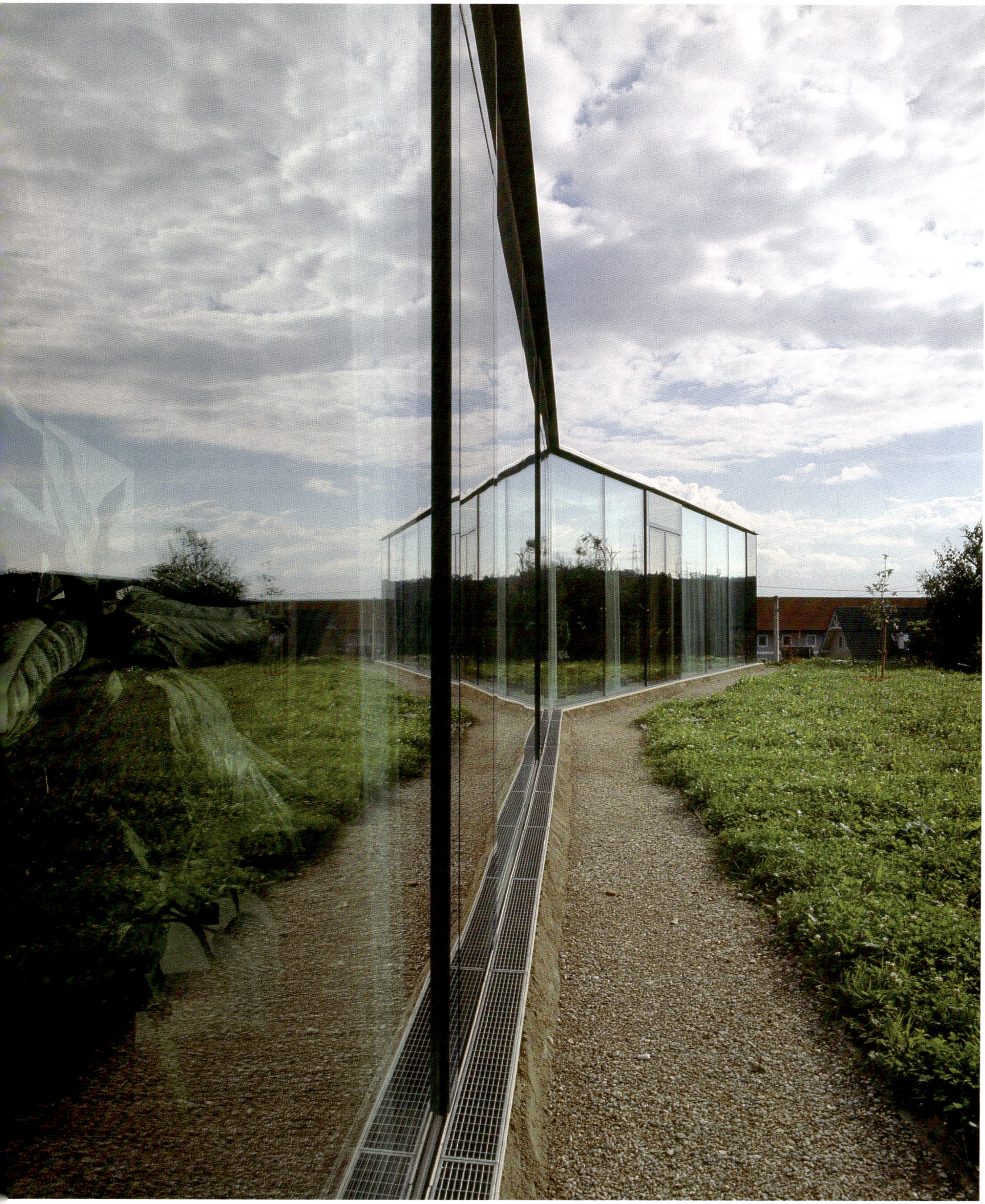

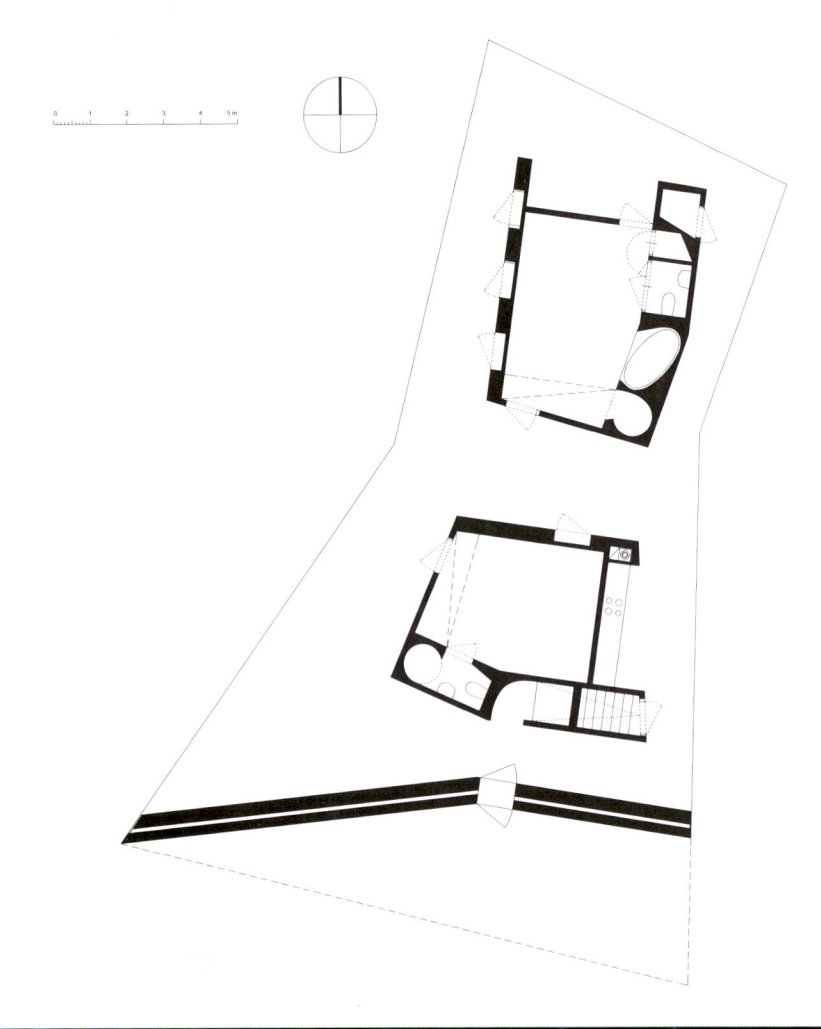

The design process of the house developed into a deep engagement with Mies van der Rohe's houses, in particular with the Farnsworth House, and the question of making a space which was open to the surroundings yet private. It became an investigation into how an open-plan space can effectively determine one's lifestyle, whereas a well orchestrated spatial layout can be liberating. The client spared no efforts to understand the conceptual approach of Mies' architecture, including educational journeys.

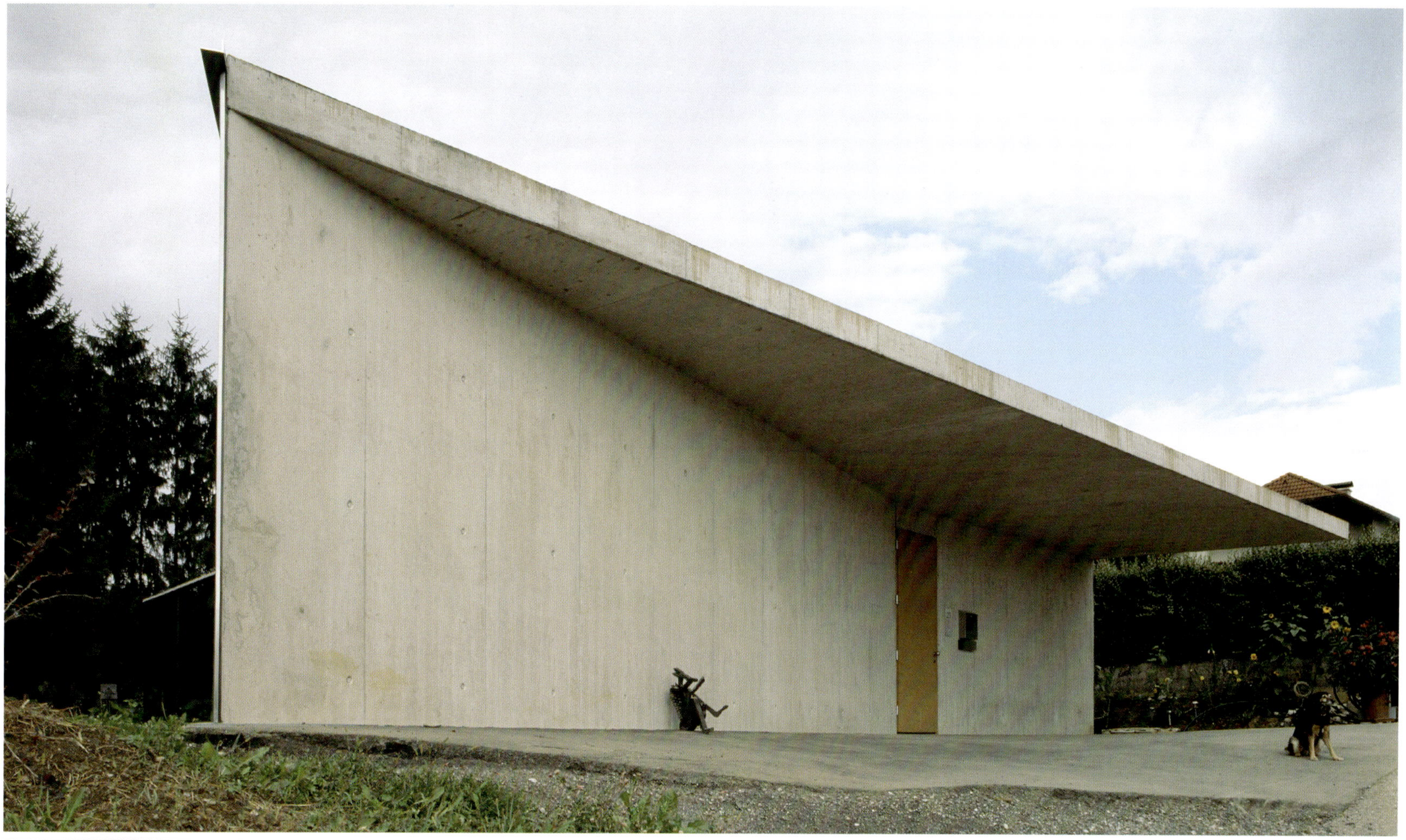

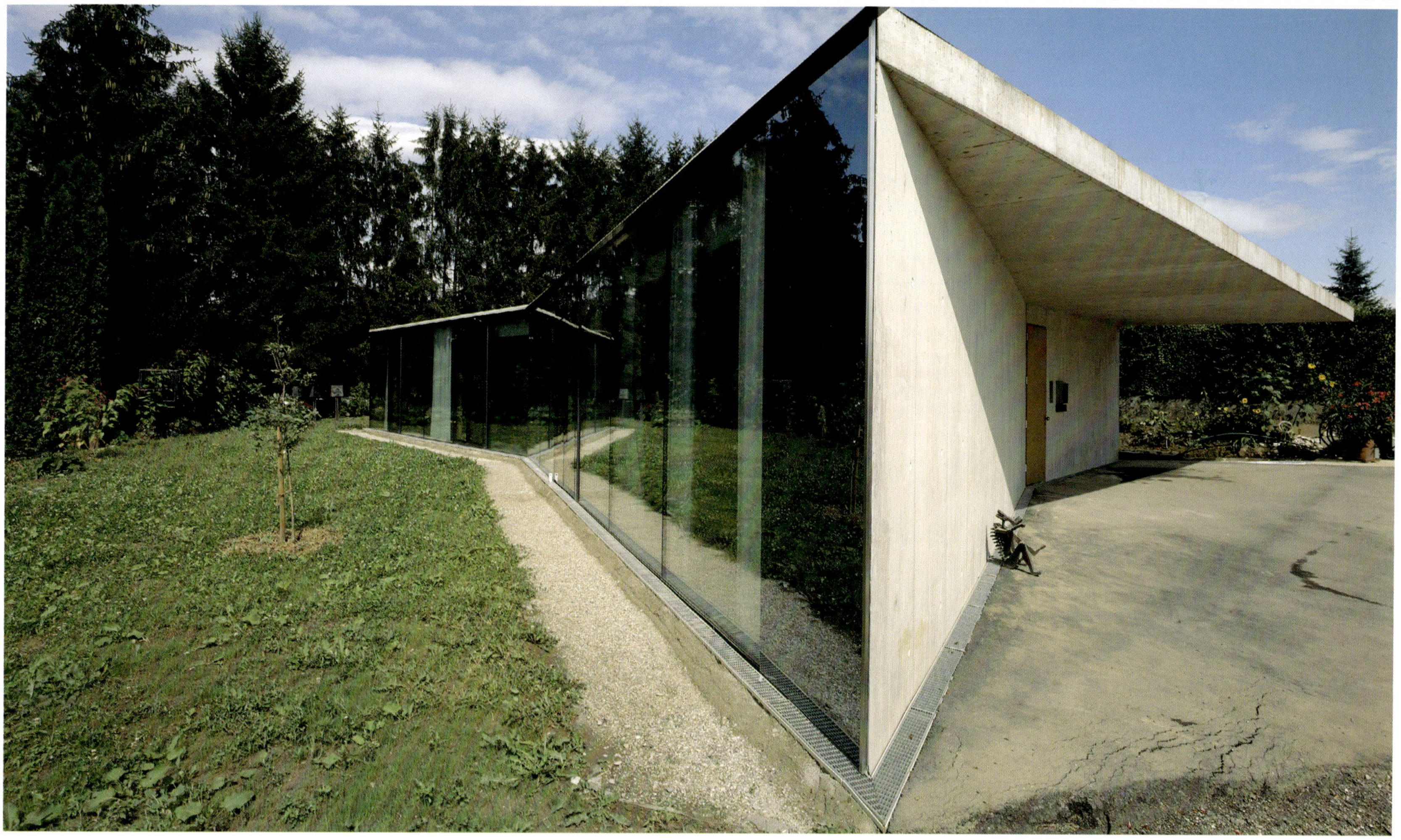

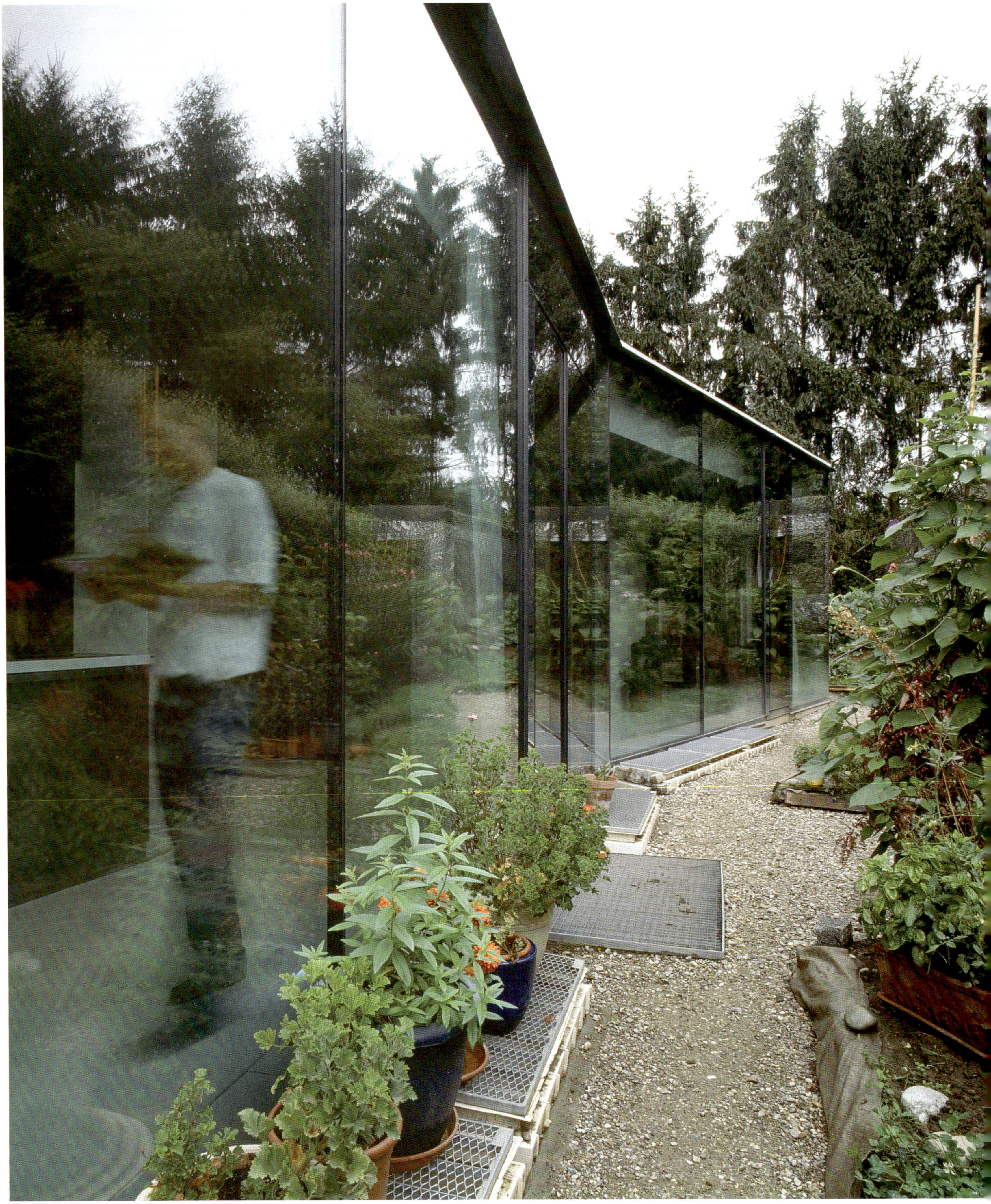

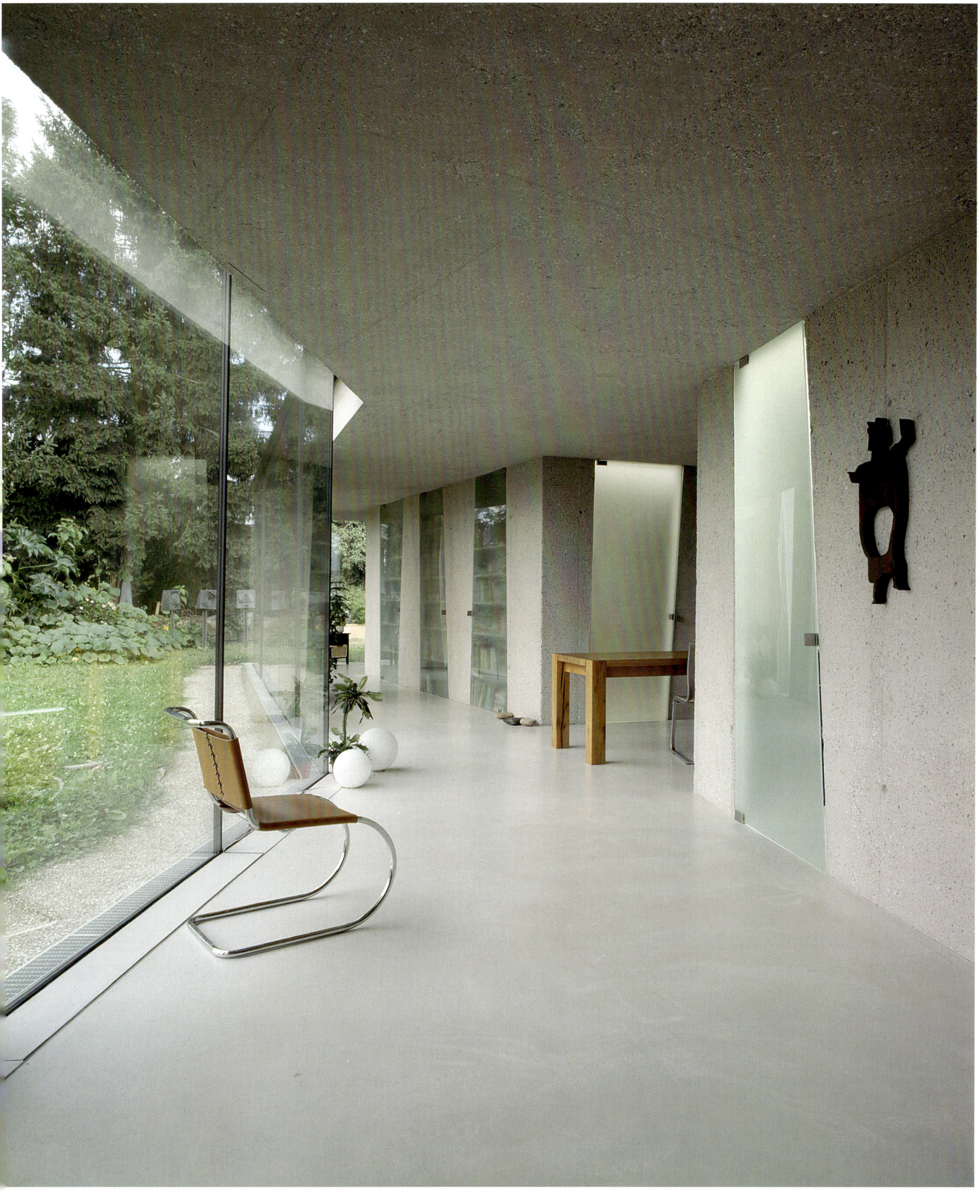

Michael Shamiyeh / BAU|KULTUR

The lighting system is closely related to the building's overall structure: The large niches in the library "monolith", enclosed behind frosted glass panels, become a source of diffuse light after dark. Sun enters the rooms inside the "monoliths" through wide skylights. Despite its openness and transparency, the conception, location and shape of the house make it hard to glimpse the interior. The house – which is made entirely of concrete and glass – was constructed in less than seven months with an incredibly low budget. The photographs were taken before the final garden design.

Michael Shamiyeh / BAU|KULTUR

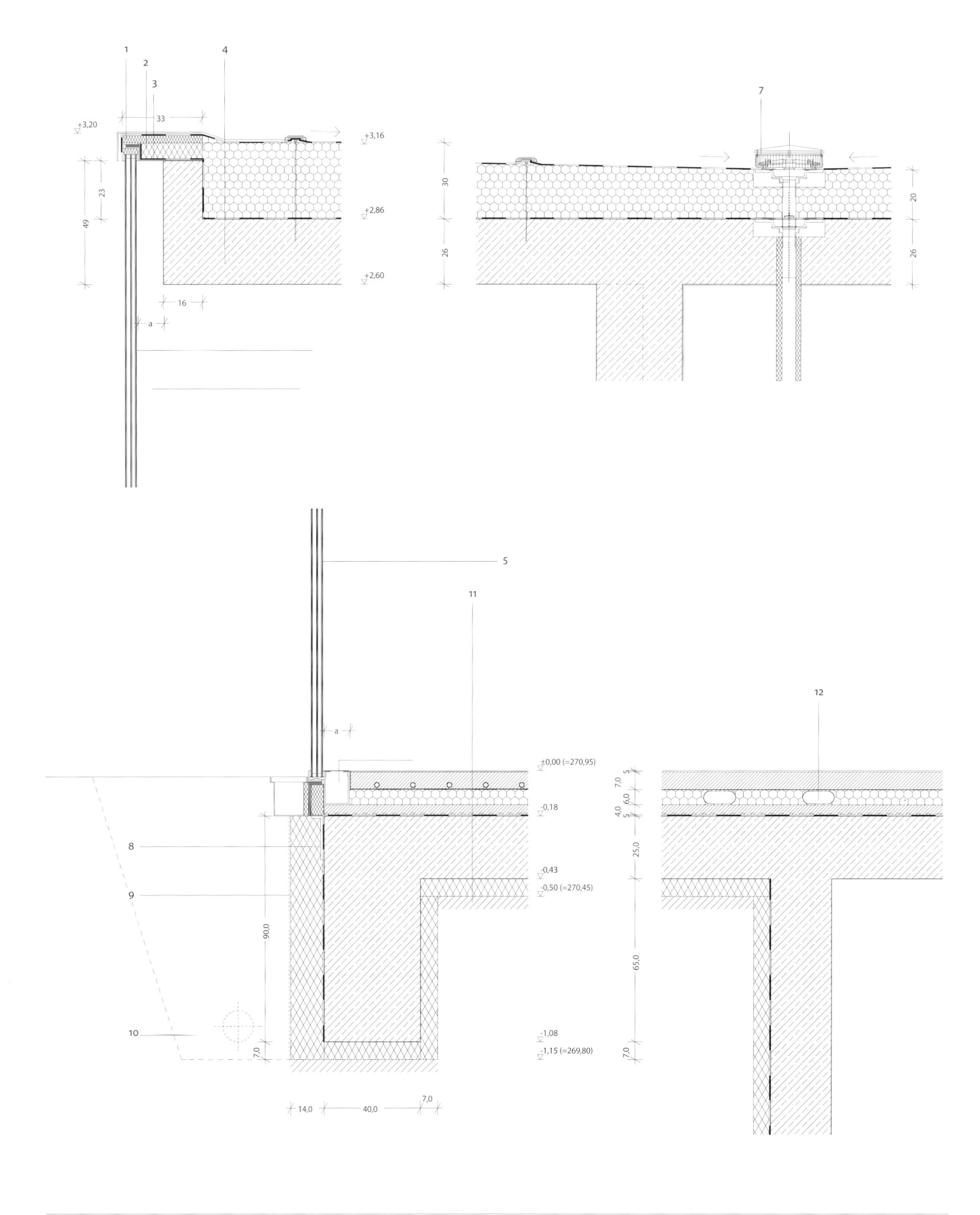

1. 3 cm insulation
2. PUR 70
3. Steel angle
4. Waterproof membrane
   30-20 cm polystyrene and roofing sheet, slope 1.5 % aprox.
   Vapor barrier
   26 cm reinforced concrete
5. Fixed glazing (outward opening doors)
6. Metal frames around door openings
7. Geberit roof drain-hole grid
8. Structural angle, façade construction
9. Synthetic textile against rodents
10. Flexible PVC drainpipe, 1.5 % slope
11. 0.5 cm epoxy resin
    7 cm floorslab
    Vapor barrier
    6 cm polystyrene + TSDPL
    4 cm protective concrete
    Separation layer
    0.5 cm damp-proof layer
    25 cm base-plate
    7 cm polystyrene
    Hygienic layer
12. 12.9 / 5.2 aeration layer embedded in soundproof container

Shuhei Endo
Transtreet G

A play area for children, an unobstructed stretch of grass for sports and a more enclosed, secluded area for quiet contemplation or reading are all integrated into this 2.5-hectare park. The design for this space includes an open, grassy area and a playground on a hill to the west; while to the east lies a sinuous concrete structure comprising a partially walled-in footpath and a waterfall terrace with surrounding pond.

The 120-meter-long footpath gently pulls away from ground level, rising to a maximum height of 2.5 meters before descending to ground level again. A curved, discontinuous wall follows the path, but with sections removed on both sides; a person walking alongside the resulting folds and gaps perceives a series of visual snapshots in which the relationship between interior and exterior is blurred. While the wall goes through multifaceted changes horizontally and vertically, the slope it follows has a certain rhythmic quality, rising and falling as a sequence of arcs, beneath which pass other footpaths.

From the uppermost point of the path, the visitor sees the waterfall terrace opening out to the west with steps placed at 90 and 45 degree angles to each other. The streams of water bounce and splash down alongside the steps, to the wide, shallow pond below.

On the east side, a grassy hillock maintains a relationship with the falling water through the placement of a series of irregular steps where it meets the wall. Stone blocks – serving as benches – have been strewn about on the grassy terrain near the main footpath.

Architect:
Transtreet G
Location:
Fukui, Japan
Photographs:
Yoshiharu Matsumura

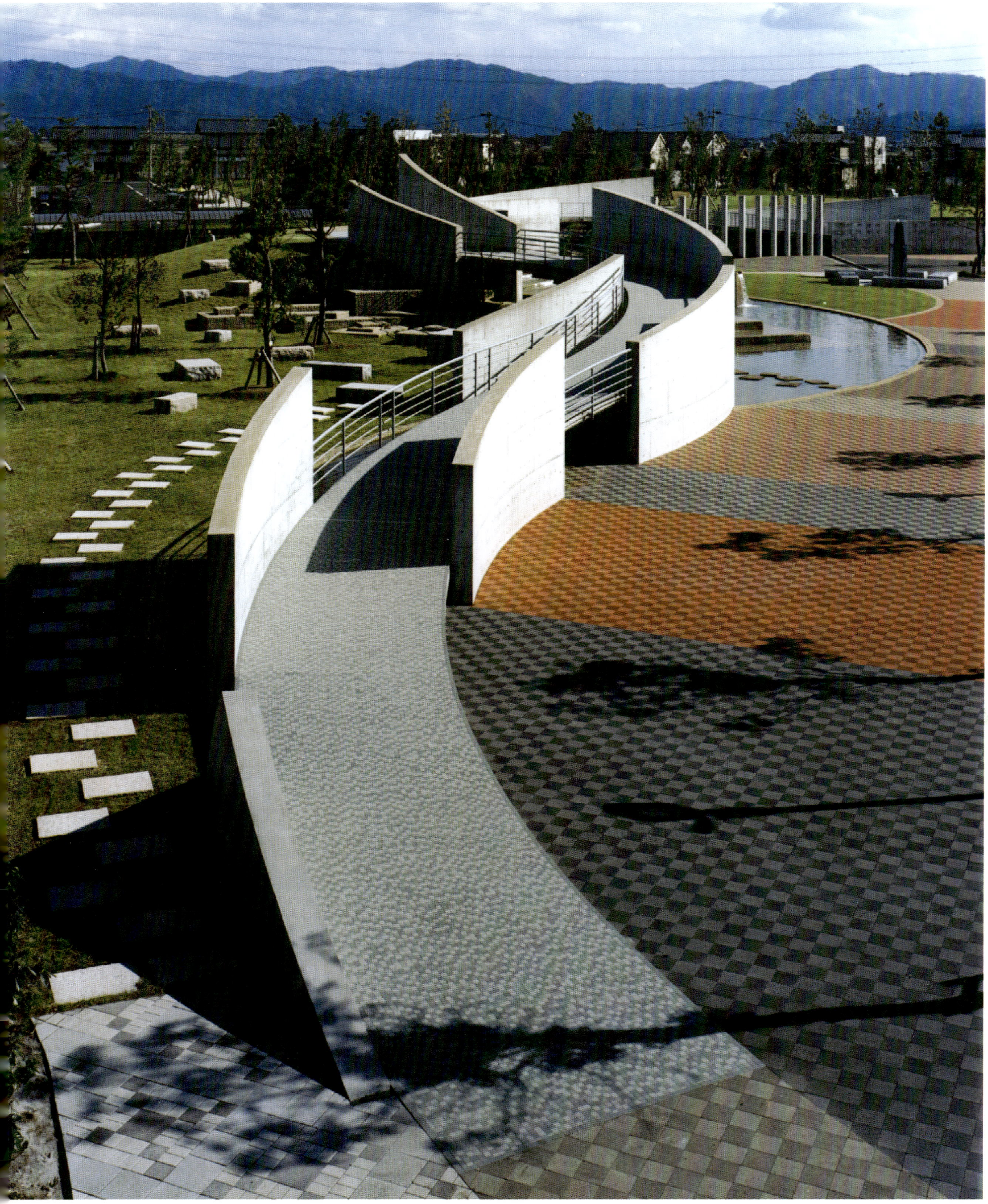

General plan

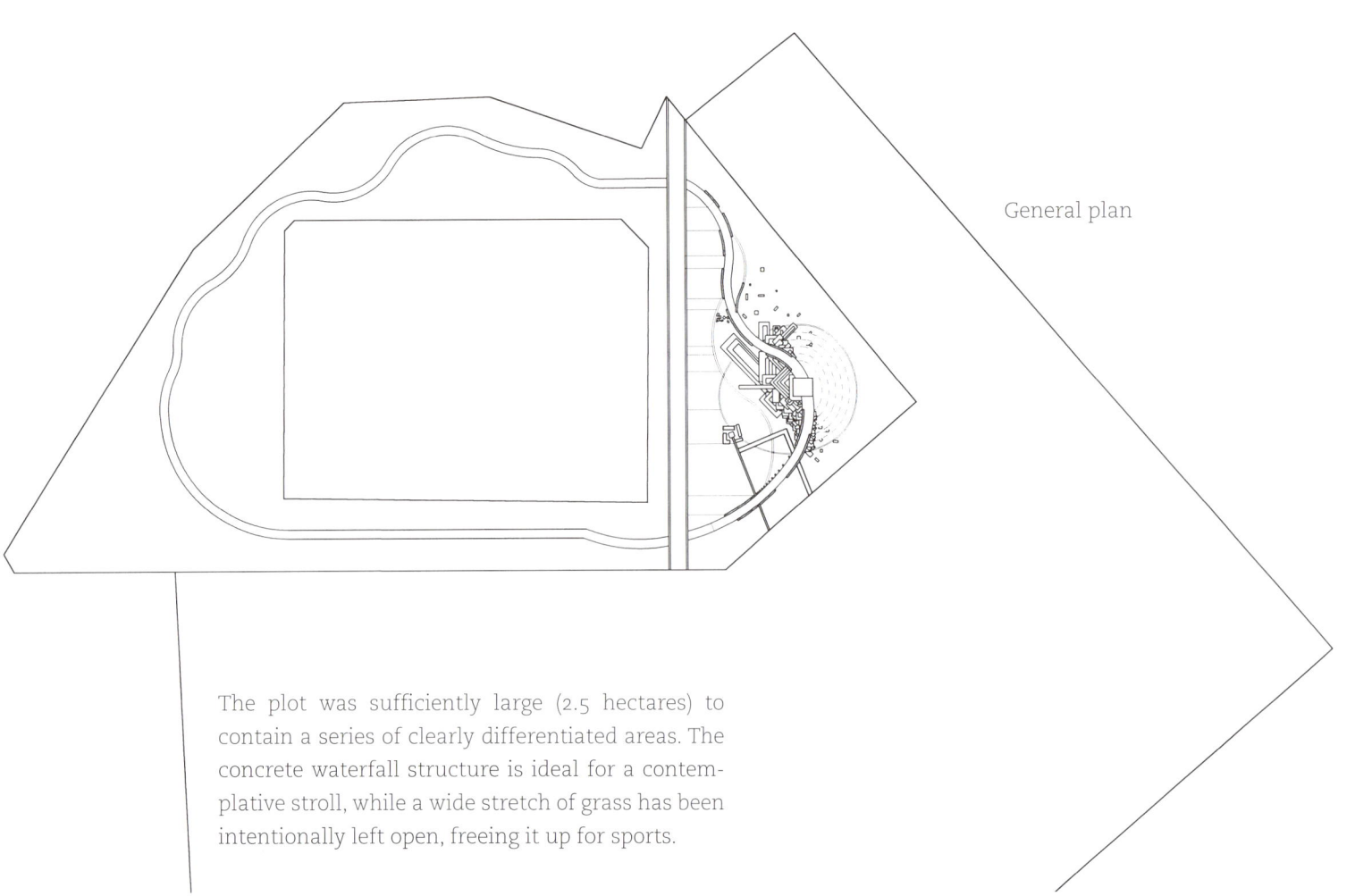

The plot was sufficiently large (2.5 hectares) to contain a series of clearly differentiated areas. The concrete waterfall structure is ideal for a contemplative stroll, while a wide stretch of grass has been intentionally left open, freeing it up for sports.

Shuhei Endo

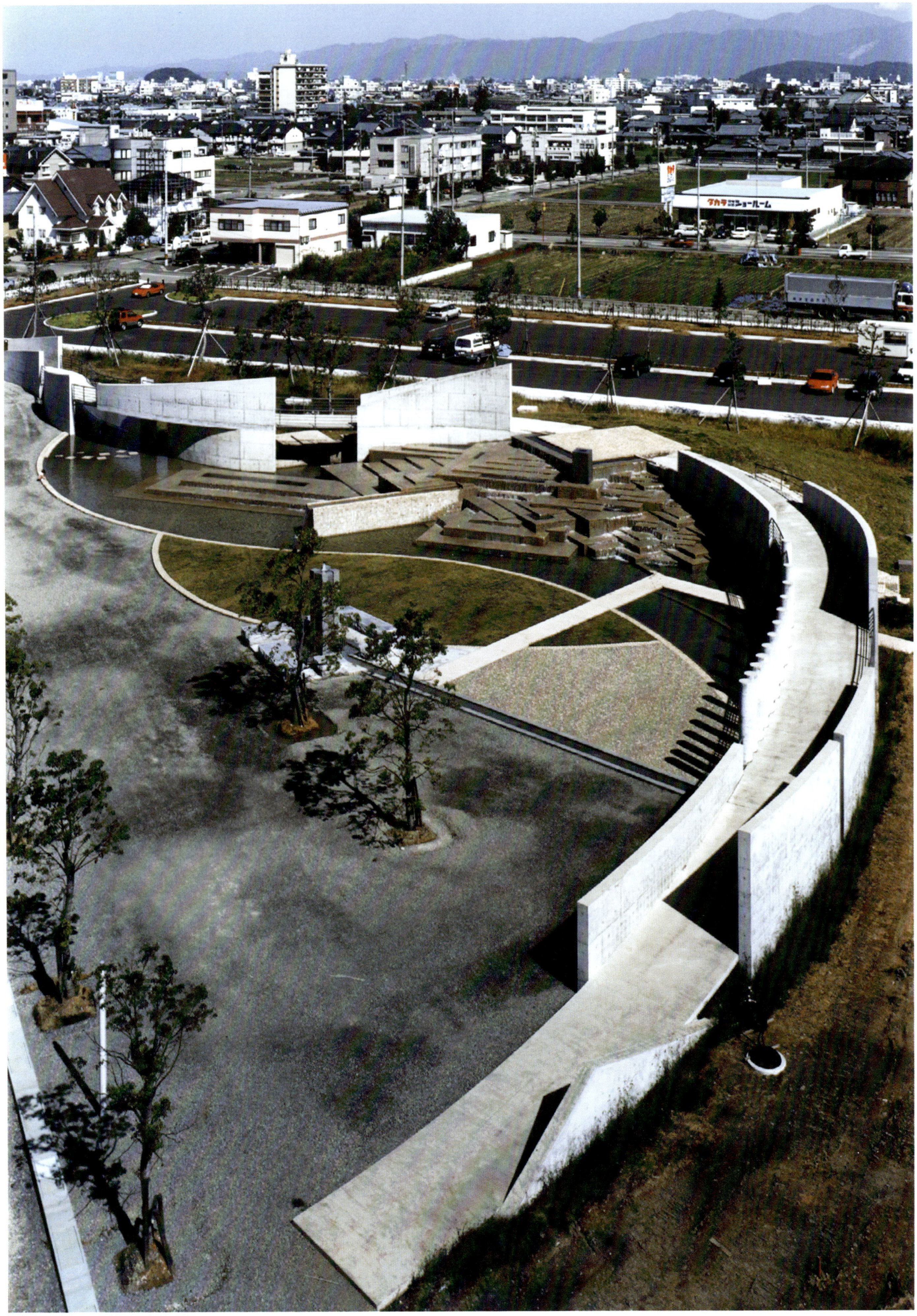

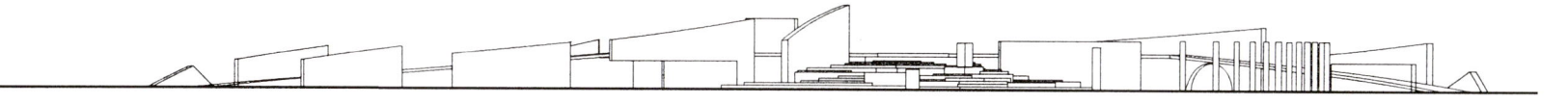

Elevations

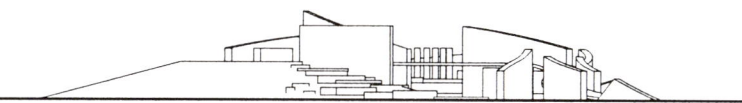

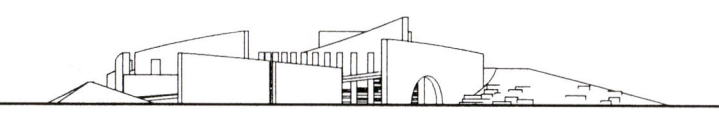

Shuhei Endo

Shuhei Endo

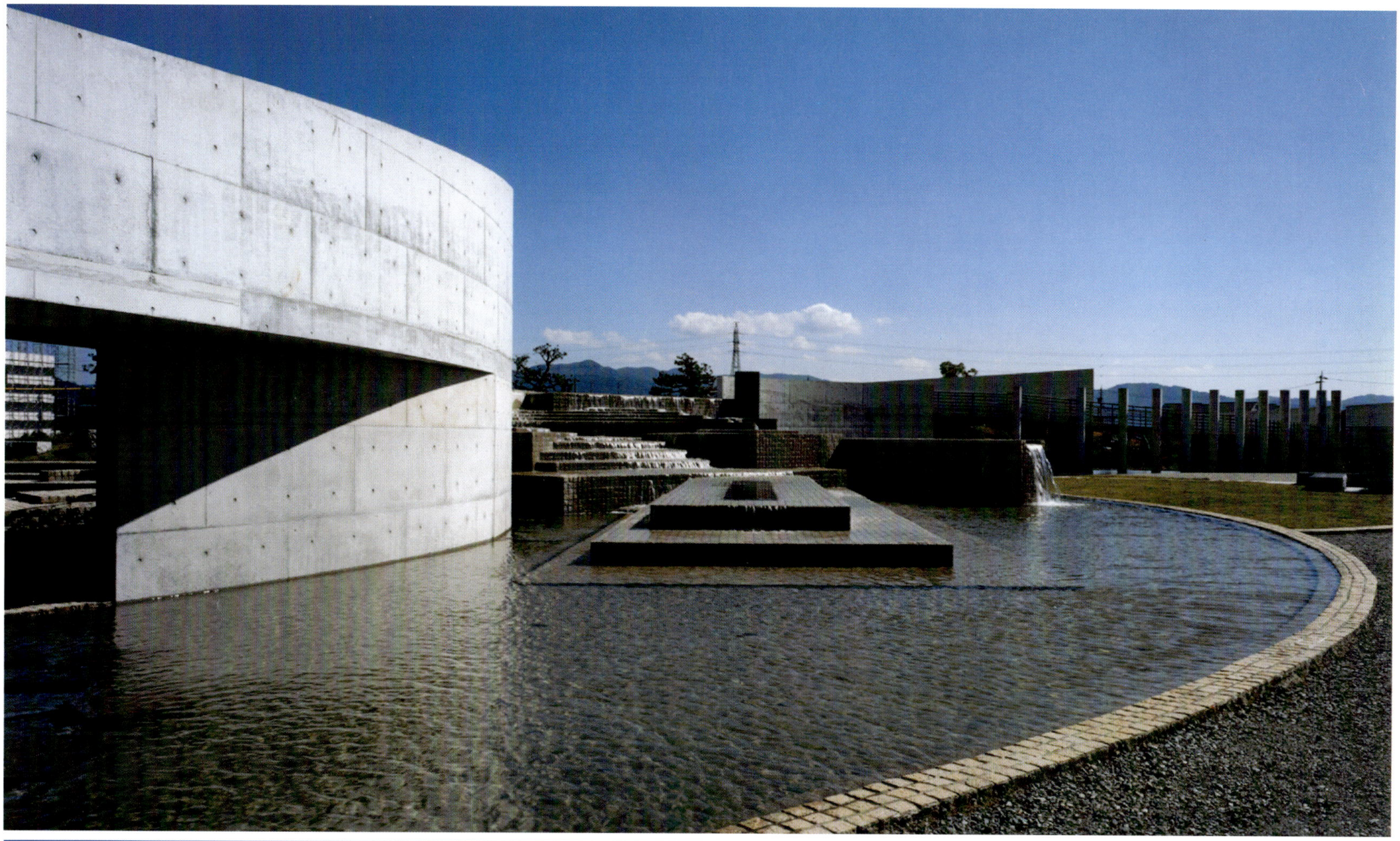

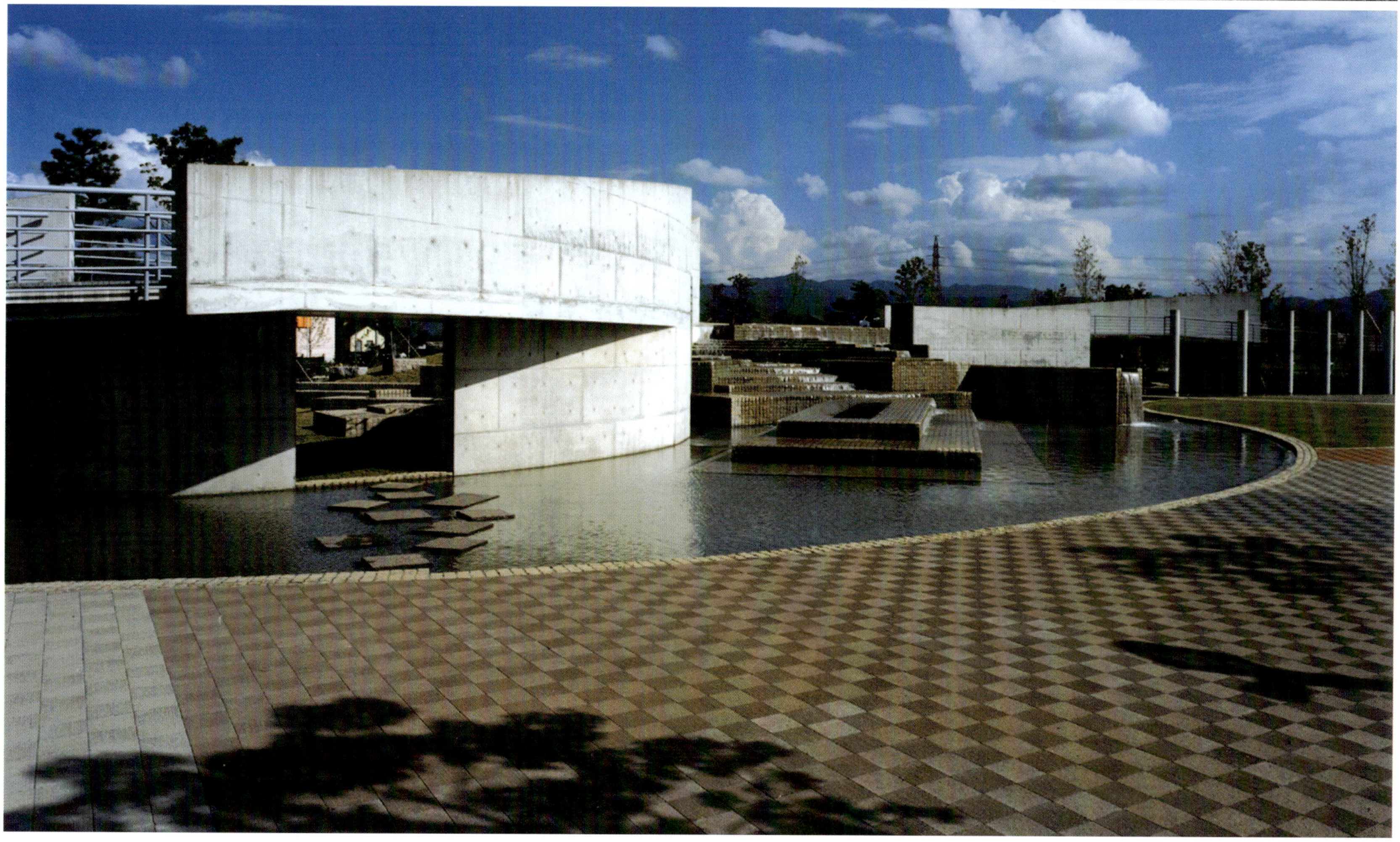

UN Studio
NMR Facilities

The internal organization of the building is expressed in its external surfaces. Inside, experiments are conducted with sensitive research equipment emitting gauss radiation. The clouds of radiation are essentially untouchable space, around which the planes of the floor, ceiling and wall surfaces are wrapped. These twin wraps contain the construction, installations and routing system of the laboratory. Together they form a loosely knotted assembly of smooth planes that fold over from floor to wall to ceiling.

The small pavilion-like laboratory for NMR (Neutron Magnetic Resonance) facilities is situated on the university campus of Utrecht, "De Uithof".

The unusual research technique itself and the molecular structures that it uncovers have strongly influenced the architecture of the laboratory. The two-story laboratory contains eight spectrometers (high frequency magnets), eight consoles and other ancillary equipment, as well as public and office spaces. The magnets all have specific behavior and requirements, creating magnetic fields of differing sizes and sensitivity. These affect the performance of other equipment present within a variable radius of the magnets. Basically, these force files should not be disturbed.

As a result, the radiating powers of the magnets constitute the virtual core of the projects, and modify the organization of the building, the materials which can be used, the disposition of the program, the equipment, and the possible routing systems. A second important structuring principle is the column-free spatial organization, which enables efficient use of the smaller center. The combination of these two central principles results in a multi-directional surface condition in which the walls fold over and meet each other to generate a situation in which all ends meet.

Architect:
UN Studio
Location:
Utrecht, the Netherlands
Photographs:
Christian Richters

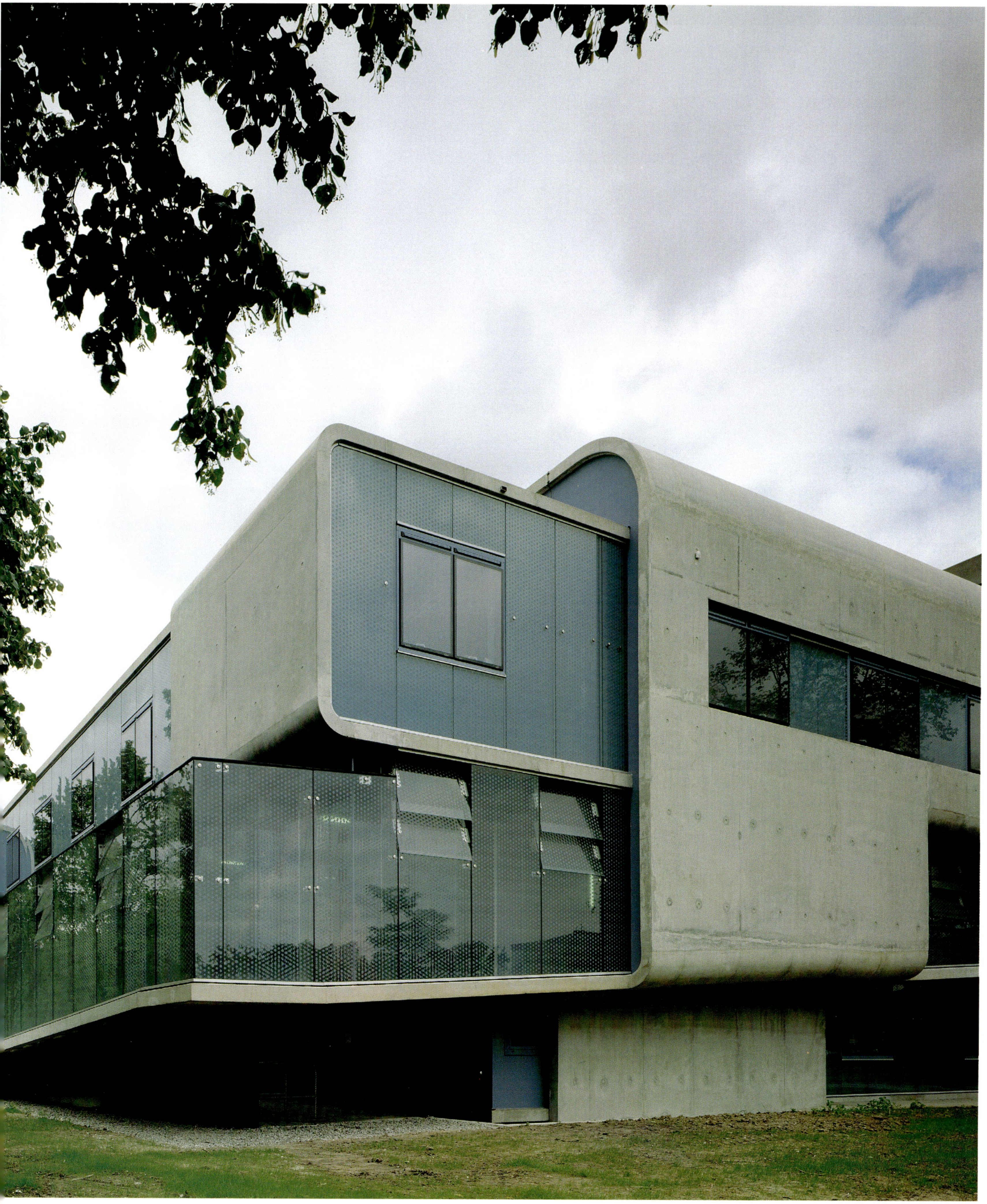

First floor plan

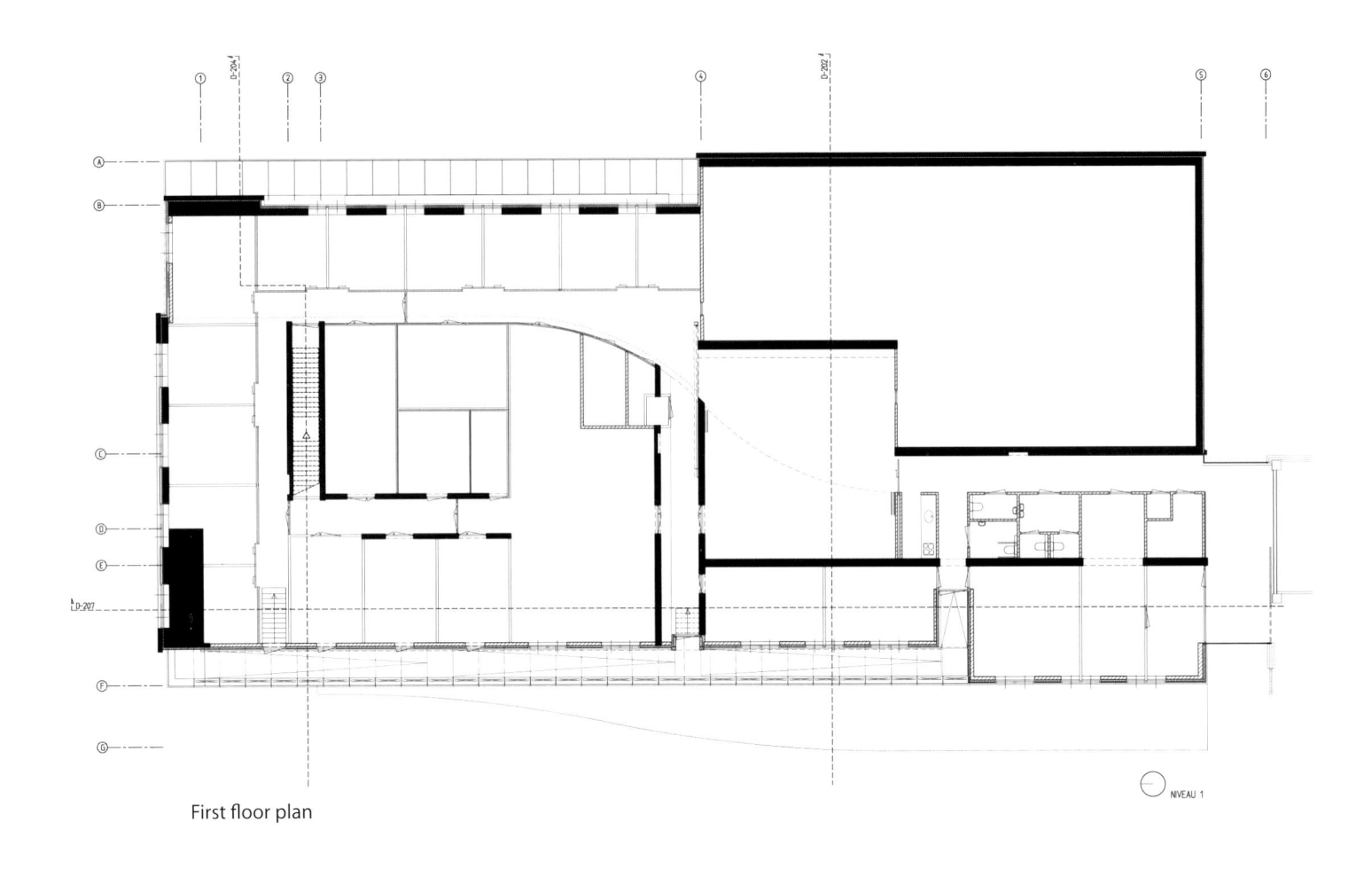

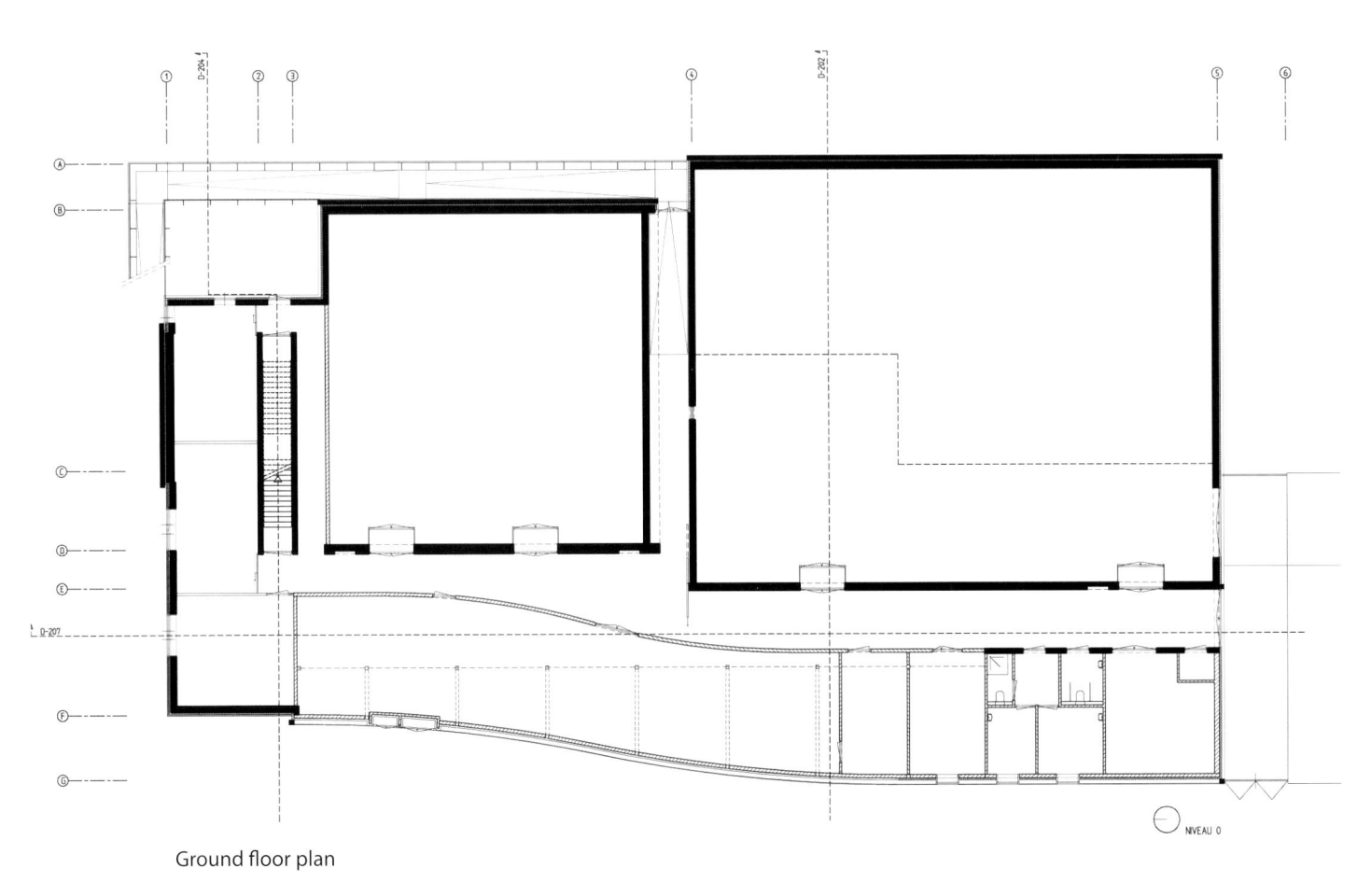

Ground floor plan

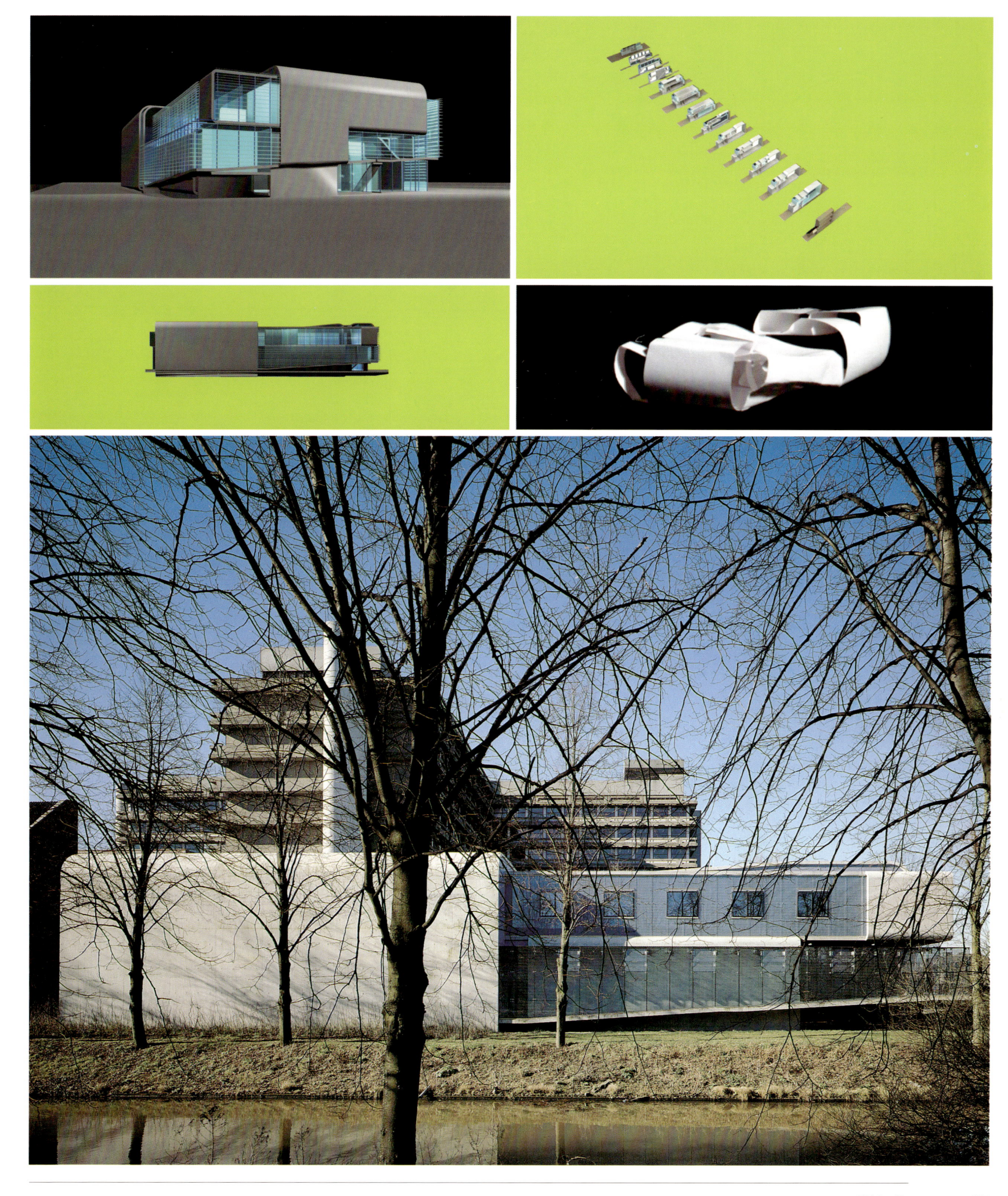

UN Studio

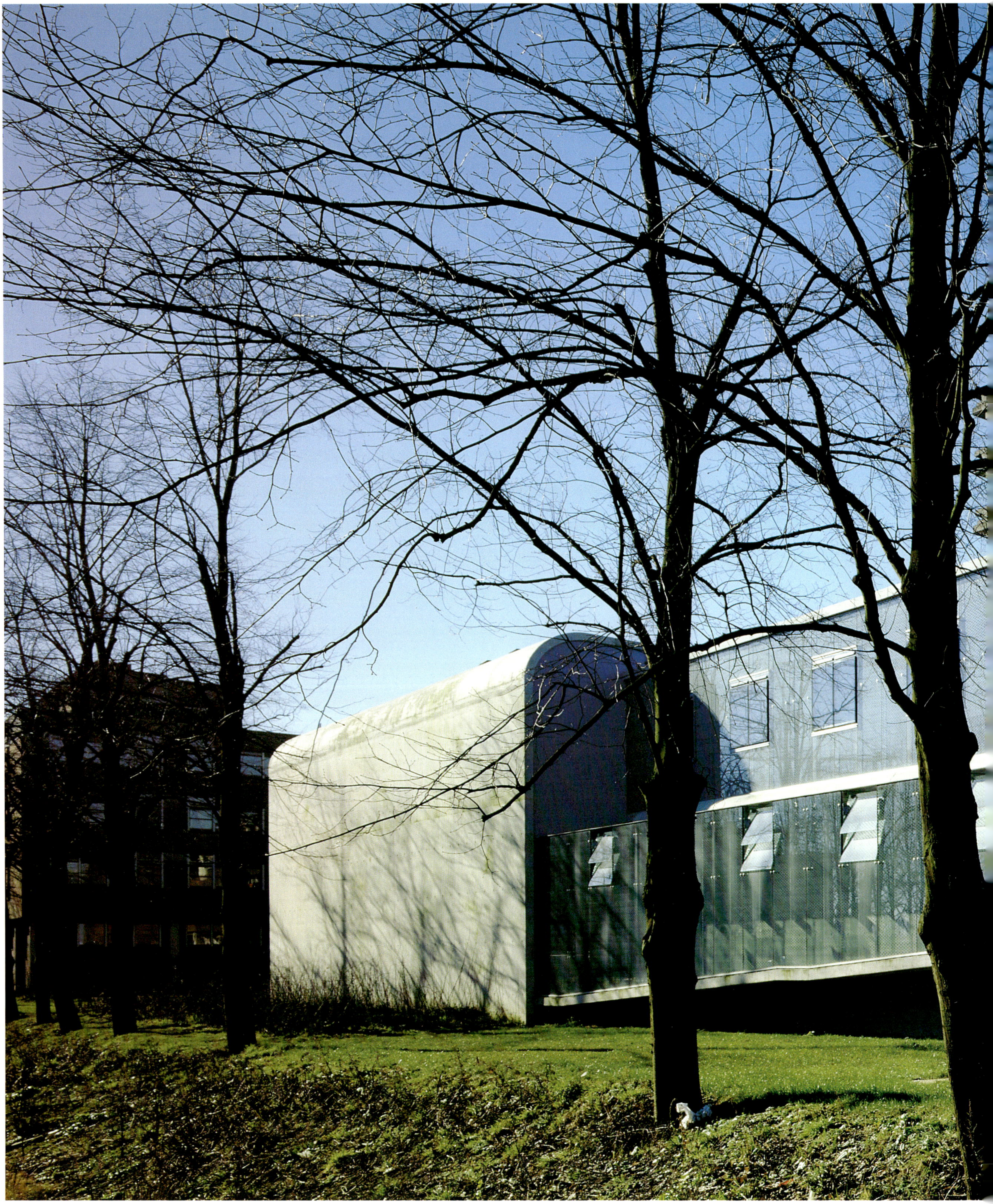

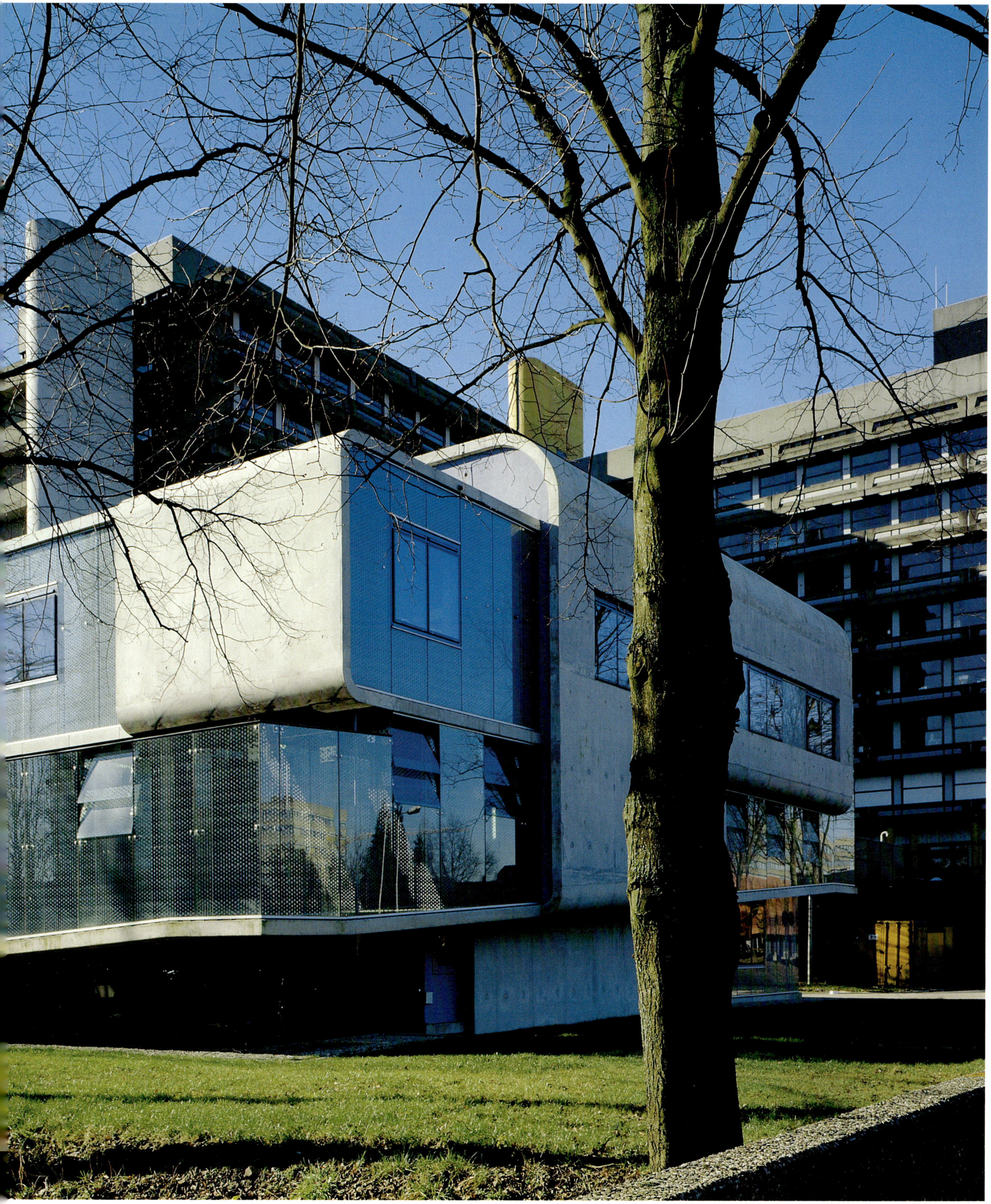

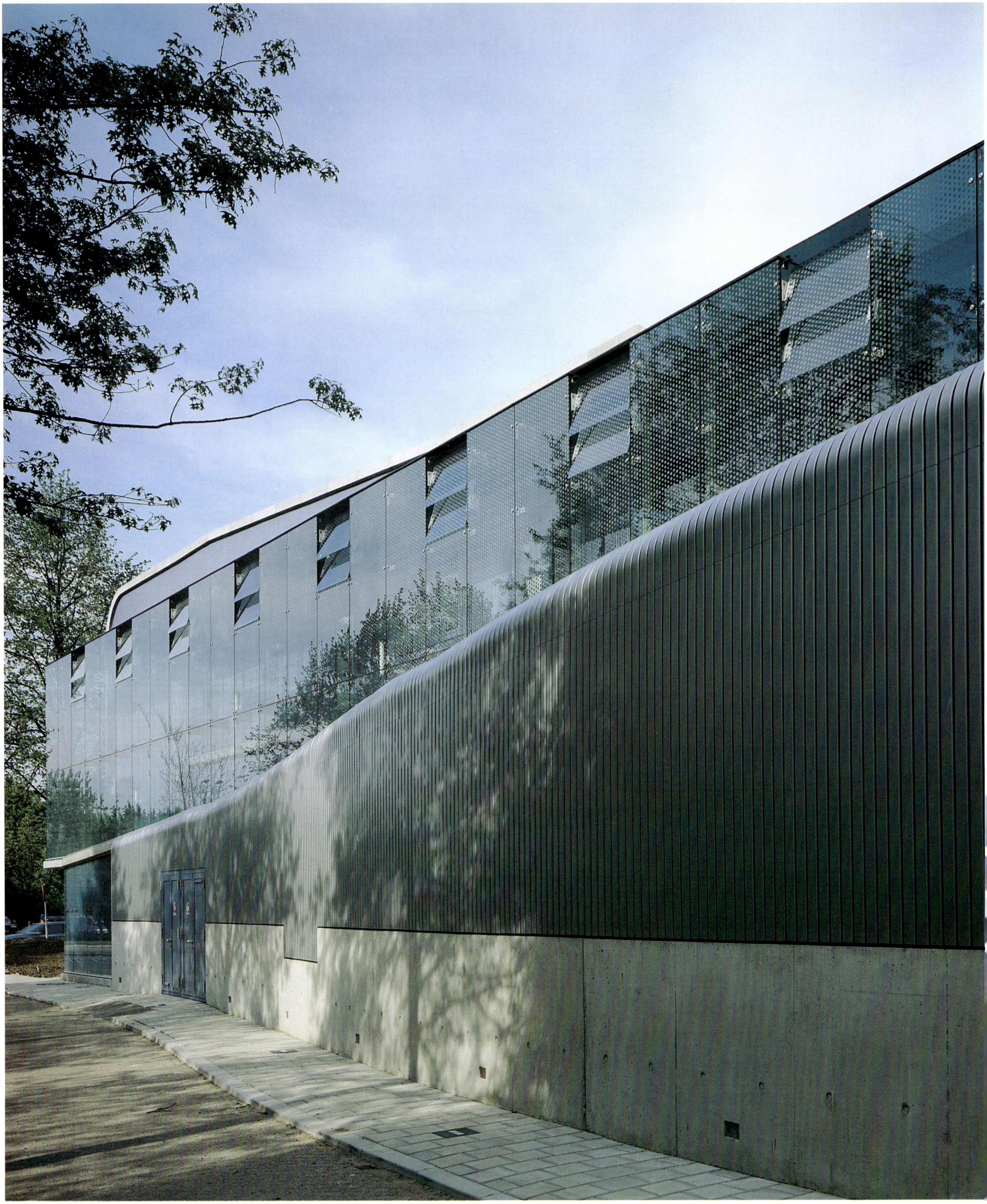

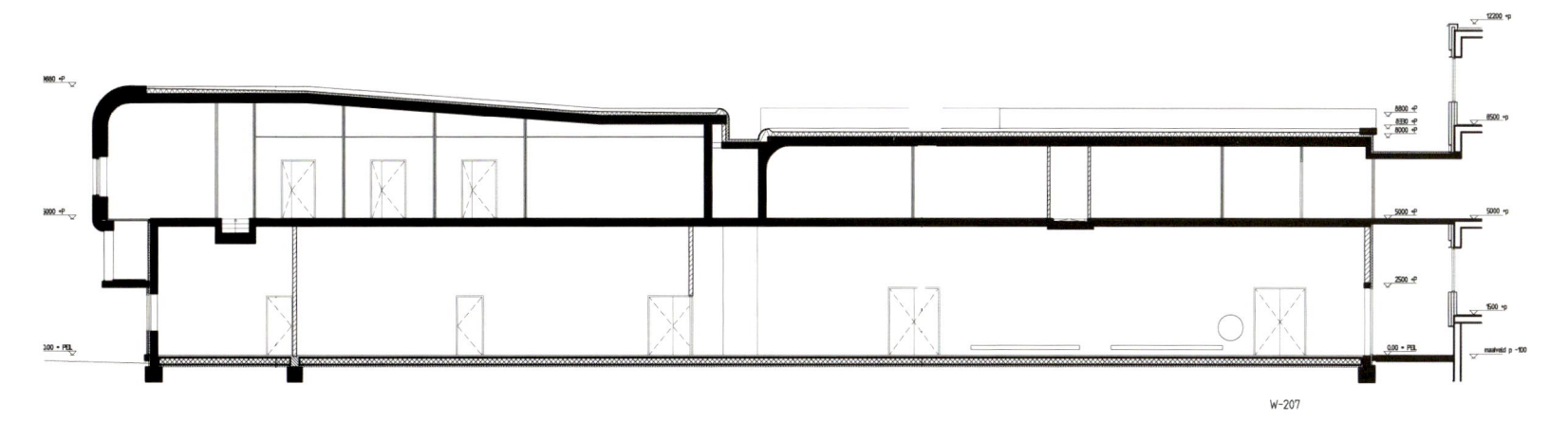

Longitudinal section

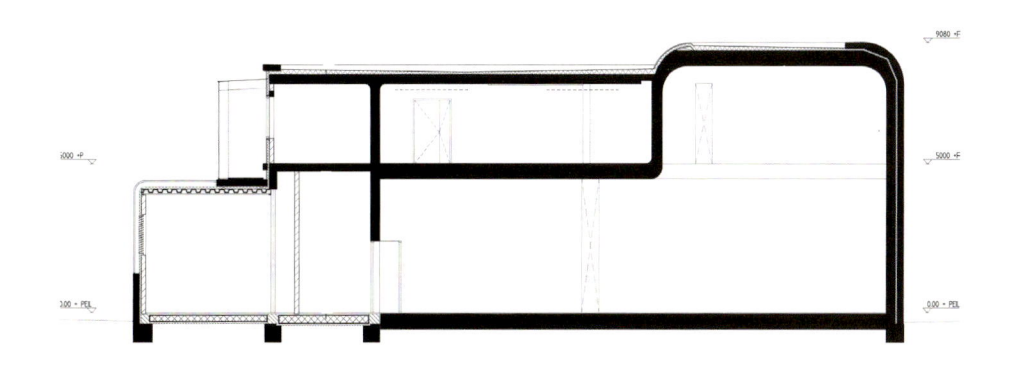

Cross-section

UN Studio

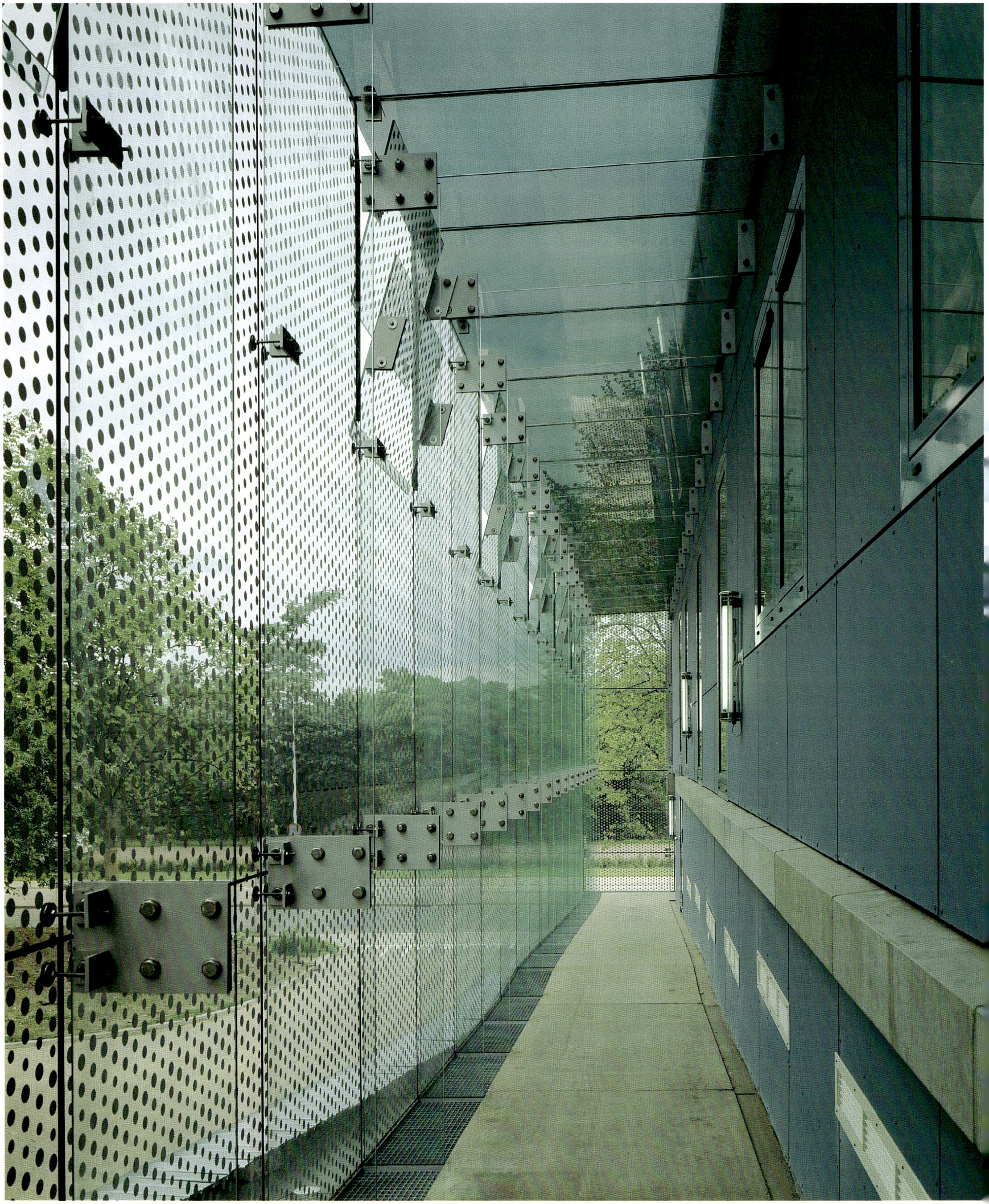

The unique demands of the laboratory dictated a column-free internal organization, which enables efficient use of the smaller center. As seen both in the exterior and interior, the walls fold over and meet each other, generating a seamless architecture.

UN Studio

Justo García Rubio
Casar de Cáceres Sub-Regional Bus Station

The brief for this project was for a small bus station building on a corner plot, which needed to suit its surroundings of white buildings typical of Cáceres. A single material and form contains everything: the covering, the interior space, the exterior image and the structure.

Set between a nursery and a school, with children passing in front of the building at all hours of the day, the architect thought to appeal to their imagination with architecture that was not indifferent to their dream world. Work therefore started in search of an adventurous form that would resolve the functional and urban requirements, among others.

The result was a form made from white concrete, which rises to become a sheet; a structure with a stability that originates from its form and which folds over on itself to fulfill all the program requirements. This was not meant to be a place just for getting on or off the bus: it was to be a unique experience for travelers departing on or arriving from a journey.

The form is a white concrete band which, like a logo, marks out the place that presides over the comings and goings of children and the departure and arrival of passengers. Passengers generally arrive at the station from the town center, having passed under vaults that support houses that cover the crosswise streets. The access to the station under the small sheet at the end of the street produces a similar sensation. This welcomes passengers and draws them into its scale and the scale of the nearby low houses, shielding them as it becomes a floor and at the same time the basement's weightless ceiling.

The sheet twists and turns providing a formal solution to the corner position of the site, and clearly separating the passenger entrance from the bus exit. Buses enter following a circular route. They park under the large sheet and, to exit, withdraw and continue along the circular route under the sheet to go out to the crossroads. The basement relieves the ground floor of service functions such as the store and bar; and allows a more complete view of the band above ground. The start of the band, which is the floor of the passenger zone with a small gradient, suggests the idea of movement throughout the complex.

Architects:
Justo García Rubio
Location:
Casar de Cáceres, Spain
Photographs:
Justo García Rubio

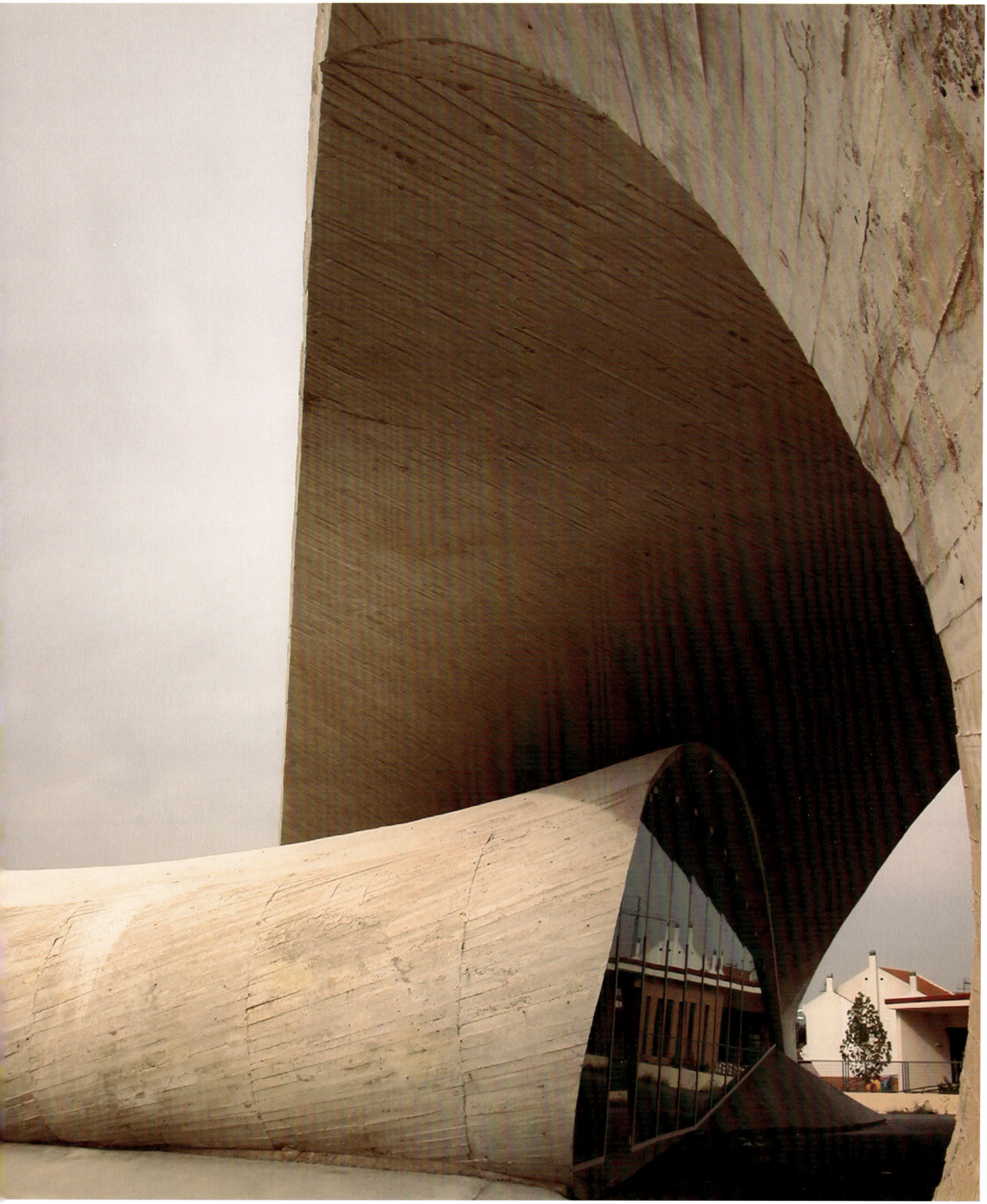

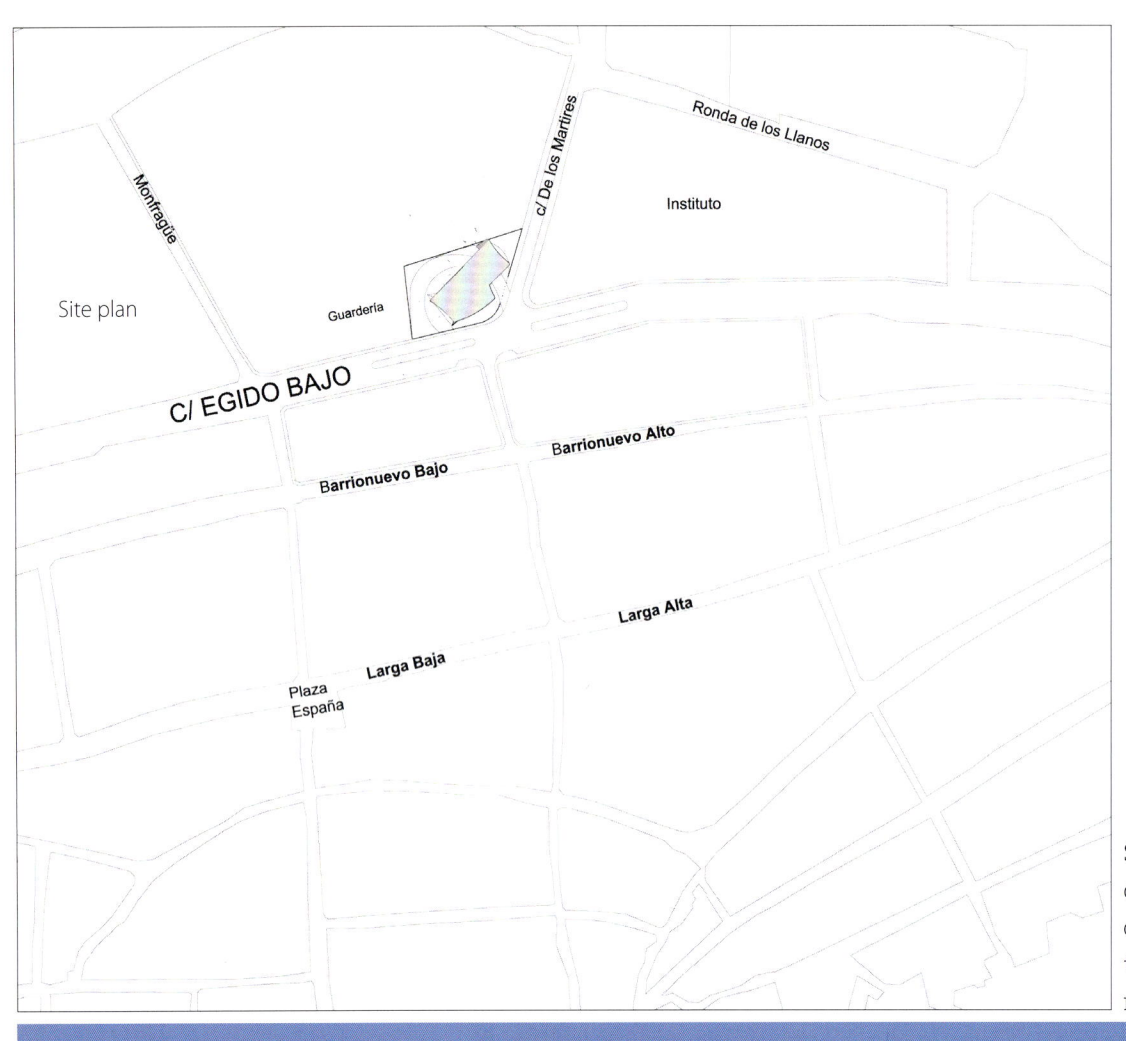

Site plan

Set between a nursery and a school, with children passing in front of the building at all hours of the day, the architect thought to appeal to their imagination with an architecture that was not indifferent to their dream world.

224   Justo García Rubio

East elevation

West elevation

Justo García Rubio

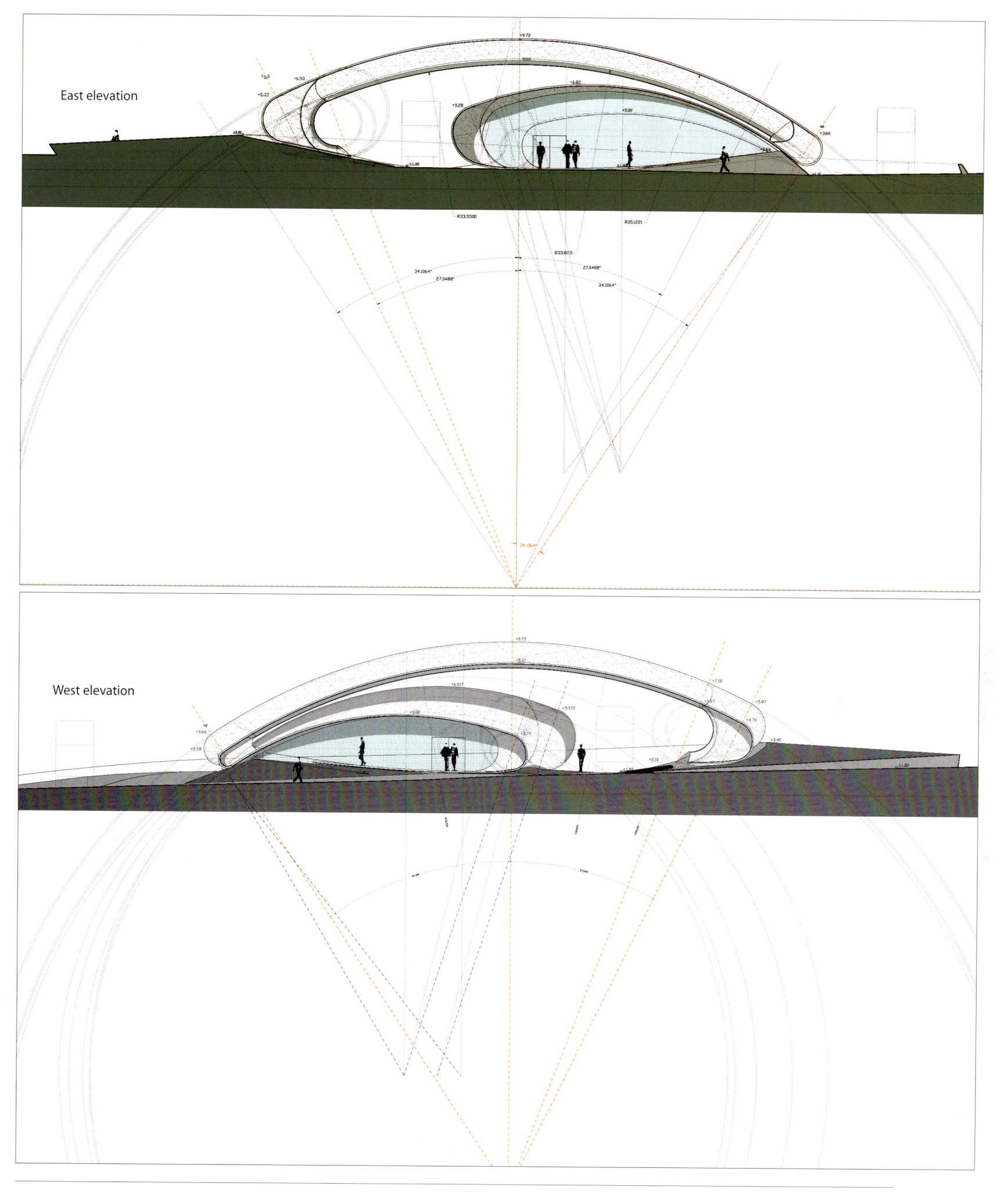

South elevation

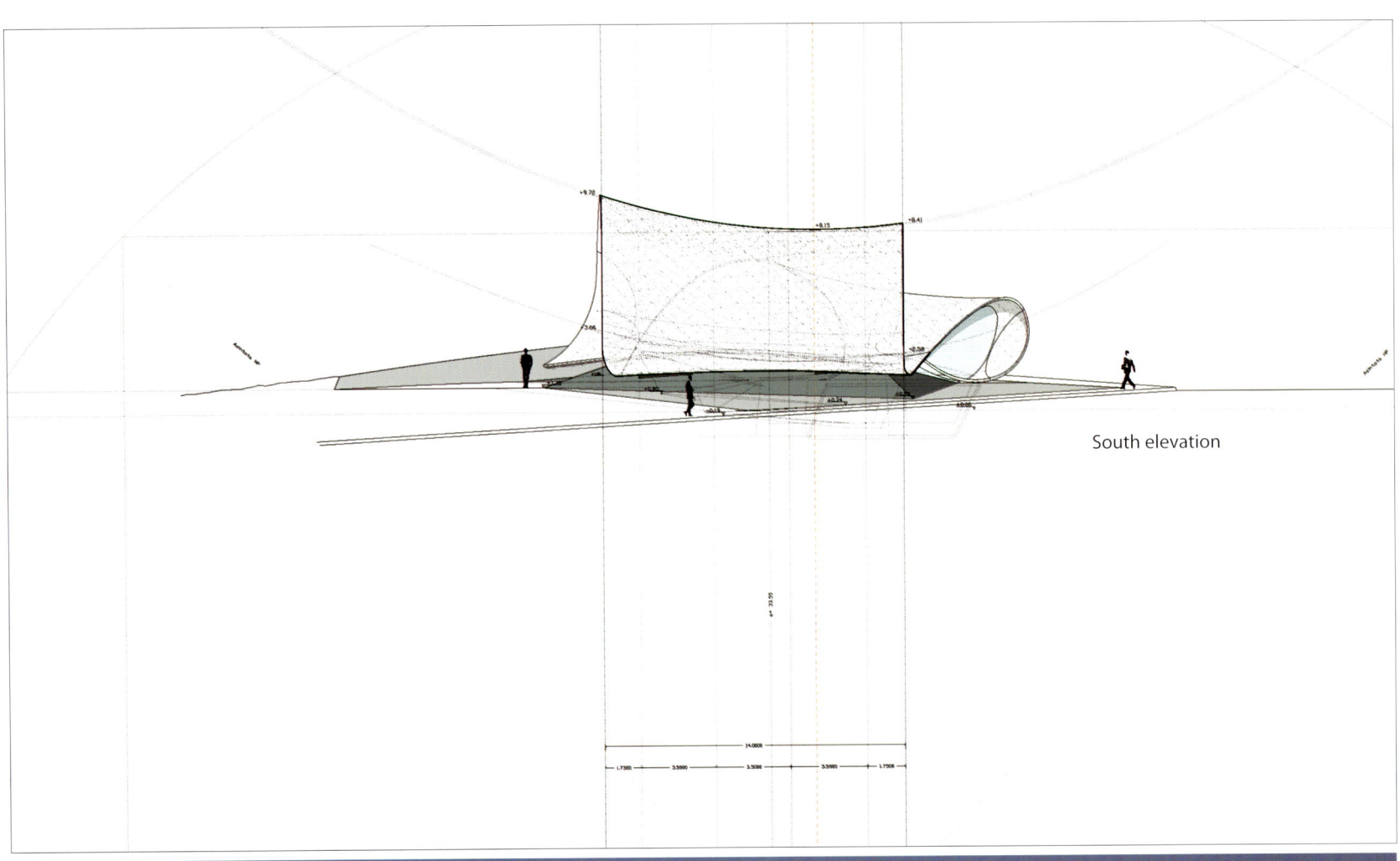

North elevation

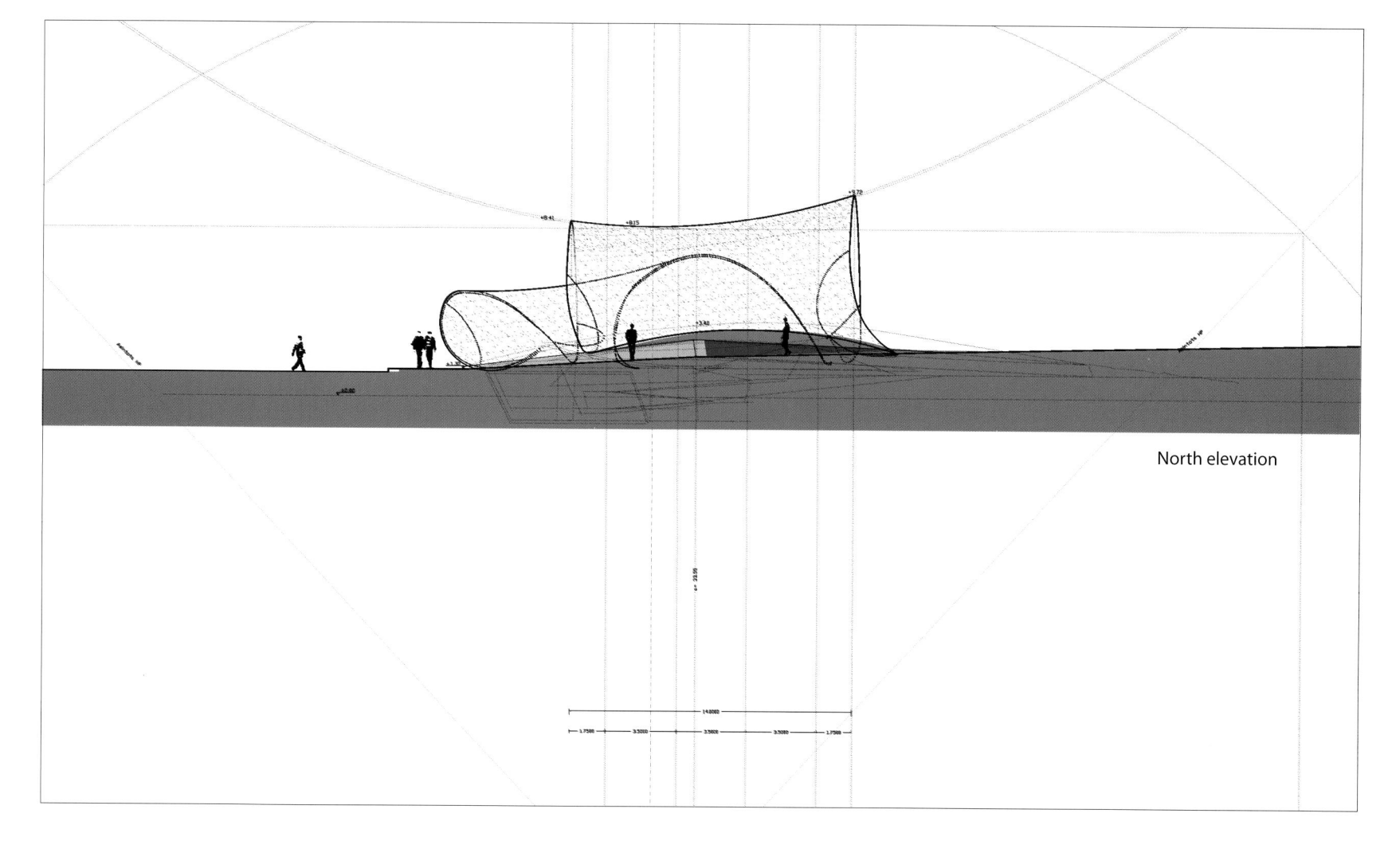

Ground floor plan

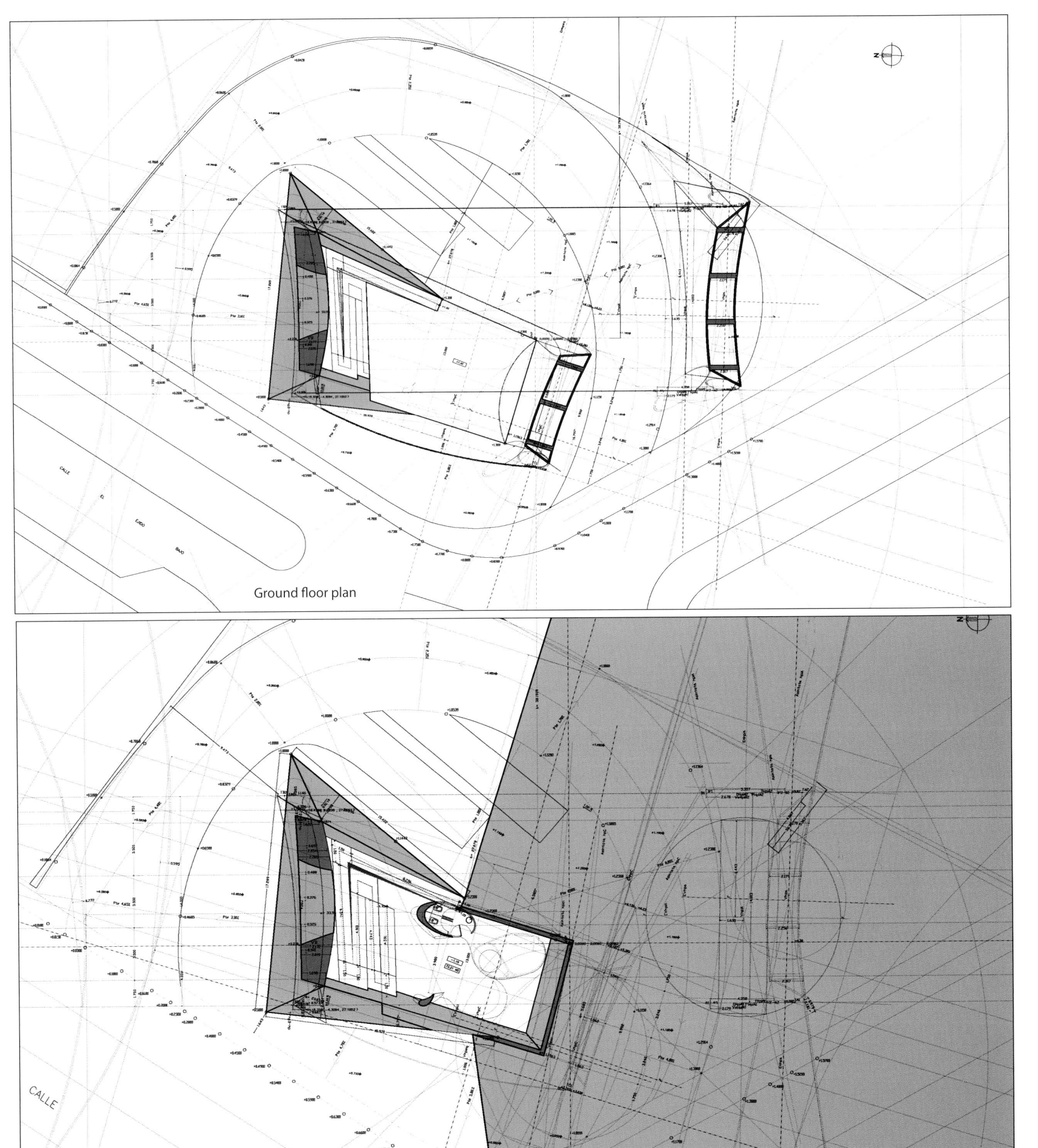

Basement floor

Roof plan

Justo García Rubio

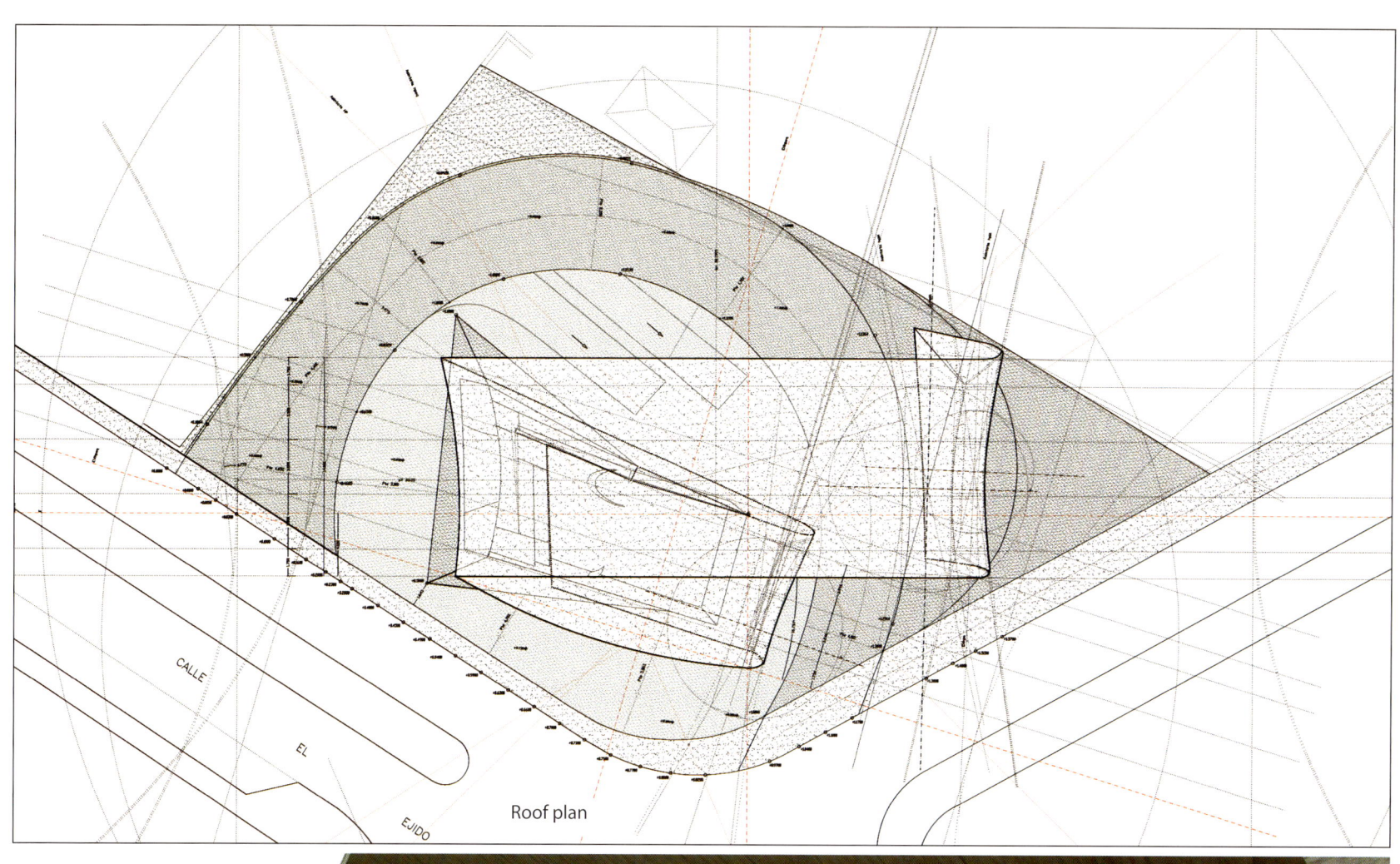

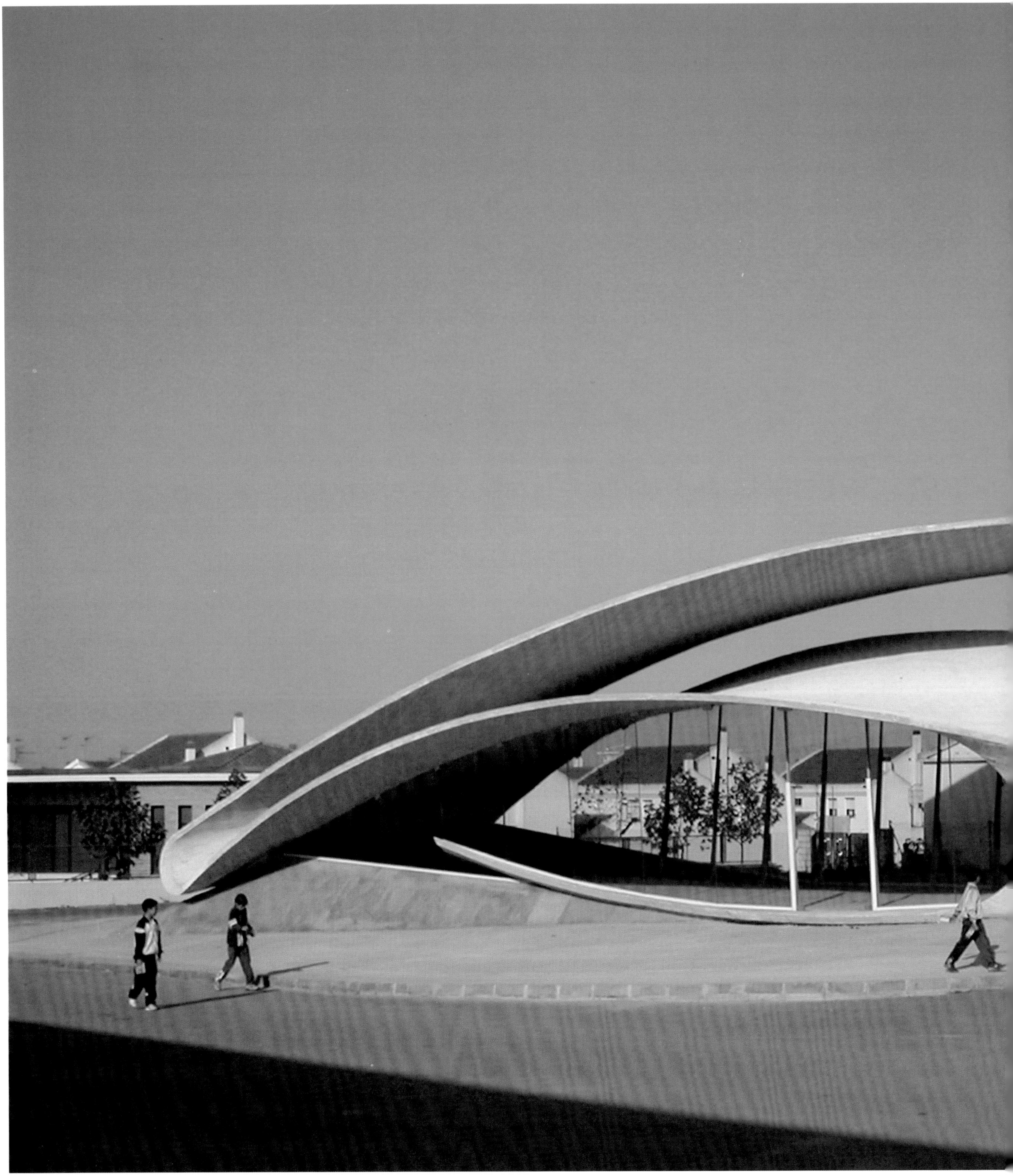

Justo García Rubio

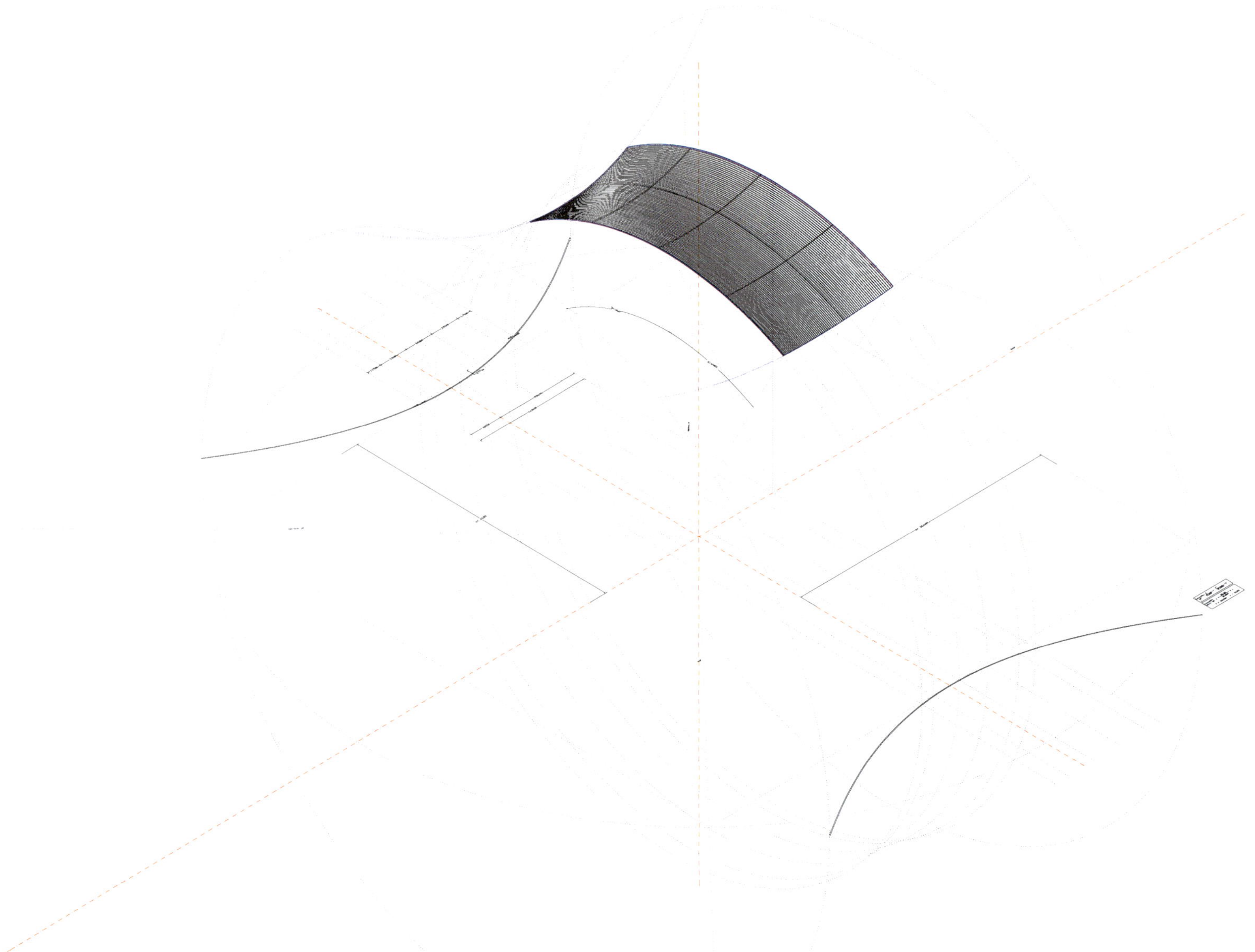

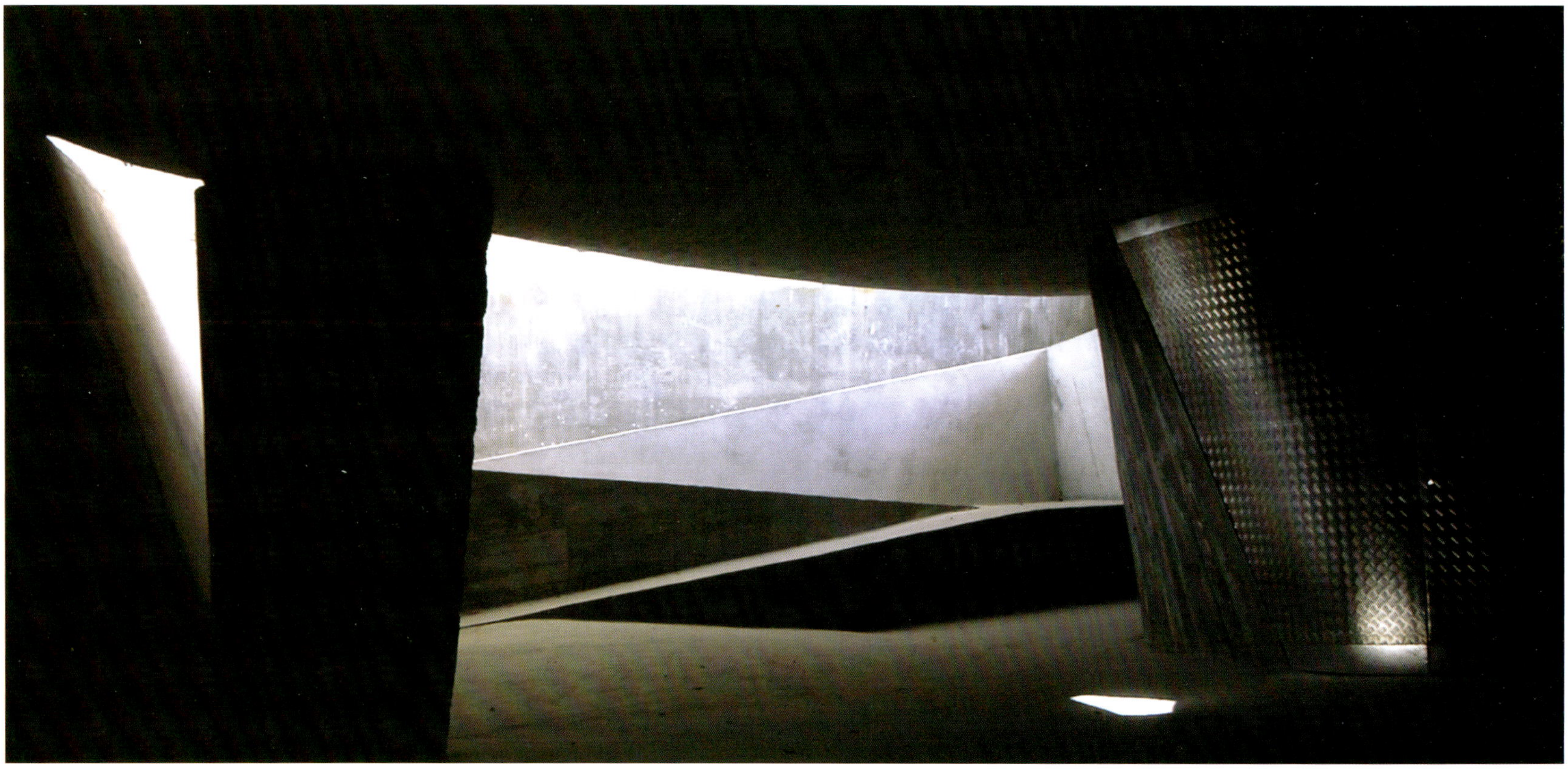

Justo García Rubio

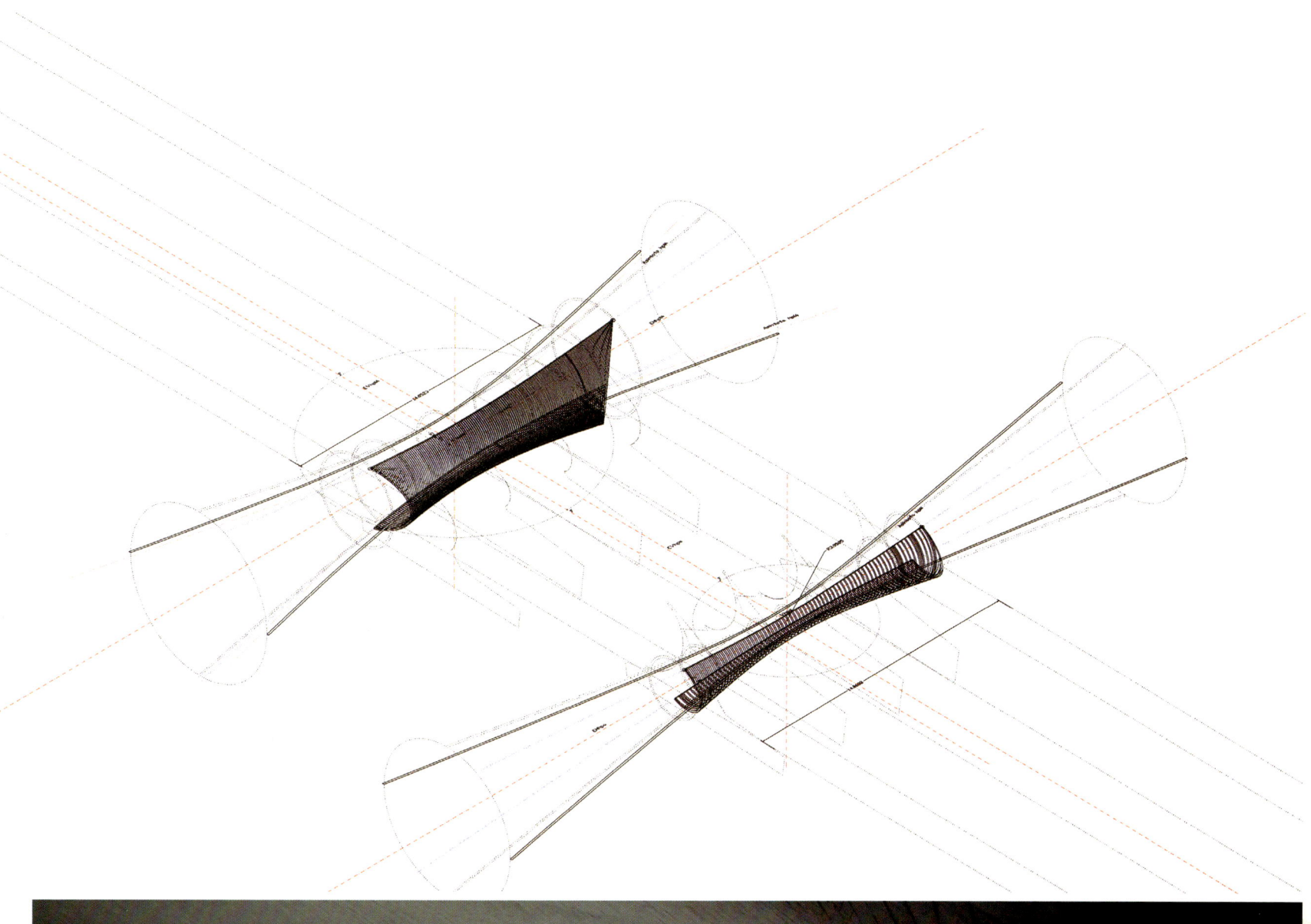

Pezo von Ellrichshausen Architects
Poli House

This house located on the Coliumo Peninsula (550 km south of Santiago de Chile); a rural setting sparsely populated by farmers, fishermen and summer tourists. The construction is a compact figure without scale references or any intention of smoothing its roughness. Once the position of the volume was established, as close as possible to the cliff edge, it was necessary to elevate the floor in order to capture two things: both the sensation of a natural podium surrounded by vastness, and the sight of the foot of the cliffs, where the sea explodes against the rocks.

Following this operation, the interior floor was divided into three platforms that adapt to the slope in a zigzag. The triple height space of the lower platform, oriented to the northwest, represents the vetrical dimension of the site; its drop, the sense of vertigo and gravity.

The building functions both as a summer house and a cultural center, hosting activities such as reunions, workshops and exhibitions. This established a contradictory proposal: the interior would have to mediate between a very public aspect and a very intimate and informal one. That is, it had to be both monumental and domestic without any of the negative aspects of either one affecting the other.

The architects decided to organize all the service functions in an over-dimensioned perimeter (the functional width), inside a thick wall that acts as a buffer. Inside this hollowed mass is the kitchen, the vertical circulations, the bathrooms, the closets and a series of interior balconies (which protect the northern and western windows from the sun and the rain). If necessary, all the furniture and domestic objects can be stored inside this perimeter, freeing the space for multiple activities.

The entire house was built with hand-made concrete, using untreated wooden shuttering. The work was done, with a small mixer and four wheelbarrows, in horizontal strata that matched the height of half a wooden board. The same battered wood of the shuttering was then used to wrap the interior and to build sliding panels that function both as doors to hide the services of the perimeter and as security shutters that cover the windows when the house is left empty.

Architect:
Mauricio Pezo,
Sofía von Ellrichshausen
Location:
Coliumo, Chile
Photographs:
Cristóbal Palma

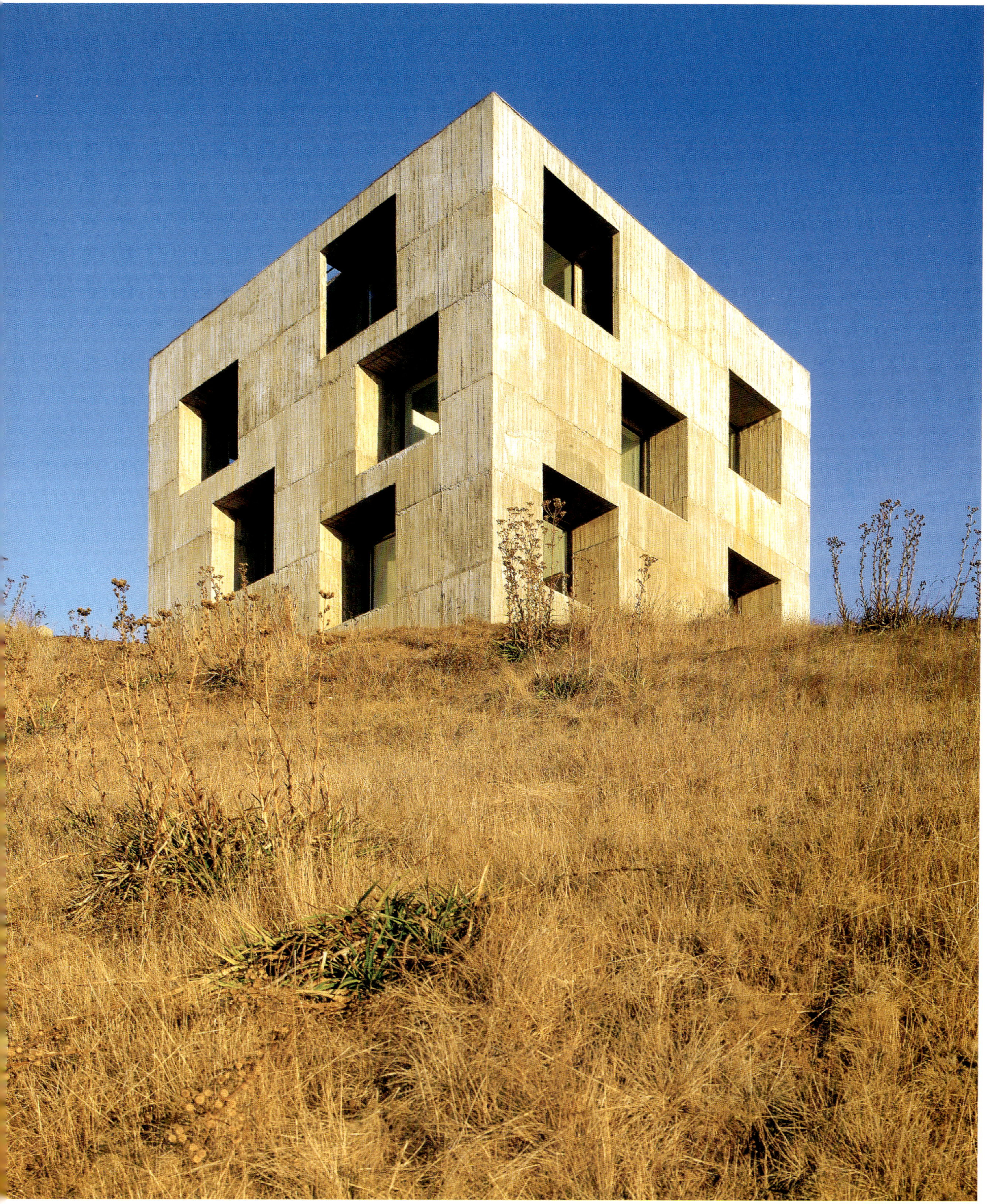

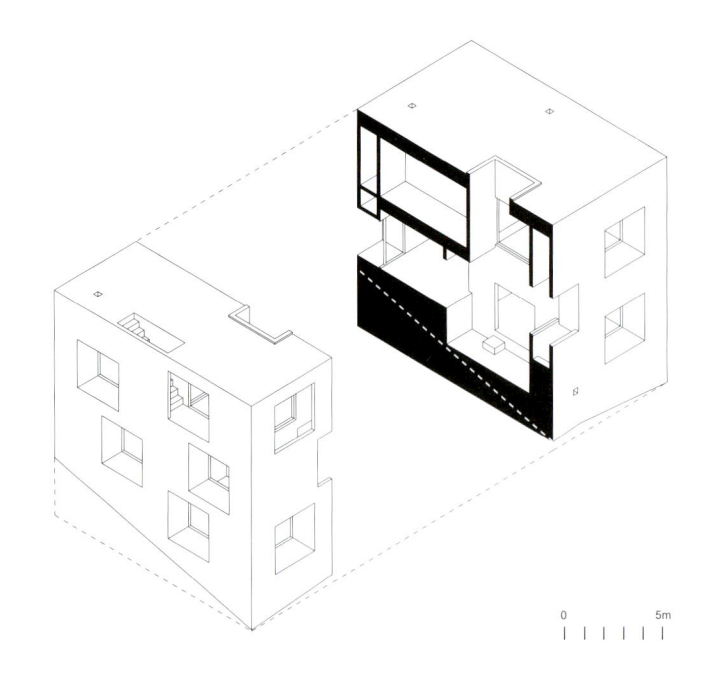

Pezo von Ellrichshausen Architects

0   5

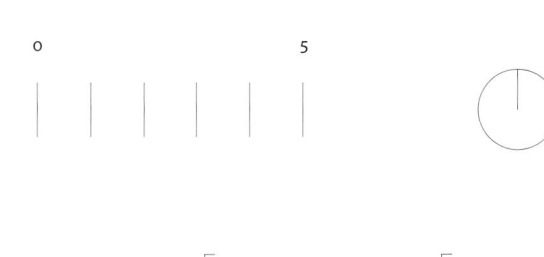

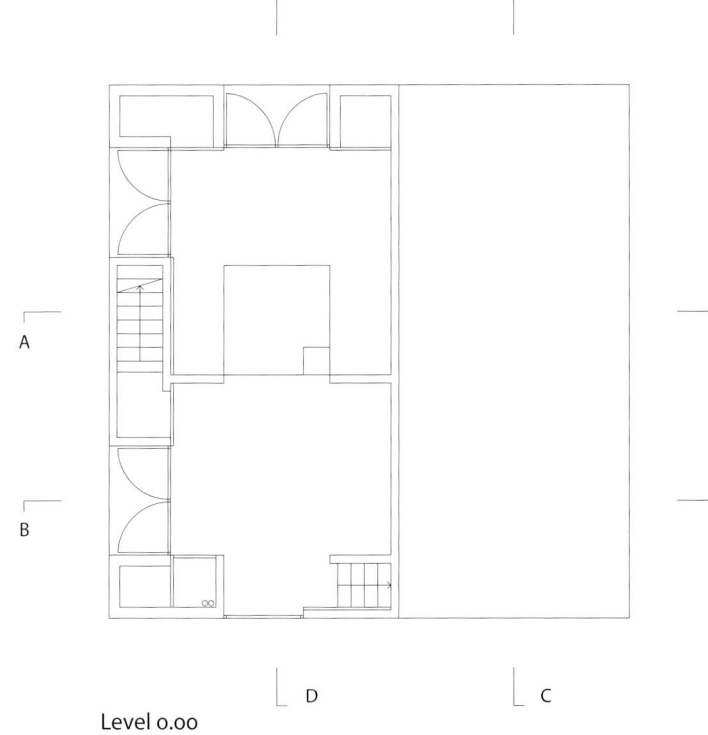

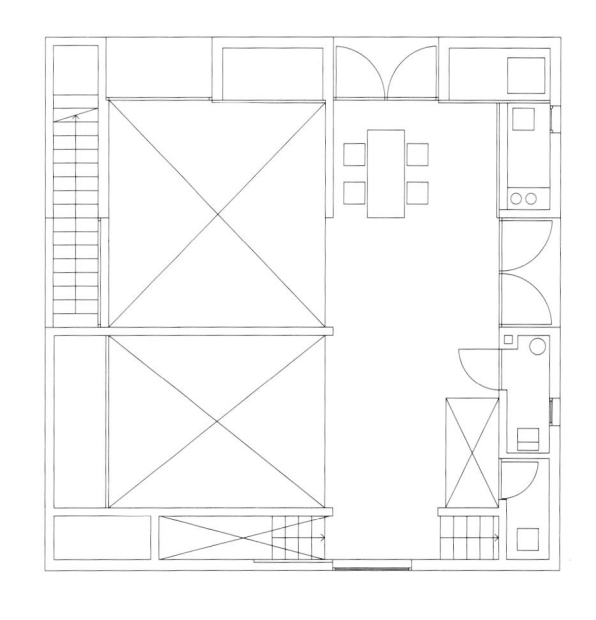

A
B

D   C

Level 0.00

Level + 1,50

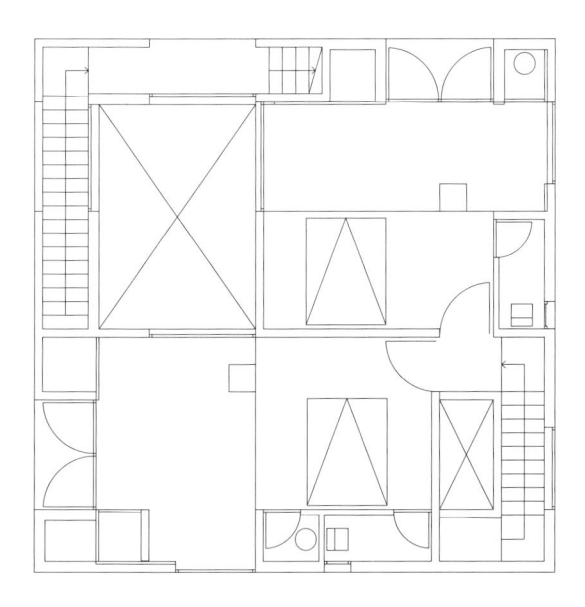

Level + 4.50

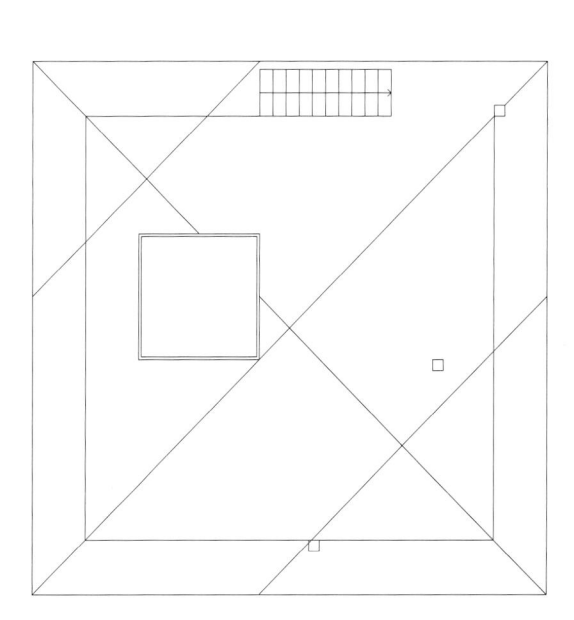

Level + 7.60

Pezo von Ellrichshausen Architects   **237**

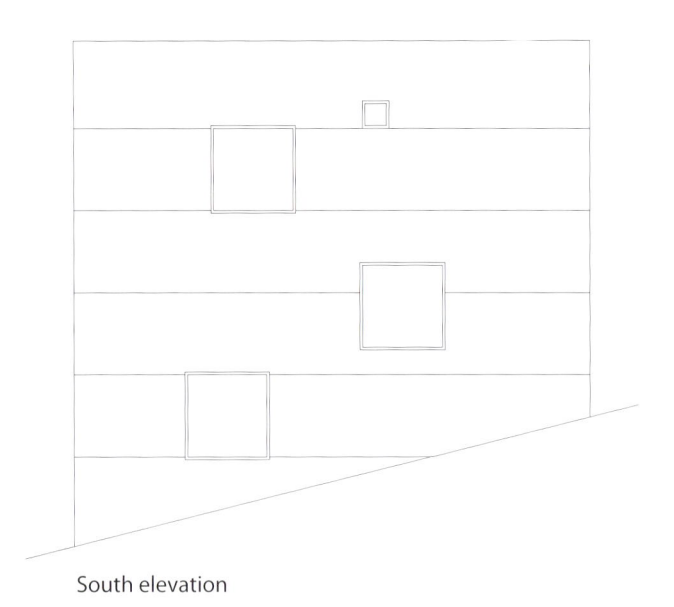

South elevation

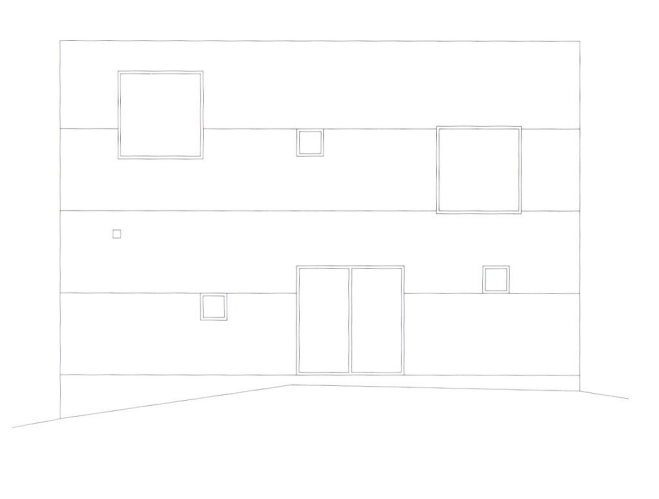

East elevation

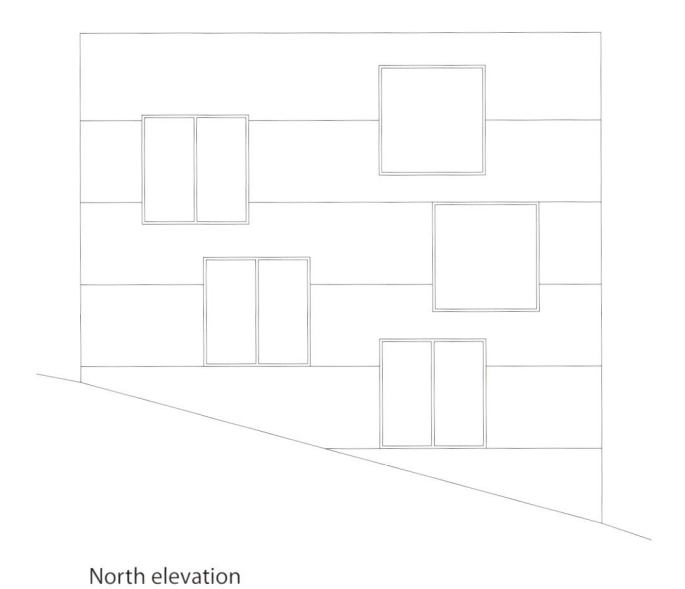

North elevation

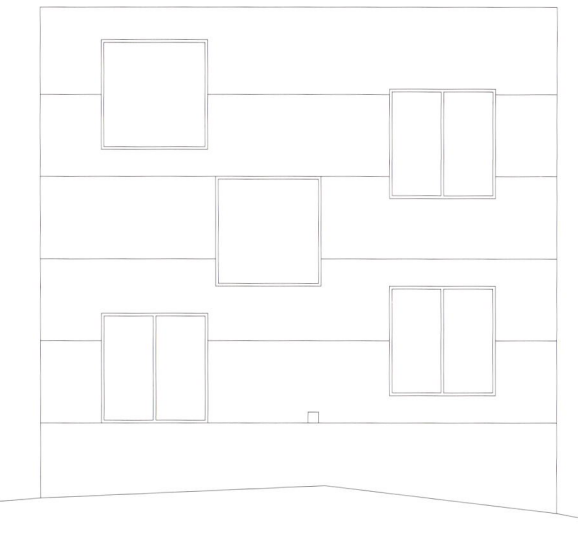

West elevation

Despite the temptation of reaching up to the cliff edge, the resistance of the ground obliged the architects to confine the operation to a small plot set back from this vertiginous border, creating a compact figure without scale or references to soften its severity.

Pezo von Ellrichshausen Architects

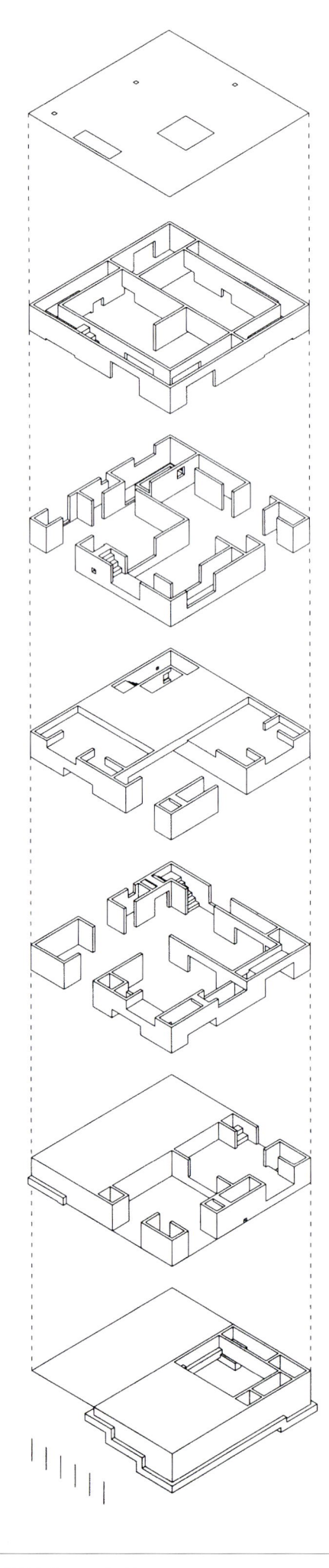

Pezo von Ellrichshausen Architects

Section AA

Section BB

Section CC

Section DD

Pezo von Ellrichshausen Architects

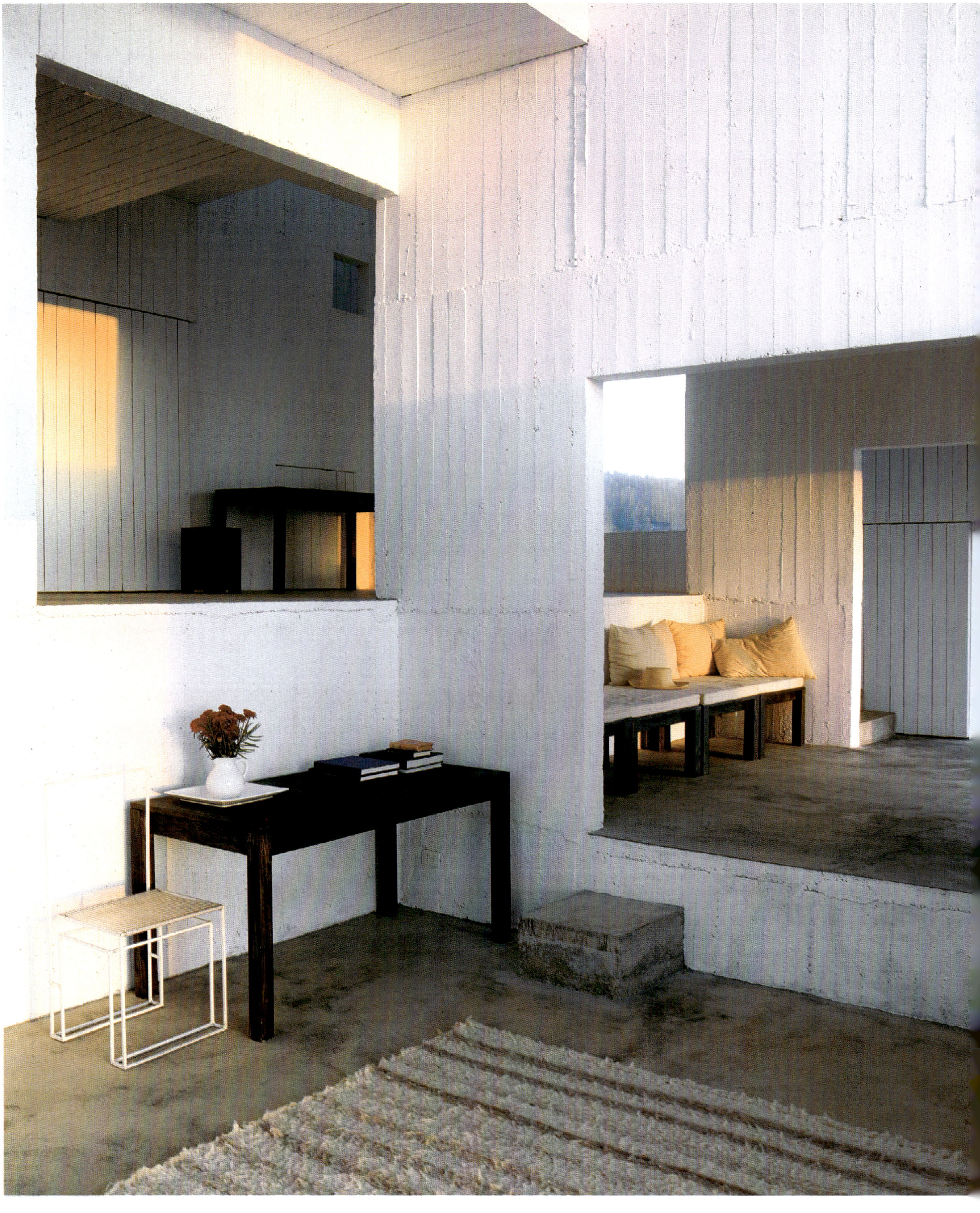

The entire house was built with hand-made concrete, using untreated wooden shuttering. The work was done, with a small mixer and four wheelbarrows, in horizontal strata that matched the height of half a wooden board. The same battered wood of the shuttering was then used to wrap the interior and to build sliding panels that function both as doors to hide the services of the perimeter and as security shutters that cover the windows when the house is left empty.

Pezo von Ellrichshausen Architects

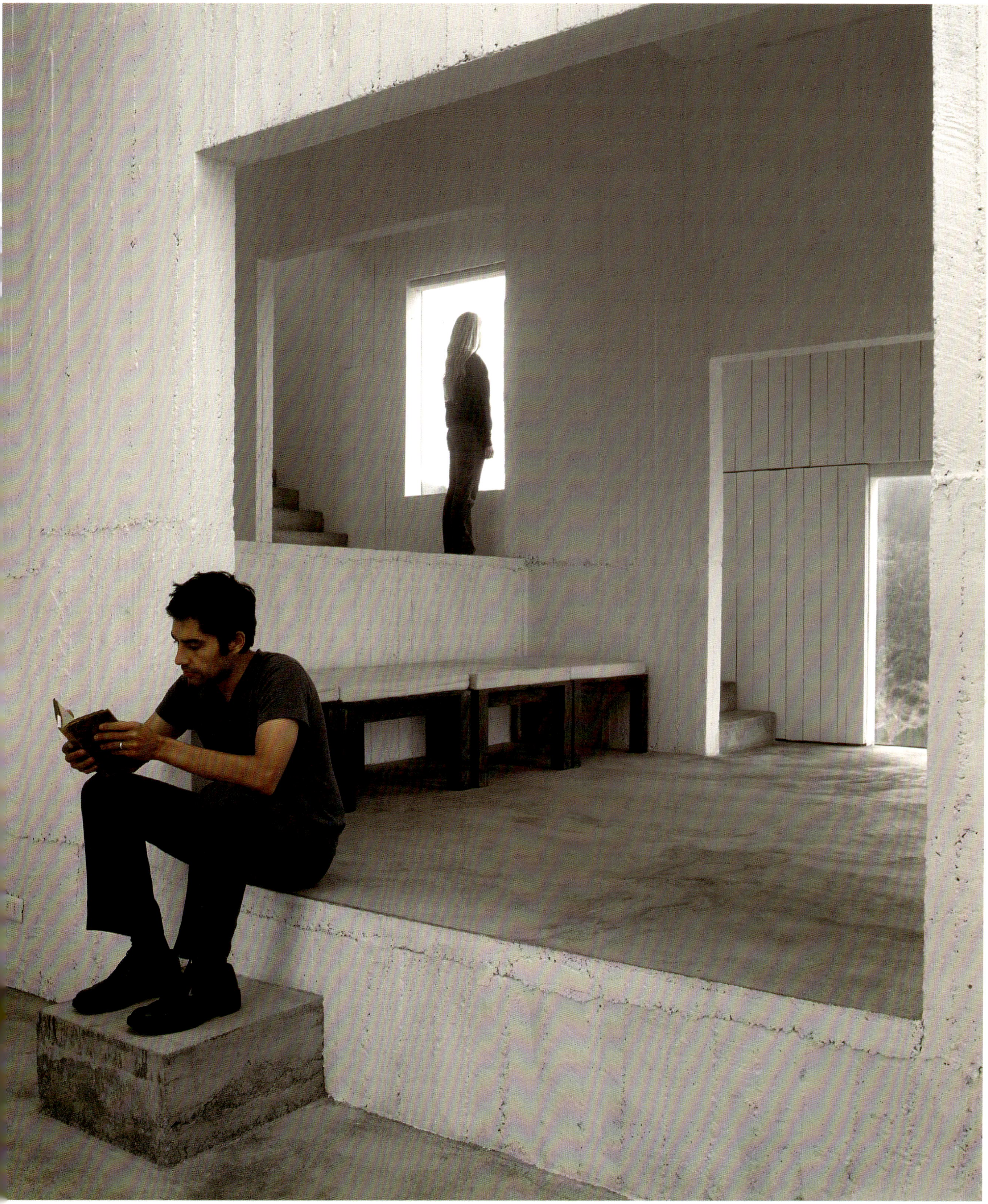

Designliga

Bench

The objective behind this project was to develop a store concept for Bench's flagship store in Berlin, which could also be transferable to other stores. As well as being functional, the design needed to communicate the company's brand image. The interior of the store is an abstraction of urban spaces and their elements, using materials from urban landscapes, thus blurring the distinction between interior and exterior. The formal language is at once both completely new and familiar. A spacious room welcomes the visitor into the store where key items of the current Bench collection are highlighted on the display furniture. These display objects can flexibly be rearranged within the room, stacked and grouped together, and also act as seats. On the walls further items from the collection are displayed along with works of collaborating artists. On the left-hand side of the middle section of the store is the cash desk, whose position allows staff to be able to clearly see people entering the shop, and vice-versa. The right-hand side of this section provides a space for changing rooms. Passed this section is the store's central element, 'the tube', which contains the majority of the clothing items. At the back of the shop are two more changing rooms, which save shoppers from having to walk back to the front of the shop to try on the clothing. The two dominant materials used throughout the space are wood and concrete. Wooden bars from the classic 'park bench' were central to the design. This visual link to the brand can be first seen on the store's façade where the bars have been used both above and below the window. Inside, the bars lead from the window to create a bench in the store's interior. They wrap around the central pillar in the shop's front section visually leading the visitor towards the back of the store, where they have been used to create the tube. The spaces between the bars allow light to enter this space, which is artificial from one side and natural on the other. The concrete used for the furnishings, i.e. the innovative display stands / seats and the cash desk, forms an interesting contrast to the organic quality of the wood. Both materials help to blur the borders between inside and out.

Architects:
Designliga
Location:
Berlin, Germany
Photographs:
contributed by Designliga

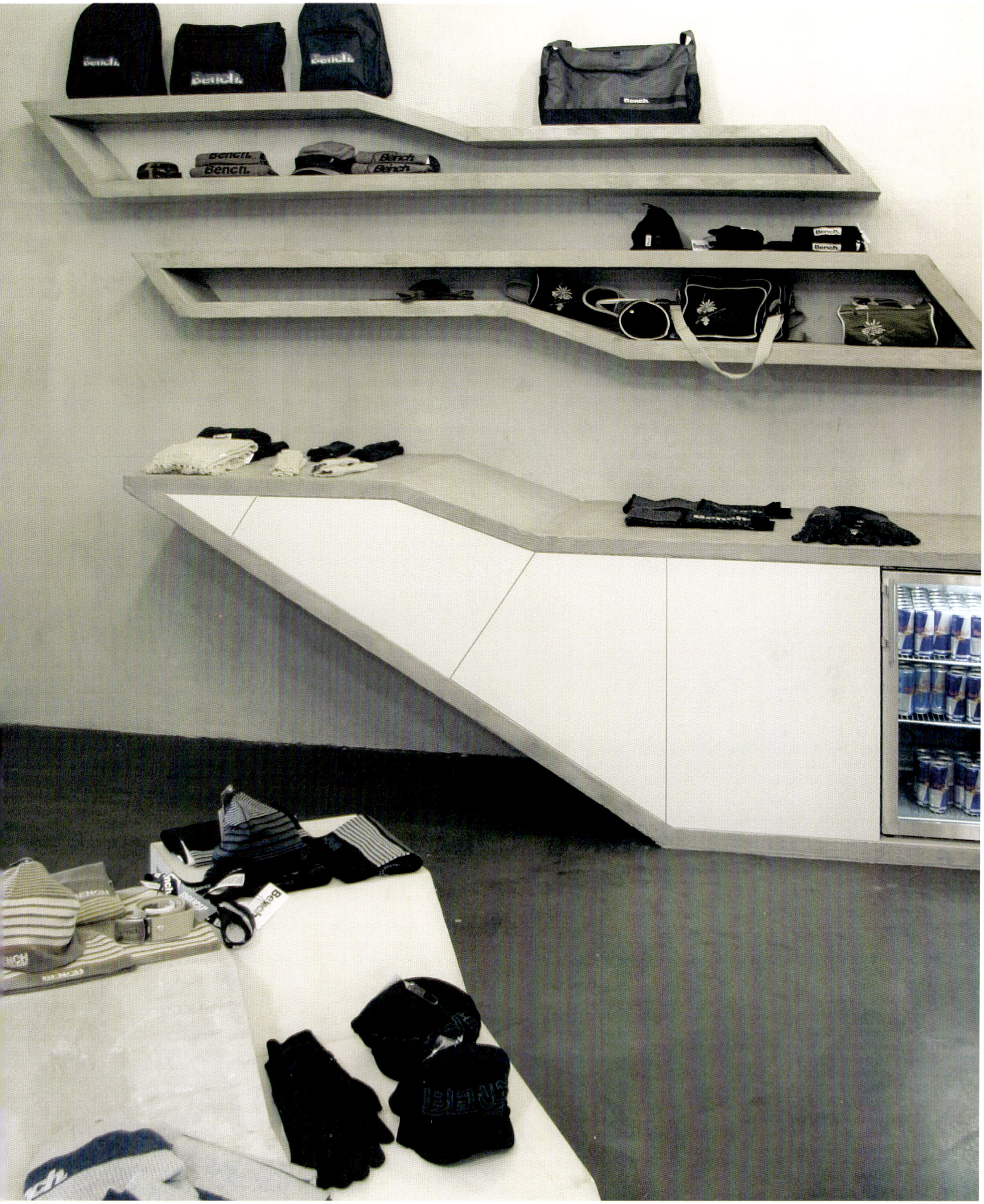
Bench.

Designliga

Designliga 249

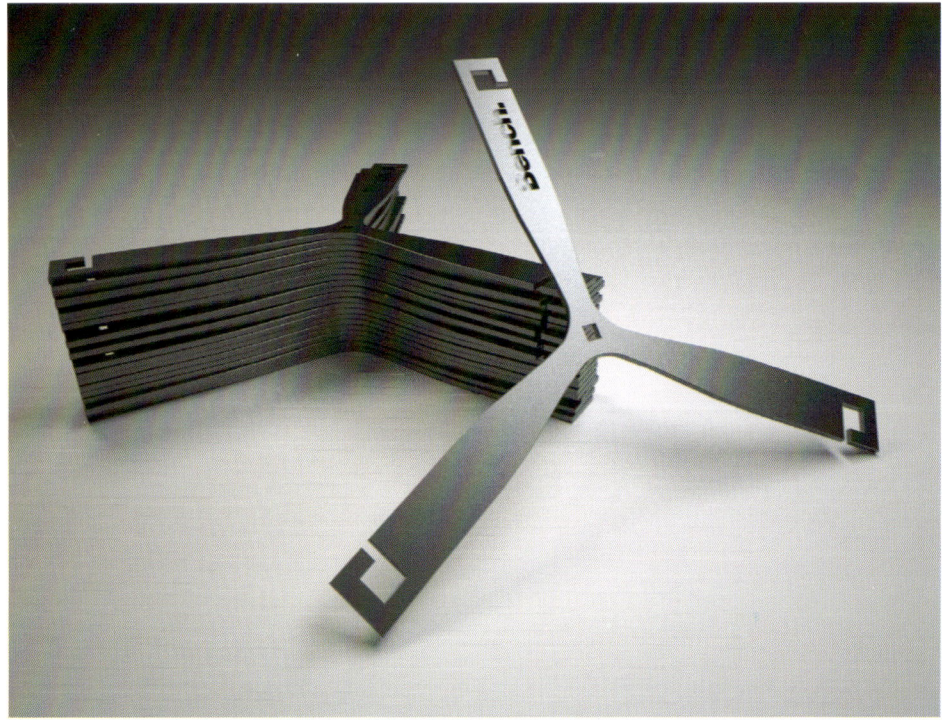

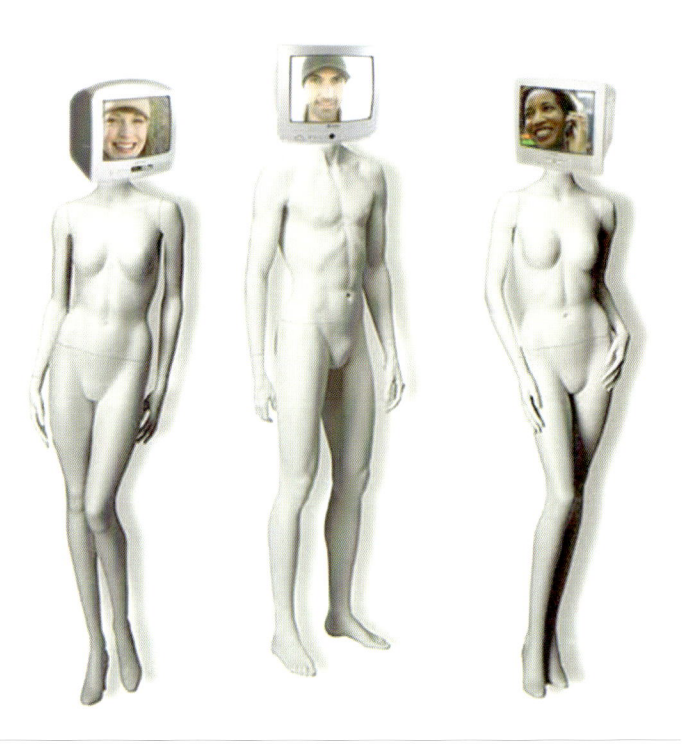

Designliga

The mannequins in the store window offer a quirky start to the shopping experience. Screens have been attached to the bodies in place of heads. These normally display random head photographs and drawings. However when sensors pick up motion around the store window the monitors connect to cameras, which are focused on the area in front of the window. This creates interaction between the store and passers-by as they try to position their faces to fit properly on the mannequins' bodies.

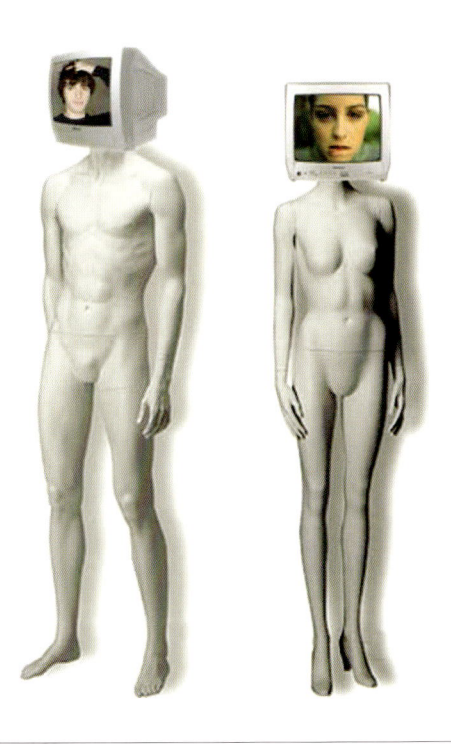

Designliga

252 Designliga

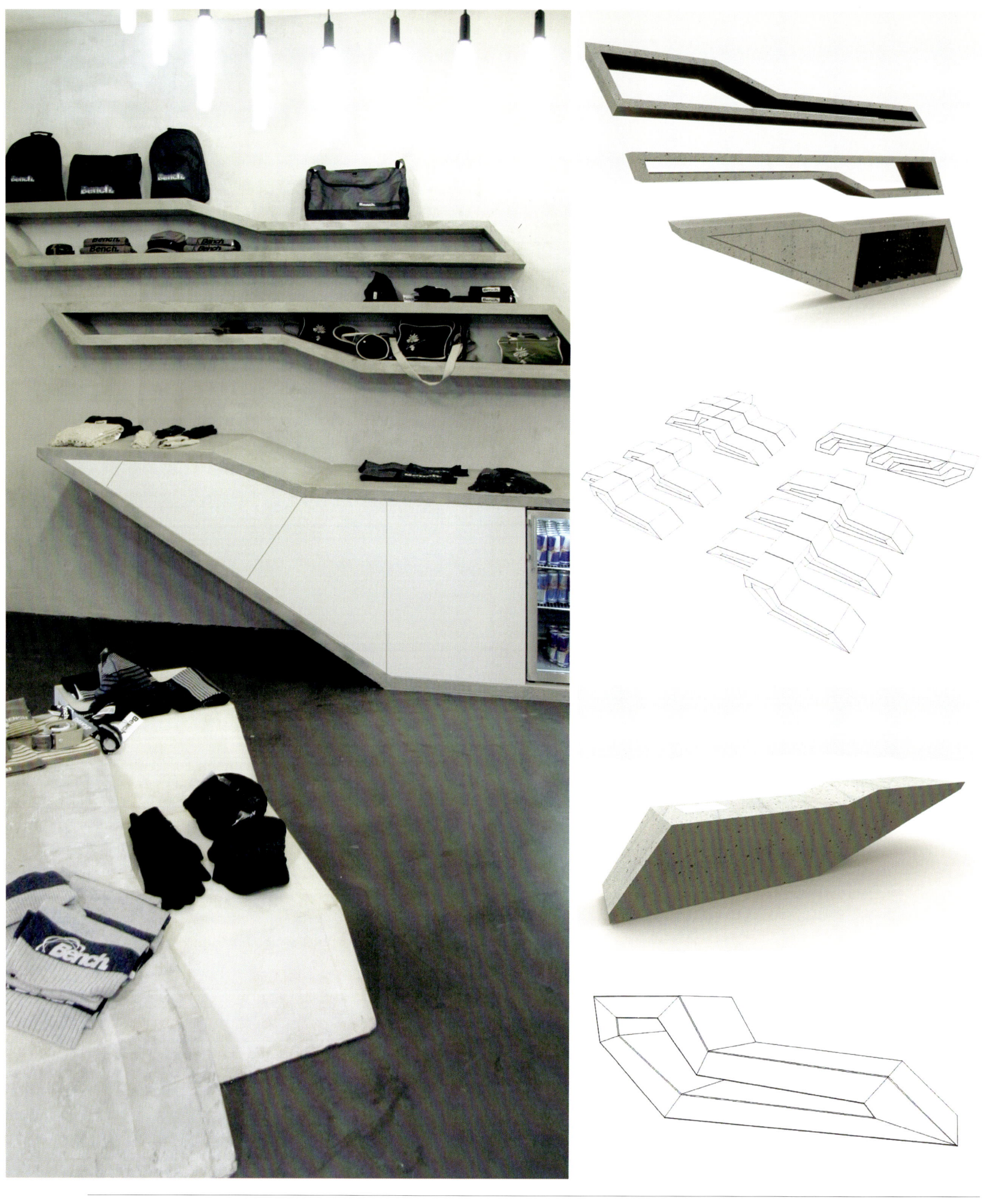

Designliga 253

Kei'ichi Irie + Power Unit Studio
Y House

This project for a family house on the outskirts of the city of Chita in Japan, began with a reflection on the part of the architects on the pathos they saw in the suburban landscpae. They argue that modernization, industrialization, and the IT revolution had destroyed these landscapes, and the little that they had retained of nature. Cities in pre-modern times found ways of reconciling themselves and co-existing with nature. But the suburbs have abandoned it, swayed by stereotyped urban models. To this day, excessive faith in industrial development and the forces of technology is causing hideous violence across the country. Such travesties will continue to be perpetrated in suburbs throughout Japan as long as there are those who believe that urban recovery may be improved by means of industry, science and technology. Dignity and serenity of landscape are on the way to extinction.

Y house is located in a row of houses on a hillside. A landscape with retaining walls among the wilderness as a result of development. Faced with their inability to reverse such devastation, the architects set themselves the task of building a house that was neither destructive nor violent.

Their strategy was to create a space isolated from the painful surrounding landscape. Once inside the building, the floor slopes down, following the topography of the site, to a large cantilevered terrace, directly open to the forest. The only major opening in this house, it frames the forest scenery through full height sliding glass doors with black frames. The opening facing the street allows daylight into the interior through translucent glass whcih simultaneously negates any view, except for one black-rimmed window which frames a small view of the town.

Walls on both sides of the cantilevered space are slanted outwards to avoid any similarity with the surrounding retaining walls. These slanted surfaces intersect, preliminary to becoming floors or walls, and resonate with each other to create a soundless acoustic space. The walls of the house, slabs of reinforced concrete only 15 cm thick resonate like the body of a violin.. The uniform thickness (15 cm) of all the surfaces allowed the architecture to take on such this musical quality. Motions such as the slow sway of forest trees, birds' flight, or falling rain animate the space with varied speeds. They reverberate between the slanted surfaces to reach the ear.

Architect:
Kei'ichi Irie + Power Unit Studio
Location:
Chita, Aichi, Japan
Photographs:
Hiroyuki Hirai

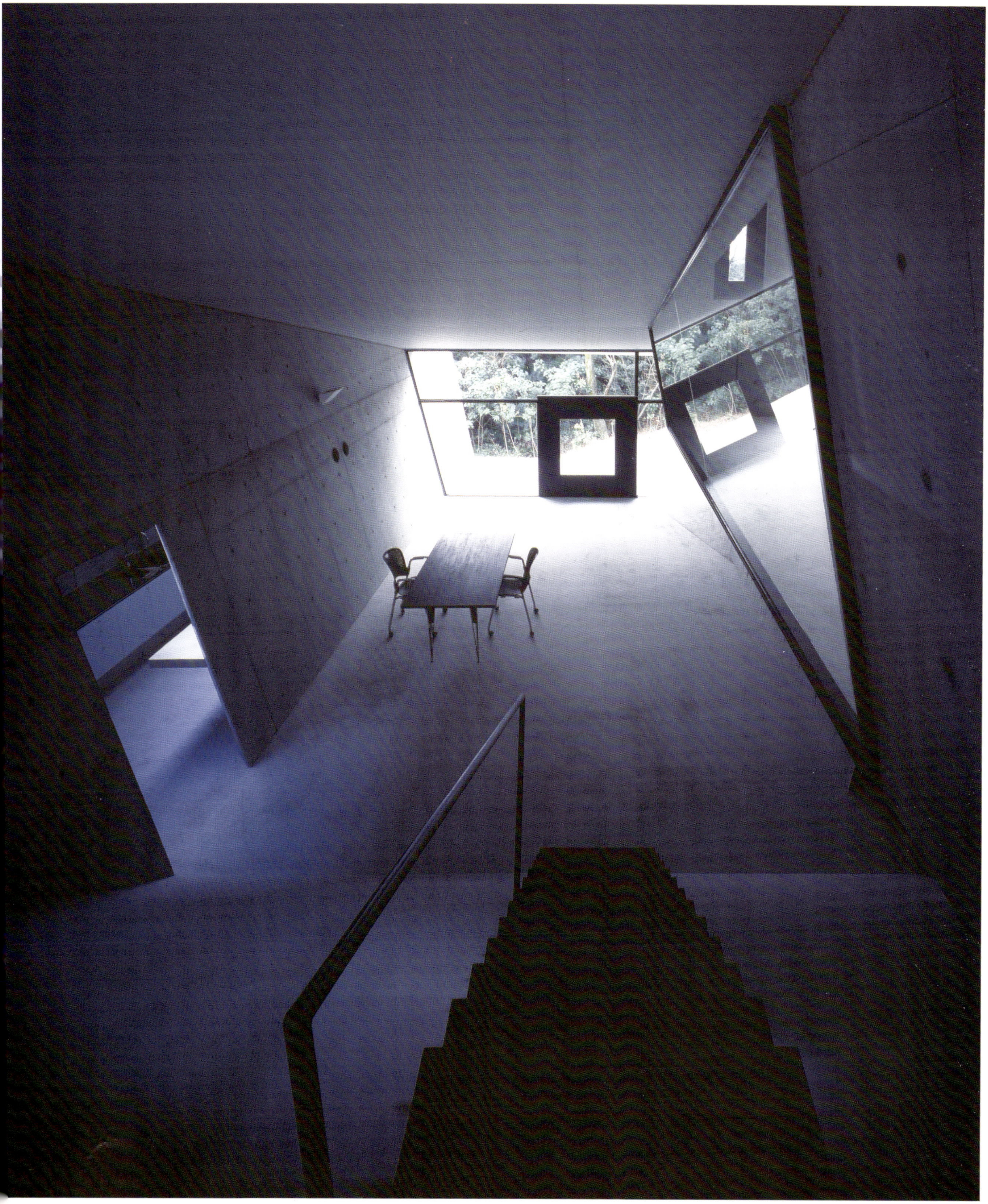

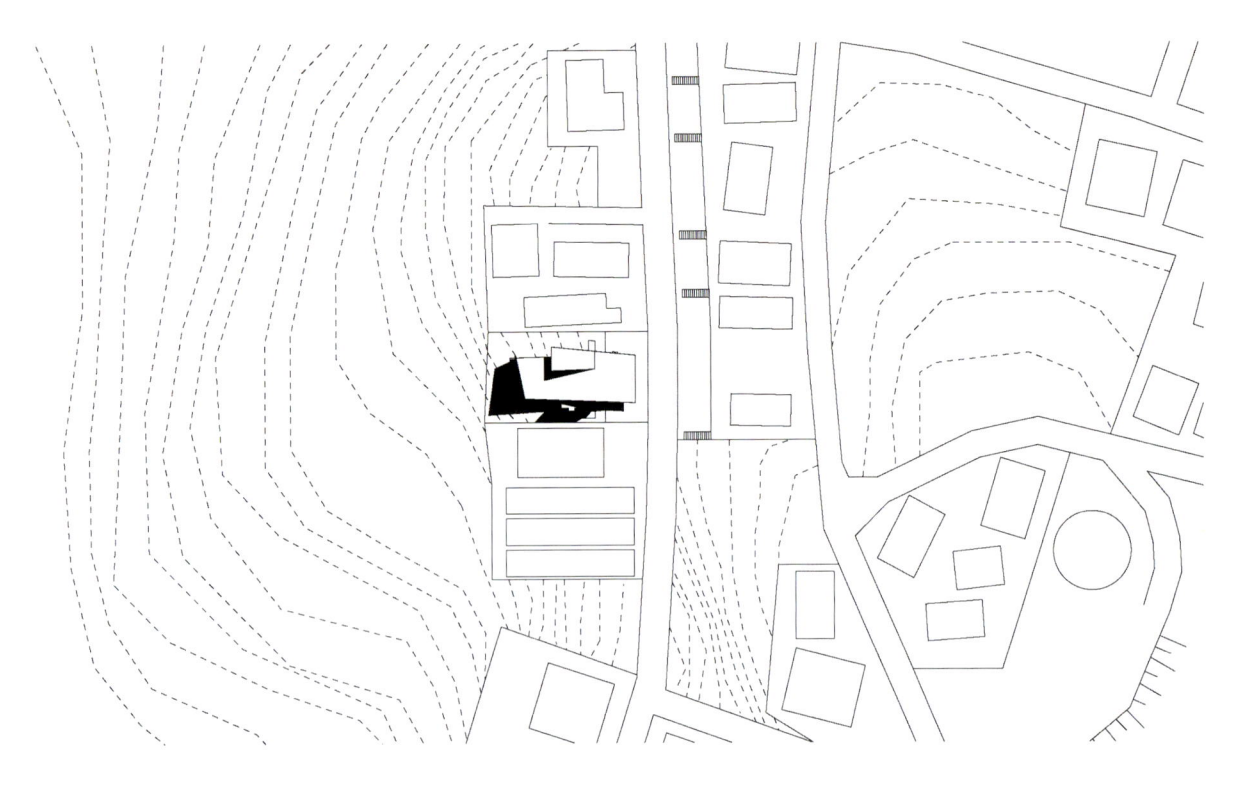

Y house is located in a row of houses on a hillside. Faced with their inability to reverse the devastation that urban development had already brought to the site, the architects set themselves the task of building a house that was neither destructive nor violent.

Site plan

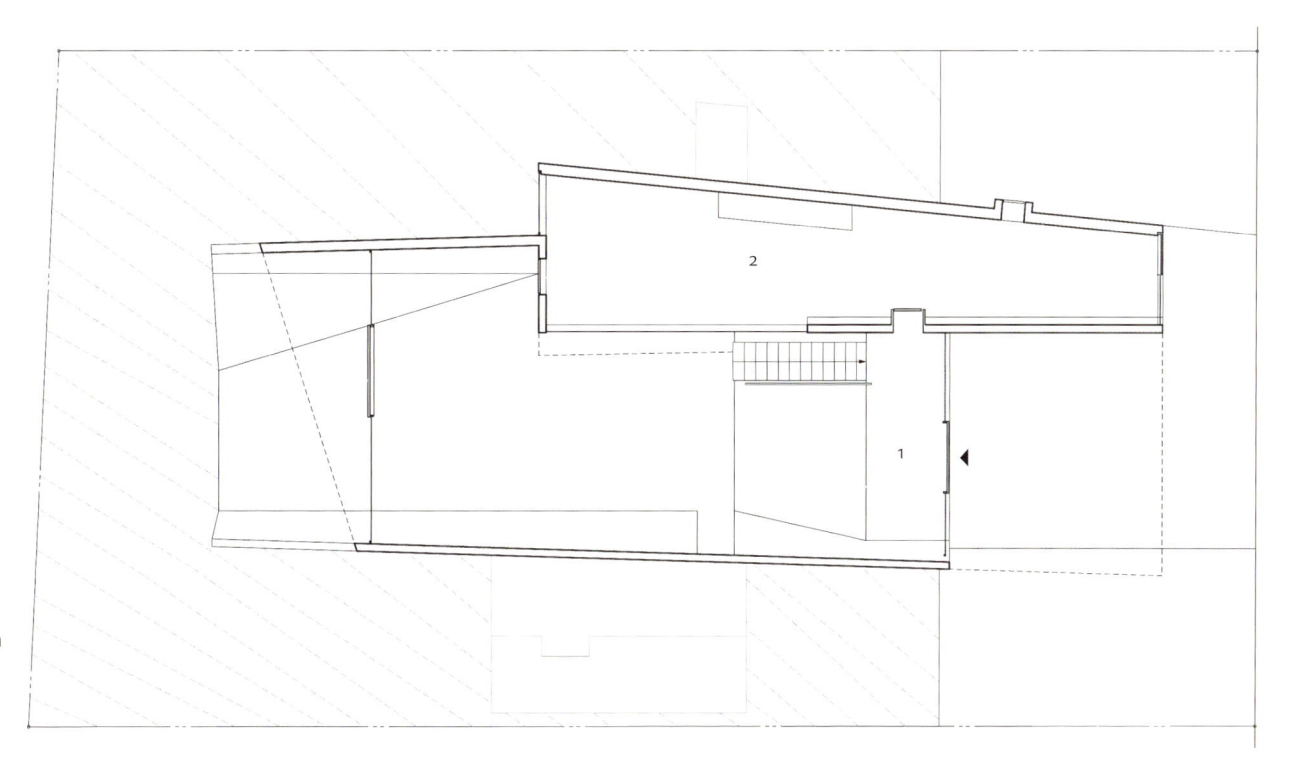

Ground floor plan
1. Entrance
2. Bedroom

Kei'ichi Irie + Power Unit Studio

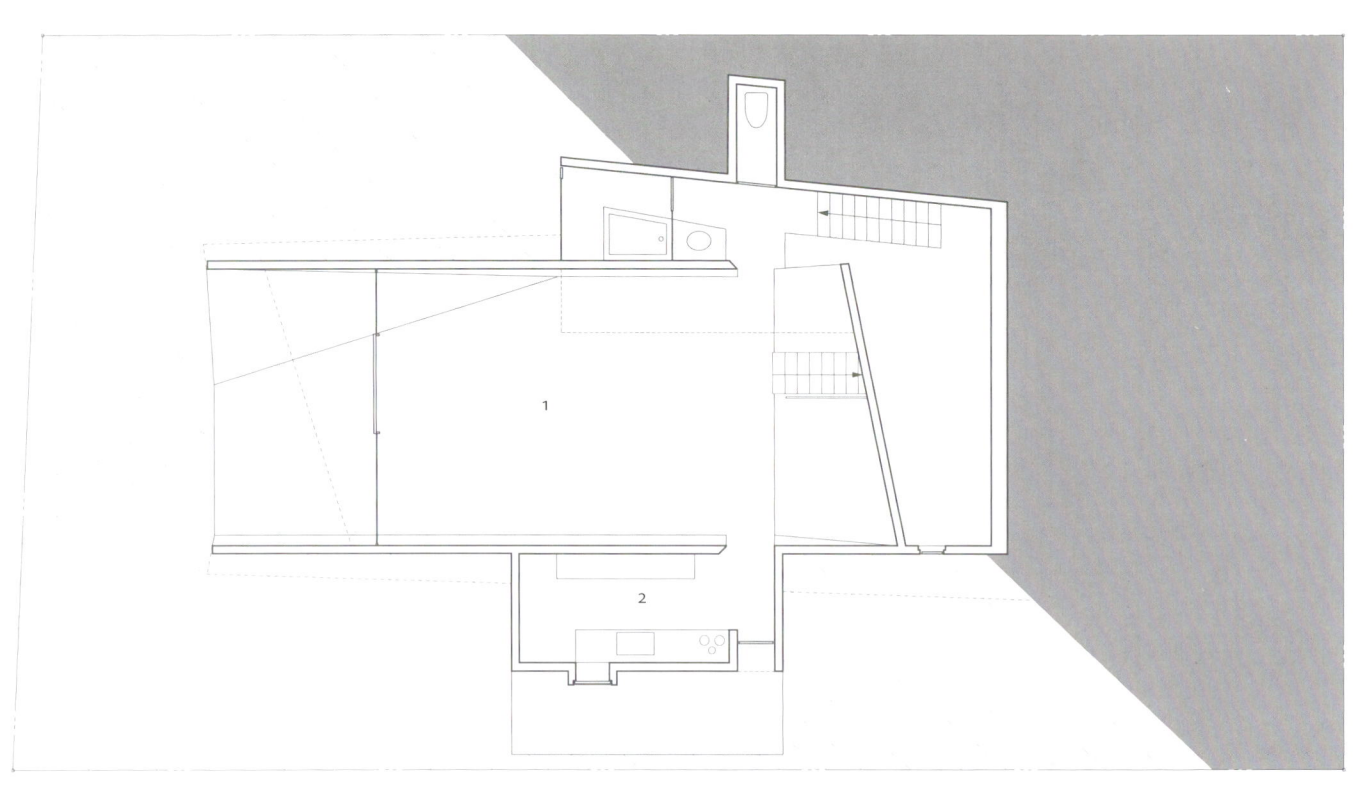

Floor plan, level -1
1. Living / Dining
2. Kitchen

258 Kei'ichi Irie + Power Unit Studio

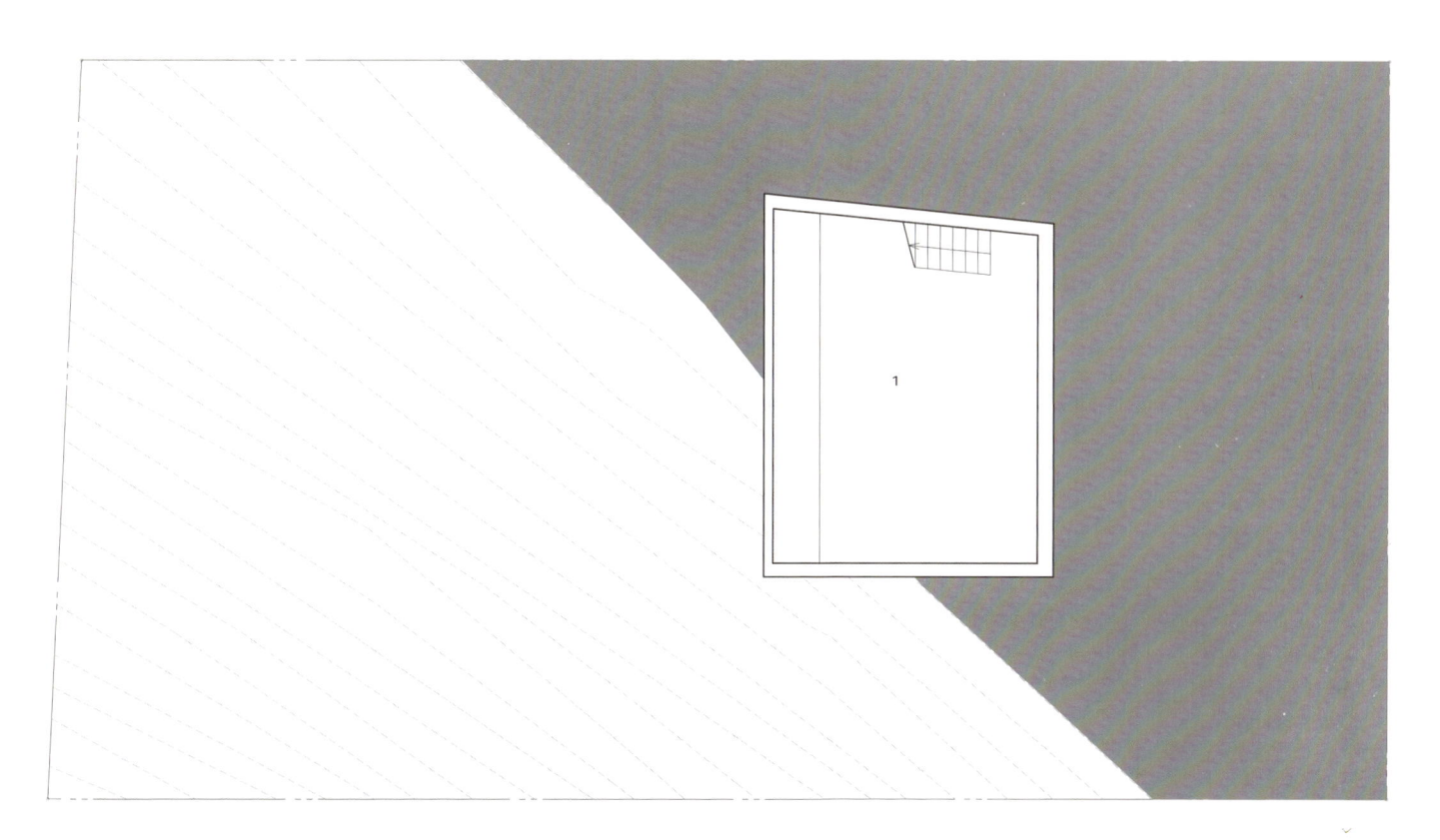

Floor plan, level -2
1. Bedroom

Kei'ichi Irie + Power Unit Studio

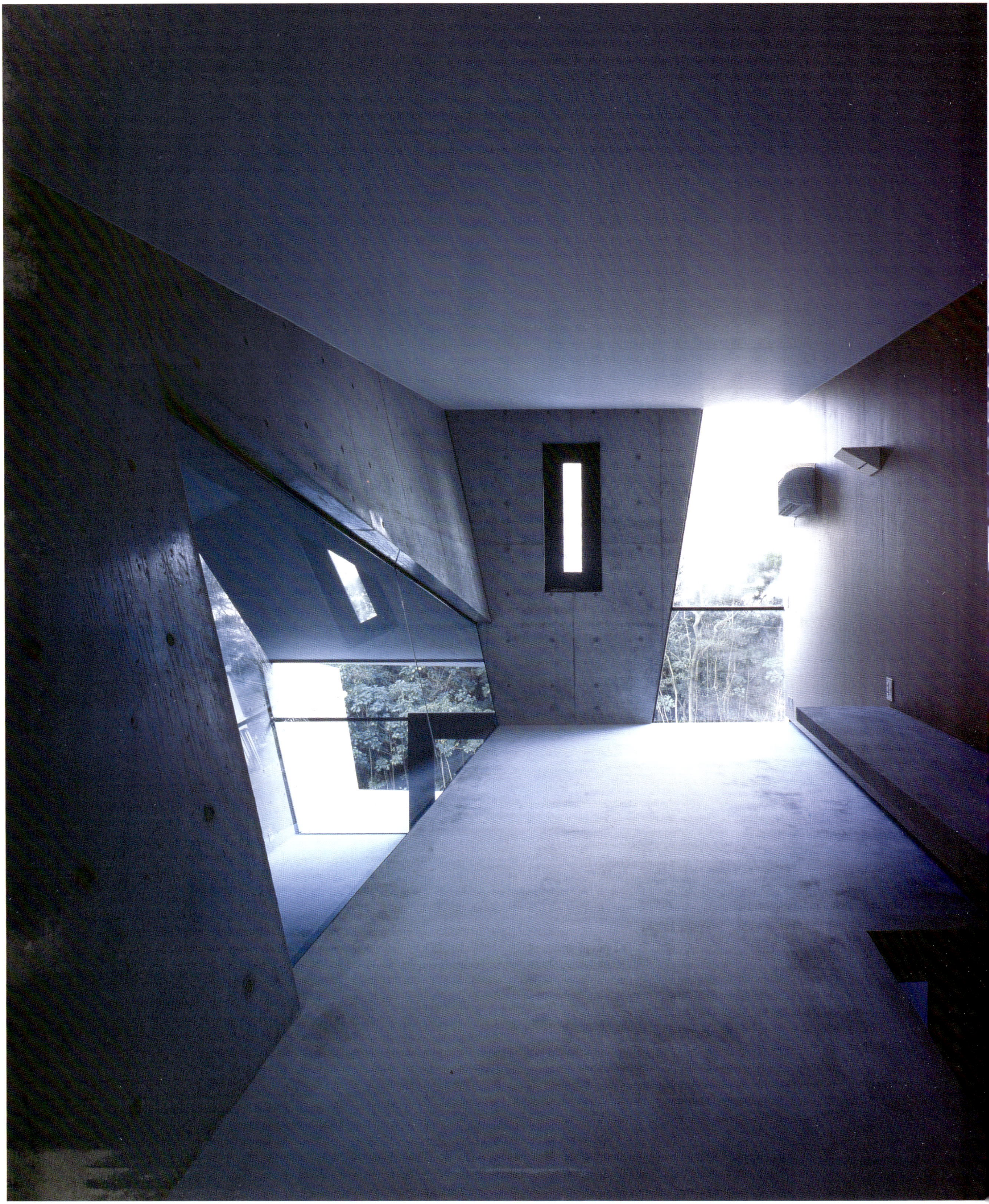

Longitudinal section
1. Entrance
2. Bedroom
3. Living / Dining

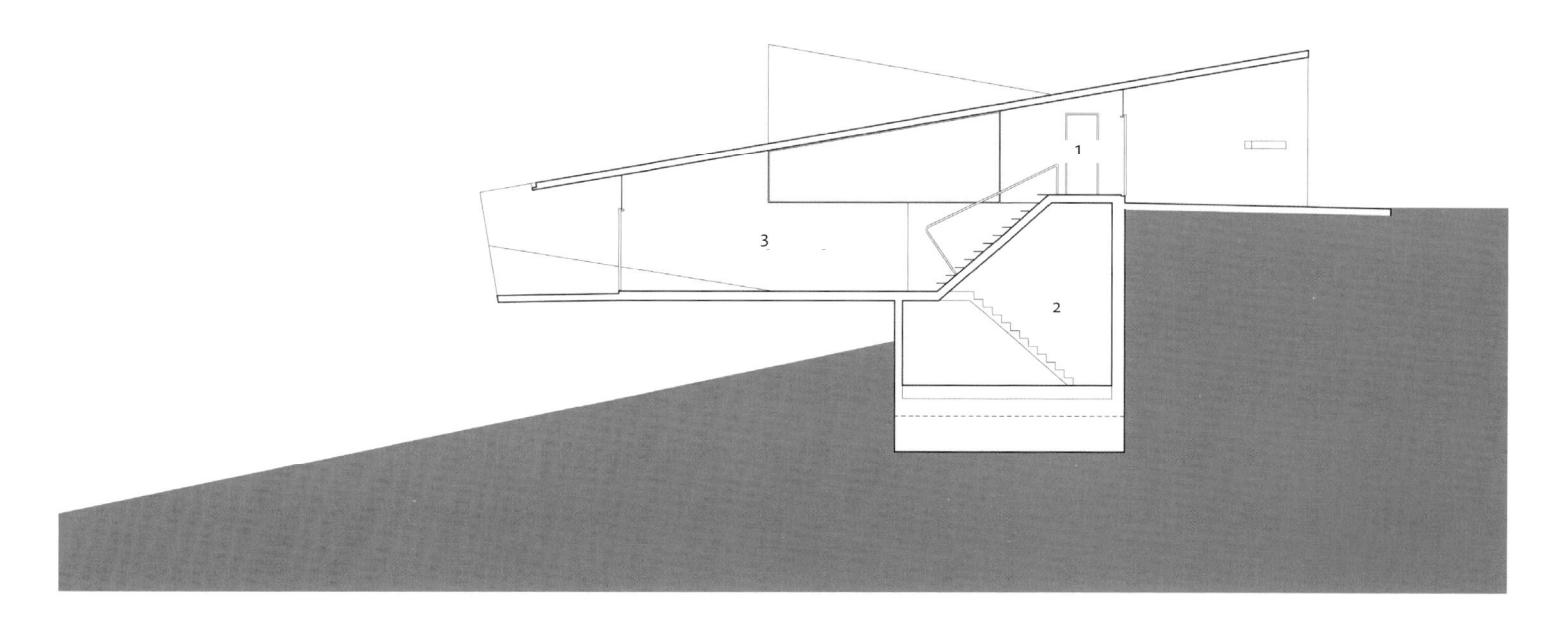

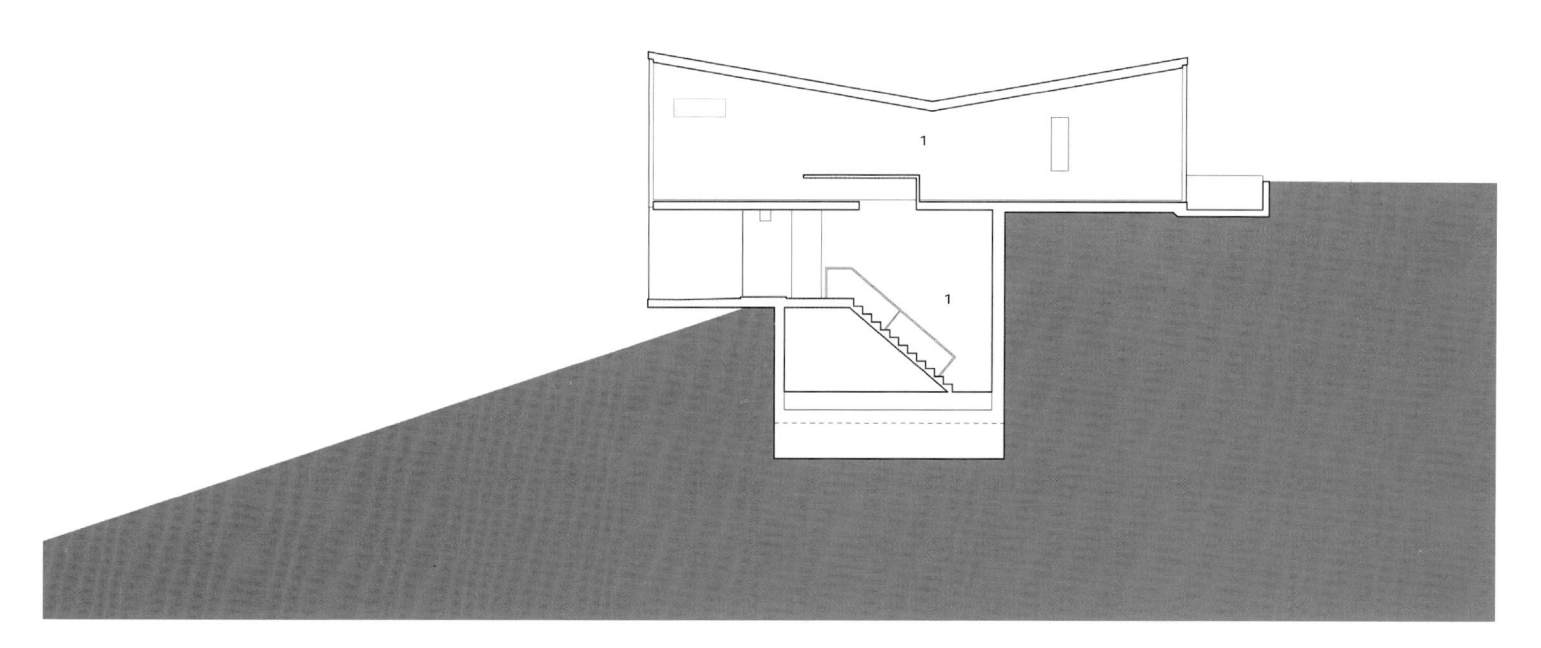

Longitudinal section
1. Bedroom

Kei'ichi Irie + Power Unit Studio   **261**

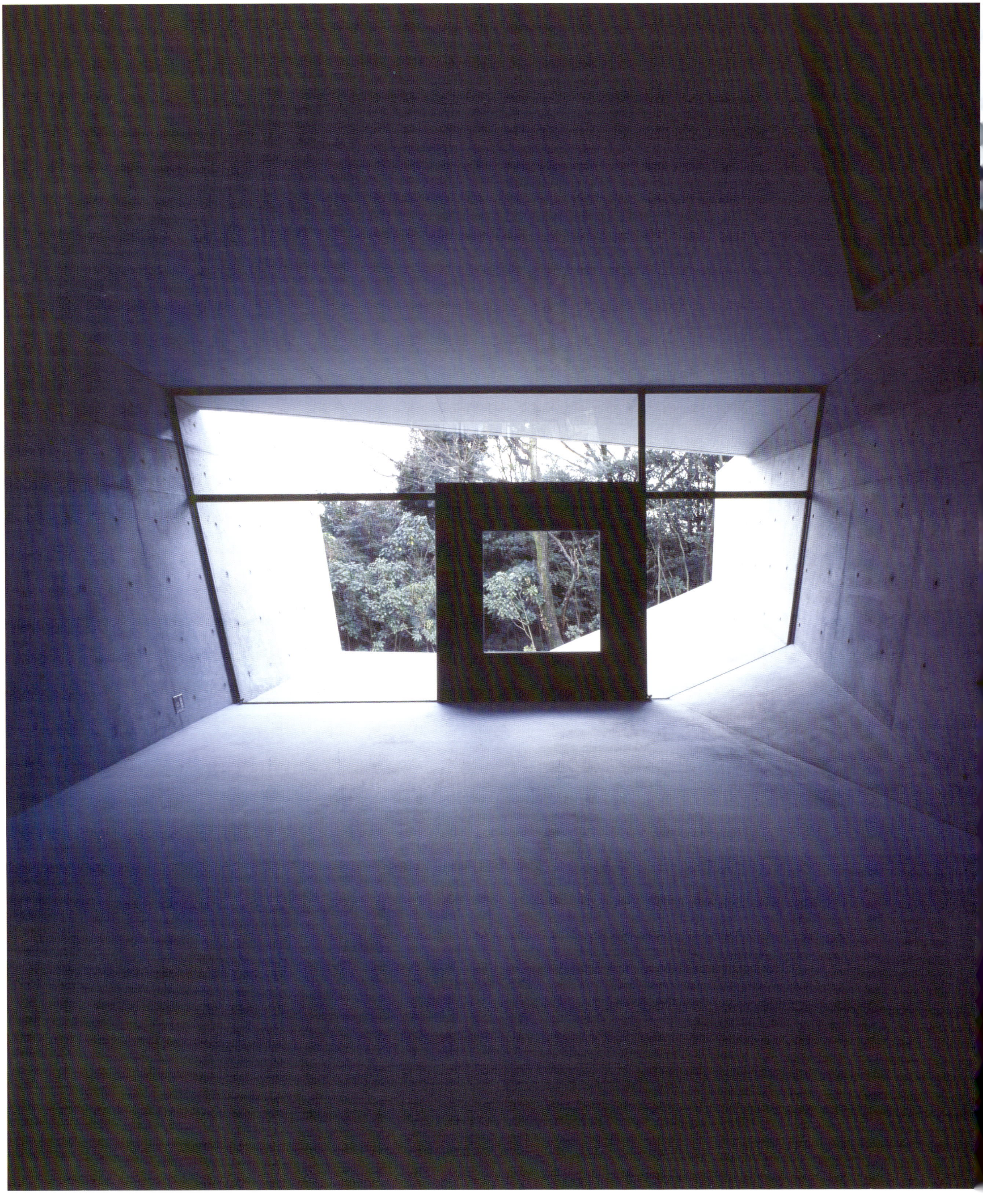

Construction section

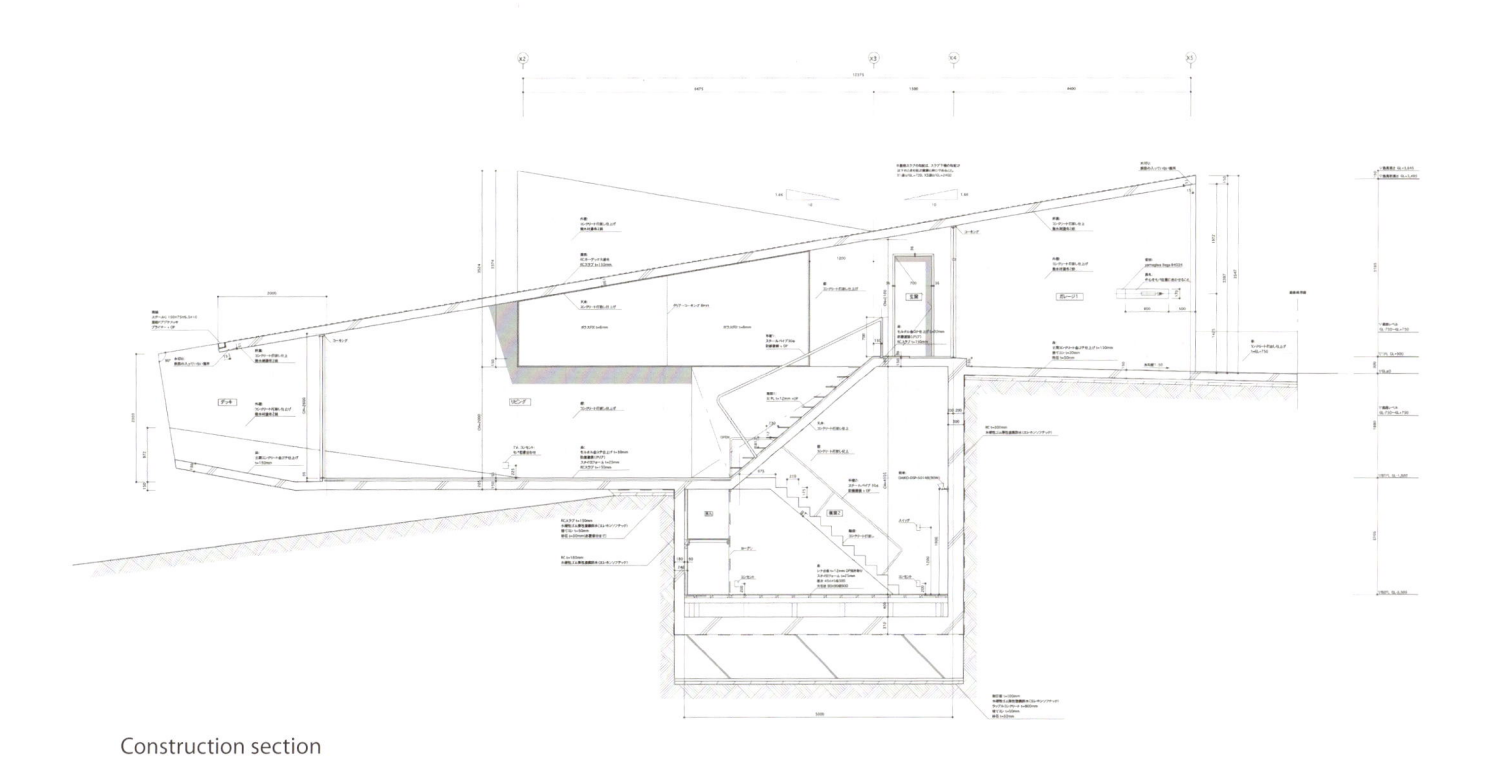

Kei'ichi Irie + Power Unit Studio

Mathias Klotz (KLOTZ & ASSOC.)
Eleven Women House

The Eleven Women House is a summer residence located on a sand-dune slope 160 km from the Chilean capital. Parents, siblings and friends gather here for the weekend or for as long as a few weeks, especially during the summer.

The name "Eleven Women" comes from the fact that the house belongs to a previously divorced couple whose combined family totals eleven daughters, whose ages range between 8 and 18.

The site has a steep slope towards the sea and enjoys great views of the Pacific Ocean that had to be taken advantage of. It is for this reason that the plan was developed in three differentiated levels, with a further level, under the swimming pool, containing the guest quarters. All bedrooms face the ocean.

The Eleven Women House was challenged by a vast plan on a site which, although big, was highly restricted by the building code and the topographical conditions. The resulting volume and the built area are the maximum permitted in both cases.

The first stage in the house's construction consisted in a 9 m (30 ft) deep cut, which would allow the entrance of light and fresh air through the east façade where the main entrance is located. This cut resulted in a substantial containment wall, created using an armed ground system, which permitted the growth of vegetation and minimized the physical and visual impact of the construction.

The dwelling was designed as a monolithic volume of reinforced concrete which houses a play room and a TV room at the lower level, the bedrooms and living room for the siblings at ground floor and the kitchen and main living room and bedroom at the upper level.

The formwork was made using pine boards arranged horizontally except for the main bedroom, where they were arranged vertically in order to introduce a visual differentiation.

The roof is used as a terrace and entrance patio, and the floor slab contains several skylights that light the kitchen and living room, as they do not receive direct natural light until sunset. All floors were clad in travertine so as to achieve the same spatial continuity attained in the ceilings, where the concrete slab crosses all rooms without interruption. Partitions were painted white and doors are frameless in order to achieve the same objective.

The landscaping uses local species, keeping in mind that the native vegetation of this coast need to be guarded and strengthened. Access to this steep site was solved with the construction of pre-cast concrete terraces emulating steps and paths.

Architect:
Mathias Klotz (KLOTZ y ASOC.)
Location:
Beranda, Chile
Photographs:
Cristóbal Palma

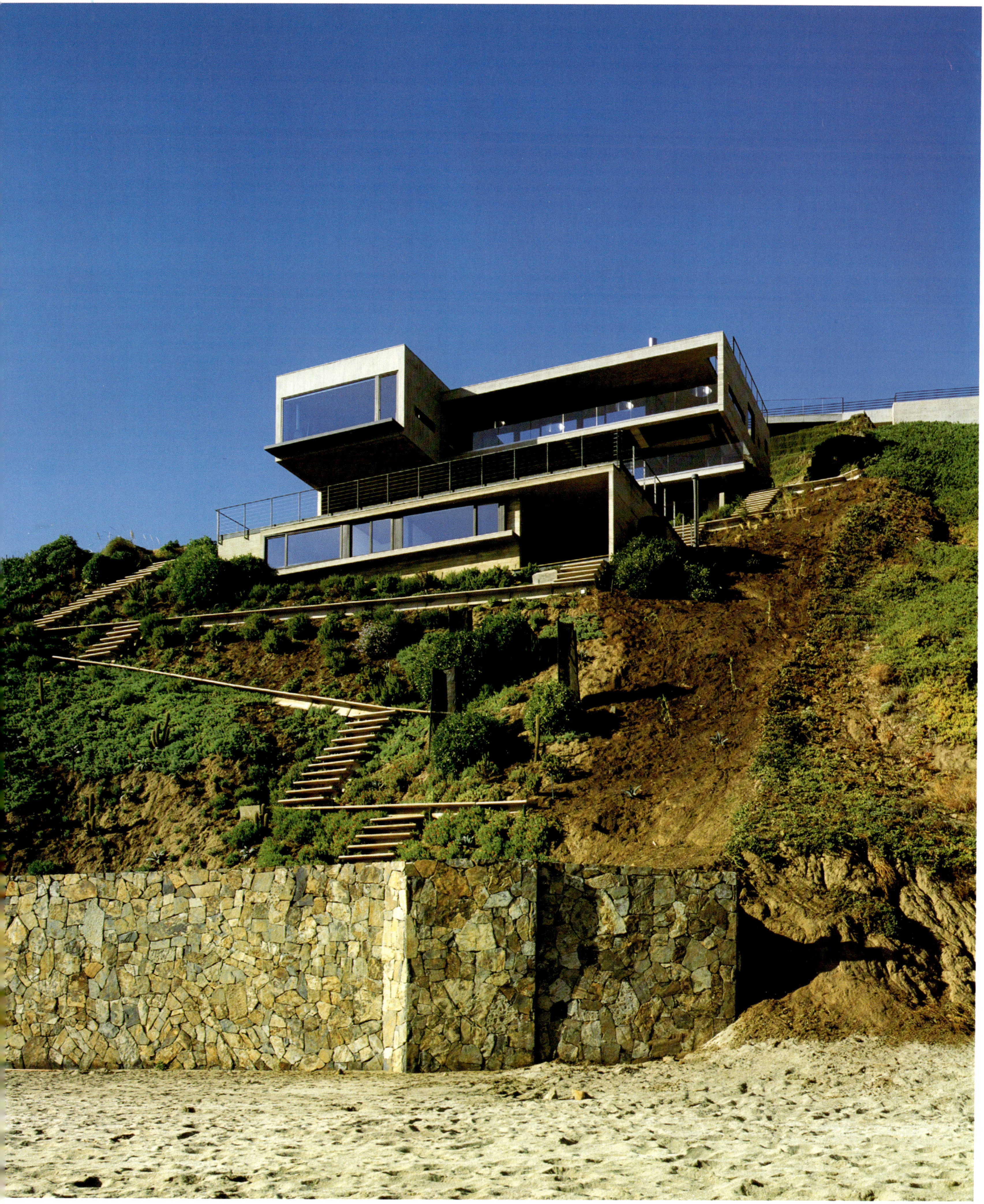

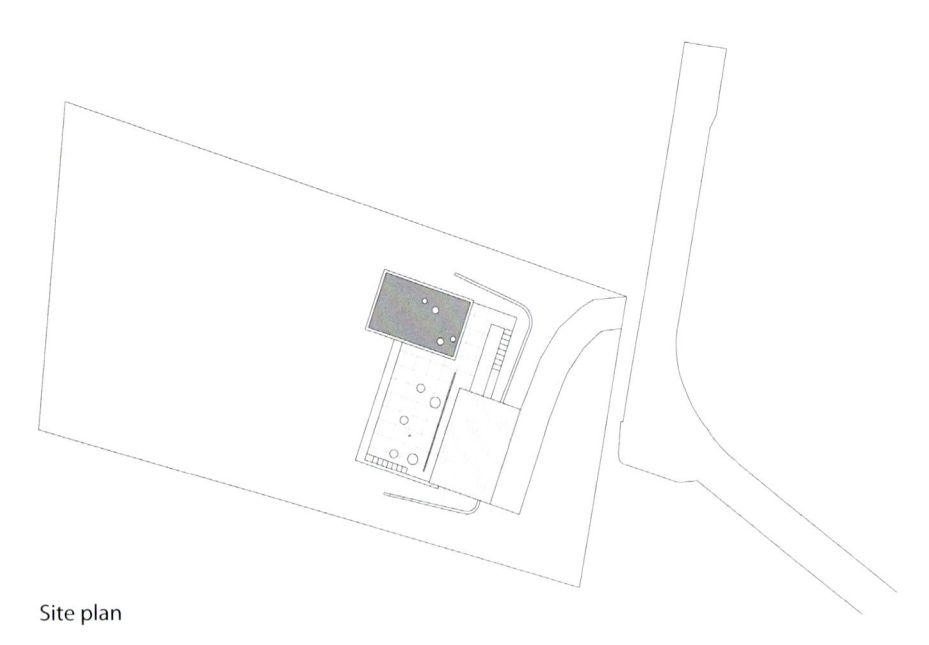

The site has a steep slope towards the sea and enjoys great views of the Pacific Ocean that had to be taken advantage of. It is for this reason that the plan was developed in three differentiated levels, with a further level, under the swimming pool, containing the guest quarters.

Site plan

Mathias Klotz (KLOTZ & ASSOC.)

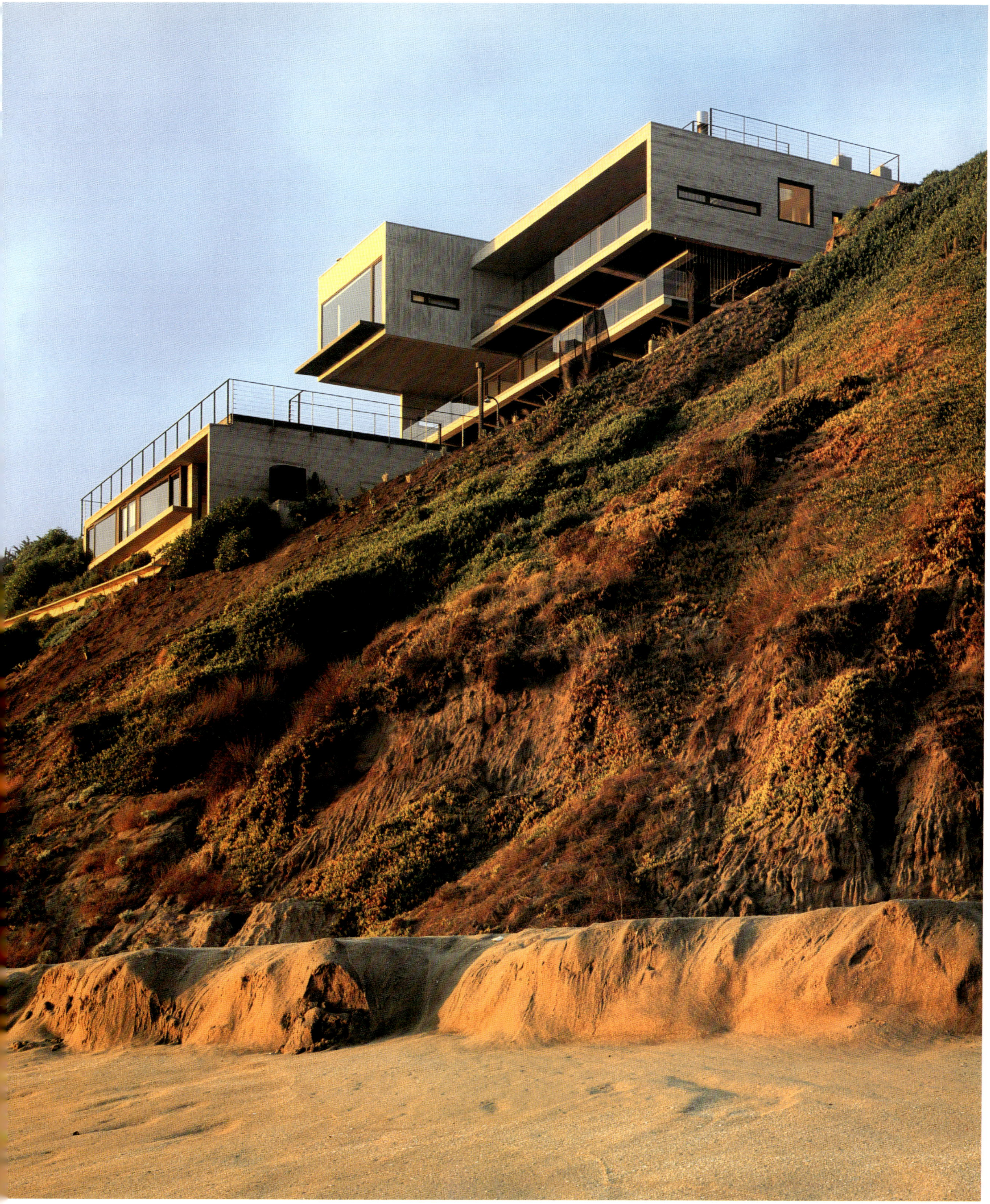

Floor plan, level +1

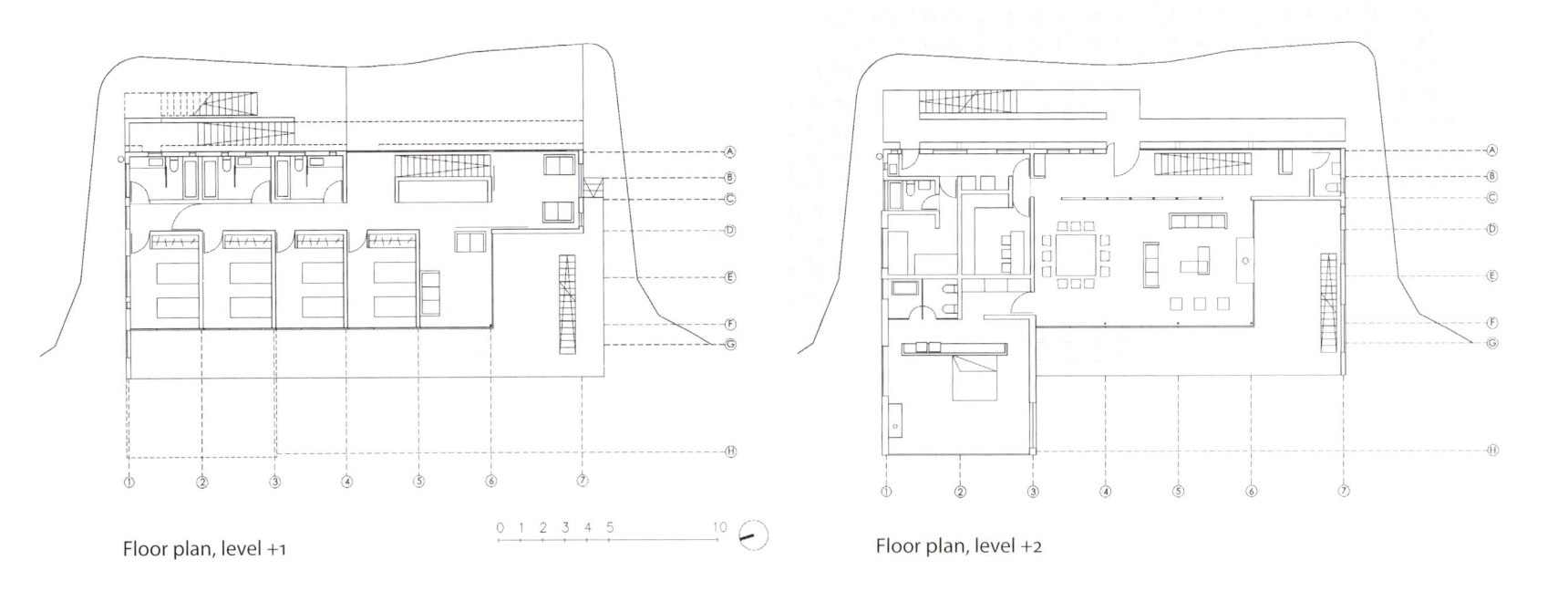

Floor plan, level +2

Mathias Klotz (KLOTZ & ASSOC.)

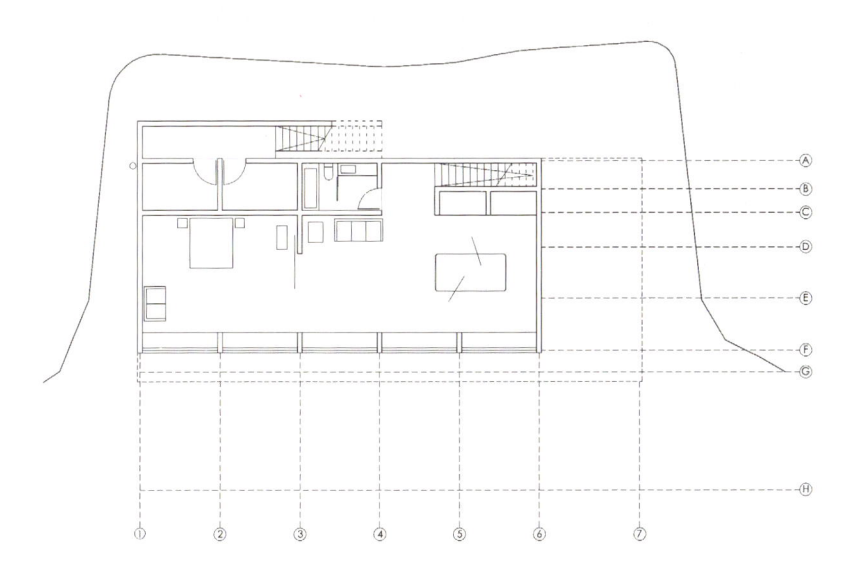

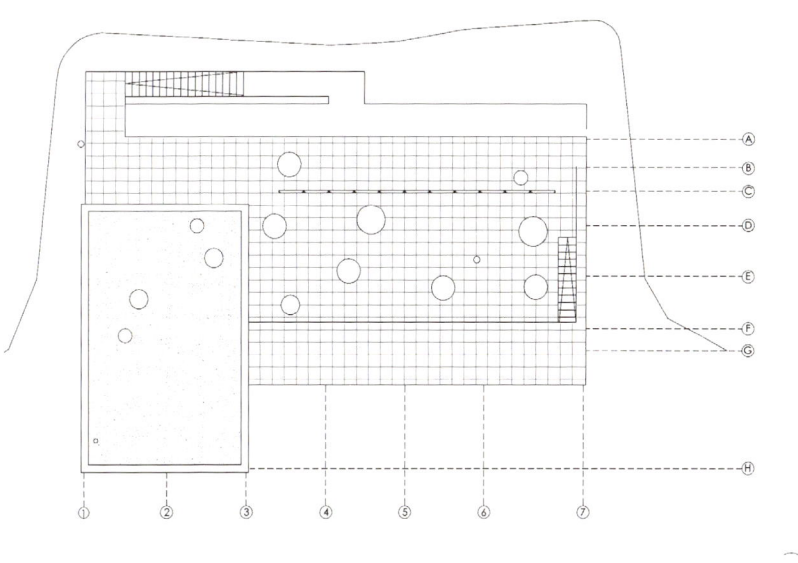

Basement plan

Roof plan

Mathias Klotz (KLOTZ & ASSOC.)

Section A

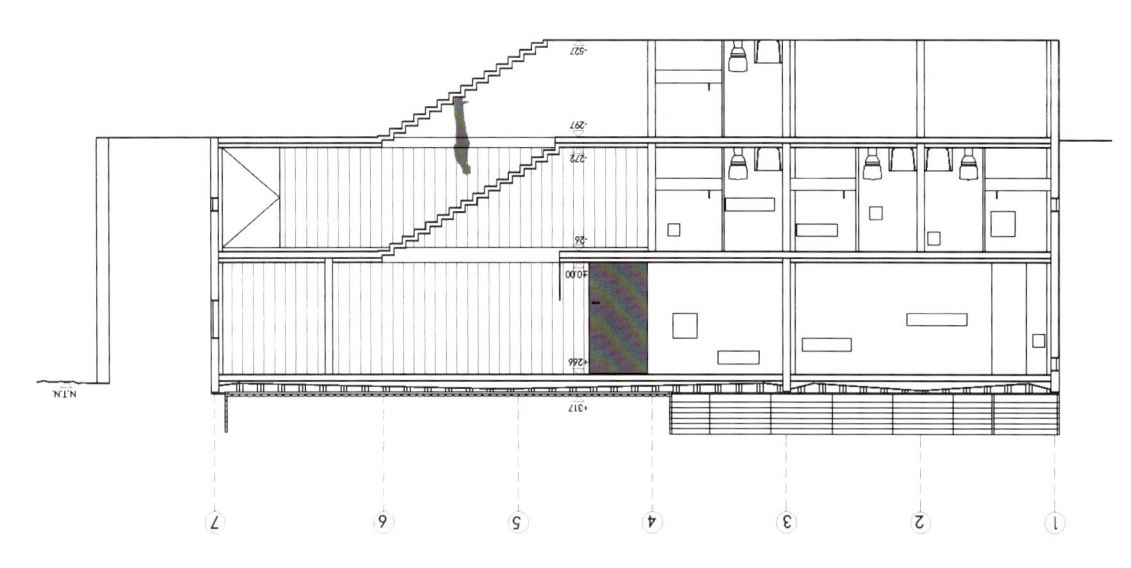

All floors were clad in travertine so as to achieve the same spatial continuity attained in the ceilings, where the concrete slab crosses all rooms without interruption. Partitions were painted white and doors are frameless in order to achieve the same objective.

Mathias Klotz (KLOTZ & ASSOC.)

Section C

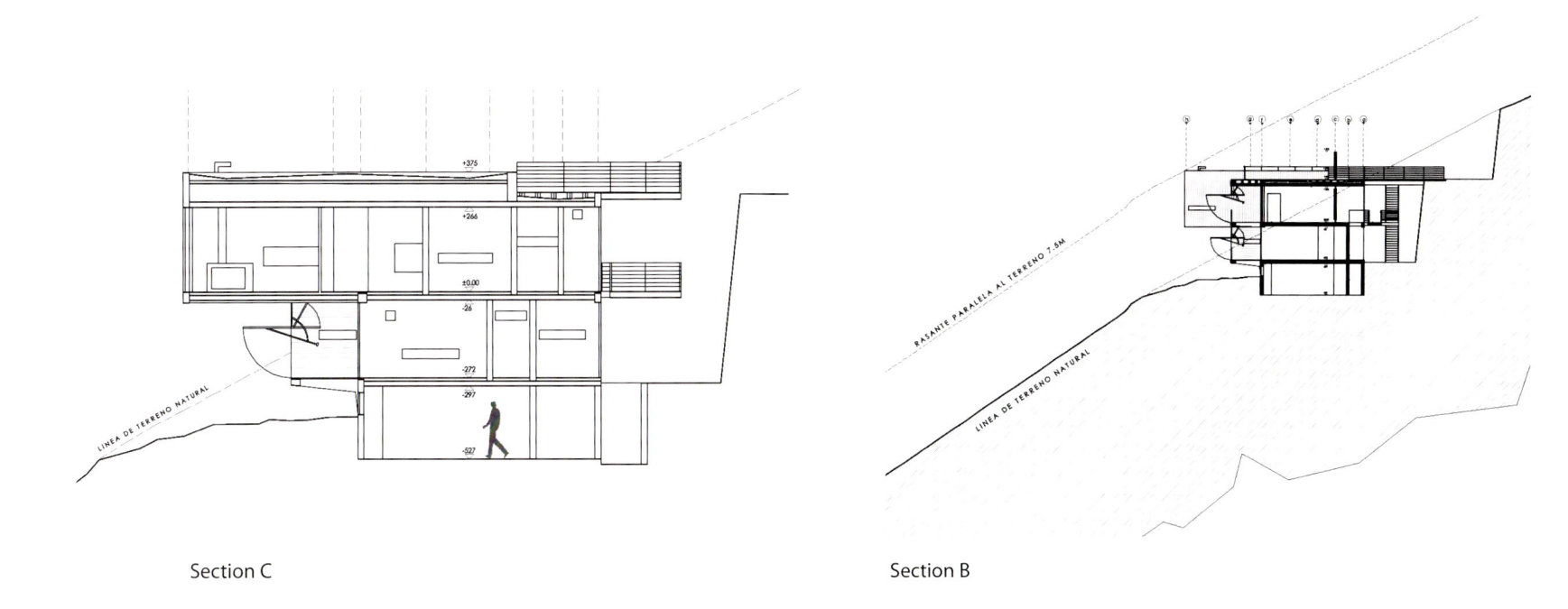

Section B

Mathias Klotz (KLOTZ & ASSOC.)

South façade

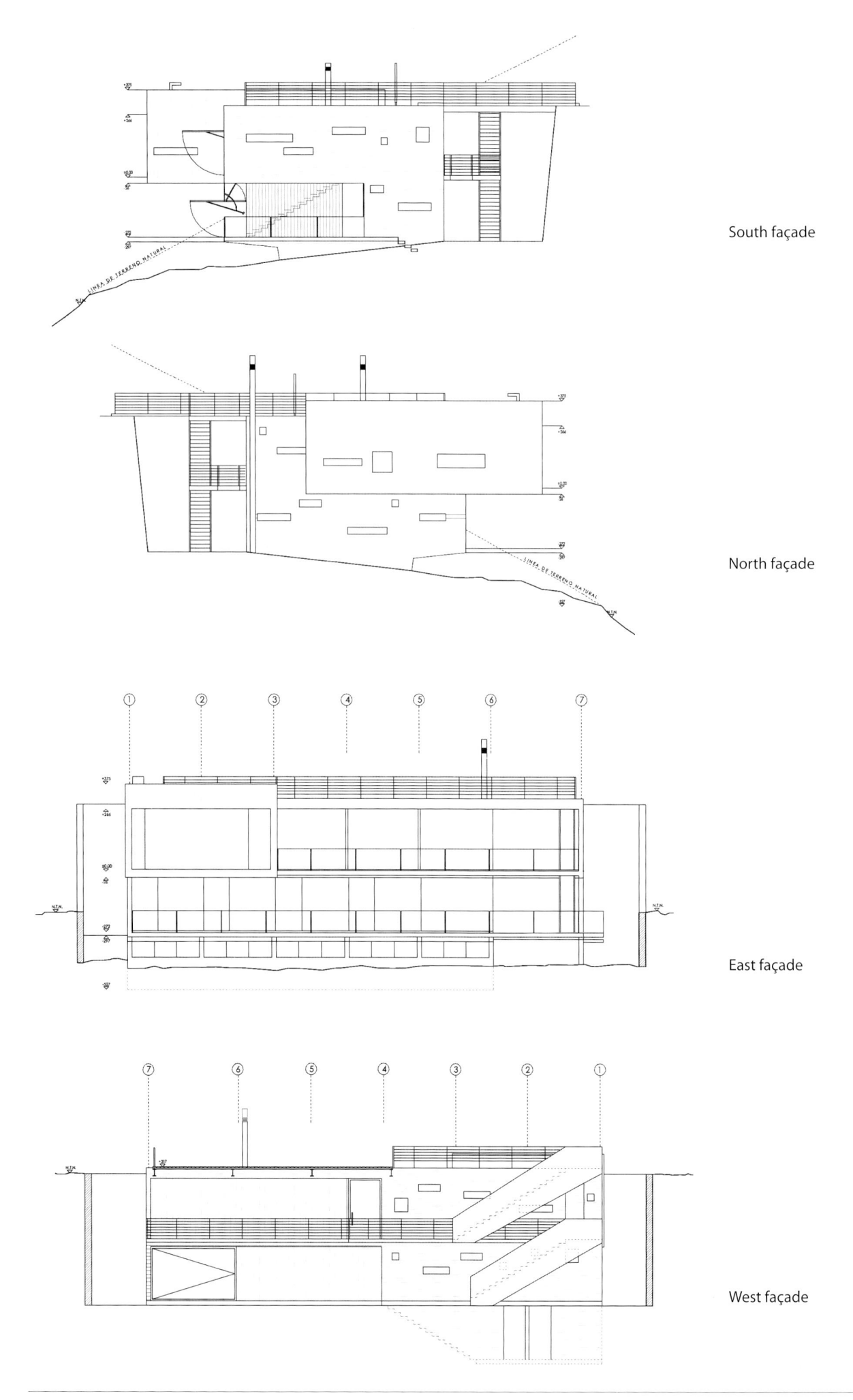

North façade

East façade

West façade

Mathias Klotz (KLOTZ & ASSOC.)

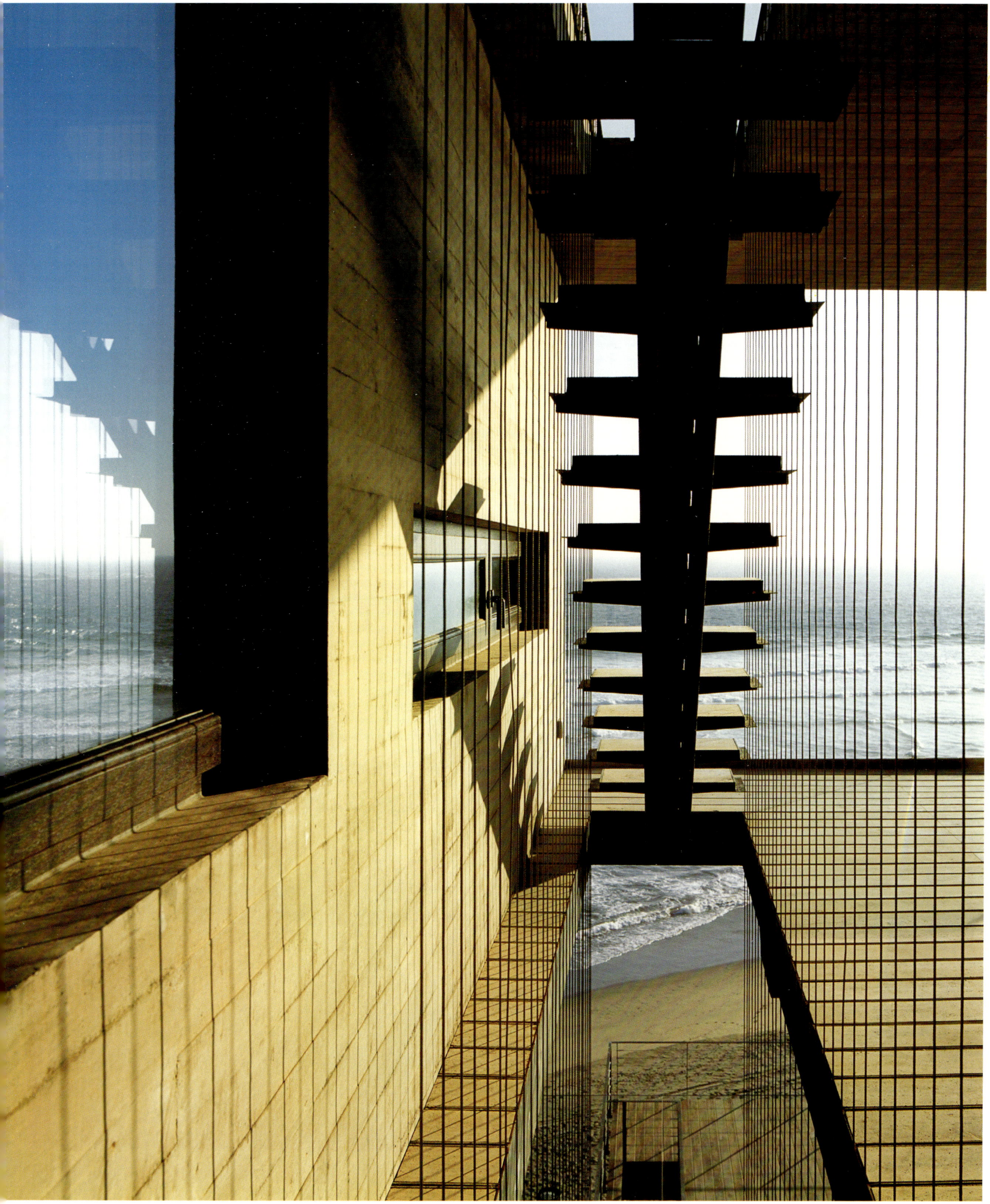

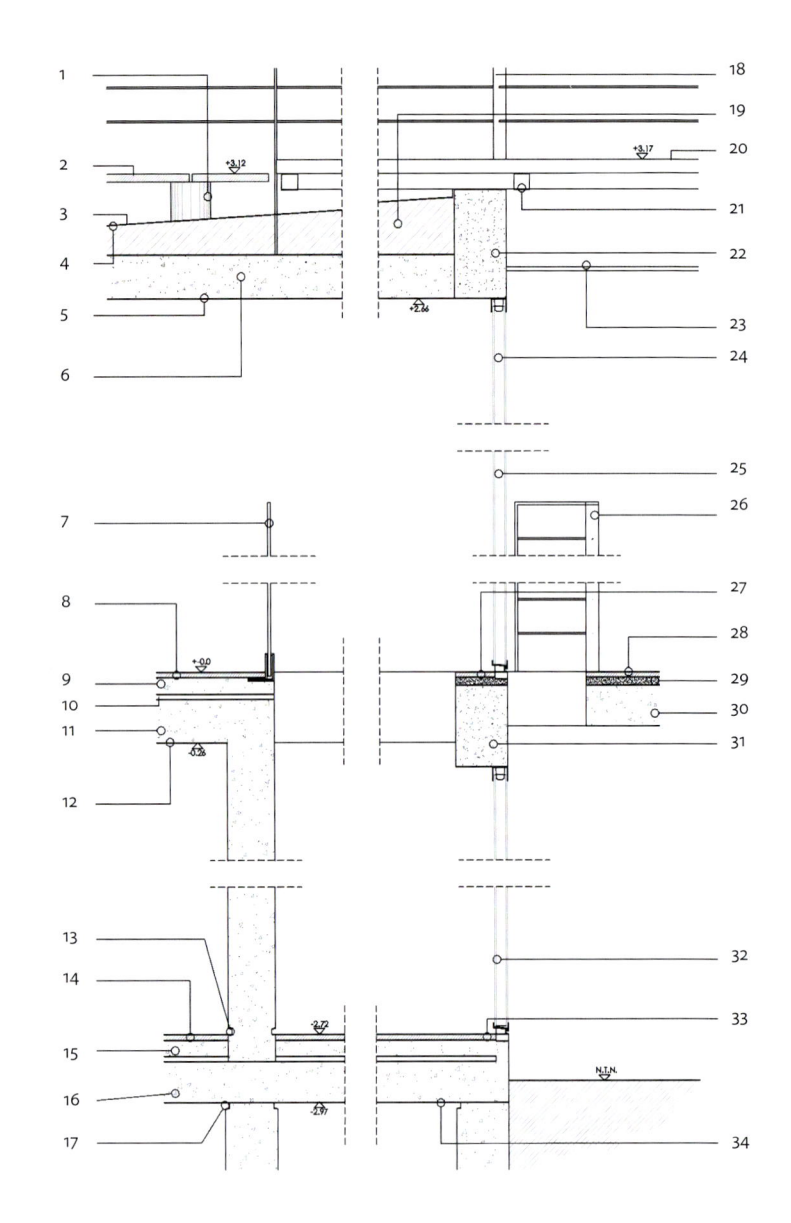

1. QHC Concrete + L.Geotextile ledge
2. High grade cement tablet 50 × 50
3. QHC 173 waterproofing
4. Geotextile laminate
5. Roof of exposed reinforced concrete pieces from 3 in mold, tongue and groove
6. Reinforced concrete slab according to calculations = 16 cm
7. Glass handrail according to detail
8. National travertine marble 20 mm
9. Light concrete covering slab for pipes and underfloor heating
10. Expanded polystyrene 2 cm
11. Reinforced concrete according to calculations = 16 cm
12. Roof of exposed reinforced concrete pieces from 3 in mold, tongue and groove
13. Edging 1.5 × 2 cm
14. National travertine marble 20 mm
15. Lightweight concrete covering slab for pipes and underfloor heating
16. Reinforced concrete slab according to calculations = 15 cm
17. Edging 1.5 × 2 cm
18. Handrail according to detail, attached to slab
19. Lightweight concrete covering slab
20. Stained pine decking 3 × 4 in. with Siladecor sealant
21. Metal frame 60 × 60 × 4 mm
22. Reinforced concrete beam, 3 in. mold, tongue and groove and brushed
23. Metal beam+attachment according to calculations
24. Profilit window VPr 01
25. Profilit window VPr 01
26. Metal handrail according to detail
27. National travertine marble 20 mm
28. High grade cement tablet 50 × 50
29. Setback 3 cm
30. Reinforced concrete slab according to calculations
31. Reinforced concrete beam, 3 in. mold, tongue and groove and brushed
32. Profilit window VPr02
33. National travertine marble 20 mm
34. Roof of exposed reinforced concrete pieces from 3 in. mold, tongue and groove

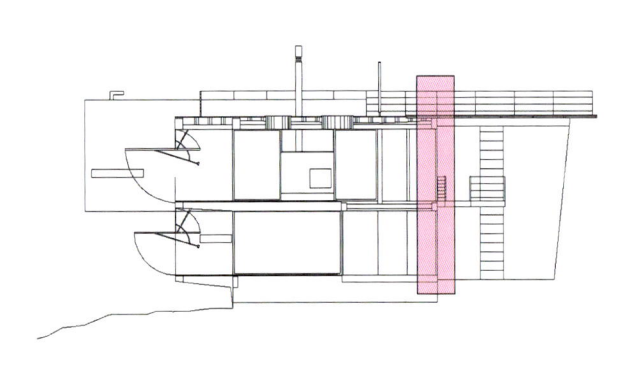

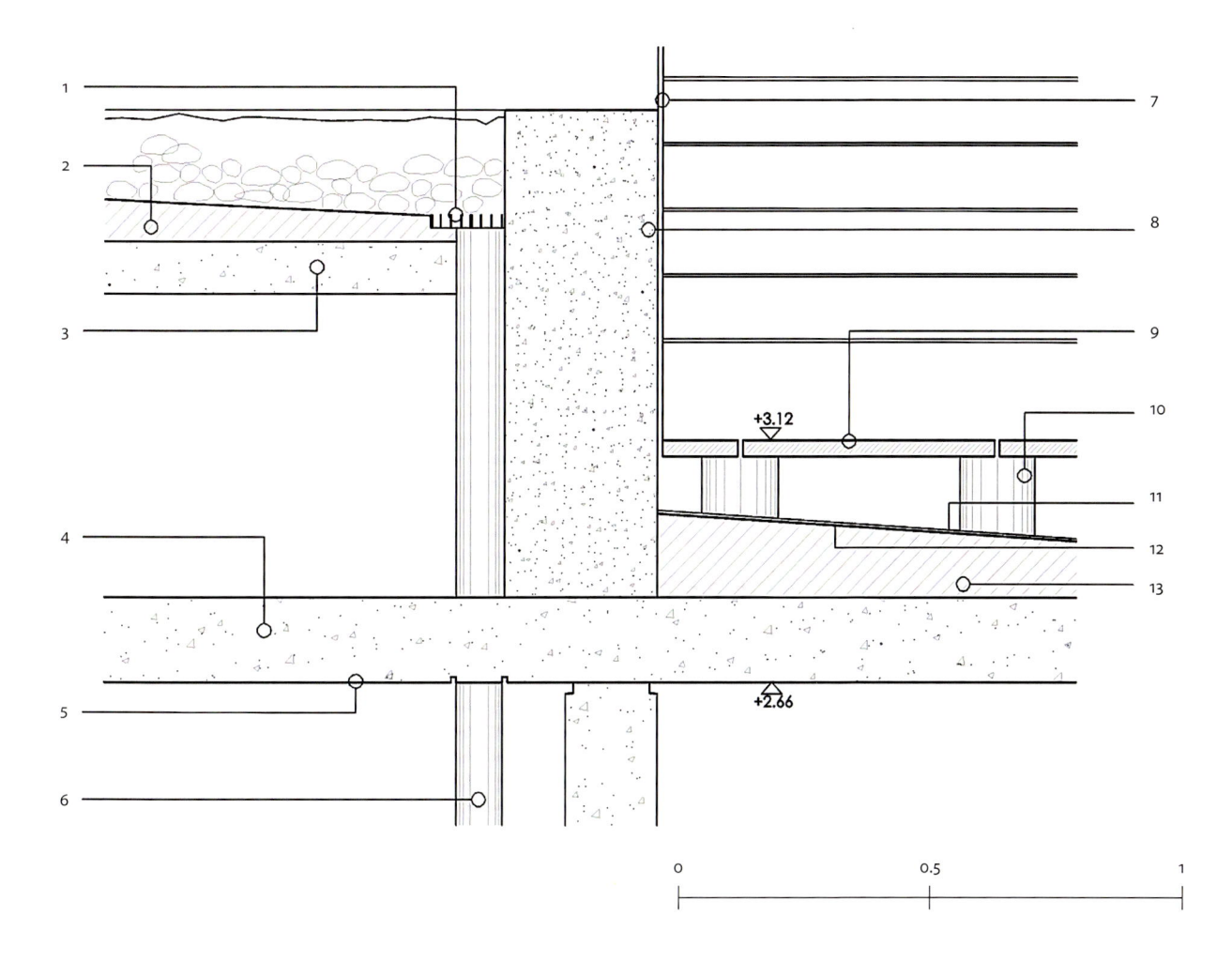

Permanent shuttering area

1. Grill with 1 cm bars
2. Lightweight concrete covering slab
3. Reinforced concrete slab according to calculations = 10 cm
4. Reinforced concrete slab according to calculations = 16 cm
5. Roof of exposed reinforced concrete pieces from 3 in. mold, tongue and groove
6. Rainwater downspout diam. 9 cm
7. Metal handrail according to detail attached to slab
8. Exposed reinforced concrete beam, 3" mold, tongue and groove and brushed
9. High grade cement tablet 50 × 50
10. QHC Concrete + L.Geotextile ledges
11. GHC 1/3 waterproofing
12. Geotextile laminate
13. Lightweight concrete covering slab sloped depending on floor

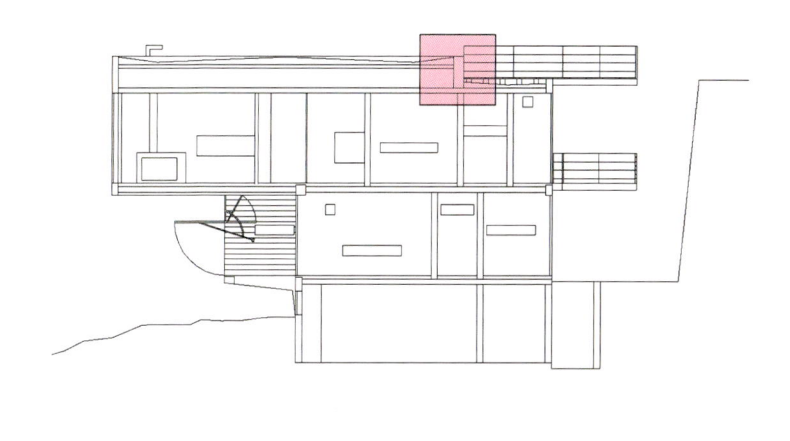

Mathias Klotz (KLOTZ & ASSOC.)

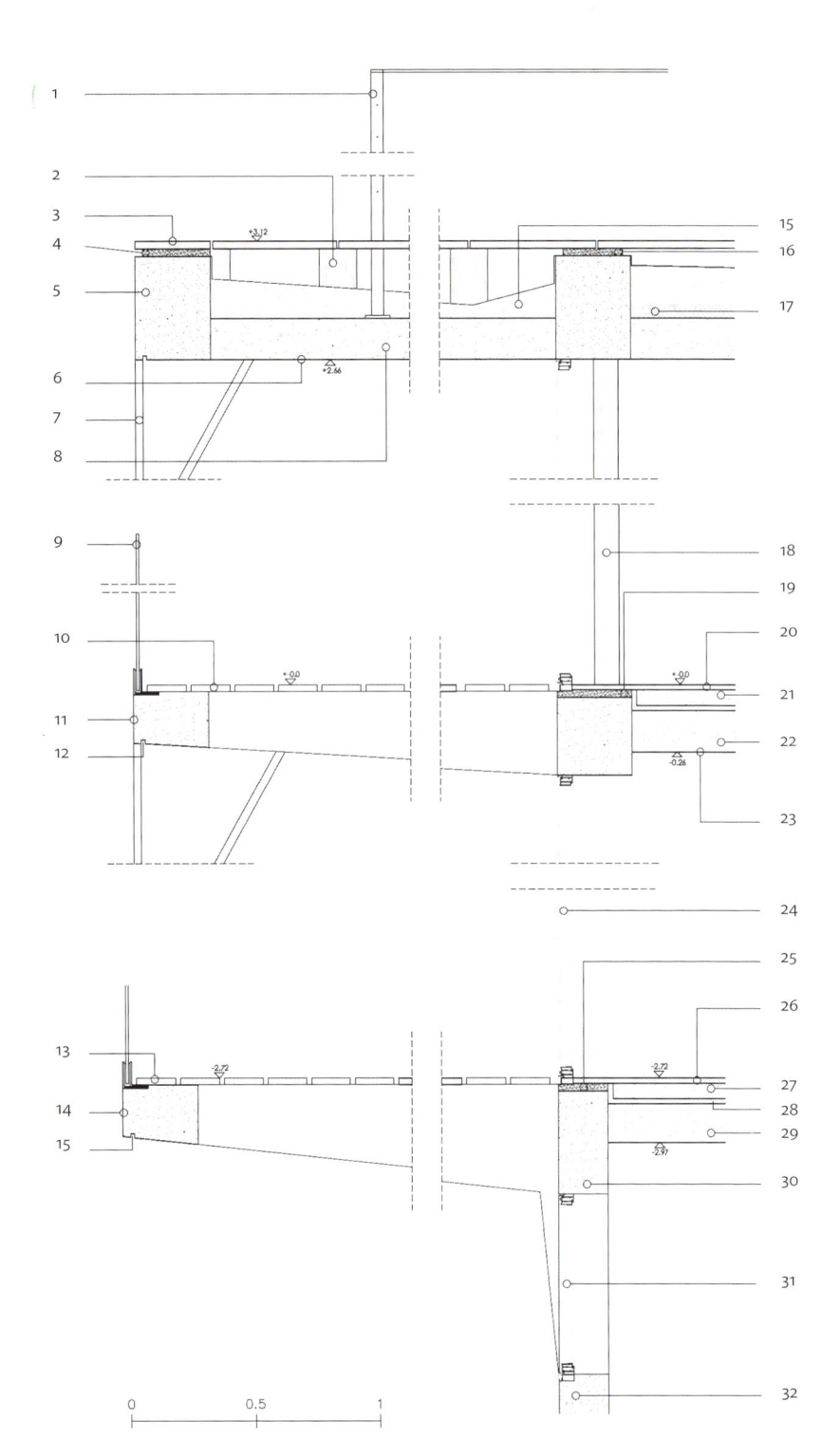

1. Metal handrail according to detail attached to slab
2. QHC Concrete + L.Geotextile ledges
3. High grade cement tablet 50 × 50
4. Setback 3 cm
5. Exposed reinforced concrete beam, 3 in. mold, tongue and groove and brushed
6. Roof of exposed reinforced concrete pieces from 3 in. mold, tongue and groove
7. Metal grate fixed to the slab
8. Reinforced concrete slab according to calculations = 16 cm
9. Glass handrail according to detail
10. National travertine marble slabs 15 x 120 cm folded metal covering plate for every 10mm each slab
11. Exposed reinforced concrete beam, 3 in. mold, tongue and groove and brushed
12. Raincaps 15 × 15 mm
13. National travertine marble slabs 15 x 120 cm folded metal covering plate for every 10mm each slab
14. Exposed reinforced concrete beam, 3 in. mold, tongue and groove and brushed
15. Raincaps 15 × 15 mm
16. Lightweight concrete covering slab
17. Setback
18. Expanded polystyrene 5 cm, 30 kg/m³
19. P.M according to calculations
20. Setback 3 cm
21. National travertine marble 20 mm
22. Light concrete covering slab for pipes and underfloor heating
23. Reinforced concrete slab according to calculations = 16 cm
24. Roof of exposed reinforced concrete pieces from 3 in. mold, tongue and groove
25. VC 03 according to detail
26. Setback 3 cm
27. National travertine marble 20 mm
28. Light concrete covering slab for pipes and underfloor heating
29. Expanded polystyrene 2 cm
30. Reinforced concrete slab according to calculations = 15 cm
31. Exposed reinforced concrete beam, 3 in. mold, tongue and groove and brushed
32. VC 06 according to detail

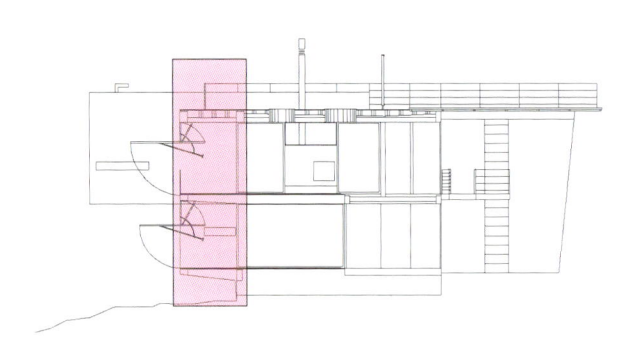

Mathias Klotz (KLOTZ & ASSOC.)

Mathias Klotz (KLOTZ & ASSOC.)